मध्य प्रदेश कर्मचारी चयन मण्डल

**मध्य प्रदेश**
शासन, स्कूल शिक्षा विभाग के अन्तर्गत

# उच्च माध्यमिक शिक्षक

पात्रता परीक्षा (ऑनलाइन)

## अंग्रेजी भाषा

**मध्य प्रदेश कर्मचारी चयन मण्डल**

# मध्य प्रदेश

**शासन, स्कूल शिक्षा विभाग के अन्तर्गत**

# उच्च माध्यमिक शिक्षक

पात्रता परीक्षा (ऑनलाइन)

## अंग्रेजी भाषा

लेखक
दीपाली

arihant
SUCCESS AND NOTHING LESS

**arihant**
SUCCESS AND NOTHING LESS

## ARIHANT PUBLICATIONS (INDIA) LIMITED



卐 **Administrative & Production Offices**

**Regd. Office**

'Ramchhaya' 4577/15, Agarwal Road, Darya Ganj, New Delhi -110002
Tele: 011- 47630600, 43518550

卐 **Head Office**

Kalindi, TP Nagar, Meerut (UP) - 250002
Tel: 0121-7156203, 7156204

卐 **Sales & Support Offices**

Agra, Ahmedabad, Bengaluru, Bareilly, Chennai, Delhi, Guwahati, Hyderabad, Jaipur, Jhansi, Kolkata, Lucknow, Nagpur & Pune.

卐 **PRICE** ₹225.00

卐 **PO No :** TXT-XX-XXXXXXX-X-XX

Published by Arihant Publications (India) Ltd.

For further information about the books published by Arihant, log on to www.arihantbooks.com or e-mail at info@arihantbooks.com

# CONTENTS

# SYLLABUS

## PART A

1. Use of Articles, Prepositions, Conjunctions, Verbs, Modals, Adverbs, Tenses, Finite – Non Finite Clauses, Determiners, Prefix & Suffix, Number, Gender, Pronouns.
2. Transformation of Sentences- Active to Passive, Direct to Indirect Narration.
3. Vocabulary, Opposites, Synonyms, One Word Substitution, Homonyms.
4. Reading Comprehension (Unseen Passage), Note-Making.

## PART B

### Fiction

1. Jane Austen - Pride and Prejudice
2. Charles Dickens - A Tale of Two Cities
3. Indian: Anita Desai - Bye-Bye Blackbird
4. Khushwant Singh - The Portrait of a Lady

### Drama

1. Bernard Shaw - Arms and the Man
2. William Shakespeare - The Tempest, Hamlet
3. Indian: Rabindranath Tagore - The Poet and Pauper , Gitanjali, True Worship

### Poetry

1. P.B. Shelley- Ode to a Skylark
2. Indian: Sarojini Naidu - The Broken Wings
3. Rabindranath Tagore - Gitanjali (Song No.1)
4. William Wordsworth - The World is Too much With us, The Tables Turned , The Solitary Reaper, I Wandered Lonely as a Cloud
5. Robert Frost – After Apple Picking, The Road Not Taken, Stopping by Woods on a Snowy Evening
6. Robert Browning - The Last Ride Together

### Prose

1. Francis Bacon - Of Studies, Of Friendship
2. William Hazlitt - Father's Letter
3. Charles Lamb- Dream Children
4. Indian: Jawaharlal Nehru- Teenage, Discovery of India
5. Nirad C. Chaudhuri - My Mother

### Figures of Speech and Forms of Poetry

1. Figures of Speech- Simile, Metaphor, Personification, Paradox, Irony
2. Forms of Poetry - Sonnet, Ode, Lyric, Elegy, Satire
3. Indian Writing in English

### Short Story

1. R.K.Narayan - Swami and Friends

### Novel

1. R.K.Narayan - The Guide
2. Mulk Raj Anand - The Lost Child

# PART A

- Parts of Speech
- Determiners/Articles
- Modals
- Finite-Non Finite Clauses
- Tense
- Direct to Indirect Narration
- Active and Passive Voice
- Synonyms
- Antonyms
- Homonyms
- One Word Substitutions
- Vocabulary
- Prefix and Suffix
- Reading Comprehension (Unseen Passage)
- Note-Making

Chapter 01

# Parts of Speech

## (Noun, Pronoun, Verb, Adverb, Preposition and Conjunction)

Parts of speech is a term in traditional grammar for one of the eight main categories into which words are classified according to their functions in sentences. *These categories are explained below*

## NOUN

A noun is defined as the name that is given to any person, place, thing or an idea.

(i) The **Sun** shines brightly

(ii) The **Jasmine** smells sweet.

### Kinds of Noun

*The kinds of noun are as follows*

#### Proper Noun

A proper noun is the name given to a particular person or a place. A proper noun always begins with a capital letter. e.g.

(i) **Maria** lives in the **United States of America.**

(ii) **World War I** started in the year 1914.

#### Common Noun

A common noun is a name given in common to every person or thing of the same class or kind. Common nouns are not written in capital letters. e.g.

(i) India is a **country.** (ii) Daniel is a **boy.**

Differences between Proper Noun and Common Noun

| Proper Noun | Common Noun |
|---|---|
| India | country |
| Daniel | boy |
| Maruti Suzuki | car |
| Mc Donald | restaurant |
| Kolkata | city |

#### Abstract Noun

An abstract noun is a word that is used to indicate an idea, activity, action, a quality or a state.

- **Idea** A thought, suggestion, belief, dream etc.
- **Action** movement, operation, laughter etc.
- **Quality** Hardness, honesty, goodness, kindness etc.
- **State** Death, darkness, childhood, poverty etc.

e.g.

(i) We are studying **Mathematics.**

(ii) Ken thought of a brilliant **idea** for his story.

#### Collective Noun

A collective noun is the name that is given to a group/number of persons or things in collection.

e.g.

(i) A **staff** of employees. (ii) A **troupe** of dancers.

#### Material Noun

Material noun are names of substances of which things are made.

e.g.

(i) I bought a **gold** ring.

(ii) **Plastic** toys are very colourful.

According to grammatical distinction, the nouns can be classified as either countable or uncountable.

#### Countable Noun

The countable noun represents the names of the people or the object that we can count.

e.g.

(i) There are **two books** in my bag.

(ii) Our house has **six rooms.**

#### Uncountable Noun

The uncountable noun represents the names of the people or the object that we cannot count but can measure or weigh.

e.g.
(i) There is no **information** about him.
(ii) Have you got some **water?**

There are certain nouns that can be used a both as countable and uncountable according to the context.
e.g.
(i) Could you bring us **three coffees** and **two teas** (Countable).
(ii) I drink a lot-of coffee but I don't drink much **tea** (Uncountable).

In example (i) coffee and tea is used as countable noun.
In example (ii) coffee and tea is used as uncountable noun.

## Number

According to numbers, the nouns can be categorised as singular and plural.

### Singular Number

A noun that represents one person or one thing is known as singular number. e.g.
(i) It is a very tall **tree.**
(ii) I am writing with **a blue pen.**

### Plural Number

A noun that represents more than one person or a thing is known as a plural number.
e.g.
(i) The **boys** are playing in the ground.
(ii) The **cows** are eating grass.
(iii) I like to read **stories.**

### Rules for Changing the Singular into Plural

#### Rule 1

Noun that end with a consonant are made plural by adding '-s' to the singular.

| | | | |
|---|---|---|---|
| Parrot | Parrots | Egg | Eggs |
| Boat | Boats | Actor | Actors |
| Cook | Cooks | Hat | Hats |

#### Rule 2

Noun that end with -s, -ss, -ch, -sh, -z, -x are pluralised by adding '-es'.

| | | | |
|---|---|---|---|
| Bus | Buses | Glass | Glasses |
| Bench | Benches | Bush | Bushes |
| Quiz | Quizes | Tax | Taxes |

#### Exception

| | | | |
|---|---|---|---|
| Stomach | Stomachs | Monarch | Monarchs |

#### Rule 3

Noun that end with -o and there is a consonant before -o then plural is made by adding '-es'.

| | | | |
|---|---|---|---|
| Tomato | Tomatoes | Mosquito | Mosquitoes |
| Mango | Mangoes | Hero | Heroes |

#### Exception

| | | | |
|---|---|---|---|
| Photo | Photos | Zero | Zeros |

#### Rule 4

Noun that end with -y and there is a consonant before -y, then plural is made by changing 'y' to 'i' and adding '-es'.

| | | | |
|---|---|---|---|
| Fly | Flies | Story | Stories |
| Baby | Babies | Family | Families |
| Copy | Copies | Library | Libraries |

#### Rule 5

Noun that end with -y and there is a vowel before -y, then plural is made by adding '-s'.

| | | | |
|---|---|---|---|
| Boy | Boys | Day | Days |
| Key | Keys | Way | Ways |
| Toy | Toys | Essay | Essays |

#### Rule 6

Noun that end with double vowel are pluralised by adding '-s'.

| | | | |
|---|---|---|---|
| Tree | Trees | Bee | Bees |
| Zoo | Zoos | Radio | Radios |
| Portfolio | Portfolios | Bamboo | Bamboos |

#### Rule 7

Some noun are pluralised by the change in their inside vowel.

| | | | |
|---|---|---|---|
| Tooth | Teeth | Foot | Feet |
| Mouse | Mice | Man | Men |

#### Rule 8

Noun that end with -f or -fe are pluralised by adding '-es' after -f or -fe is changed to '-v'.

| | | | |
|---|---|---|---|
| Knife | Knives | Thief | Thieves |
| Wife | Wives | Life | Lives |

#### Exception

| | | | |
|---|---|---|---|
| Roof | Roofs | Safe | Safes |
| Chief | Chiefs | Proof | Proofs |
| Scarf | Scarfs/Scarves | | |

#### Rule 9

Compound noun are pluralised by adding '-s' to the principal word.

| | |
|---|---|
| Step-son | Step-sons |
| Brother-in–law | Brothers-in–law |
| Pea-cock | Pea-cocks |
| Passer-by | Passers-by |

#### Exception

Man–Servant → Men–Servants
Lord– Justice → Lord– Justices

#### Rule 10

Noun that end with '-man' are made plural by changing '-man' into '-men'.

| | | | |
|---|---|---|---|
| Woman | Women | Postman | Postmen |
| Watchman | Watchmen | Chairman | Chairmen |
| Milkman | Milkmen | Fellowman | Fellowmen |

## Gender

According to gender, the noun can be classified as masculine, feminine, common and neuter gender.

### Masculine Gender

A noun that represents a male is known as the masculine gender.

e.g. boy, man, lion, king etc.

### Feminine Gender

A noun that represents a female is known as the feminine gender.

e.g. girl, woman, lioness, actress, queen etc.

### Common Gender

A noun that represents either a male or a female is known as the common gender.

e.g. friend, guardian, guest, infant, owner, parent, passenger, pig, pupil etc.

### Neuter Gender

A noun that represents a thing that is non-living is called a neuter gender.

e.g. box, bread, butter, chair, chalk etc.

All non-living objects fall into this category.

## Rules for Changing Masculine into Feminine

### Rule 1

Masculine can be changed into feminine by adding '-ess'.

| | |
|---|---|
| Poet | Poetess |
| Lion | Lioness |
| Host | Hostess |
| Giant | Giantess |

### Exception

| | |
|---|---|
| God | Goddess |

### Rule 2

In some noun; that have an ending in 'r', after masculine can be changed into feminine by adding '-ess' removing the 'vowel' before the last letter.

| | | | |
|---|---|---|---|
| Tiger | Tigress | Monitor | Monitress |
| Actor | Actress | Editor | Editress |

### Rule 3

Masculine can be changed into the feminine by using a completely different word.

| | | | |
|---|---|---|---|
| King | Queen | Hero | Heroine |
| Uncle | Aunt | Husband | Wife |

### Rule 4

Feminine of the compound noun are made by changing the masculine word of the compound noun that comes to the front.

| | |
|---|---|
| He-bear | She-bear |
| Bull-calf | Cow-calf |
| He-goat | She-goat |
| Son-in-law | Daughter-in-law |

### Rule 5

Feminine of some masculine are made by removing the last vowel and consonant and then by adding '-ess'.

| | |
|---|---|
| Governor | Governess |
| Murderer | Murderess |

### Exception

| | |
|---|---|
| Duke | Duchess |

### Rule 6

Compound noun change their gender by changing masculine word into feminine coming later.

| | |
|---|---|
| Headmaster | Headmistress |
| Grandfather | Grandmother |
| Milkman | Milkmaid |
| Peacock | Peahen |

# PRONOUN

A pronoun is a word, which is used in a place of a noun.

(i) **She** is going to temple.
(ii) **He** is taking bath.

## Kinds of Pronoun

*There are following kinds of pronoun*

### Personal Pronouns

Words used in place of noun referring to persons.

'I, we, you, he, she, it, they' etc.

| Person | Subjective Case | | Objective Case | | Possessive Case | |
|---|---|---|---|---|---|---|
| | Singular | Plural | Singular | Plural | Singular | Plural |
| First | I | We | Me | Us | My, Mine | Our, Ours |
| Second | You | You | You | You | Your | Yours |
| Third | He, She, It | they | Him, Her, It | Them | His, Her, Its | Their, Theirs |

### Demonstrative Pronouns

- Words used for noun to point out objects. 'This, that, these, those' etc. e.g.
  (i) **This** is my book. (ii) **That** is her house.
- In the following examples 'This' and 'That' are used as *demonstrative adjectives.*
  (i) **This** book. (ii) **That** house.

### Relative Pronouns

Words used for noun to express functions relating to who, which, that, whose, whom etc.

e.g.

(i) The man **who** has just entered the room is my friend.
(ii) The book **that** I bought is very costly.

### Interrogative Pronouns

Words used for noun to ask questions. 'Who, What, Which, Whose, Whom' etc.

e.g.

(i) **Who** took my bag? (ii) **Whom** did you meet?

### Indefinite Pronouns

Words used for noun in vague and general meaning 'everybody, nobody, somebody, either, neither, all, much, several, each, others, another' etc.

e.g.

(i) **All** that glitters is not gold.

(ii) I will try to think of **somebody** who can help you.

### Reflexive Pronouns

Words used as forms of personal pronouns for emphasis. 'Myself, ourselves, himself, herself, themselves, yourself' etc. e.g.

(i) I shall do this work **myself**.

(ii) She cut her finger **herself**.

### Distributive Pronouns

Used for individuals and objects referring to them as one at a time. Either, neither, each, every, none, anyone etc.

e.g.

(i) **Either** of the sisters is staying here.

(ii) **Neither** of his arms is defective.

### Reciprocal Pronouns

Words used to point out mutual relationship. 'Each other, one another' etc.

e.g.

(i) The brothers love **each other**.

(ii) Indians should not fight with **one another**.

## Rules of Pronoun

### Rule 1

- When the subject of the verb is the receiver of the action, the action is said to be reflected. Such verbs are used reflexively.
- Acquit, absent, avail, reconcile, amuse, resign, avenge, revenge, enjoy, exert, apply, adapt, adjust, pride, over-reach etc are used reflexively. e.g .

(i) You should **avail** yourself of every chance in life. *(Correct)*

(ii) They **enjoyed** picture last evening. *(No reflexive pronoun is needed)*

(iii) They **enjoyed** during summer vacation. *(Place 'themselves' after 'enjoyed')*

(iv) He **resigned** himself to his failure. *(Correct)*

(v) The former DM **acquitted** very efficiently. *(Place 'himself' after 'acquitted')*

### Rule 2

The following verbs are not used reflexively.

Keep, stop, turn, qualify, bathe, move, rest, hide are not used reflexively. e.g.

(i) You should **keep** yourself from bad boys. *(Drop 'yourself')*

(ii) He has **qualified** himself for the post. *(Drop 'himself')*

(iii) He **hid** himself in the room. *(Drop 'himself'Int. verb)*

(iv) The thief **hid** money under the carpet. *(Correct) (Tran verb)*

### Rule 3

A reflexive pronoun cannot act as a subject or object of a verb unless it is preceded by pronoun or noun concerned. e.g.

(i) **Myself** will see to it that you get your share of property. *(Change 'myself' into 'I')*

(ii) **Yourself** and he reached there in time. *(Change 'yourself' into 'you ')*

(iii) I **myself** like him. *(Correct)*

(iv) Raj will do it for **myself** and my sister. *(Change 'myself' to 'me')*

### Rule 4

The verb 'to be' should be followed by subjective form when the complement is pronoun. e.g.

(i) It is **me** who have brought you home. *(Change 'me' into 'I')*

(ii) Was it **her** who did it for you? *(Change 'her' into 'she')*

(iii) It will be **us** who will buy a new house. *(Change 'us' into 'we')*

### Rule 5

Verbs and prepositions are followed by objective case of a pronoun. e.g.

(i) Between **you** and I, Suhani is intelligent. *(Say 'me')*

(ii) She is teaching Rohit and **she**. *(Say 'her')*

(iii) Let **they** go. *(Say 'them')*

### Rule 6

- Good manners require that the order of singular pronouns should be second person, third person and first person.
- But, in plural, 'we' is used before 'you' and 'they' after 'you'. The latter order is also observed while referring to unpleasant acts.

e.g.

(i) **I** and **you** will attend her wedding tomorrow. *(Correct use is 'You' and 'I')*

(ii) **She** and **you** will share the mangoes. *(Use 'You' and 'She')*

(iii) **You**, Mohan and **I** will watch movie tonight. *(Correct)*
(iv) **We, you** and **they** are leaving for Mumbai tomorrow. *(Correct)*
(v) **You** and **I** will be punished. *(Unpleasant act, Correct use is 'I and you')*

**Rule 7**

The relative pronoun should be expressed according to its relation with the verb of the adjective clause, 'who' is used as a subject of a verb of adjective clause and 'whom' is used as an object of a verb of adjective clause.

e.g.
(i) He was talking of the women, **who** he said, he met in America. *(Use 'whom' in place of 'who')*
(ii) She is the kind of lady, **whom** everybody knows, is intelligent. *(Use 'who' in place of 'whom')*

**Rule 8**

The use of 'but' as a relative pronoun.

e.g.
(i) There was none **but** wept. *(Who did not weep)*
(ii) There is no country **but** is corrupt. *(Which is not corrupt)*

**Rule 9**

The use of the 'same' as pronoun is wrong.

e.g.
(i) I shall give you a book and **the same** is very useful. *(Say 'it' in place of 'the same')*
(ii) He bought a house and is living in **the same**. *(Say 'it' in place of 'the same')*

**Rule 10**

- 'Which' is used in place of 'who' when we are referring to a choice between two or more than two things or persons.

e.g.
(i) Of the two sisters **who** is more intelligent. *(Use 'which' in place of 'who')*
(ii) **Who** is your father in the crowd? *(Use 'which' in place of 'who')*
(iii) **Who** is better of the two dancers in our society? *(Place 'the' before better and change 'who' into 'which')*

**Rule 11**

**Possessive Case** We don't use noun after possessive case of a pronoun.

e.g.
(i) This book is **mine**.
(ii) This shirt is **yours**.
(iii) **Our** is a populous country. *(Say 'Ours')*

# VERB

Verb is one of the main parts of a sentence or question in English. The verb in a sentence expresses action or being. There is a main verb and sometimes one or more helping verbs.

e.g.
He can swim.*'Swim' is the main verb; can is the helping verb.)*

A verb must agree with its subject in number (both are singular or both are plural). Verbs also take different forms to express tense.

## Types of Verbs

As we've covered, a verb can be categorised as a physical verb (e.g. to run), a mental verb (e.g. to think) or a state-of-being verb (e.g. to be).

*However, a verb will often be further categorised as one of the following*

**Action Verb** An action verb expresses an activity that a person or thing can do.

e.g.
(i) Pinki **eats** cutlets.
(ii) The tiger **chased** the rabbit in the shallow rapids.

Compare those verbs with these
(iii) Praveen **likes** cake.
(iv) The cat **is** hungry.

**Stative Verb** A stative verb expresses a state rather than an action. A stative verb typically relates to a state of being, a thought or an emotion.

e.g.
(i) I am **at** home. (ii) She **believes** in fairies.
(iii) He **feels** elated.

**Transitive Verb** A transitive verb is one that acts on something (i.e., it has a direct object).

e.g.
(i) I saw the **dog**. *(Here, the direct object is the 'dog')*
(ii) Laxman ate the **pie**. *(Here, the direct object is the 'pie')*
(iii) The postman will give Sanoj the **letter**. *(Here, the direct object is the 'letter')*

⚠ The direct object of a transitive verb can be found by finding the verb and asking "what?"
e.g.
"saw what?" (answer: *the dog*); "ate what?" (answer: *the pie*); "will give what?" (answer: *the letter*).

**Intransitive Verb** An intransitive verb is one that does not act on something (i.e., there is no direct object).

e.g.
(i) The rain **fell**. (ii) My throat **hurts**.
(iii) The cat **sneezed**.

**Auxiliary Verb** An auxiliary verb (or helping verb) accompanies a main verb to help express tense, voice or mood. The most common auxiliary verbs are be, do, and have (in their various forms). *Here are some examples of auxiliary verbs*:
(i) Rahul **has** eaten all the fruits. *(Here, the auxiliary verb 'has' helps to express tense.)*
(ii) The table **has been** prepared. *(Here, the auxiliary verbs 'has been' help to express voice (in this case, the passive voice).*

(iii) If he **were** to arrive in the next 10 minutes, we **would** be on schedule.
*(Here, the auxiliary verbs 'were and would' help to express mood (in this case, the subjunctive mood).*

**Modal Verb** A modal verb is a type of auxiliary verb used to express ideas such as ability, possibility, permission, and obligation. The modal auxiliary verbs are can, could, may, might, must, ought to, shall, should, will and would.

e.g.

(i) Leena **can** eat a lot of apples.
*(Here, the modal verb 'can' helps to express the idea of ability.)*

(ii) Leena **might** eat that apple before he gets home.
*(Here, the modal verb 'might' helps to express the idea of possibility.)*

(iii) Leena **may** eat as many apples as he likes.
*(Here, the modal verb 'may' helps to express the idea of permission.)*

(iv) Leena **should** give you some of those apples you bought.
*(Here, the modal verb 'should' helps to express the idea of obligation.)*

**Phrasal Verb** A phrasal verb is a verb made up of more than one word (usually two words). A phrasal verb has a main verb and another word (either a preposition or a participle). The phrasal verb usually has a meaning different from the main verb.

e.g.

(i) A burglar will often break a window to **break in.**
*(Here, the phrasal verb 'break in' means to enter illegally, which is different 'to break')*

(ii) If you drop the baton the team will **drop back** to last place.
*(Here, the phrasal verb 'drop back' means to fall behind, which is different 'to drop')*

**Regular and Irregular Verbs** A regular verb is one that forms its simple past tense and its past participle by adding -ed or -d to the base form of the verb.

⚠ There are spelling rules to consider too.
e.g.
love, hate, move
An irregular verb is one that does not conform to this ruling.
e.g. tell, bleed, write, bring.

# ADVERB

An adverb is a word used to add something to the meaning of a verb, adjective or another adverb. It is said to modify verbs, adjectives and adverbs.

e.g.

(i) She is walking **slowly**.
(ii) She is **very** intelligent.
(iii) A **kindly** woman helped him find his way home.

## Kinds of Adverb

*The kinds of Adverb are as follows*

- **Adverb of Time** Before, ago, lately, yet, now, soon, yesterday, already, never.
- **Adverb of Frequency** Always, once, seldom, usually, rarely etc.
- **Adverb of Place** Here, everywhere, down, near, away, backward, upward.
- **Adverb of Manner** Slowly, so, soundly, delightfully.
- **Adverb of Affirmation and Negation** Certainly, apparently, obviously, no, undoubtedly.
- **Adverb of Degree** Almost, fully, very, enough, rather, quite, too, really.
- **Interrogative Adverb** How, what, when, why.
- **Relative Adverb** When, where, why, how.
- **Adverb of Reason** Hence, thus, so, therefore.
- **Exclamatory Adverbs** Ah!, What, May, How, Bravo!

## Positioning of an Adverb

There are various rules used in context of positioning of adverb. *These are given below*

### Rule 1

- Adverbs of place are put behind the direct object or the verb.

e.g.

(i) We had not seen the man **here**.
(ii) Players stayed **behind** the crowd.

### Rule 2

- Adverbs of frequency are put before the main verb. But, if 'be' is main verb then in case the auxiliary is absent, adverb of frequency is put after 'be'.

e.g.

(i) She **often** plays on Sunday.
(ii) Rohan doesn't **always** eat pizza.
(iii) Parents are **usually** here in festivals.

### Rule 3

Adverbs of time such as 'Always, often, already, just, never, ever, sometimes, frequently, generally, recently, usually, seldom, hardly, rarely, normally etc are generally placed before the verb they modify.

e.g.

(i) My brother **comes often** every Sunday.
*(Place 'often' before 'comes')*

(ii) He **goes usually** to the movie every Friday.
*(Place 'usually' before 'goes')*

(iii) He **never** talks ill of friends. *(Correct)*

(iv) He is **always** satisfied. *(Correct)*

**Rule 4**

Adverbs of manners are placed only after the intransitive verb. However, the adverb can be placed either before or after the transitive verb.

e.g.

(i) He returned immediately. *(Correct)*

(ii) He briefly narrated the incident to me. *(Correct)*

(iii) He narrated to me the incident briefly. *(Correct)*

(iv) He **soundly slept** last night.
*(Place 'soundly' 'after' slept)*

## Rules of Adverb

**Rule 1**

Adjective qualifies a noun and a pronoun whereas adverb modifies a verb, an adjective and an adverb. e.g.

(i) Her act was **remarkable**.

(ii) She acted **remarkably** to achieve success.

**Rule 2**

If the sentence is introduced by an adverb, inverted form of the verb is used for the sake of emphasis.

e.g.

(i) Seldom he visits his parents. *(Incorrect)*

(ii) Seldom does he visit his parents. *(Correct)*

(iii) He seldom visits his parents. *(Correct)*

**Rule 3**

- Use of **else** and **other**.
- 'Else' should be followed by 'but'.
- 'Other' and 'otherwise' are followed by 'than'.

e.g.

(i) It is nothing else **than** sheer madness.
*(Use 'but' in place of 'than')*

(ii) She had no other alternative **but** stay here.
*(Use 'than' in place of 'but')*

(iii) She has no one else to look after her **except** me.
*(Use 'but' in place of 'except')*

**Rule 4**

Both 'never' and 'not' are adverbs. The use of 'never' for 'not' is incorrect

e.g.

(i) I **never** went to Ooty last year.
*(Use **'did not go'** in place of 'never')*

(ii) I never remember to have said so. *(Correct)*

(iii) I remember **never** to have said so.
I do not remember to have said so.
*(Use 'do not' in place of 'never and use them before the main verb')*

(iv) I never allow my son to go out in dark.
*(Correct/Habitual action)*

**Rule 5**

- Note the use of phrases
- 'Seldom or ever, 'seldom, if ever' 'little or nothing', 'little, if anything'.
- The phrases 'seldom or ever' and little or anything are wrong in use.

e.g.

(i) We seldom or ever meet our relatives these days.
*(Incorrect)*

(ii) We seldom or ever (Seldom, if ever) meet our relatives these days. *(Correct)*

**Rule 6**

- Negative adverbs should not be used with the words negative in meaning. So, two negatives should be avoided.
- Seldom, nowhere, never, nothing, hardly, scarcely, neither, barely, rarely are some of the adverbs expressing negative meaning.

e.g.

(i) I rarely went to meet **nobody** across the road.
*(Use 'anybody' in place of 'nobody')*

(ii) She hardly knows **nothing** about the family.
*(Use 'anything' in place of 'nothing')*

(iii) I hardly know **somebody** in the town.
*(Say 'anybody in place of 'somebody)*

(iv) He does nothing without **never** consulting me.
*(Use 'ever' for 'never')*

**Rule 7**

Given below are some of the examples of the words being treated as adverbs whereas they are adjectives or nouns.

e.g.

(i) Manly, masterly, slovenly, monthly, weekly, sickly, friendly, orderly, gentlemanly are adjectives and should not be confused with adverbs.

(ii) Coward, miser, niggard are nouns. 'Cowardly, miserly, niggardly' are adjectives. 'In a cowardly, miserly, niggardly manner, are used as adverbs.

(iii) Fast, straight, outright, direct, hard, hardly, late, light, high, safe, quiet etc are used both as an adjective and adverb.

(iv) 'Loudly and aloud are adverbs though different in meanings. 'Loud' is an adjective.

(v) Late, lately are both an adjective and an adverb. 'Lately' is an adverb.

(vi) Hard is both an adjective and adverb used in affirmative sense. 'Hardly' is an adverb used in negative meaning.

**Rule 8**

- The use of very, much, so, too, enough, rather.
- 'Very' modifies present participle used as adjective, adverb and adjective in positive degree. 'Much' is used with comparative degree and past participle. e.g.

(i) It is a **much** interesting picture. *(Use 'very' in place of 'much')*

(ii) I was **very** exhausted in the evening. *(Use 'much' in place of 'very')*

(iii) She did this work very quickly. *(Correct)*

- 'So' and 'too' should not be used without 'that' (Adverb clause) and 'to' (Infinitive) respectively.
- 'Very' and 'much' may be used in the place of 'so' and 'too'.

e.g.

(i) My brother is **so** healthy. *(Use 'very' in place of 'so')*

(ii) She is **very** kind. *(Here, 'very' means 'to a great extent')*

(iii) She is **too** poor to study further. *(Correct)*

(iv) She is so poor that she cannot study further. *(Correct)*

(v) She is **too** healthy. *(Over healthy say 'very' for 'too')*

(vi) It is too bad. *(Correct)*

### Rule 9

- Use of 'very much, too much, much too'.

e.g.

(i) I am disturbed **very much** by this.

(ii) The cost of the pen is **very much**.

- Too much is used to indicate a situation of having something in plenty and one doesn't like it.

e.g.

(i) **Too much** of anything is bad.

(ii) Some people have **too much** of problems.

- 'Much too' is used to imply stress on the quantity that is already too much.

e.g.

(i) He seems to be **much too** wise.

(ii) This phone seems to be **much too** costly.

### Rule 10

- Use of 'Only'
- 'Only' is used to show the 'alone' case.

e.g.

(i) **Only** he was left there.

(ii) The accident broke his bicycle **only**.

- 'Only' is used to show the meaning 'solely'.

e.g.

(i) **Only** she can do this work.

(ii) She does **only** solo performances.

(iii) This compartment is reserved for the blinds **only**.

# PREPOSITION

Preposition is a word that shows positional relation of a noun or a pronoun with the sentence.

e.g.

(i) Who is **in** the room?

(ii) She is standing **on** the table.

Here, **bold** words are prepositions.

## Prepositions Before Particular Words

*The use of vorious preposition before particular words are given below*

### Travel and Movement

- From, to, at, in, by, on, into, onto, off, out, out of. e.g.

(i) We travel daily **from** Meerut to Delhi.

(ii) I need a pencil **to** write with.

- Arrive at/in, get to (Reach). e.g.

(i) They **arrived in** India in March.

(ii) I **arrived at** Patel Bridge.

(iii) I **go to** the Bus stand late.

e.g.

(i) They went home **by** bus. *(With Preposition)*

(ii) She returned **to** her home late. *(With Preposition)*

### Above and Over

(i) 'Above' and 'over' both mean 'higher than' and sometimes either can be used.

(ii) But 'over' can also mean 'covering' 'on the other side of', 'across', from one side to the other and in every part of the region. e.g.

(i) White flags were waved **above** the buildings.

(ii) There is a bridge **over** the river.

### Under, Below and Beneath

- 'Below', 'under', both mean lower than, but 'under' usually denotes physical contact. e.g.

(i) She kept money **under** the bed.

(ii) The old man was crushed **under** the car.

- However, 'below' is used when there is a space between the two surfaces. e.g.

(i) They live **below** us.

(ii) He placed the lamp **below** the Almirah.

- 'Under' can mean junior in ranks. e.g.

(i) He is **under** me.

(ii) I was wearing a sweater **under** the jacket.

- 'Beneath' has the same meaning as 'under', but it is better to use it for abstract meanings. e.g.

(i) He would think it **beneath** him to do such small work.

(ii) It is **beneath** his dignity to beg for money.

### Time and Date

(Use at, on, by, in) at dusk, at noon, at dawn, at midnight, at midday, at sixteen (at night, at six, at 7:30, in/on the morning/afternoon/evening night, (Of a certain date).

e.g.

(i) We left **on** the evening of sixth **at** 5:30 pm.

(ii) We left **in** the evening/afternoon.

### On Time, In Time and In Good Time

- On time (At time arranged, neither before nor after)
  e.g. The train is running **on time**.
- In time (Not late)
  e.g. Passengers should be **in time** for their train.
- In good time (with comfortable margin)
  e.g. I arrived at the theatre **in good time**.

### At the Beginning/At the End, In the Beginning/In the End, At First, At Last

- **At the beginning** of a book, there is a foreward.
  *(Literally at the beginning)*
- At the end, there may be an index.
- 'In the beginning at first' = In the early stage. It implies that later there was change.
  e.g. **In the beginning**, we used hand tools, later we had machines.
- 'In the end /At last' eventually after sometime
- e.g. At first, he opposed marriage but **in the end** he gave his consent.

## Rules of Usage of Preposition

### Rule 1

A preposition is usually placed before its object but sometimes it is placed after it in following cases

- When the 'object' of the preposition is in the interrogative pronoun : what, who, whom, which, where etc, the preposition takes end or front position.

e.g.
(i) **What** are you thinking **of**?
(ii) **Who** are you talking **to**?
(iii) **Whom** are you talking **to**?

- When the 'object' of the preposition is a relative pronoun 'that' the preposition takes end position.

e.g.
(i) This is the book that I have been looking **for**.
(ii) This is the picture that she always talks **of**.
(iii) Here is the magazine that you asked **for**.

- When an infinitive qualifies a noun, the preposition should be placed after the infinitive, if required.

e.g.
(i) It is not a safe place **to** live. (say live in)
(ii) He gave me a pen **to** write. (say write with)

### Rule 2

- As a rule no preposition is placed after the following verbs when these verbs- are used in active voice.

  'Stress, emphasise, discuss (Matter), investigate, comprise, accompany, consider, violate, demand, resemble, pervade, precede, succeed, reach (At), resign (Post), attack, invade, resist, enter (Come into), eschew, befall, order, direct, join, sign, affect, ensure, board, describe, await, lack, regret, concern.

- **Omission of 'to'** with verbs of communication before the object. 'advise- tell-ask' beg, command, encourage, request, inform, order, urge.

  e.g.
  (i) I advised to him to go. (Drop to after advised)
  (ii) I informed to the police of the accident. (Drop to)

### Rule 3

- Omission of preposition before indirect object.
  'Bring, give, lend, promise, leave, sell, buy, show, take, fetch, tell, hand, send, sing, read, cost, play (An instrument), find, get, ask, offer etc.

e.g.
(i) I shall **fetch** you books from market.
*Or*
I shall **fetch** books for you from market.
(ii) Her father **left** him large property.
Or
Her father **left** large property to him.

- Note the placement of proper object (Direct/Indirect) with the use of the following verbs with special reference to the preposition.
  The use of verbs 'provide, supply, furnish, entrust, present'.
  e.g.
  I provided him money. *(Incorrect)*
  I provided him **with** money. *(Correct)*
  Or
  I provided money **to** him. *(Correct)*
- The correct use of 'rob, fine, inform, explain, recommend, compensate, suggest, propose', in relation to objects.

e.g.
(i) **Rob** a person of something.
(ii) **Fine** someone (Ten rupees etc).
(iii) **Inform** someone of something.
(iv) **Explain** something to a person.
(v) **Recommend/Suggest/Propose something/somebody** to others
(vi) **Compensate** someone for something.

### Rule 4

- 'Than and But' as Preposition

  **Than and But** are usually conjunctions. However, they may be sometimes used as prepositions.

  e.g.
  (i) I did not see any other person **than** your brother.
  (ii) I did not see anybody else **but** your brother.
- 'A' in the following sentences has been used as a preposition, though in a weakened form of (in).
  e.g.
  (i) He earns fifty rupees **a** day.
  (ii) She visits me once **a** month.

### Between and Among

- 'Between' is used while referring to two persons/things. It may also be used for two or more in choice.
- 'Among' is used while referring to more than two persons/things.

e.g.
(i) The two brothers divided the property **between** themselves.
(ii) The two brothers and their sisters divided the property **among** themselves.

### Before and Ago

- 'Before' denotes the preceding action and can also be used in place of 'Ago'.
- 'Ago' refers to the past action.

e.g.
(i) She left India two days **ago/before.**
(ii) She had left India **before** she was married.
(Conjunction) (Preceding action)

### In and At

'In' refers to towns, cities and countries in a wider sense while 'At' is used for speaking of comparatively smaller places.

e.g.
(i) He lives **in** Delhi.
(ii) He lives **at** Rohini in Delhi.

### In and Into

'In' denotes position whereas 'Into' shows movement and entrance.

e.g.
(i) The students are **in** the classroom.
(ii) The students came **into** the classroom.

### Beside and Besides

- '**Beside**' means 'by the side of'.
- '**Besides**' means 'in addition to'.

e.g.
(i) She sat **beside** him at the party.
(ii) **Besides** studying, he is also working somewhere.

### By and With

- 'By' is used for 'doer' of the action.
- 'With' is used to denote the instrument.

e.g.
(i) He struck the dog **with** a stick.
(ii) A dog was struck **by** him.

### From and Between

- 'From' is normally used with 'to/till/until'.
- 'Between' is used with 'and'.

e.g.
(i) He works in the office **from** ten to five.
(ii) The reception will be held **between** 5 pm and 9 pm.

# CONJUNCTION

A word which joins together sentences and words, and, but, or, so, etc are the some examples of conjunctions

e.g.
(i) Rahul and Rashmi are friends.
↓
Conjunction
(ii) We loved him but he always hated us.
↓
Conjunction

## Kinds of Conjunctions

*There are three kinds of conjunctions*

1. **Co-ordinate Conjunction** Conjunctions that joins two independent clauses or co-ordinate clauses.
   e.g. Mohan is honest but poor.
   ↓
   Co-ordinate Conjunction
   Here, 'but' is co-ordinate conjunction, as it joins two independent sentences.
2. **Sub-ordinate Conjunction** Conjunctions that join a dependent clause to the co-ordinate clause in a complex sentence.
   e.g. He escaped punishment though he was late.
   ↓
   Sub-ordinate Conjunction
   In the above example, 'though' connects the In dependent clause 'escaped punishment' with the dependent clause 'He was late'.
3. **Correlative Conjunction** Conjunction that are used in pairs are correlative conjunctions.
   e.g. He is not only rich but honest also.
   Here, 'not only but also' is a correlative conjunctions.

## Use of Conjunctions

1. It is proper to use 'Nor' after 'Neither' and 'or' after 'either'.
   e.g. You are neither fatty **or** slim. *(Incorrect)*
   You are neither fatty **nor** slim. *(Correct)*
2. 'Even if' and 'But' should be used together in any sentence.
   e.g. Even if I am well **yet** I can't work. *(Incorrect)*
   Even if I am well, **but** I can't work. *(Correct)*
3. 'Both' and 'And' are used in pair.
   e.g. Both Reema **or** Rani are beautiful. *(Incorrect)*
   Both Reema **and** Rani are beautiful. *(Correct)*
4. 'Whether' and 'or/not/or no' are used in pair.
   e.g. I can't say that he will go or not. *(Incorrect)*
   I can't say whether he will go or not. *(Correct)*
5. 'Other' and 'Than' are used in pair.
   e.g. You have other job **that** to do. *(Incorrect)*
   You have **other** job **than** this to do. *(Correct)*

6. 'Lest' and 'Should' be used together, lest expresses negative meaning so no other negative word should be used with it.
   e.g. Go there lest you **may** miss the bus. *(Incorrect)*
   Go there lest you **should** miss the bus. *(Correct)*
7. 'Although' and 'Yet' should be used in pair.
   e.g. Although, she is fresher **but** she is confident. *(Incorrect)*
   Although, she is fresher **yet** she is confident. *(Correct)*
8. To show two simultaneous actions, 'While' is used, but if actions happen in order, 'When' is used to denote them.
   e.g. **When** I was in the club, I saw him. *(Incorrect)*
   **While** I was in the club I saw him. *(Correct)*
9. 'Until' and 'Unless' are used to show time and condition respectively. These words have negative sense so no negative word is used with these words.
   e.g. **Until** you work hard you cannot do well. *(Incorrect)*
   **Unless** you work hard you cannot do well. *(Correct)*
10. 'So' and 'So That' are used to show cause and purpose.
   e.g.
   He is fool **so that** he is not famous. *(Incorrect)*
   He is a fool **so** he is not famous. *(Correct)*
11. When verbs like treat, regard, describe, present, define, depict then 'as' is used before noun. e.g.
   Do not treat an animal an animal. *(Incorrect)*
   Do not treat an animal **as** an animal. *(Correct)*
12. 'Such' and 'As' are used in pair. e.g.
   Such works are tough **that** take time. *(Incorrect)*
   Such works are tough **as** take time. *(Correct)*
13. When the subject of the sentence involves itself in the work just after the other then we use "No sooner ...... than".
   e.g. **No sooner** had I reached my home **than** the guests went.
14. When there is no remarkable time gap between the two actions then we use "Hardly/Scarcely/Barely .......... when"
   e.g. **Hardly** had she gone out **when** her friend came.
15. When there is a contrast between two situations or two ideas then we use "Nothing ...... but"
   e.g. He is **nothing but** a volunteer in this organisation.

# Practice Questions

**Directions** *(Q. Nos. 1-5) Choose the appropriate noun from the options given below to complete the sentence.*

**1.** The ....... still has not taken our order.
(a) porter (b) manager
(c) waiter (d) shopkeeper

**2.** The Nile is the longest of all the .......
(a) lakes (b) oceans (c) seas (d) rivers

**3.** I do not travel with much .......
(a) furniture (b) food (c) work (d) luggage

**4.** ....... is on the banks of river Hooghly.
(a) Kelkata (b) Kolkata
(c) Calcutta (d) None of these

**5.** Our ......... fought with great courage during the Kargil War.
(a) men (b) soldiers
(c) politicians (d) students

**Directions** (Q. Nos. 6-10) *Which type of noun the underlined word is?*

**6.** Solomon was the wisest of all kings.
(a) Common noun (b) Proper noun
(c) Abstract noun (d) Collective noun

**7.** The soldiers were rewarded for their bravery.
(a) Common noun (b) Proper noun
(c) Abstract noun (d) Material noun

**8.** The French army was defeated at Waterloo.
(a) Common noun (b) Collective noun
(c) Proper noun (d) Abstract noun

**9.** Gold is a precious metal.
(a) Proper noun (b) Common noun
(c) Abstract noun (d) Material noun

**10.** Banana is a very nutritious fruit.
(a) Proper noun (b) Common noun
(c) Collective noun (d) Abstract noun

**Directions** *(Q. Nos. 11-15) Choose the correct corresponding noun of the given words.*

**11.** Succeed
(a) Succeeded (b) Success
(c) Succession (d) Succeeding

**12.** Write
(a) Writing (b) Written
(c) Writer (d) Wrote

**13.** Laugh
(a) Laughter (b) Laughed
(c) Laughingly (d) Laughing

**14.** Vacant
(a) Vacated (b) Vacate
(c) Vacancy (d) Vacantly

**15.** Know
(a) Knew (b) Known
(c) Knowledge (d) Knowing

**Directions** *(Q. Nos. 16-17) Match the words in List I with their appropriate options in List II.*

**16.**

| | List I (Word) | | List II (Collective Noun) |
|---|---|---|---|
| A. | Keys | 1. | Committee |
| B. | Flowers | 2. | Bunch |
| C. | Members | 3. | Herd |
| D. | Cattle | 4. | Bouquet |

**Codes**

| | A | B | C | D | | A | B | C | D |
|---|---|---|---|---|---|---|---|---|---|
| (a) | 4 | 1 | 2 | 3 | (b) | 2 | 4 | 1 | 3 |
| (c) | 1 | 3 | 2 | 4 | (d) | 3 | 4 | 2 | 1 |

**17.**

| | List I (Word) | | List II (Types of Noun) |
|---|---|---|---|
| A. | Jawaharlal Nehru | 1. | Collective |
| B. | Fleet | 2. | Common |
| C. | Chairs | 3. | Abstract |
| D. | Happiness | 4. | Proper |

**Codes**

| | A | B | C | D | | A | B | C | D |
|---|---|---|---|---|---|---|---|---|---|
| (a) | 2 | 1 | 3 | 4 | (b) | 4 | 1 | 2 | 3 |
| (c) | 4 | 3 | 2 | 1 | (d) | 3 | 2 | 1 | 4 |

**18.** The noun which is used both as singular and plural.
(a) Tie (b) Coat
(c) Shirt (d) Trousers

**19.** Choose correct list of plural nouns.
(a) Fan, sheep, table, boys
(b) Sheep, oxen, books, mice
(c) Bag, watch, sheep, bottles
(d) Knife, books, chairs, bottles

**20.** Which of the following is not a singular noun?
(a) Toe (b) Ankle (c) Knee (d) Feet

**Directions** *(Q. Nos. 21-35) Fill in the blanks by choosing the correct option.*

**21.** Leena and Payal are very excited because .......... are going to Disneyland.
(a) that (b) those
(c) there (d) they

**22.** Mahima and Kajal are doctors and ........ profession is very noble.
(a) her (b) hers
(c) them (d) their

**23.** ........... wants to go to a hill station in summer.
(a) Everyone (b) Someone
(c) Anyone (d) No one

**24.** One should always keep ........ word.
(a) his (b) her
(c) their (d) All of these

**25.** ........... Suresh and Mayank had been ex-monitors of my class.
(a) They (b) Them
(c) Both (d) Those

**26.** After accident, Sanjeev is unable to move .......... legs.
(a) those (b) his
(c) its (d) himself

**27.** My sister and .......... went to watch a movie yesterday.
(a) me (b) my
(c) I (d) her

**28.** Would you please call ...........?
(a) herself (b) hers
(c) both (a) and (b) (d) None of these

**29.** "The children ...........work is neat and finished in time will get two marks extra," said the teacher.
(a) which (b) whose
(c) that (d) where

**30.** Did you draw this picture............?
(a) myself (b) itself
(c) yourself (d) himself

**31.** Neha is the girl .......... laptop was stolen today.
(a) her (b) hers
(c) whose (d) whom

**32.** This is the car .......... had an accident
(a) who (b) which
(c) whose (d) whom

**33.** Shishir is boy ......... father works at SBI.
(a) who (b) whose
(c) whom (d) which

**34.** Karuna and Jyoti have not met .......... for a long time.
(a) herself (b) themself
(c) themselves (d) each other

**35.** Students helped .......... with their reports.
(a) each other (b) himself
(c) herself (d) themselves

**Directions** *(Q. Nos. 36-45) Fill in the blanks with the correct adverb. Choose from the options given:*

**36** I ........... want to know what happened.
(a) exactly (b) purely
(c) simply (d) highly

**37.** Don't worry. It's ........... safe. You won't fall.
(a) finely (b) deeply
(c) fully (d) completely

**38.** The future will be ........... shaped by technology.
(a) merely (b) specially
(c) largely (d) purely

**39.** Everything will be ........... cheaper in the sales.
(a) widely (b) greatly
(c) considerably (d) particularly

**40.** There's nothing ........... similar to this product.
(a) closely (b) remotely
(c) nearly (d) wildly

**41.** They succeeded in .......... exploiting their opportunities.
(a) hardly (b) entirely
(c) fully (d) deeply

**42.** Nobody answering the phone doesn't ........... mean there is no one there.
(a) necessarily (b) surely
(c) wholly (d) strictly

**43.** It's ........... true that education is becoming global.
(a) exactly (b) reliably
(c) certainly (d) fully

**44.** We were ........... considering selling the house.
(a) heavily
(b) seriously
(c) brightly
(d) fully

**45.** It was a long time ago, but I ........... do remember when we first arrived in our new home.
(a) specially (b) surely
(c) seriously (d) strictly

**Directions** *(Q. Nos. 46-55) The sentences given below, have three parts, indicated by (1), (b) and (c). Read each sentence to find out whether there is an error. If you find an error in any parts (1), (b) or (c). Indicate your response by blackening the letter related to that part in the answer sheet provided. If a sentence has no error, indicate this by blackening (d), which stands for 'No error'. (Ignore the errors of punctuation, if any.)*

**46.** Order has been issued (1)/ for his transfer to another district (b)/ but he has not received them so far. (c)/ No error (d)

**47.** Although, she has studied (1)/ English for almost a year (b)/ she is yet to learn the alphabets. (c)/ No error (d)

**48.** There are two sets of books (1)/ which are lying (b)/ unused in the library. (c)/ No error (d)

**49.** Children are prone (1)/ to making mischiefs (b)/ if they have nothing to do. (c)/ No error (d)

**50.** Sheeps are economically useful (1)/ and so they are reared (b)/ in the hills. (c)/ No error (d)

**51.** I have not gone through (1)/ the letter and so I am not aware (b)/ of its content. (c)/ No error (d)

**52.** I shall not attend the meeting (1)/ since I have many works to complete (b)/ within alloted time. (c)/ No error (d)

**53.** You should always be (1)/ true to your words (b)/ if you are to succeed in life. (c)/ No error (d)

**54.** It is a pity (1)/ that even five years old boys (b)/ are engaged in hazardous factories. (c)/No error (d)

**55.** I gave him (1)/ two hundred rupees notes (b)/ for depositing. (c)/ No error (d)

**Directions** *(Q. Nos. 56-65) Find the correct verb to fill in the blanks, so that the meaningful sentences could be framed.*

**56.** I want to while away my time ......... new places in world.
(a) visit (b) visiting
(c) visits (d) visited

**57.** I studied hard because I knew that test would ......... difficult.
(a) being (b) been
(c) can (d) be

**58.** I am reading a novel that my mother ......... bought last year.
(a) is (b) will
(c) be (d) had

**59.** I had left, when my husband ....... .
(a) arrived (b) arrive
(c) is arrive (d) was arrive

**60.** If he comes, we ......... go with him.
(a) could (b) be
(c) shall (d) being

**61.** I ......... for my pen. Have you seen it?
(a) will look (b) looking
(c) look (d) am looking

**62.** You can keep my iPod if you like. I ......... it any more.
(a) don`t use (b) doesn`t use
(c) didn`t use (d) am not using

**63.** My school ......... a food-and-fun fair next month to raise money for the school building-fund.
(a) holds (b) is holding
(c) can hold (d) will hold

**64.** Our lecturer let us ......... the problem in groups before the class started.
(a) discussing (b) to discuss
(c) discuss (d) discussed

**65.** When we went there we found that the lion ......... .
(a) had disappeared (b) was disappeared
(c) has disappeared (d) disappeared

**Directions** *(Q. Nos. 66-85) Fill in the blanks with the correct preposition by choosing the appropriate option.*

**66.** He reminds me ____ you in some ways. You have similar temperaments.
(a) about (b) of (c) at (d) off

**67.** The electric fence is designed to prevent people ____ entering his garden.
(a) of (b) at
(c) from (d) off

**68.** The judge banned him ____ driving for six months after he was found guilty of speeding.
(a) from (b) of
(c) about (d) since

**69.** She takes great interest ____ discussing political issues.
(a) at (b) in
(c) for (d) since

**70.** The police wouldn't provide the press ____ any information about the crime.
(a) by (b) with
(c) of (d) in

**71.** The salesman failed to interest me ____ any of his products.
(a) into (b) about
(c) in (d) from

**72.** His bodyguards protect him ____ potential harm.
(a) from (b) with
(c) about (d) off

**73.** My uncle deals ____ spices and condiments.
(a) with (b) in
(c) until (d) for

**74.** Tomatoes are rich ____ antioxidants that are good for health.
(a) in (b) for
(c) to (d) from

**75.** The teacher stressed ____ the importance of planning.
(a) on (b) about
(c) for (d) in

**76.** Most people agree that kindergarten contributes ____ the child's mental development.
(a) to (b) for
(c) of (d) from

**77.** Since Jennifer was a year younger than her friends, she had a hard time keeping ____ with them.
(a) up (b) along
(c) in (d) through

**78.** In most countries, children start primary school ____ the age of six.
(a) by (b) in
(c) at (d) upto

**79.** Although he studied hard, he couldn't succeed ____ getting a high score in his test.
(a) at (b) in
(c) for (d) by

**80.** There are different sets of language learning sets available ____ all age groups.
(a) for (b) of
(c) upto (d) at

**81.** All candidates are looking forward ____ the announcement of our test scores.
(a) for (b) of
(c) to (d) about

**82.** Since I am busy preparing ____ the exam which is tomorrow, I can't go out with you tonight.
(a) with (b) for
(c) of (d) in

**83.** The students walk five kilometers to school, so they need to get up very early ____ the morning.
(a) at (b) in
(c) for (d) to

**84.** As our school was next to our house, I used to come home ____ lunch time.
(a) in (b) during
(c) at (d) for

**85.** I was born ____ 23rd ____ April, so there is no school when it's my birthday.
(a) in, of (b) on, off
(c) of, in (d) on, of

**Directions** *(Q. Nos. 86-95) Fill in the blanks by selecting the most appropriate conjunctions from the options given below.*

**86.** This old woman spoke ____ English ____ Russian.
(a) either, nor (b) neither, nor
(c) only, but (d) although, yet

**87.** She tried to learn English _____ it was too difficult.
(a) and (b) but
(c) so (d) since

**88.** Last night I went to sleep _____ I was very tired.
(a) since (b) for
(c) and (d) so

**89.** We have tickets for the cinema _____ the opera.
(a) yet (b) and
(c) or (d) nor

**90.** Would you like orange juice _____ cola?
(a) and (b) or
(c) but (d) since

**91.** This is Mary. She is very rich _____ unhappy.
(a) and (b) but
(c) so (d) or

**92.** She is good at Maths _____ her favourite subject is History.
(a) or (b) but (c) so (d) and

**93.** He easily passed the exams _____ he studied quite seriously.
(a) for (b) and
(c) so (d) but

**94.** I'm Polish _____ my mother is Russian.
(a) yet (b) but
(c) so (d) or

**95.** Rohan needed some money _____ he borrowed it from his parents.
(a) and (b) so
(c) but (d) since

## ANSWERS

| | | | | | | | | | | | | | | | | | | | |
|---|---|---|---|---|---|---|---|---|---|---|---|---|---|---|---|---|---|---|---|
| 1. | (c) | 2. | (d) | 3. | (d) | 4. | (b) | 5. | (b) | 6. | (b) | 7. | (c) | 8. | (b) | 9. | (d) | 10. | (b) |
| 11. | (b) | 12. | (c) | 13. | (a) | 14. | (c) | 15. | (c) | 16. | (b) | 17. | (b) | 18. | (d) | 19. | (b) | 20. | (d) |
| 21. | (d) | 22. | (d) | 23. | (a) | 24. | (d) | 25. | (c) | 26. | (b) | 27. | (c) | 28. | (d) | 29. | (b) | 30. | (c) |
| 31. | (c) | 32. | (b) | 33. | (d) | 34. | (d) | 35. | (d) | 36. | (c) | 37. | (d) | 38. | (c) | 39. | (c) | 40. | (b) |
| 41. | (c) | 42. | (a) | 43. | (c) | 44. | (b) | 45. | (b) | 46. | (a) | 47. | (c) | 48. | (a) | 49. | (b) | 50. | (a) |
| 51. | (c) | 52. | (b) | 53. | (b) | 54. | (b) | 55. | (b) | 56. | (b) | 57. | (d) | 58. | (d) | 59. | (a) | 60. | (c) |
| 61. | (d) | 62. | (a) | 63. | (b) | 64. | (c) | 65. | (a) | 66. | (b) | 67. | (c) | 68. | (a) | 69. | (b) | 70. | (b) |
| 71. | (c) | 72. | (a) | 73. | (b) | 74. | (a) | 75. | (a) | 76. | (a) | 77. | (a) | 78. | (c) | 79. | (d) | 80. | (a) |
| 81. | (c) | 82. | (b) | 83. | (d) | 84. | (b) | 85. | (d) | 86. | (b) | 87. | (b) | 88. | (a) | 89. | (b) | 90. | (b) |
| 91. | (b) | 92. | (b) | 93. | (a) | 94. | (b) | 95. | (b) | | | | | | | | | | |

Chapter 02

# Determiners/Articles

Determiners are words that come at the beginning of noun phrases, before adjectives. These words help to show how much or how many we are talking about.

## Classification of Determiners

Determiners can be classified into following categories

1. Demonstrative Determiners
2. Possessive Determiners
3. Quantifiers
4. Articles

## Use of Determiners

### 1. Demonstrative Determiners

These determiners show where an object or person is in relation to the speaker.

There are four basic determiners, 'this, these, that and those'. e.g.

(i) Whose house is *this*?
(ii) *Those* days were really good old days.
(iii) I know nothing about *that* murder,
(iv) Are *these* books Yours?

### 2. Possessive Determiners

Possessive determiners or possessive adjectives tell us who owns something. We use a possessive determiner before a noun to show who owns the noun we are talking about. They come in front of any other adjectives. e.g.

(i) This is **your** book.
(ii) That is **our** beautiful house.

We use different possessive determiners depending on who owns the thing we are talking about.

| Subject | Possessive Determiner | Used with Type of Noun |
|---|---|---|
| I | my | first person singular |
| We | our | first person plural |
| You | your | second person singular/plural |
| They | their | third person plural |
| He | his | third person singular masculine |
| She | her | third person singular feminine |
| It | its | third person singular neuter |

**My**, **her**, **his** and **its** are used with singular nouns, while **our** and **their** are used with plural nouns. **Your** can be used with either singular or plural nouns, depending on the sense.

e.g. (i) This is **my** book. (ii) The dog licked **its** paw.
(iii) Which is **their** car?

All three of you, have you done **your** homework?

### 3. Quantifiers

Quantifiers answer the simple questions like. 'How much, how many'?

Some of the most common quantifiers are 'A few, A little, much, many, a lot of, most, some, any, enough'. Some definite numeral determiners are 'One, Two, Three'. e.g.

– The **second** boy in the **third** row is my brother.

### 4. Articles

An article is a word used to modify a noun, which is a person, place, object or idea..... Usually adjectives modify noun through description but articles are used instead to point out or refer to noun.

Articles impart effectiveness and accuracy to the noun. Articles also come in the category of determiners.

There are two kinds of Articles

1. Indefinite Article– A, An
2. Definite Article– The

#### Rules of Articles

#### The Use of Indefinite Articles 'A', 'An'

#### Rule 1

A student must note that the choice between 'A' and 'An' is determined primarily by sound.

- 'A' is used before a word beginning.

(a) With a consonant. e.g.
(i) A boy (ii) A child

(b) With a vowel giving the sound of a consonant. e.g.
(i) A one eyed man (ii) A university student

- 'An' is used before a word beginning.

(a) With a vowel. e.g.

(i) An elephant (ii) An apple

(b) With a mute 'h'. e.g.

(i) An hour (ii) An heir

(c) With a consonant pronounced with the sound of a vowel. e.g.

(i) An LL.B student (ii) An M.P.

**Rule 2**

Indefinite article 'A'/'An' is used when we talk of a thing or a person that is indefinite or that is mentioned for the first time. (in the sense of 'one').

Indefinite article is also used to express a class (in the sense of 'any')

- Before a singular/countable common noun when it is mentioned for the first time representing no particular person or a thing. e.g.
  (i) I need **a** book. *(one)*
  (ii) Twelve inches make **a** foot. *(one)*
- Before a singular countable noun which is used to single out some person/something as a representative of a class of things, animals and persons. e.g.
  – A cow is **a** useful animal. *(any in the sense of class)*
- To make a common noun of a proper noun to express quality. e.g.
  – **A** Shylock is living in my neighbourhood. *(a cruel miser)*
- In certain expressions of quantity with certain numbers and expressions of 'Price/rate, speed, ratio'. e.g.
  – Rupees ten **a** kilo.
- When 'A/An' represent a weakened form of preposition 'in'. e.g.
  – He earns fifty thousand rupees **a** year.
- In exclamations with 'what' or 'how' before singular countable nouns. e.g.
  (i) What **a** hot day! (ii) What **a** pretty girl!
- Note the position of indefinite article in the following adverbs 'Rather, very, much, quite, so, too, such, as'. e.g.
  (i) It is *rather* a nuisance.
  (ii) It is *rather* a good step (or a rather good step).
- Before certain phrases. e.g.
  (i) In a hurry (ii) A pity
  (iii) Take a liking (iv) Feel a shame
- Before the words denoting numbers. e.g.
  (i) A hundred (ii) A dozen
- Before the verbs used as noun. e.g.
  (i) For a swim (ii) For a talk

⚠ Indefinite article 'A' is used. In the sense of 'any' to single out a person, a thing or an animal as a representative of a class. e.g.
(i) A son should be obedient.
(ii) A cow is a useful animal.

## Use of Definite Article 'The'

- When we talk of a particular person or a thing that has already been mentioned, known or under discussion. e.g.
  (i) **The** book (which you mentioned) is not available in the market.
  (ii) Let us study **the** lesson carefully. (lesson in hand)
- Before proper nouns (unique objects) when they refer to the names of historical buildings, mountain ranges, planets, rivers, oceans, gulfs, groups of island, holy books, ordinals, descriptive names of countries, states, newspapers, magazines, deserts, superlative degree, names of trains, hotels, shops, trains. e.g.
  (i) The Persian Gulf (ii) The Indian Ocean
  (iii) The Ganges (iv) The Himalayas
  (v) The Ramayana (vi) The Vedas
  (vii) The Sun (viii) The Earth

⚠ 'The' is not used before **Aravali** and **Everest** because they are not mountain ranges.

- When a singular noun expresses a class of animal or things. But 'the' is avoided with their plural forms and persons to express a class.
  e.g.
  (i) The dog is a faithful animal.
  (ii) The rose is a sweet flower.
  (iii) The cow is economically useful.
  (iv) Dogs are faithful.
  (v) The cows are economically useful. *(Delete 'the')*
  (vi) The son should be obedient.
  *(Delete 'The', use 'A'. 'The' before a person does not express a class of persons)*
- 'Man/Woman/Mankind' used in general sense to represent human race are used without article. e.g.
  – Man is mortal. *(Used in general sense)*
- Before an adjective when it represents a class of persons. e.g.
  (i) The rich should help the poor.
  (ii) The old are respected by the young.
- Before musical instruments. e.g.
  (i) He can play **the** flute.
  (ii) She is fond of playing **the** harmonium.
- As an adverb with a comparative sense. (Double comparison). e.g.
  (i) **The** sooner, **the** better.
  (ii) **The** higher you go, **the** colder it is.
- Before comparative degree in case of a choice. e.g.
  (i) She is **the** weaker of the two sisters.
  (ii) Which is the more beautiful of the two sisters?
- Before proper noun for the sake of comparison. e.g.
  (i) Surdas is **the** Milton of India.
  (ii) Kalidas is **the** Shakespeare of India.
- Before sports, cups and trophies. e.g.
  (i) India won **the** Singer Cup last year.
  (ii) A number of teams are taking part in **the** World Cup.

- Before physical positions. e.g.
  (i) The top of **the** mountain.
  (ii) The back of the house.
- With the cardinal points. e.g.
  (i) **The** Sun rises in **the** East.
  (ii) **The** Himalayas are to **the** North of India.
- Before a unit of measurement. e.g.
  (i) Cloth is sold by **the** metre.
  (ii) Eggs are sold by **the** dozen.
- Before caste and communities. e.g.
  (i) **The** Rajputs are brave people.
  (ii) **The** Marathas are hard working.
- Before the adjective 'same and whole' and after the adjective 'all and both' 'the' is used with plural nouns. e.g.
  (i) This is **the** same book that you gave me.
  (ii) **The** whole class was absent.
- In certain idiomatic phrases. e.g.
  (i) In **the** wrong. (ii) On **the** contrary.
- Before a common noun to give it the force of a superlative. e.g.
  (i) She is **the** woman.
  (ii) Netaji was **the** leader.
- Before a common noun to give it the sense of an abstract noun (feelings, qualities etc.) e.g.
  (i) **The** judge in him. *(sense of justice)*
  (ii) **The** mother in her. *(feelings of a mother)*
- Before inventions. e.g.
  (i) **The** telephone. (ii) **The** wireless.
- Before the name of professions used collectively. e.g.
  (i) **The** Press. (ii) **The** Bench.
- Before a noun, qualified by adjectives. e.g.
  (i) **The** former President Abdul Kalam
  (ii) **The** immortal Shakespeare.
- Before the case in apposition. e.g.
  (i) Netaji, **the** hero of modern India, ought to be remembered.
  (ii) Who can underestimate Mr Vajpayee, **the** former Prime Minister?
- Before the dates. e.g.
  (i) **The** 10th of May. (ii) **The** 5th of September.
- Before the organs of government. e.g.
  (i) **The** judiciary (ii) **The** Legislature
- Before the parts of a body of a person in place of possessive adjectives. e.g.
  (i) He hit me on **the** back.
  (ii) She caught me by **the** arm.
- Before the political parties. e.g.
  (i) The BJP (ii) **The** Labour Party
- Before the Armed forces. e.g.
  (i) **The** Army (ii) The Police
- Before the dynasties, empires, wars, revolutions, centuries. e.g.
  (i) **The** Gupta dynasty.
  (ii) **The** British empire.
- Before language to signify nationality. e.g.
  (i) **The** Chinese are hard working.
  (ii) **The** Japanese are patriots out and out.

## Omission of Articles

The article 'A/An, The' are omitted

- Before proper noun. e.g.
  (i) Shakespeare was the greatest dramatist.
  (ii) Delhi is the capital of India.

⚠ (a) When indefinite article is used before proper nouns they become **common noun.**

(b) 'The' before a proper noun is used for the sake of comparison. e.g.
  (i) This man is a Shylock. (a miser)
  (ii) Samudra Gupta was **the** Napolean of his age. *(The greatest general of his time.)*

- Before names of materials. e.g.
  (i) Silver is a useful metal.
  (ii) The tea of Assam is very famous. *(particular tea )*
- Before common noun 'the' is used in its widest sense. e.g.
  (i) Man is mortal.
  (ii) The Gods and the Goddesses are kind to him. (in the sense of deities)
- Before abstract noun as qualities, feelings and states used in general sense. e.g.
  (i) Truth is a noble quality.
  (ii) Love is a natural feeling.
- Before noun complement. (appoint, make, elect, select etc.) e.g.
  (i) The committee appointed him Captain.
  (ii) They elected him President.
- Before collective noun in general sense. e.g.
  (i) Life is complex.
  (ii) Society does not allow this.
- Before uncountable noun. (Refer to Rule 1 in the chapter on Noun) e.g.
  (i) He gave me advice.
  (ii) He passed on information to me.
- Before languages. e.g.
  (i) Chinese is a difficult language.
  (ii) He knows Russian very well. *[Rule 3(B)]*
- Before 'school, college, home, church, temple, sea, work, bed, table, hospital, market, prison, court' when their purpose is thought of rather than the actual building/place. e.g.
  (i) We go to temple on Mondays. *(for prayer)*
  (ii) I go to bed early. *(to sleep)*
  (iii) He was sent to prison after conviction. *(as a prisoner)*
- Before 'hobbies, professions and sports'. e.g. articles are omitted.
  (i) Dancing is her profession. (ii) Gardening is his hobby.

- Before names of diseases. e.g.
  (i) Cancer is a dreaded disease.
  (ii) AIDS is spreading like wild fire.
- Before regular meals except when preceded by an adjective. e.g.
  (i) I take breakfast at 8 am.
  (ii) You should take dinner early.
  (iii) They gave us a good breakfast.
  (iv) A good breakfast is necessary.
- Before parts of the body. e.g.
  – Liver is the largest organ of human body.
- Before modes of travel. e.g.
  (i) He will go by air.
  (ii) A journey by road is very comfortable.
- Before names of relations like 'Uncle, mother, father' etc in place of possessive adjectives. e.g.
  (i) Father will go to Delhi tomorrow.
  (ii) Aunt is expected any moment.

⚠ 'Father' and 'Aunt' implies 'our father' and 'our aunt'

- Before little, few. (in negative sense). e.g.
  (i) Little sugar
  (ii) Few students

- When two or more connected noun refer to the same person or thing, the article should be used before the first noun. However, the article is used before each noun if they refer to two different persons or objects.

  e.g.
  (i) The Prime Minister and the President are visiting the town today. *(Two different persons holding two different posts.)*
  (ii) The Prime Minister and President of the party is on a visit to the town today.*(One person holding two posts.)*
- Similarly, one article before the first adjective is used when two or more adjectives qualify the same noun. e.g.
  – She is wearing a black and a white saree. *(Omit 'a' before 'white')*
- If there are two articles before ordinals, use singular noun. In the case of article before one ordinal, noun should be used in plural form. e.g.
  (i) The first and the second *chapter* are very difficult. *(Incorrect)*
  (ii) The first and second *chapters* are very difficult. *(Correct)*

⚠ The article is not repeated with plural nouns. **Verb is in plural form** in the sentences given in 'C'.

# Practice Questions

**Directions** *(Q. Nos. 1-40) Fill in the blanks with suitable Determiners out of the following options.*

**1.** Do you have .......... post card? Yes I have ..........
(a) any, some (b) any, one
(c) any, none (d) some, some

**2.** She showed .......... concern for her step-daughter.
(a) a little (b) little
(c) few (d) some

**3.** Did .......... write with my pen when I was away?
(a) some (b) someone
(c) anyone (d) None of these

**4.** All the boys went to beach but only .......... could swim.
(a) few (b) a few
(c) little (d) the little

**5.** There are .......... countries in the world where population is not growing fast.
(a) any (b) many
(c) most (d) much

**6.** There was .......... accident near .......... market this morning .
(a) the, a (b) an, the
(c) a, the (d) the, the

**7.** One of the students of the class writes ......... date on .......... black board every day.
(a) a, the (b) the, a
(c) the, the (d) the, an

**8.** Dr Radha Krishnan was .......... more famous philosopher than a politician.
(a) the (b) an
(c) a (d) None of these

**9.** .......... higher you go .......... colder it is.
(a) a, the (b) the , the
(c) a, an (d) an, the

**10.** The eggs are sold by ......... dozen.
(a) a (b) an
(c) the (d) None of these

**11.** .......... doctor says it is .......... hopeless case.
(a) The, a (b) A, the
(c) The, the (d) A, a

**12.** Last month we went to see .......... National book fair with our teacher.
(a) Some (b) the
(c) a (d) an

**13.** We bought .......... books.
(a) much (b) more
(c) any (d) many

**14.** ......... of them were story books, while the others were of General Knowledge.
(a) Much (b) Any
(c) Some (d) The little

**15.** .......... man who is wearing .......... white cap is my neighbour.
(a) A, The (b) The, The
(c) The, a (d) A , a

**16.** Games keep .......... body fit.
(a) a (b) an
(c) the (d) None of these

**17.** Will she be back in .......... hour?
(a) a (b) an
(c) the (d) None of these

**18.** I met .......... European yesterday.
(a) a (b) an
(c) the (d) None of these

**19.** Did he leave the country for ........ good?
(a) a (b) an
(c) the (d) zero article

**20.** The next .......... passengers are without ticket.
(a) three (b) fewer
(c) many (d) all

**21.** There is .......... scope of his recovery.
(a) the little (b) fewer
(c) little (d) all

**22.** Does your father work in ......... Overseas Bank?.
(a) zero article (b) an
(c) the (d) some

**23.** .......... books he has written will bring him laurels.
(a) Zero article (b) A few
(c) The (d) Some

**24.** .......... of the students in my class are good at English.
(a) Zero article (b) The few
(c) Any (d) Some

**25.** Forgiveness is .......... great virtue.
(a) a (b) an
(c) the (d) zero article

**26.** He went to .......... hospital to deliver the parcel.
(a) a (b) an
(c) the (d) zero article

**27.** Did you like .......... girl's new dress?
(a) some (b) both
(c) all (d) any

**28.** Rosemary wanted to buy .......... those flowers.
(a) some (b) both
(c) all (d) any

**29.** The bottle contained .......... amount of water.
(a) the few (b) the little
(c) many (d) a little

**30.** Was there .......... student in the class?
(a) some (b) many
(c) a few (d) any

**31.** .......... number of students leave this school every year.
(a) A (b) An
(c) The (d) Zero article

**32.** .......... number of students is not increasing in this school.
(a) A (b) An
(c) The (d) Zero article

**33.** .......... sisters are known to me.
(a) Any (b) One
(c) Both (d) Zero article

**34.** It is .......... honour to work with .......... Executive Director.
(a) a, the (b) an, the
(c) the, the (d) an, zero article

**35.** I have .......... important news for you.
(a) some (b) all
(c) any (d) the

**36.** I won't let the whole empire go to .......... dogs.
(a) a (b) an
(c) the (d) zero article

**37.** .......... manuscript does not reach the printing press.
(a) Some (b) Many
(c) Many a (d) Any

**38.** .......... candidates turned up this time.
(a) Many a (b) Fewer
(c) Few (d) Any

**39.** The poor have .......... money for recreation.
(a) little (b) fewer
(c) few (d) any

**40.** He has joined as Registrar at .......... Jai Narain Vyas University.
(a) a (b) an
(c) the (d) zero article

**Directions** *(Q. Nos. 41-51) Fill in the blanks with suitable article from the options given below.*

**41.** ......... Tower of London is ........... popular tourist place.
(a) The/a (b) An/the
(c) A/an (d) The/the

**42.** Where is ...... video game I gave you yesterday?
(a) an (b) a
(c) the (d) No article

**43.** Binod has ........ terrible headache.
(a) an (b) a
(c) the (d) No article

**44.** Allahabad is situated on the bank of ......... Ganga.
(a) an (b) a
(c) the (d) No article

**45.** There is nothing like staying at ...... home for relaxation.
(a) an (b) a
(c) the (d) No article

**46.** I watched a magic show two days ago which was ....... exciting experience.
(a) the (b) a (c) an (d) No article

**47.** ....... mangoes and ....... apples are exported to other countries from India.
(a) A/the (b) The/the
(c) The/a (d) No articles

**48.** ............... Air India has shown signs of improvement.
(a) A (b) An
(c) The (d) No article

**49.** My mother bought ............. expensive saree on Mother's Day.
(a) an (b) a
(c) the (d) No article

**50.** Look, there is ......... little squirrel on this tree!
(a) an (b) the
(c) a (d) No article

**51.** I hate ....... geography and biology. ........ only subject I like is English.
(a) the/The (b) No article/The
(c) a/An (d) the/A

**Directions** *(Q. Nos.52-56) Answer the following questions by filling the blanks with the most appropriate article from the given options.*

**52.** What did you get for your birthday?
I got ........ lot of good presents.
(a) a (b) the (c) an (d) No article

**53.** Where are you going for your vacations?
I am going to ........ hill station in Himachal Pradesh.
(a) an (b) a (c) the (d) No article

**54.** Do you think your friend is lying?
No, he is the kind of ........ guy who never tells lies.
(a) the (b) an (c) a (d) No article

**55.** How is your grandfather?
He is ....... little sick, but it is nothing serious.
(a) an (b) a (c) the (d) No article

**56.** Where were you last night? I called you so many times.
Oh sorry, .........yesterday my mobile was off.
(a) the (b) an
(c) a (d) No article

**Directions** *(Q. Nos. 57-58) Match List I with List II in order to form meaningful sentences.*

**57.**

| | List I | | List II |
|---|---|---|---|
| A. | Rebecca works in | 1. | an Indian boy. |
| B. | Mike lives in | 2. | hosted by the Bhallas. |
| C. | Jane wants to marry | 3. | a book shop. |
| D. | I am not attending the party | 4. | an old house. |

**Codes**

| | A | B | C | D | | A | B | C | D |
|---|---|---|---|---|---|---|---|---|---|
| (a) | 3 | 1 | 2 | 3 | (b) | 3 | 4 | 1 | 2 |
| (c) | 2 | 4 | 1 | 2 | (d) | 2 | 3 | 4 | 1 |

***58.***

| | List I | | List II |
|---|---|---|---|
| A. | Do you have ....... pen? | 1. | an |
| B. | Is this ....... pen given by Mr Singh? | 2. | No article |
| C. | Amit is....... MBA from Rajasthan University. | 3. | the |
| D. | How do I go to ....... Lajpat nagar? | 4. | a |

**Codes**

| | A | B | C | D | | A | B | C | D |
|---|---|---|---|---|---|---|---|---|---|
| (a) | 2 | 3 | 1 | 4 | (b) | 4 | 3 | 1 | 2 |
| (c) | 3 | 2 | 1 | 4 | (d) | 2 | 1 | 3 | 4 |

**Directions** (Q. Nos. 59-60) **Choose the best option with correct use of article(s).**

***59.*** 1. Mr Sharma is a best doctor.
2. Mr Sharma is the best doctor.
3. Mr Sharma is an best doctor.
4. Mr Sharma is best doctor.

**Codes**
(a) Only 1 (b) Only 4
(c) Only 2 (d) Only 3

***60.*** 1. The train stopped at station.
2. The train stopped at a station.
3. The train stopped at the station.
4. The train stopped at an station.

**Codes**
(a) Only 1 (b) Only 4
(c) Only 2 (d) Only 3

## ANSWERS

| | | | | | | | | | | | | | | | | | | | |
|---|---|---|---|---|---|---|---|---|---|---|---|---|---|---|---|---|---|---|---|
| 1. | (b) | 2. | (b) | 3. | (b) | 4. | (b) | 5. | (b) | 6. | (b) | 7. | (c) | 8. | (c) | 9. | (b) | 10. | (c) |
| 11. | (a) | 12. | (b) | 13. | (d) | 14. | (c) | 15. | (c) | 16. | (c) | 17. | (b) | 18. | (a) | 19. | (d) | 20. | (a) |
| 21. | (c) | 22. | (c) | 23. | (c) | 24. | (d) | 25. | (a) | 26. | (c) | 27. | (d) | 28. | (c) | 29. | (d) | 30. | (d) |
| 31. | (a) | 32. | (c) | 33. | (c) | 34. | (b) | 35. | (a) | 36. | (c) | 37. | (c) | 38. | (b) | 39. | (a) | 40. | (d) |
| 41. | (a) | 42. | (c) | 43. | (b) | 44. | (c) | 45. | (d) | 46. | (c) | 47. | (d) | 48. | (d) | 49. | (a) | 50. | (c) |
| 51. | (b) | 52. | (a) | 53. | (b) | 54. | (d) | 55. | (b) | 56. | (d) | 57. | (b) | 58. | (b) | 59. | (c) | 60. | (d) |

Chapter 03

# Modals

A verb used to express the mood or attitude of a speaker is called Modal Auxiliary.

e.g.

(i) You *should* regularly go for a morning walk.

(ii) They *must* attend tomorrow's meeting.

(iii) *May* I use your pen please?

## Different Uses of Modals

1. **May and Might** These modal auxiliary verbs 'may and might' are used to express

(A) **Possibility**

(i) It *may/might* rain. (ii) You *may* fall.

(B) **Permission**

(i) *May* I come in? (ii) Yes, you *may* come in.

(C) **Wish or Prayer**

(i) *May* you enjoy marital happiness!

(ii) *May* you live long !

(D) **Purpose**

(i) She works hard so that she *may* pass.

(ii) She came so that she *might* see me.

(E) **Remote Possibility**

'Might' is used in place of 'may' to express remote possibility.

e.g.

(i) It *might* rain. (ii) He *might* be sleeping now.

Normally both 'May and Might' can be used to express possibility in present and future. However, 'might' is used when the reporting verb is in the past.

(F) **May/Might + Have** They are used to express possibility/desirability relating to the past action.

e.g.

(i) He *may/might* have left yesterday. *(It is possible he left)*

(ii) He *might* have failed. *(It is possible he failed)*

2. **Can and Could** (Able to) They are used to express

(A) **Ability** (Present, Past and Future)

She *can* write english well. *(is able to)*

(B) **Polite Request**

(i) *Could* you please do it for me?

*('Would' is also used for polite request)*

(ii) *Could* you please lend me some money?

(C) **Permission/Order**

(i) Yes, you *can* go now.

(ii) You *can* take my book.

*(Here 'can' is an alternative to 'may')*

(D) **Prohibition/Offer**

(i) You *cannot* enter the room. *(Prohibition)*

(ii) *Can* I get you some fruits? *(Offer)*

(E) **Possibility**

(i) Who is she with him?

She *could* be his wife. *(possibly)*

(ii) How old is she?

She *could* be sixteen. *(possibly)*

(F) **Could + Have** This form is used for past ability while indicating that the action did not take place.

e.g.

(i) I *could have* revealed the secret. *(but I did not)*

(ii) You *could have* borrowed money. *(but you did not)*

⚠ In all these sentences the action did not take place.

3. **Should** It is used to express

(A) **Duty/Obligation**

(i) You *should* stand by your brother.

(ii) I *should* leave now.

(B) **Change of shall in the Past tense**

(i) I told him that I *should* go there.

(ii) Did I not tell you that I *should* qualify?

(C) **Purpose**

Walk carefully lest you should fall.

(D) **Condition**

Should you work hard, you will get success.

*('should' is used in the sense of 'if'.)*

(E) **Should + Have** This form is used to express obligation in the past. It may simply the non-performance of the action.

e.g.
(i) You *should have* stood by your brother.
(ii) He *should have* left a massage.

**4. Must** It expresses

(A) **Necessity or Obligation** (in place of 'should')
(i) You *must* follow instructions.
(ii) I *must* leave now.

(B) **Order of the Speaker**
(i) You *must not* leave now.
(ii) They *must not* play here.

(C) **Strong Possibility** (in place of 'may')
(i) It is ten. The teacher *must* be in the class.
(ii) She *must* be working in the office now.

(D) **Determination**
I *must* help him.

(E) **Deduction, Inference**
(i) He has a big house. He *must* be rich.
(ii) She reads a lot. She *must* be learned.

(F) **Must + Have** This form is used for a past action or situation indicating non-performance of action.
e.g.
(i) You *must* have followed instructions.
(ii) You *must* have left them.

**5. Ought to** It expresses

(A) **Duty or Moral Obligation** It is normally used for 'should and must', when there is strong sense of moral duty, advice or indication of correct action.
e.g.
(i) You *ought to* serve your motherland.
(ii) You *ought not* to take fatty food.

(B) **Ought to + Have** This construction is used in relation to past action of duty that was not fulfilled or an action that was neglected in the past.
(i) You *ought to have* taken care of your wife.
(ii) You *ought to have* served your parents.

# Practice Questions

**Directions** *(Q. Nos. 1-5) Fill in the blanks by choosing appropriate modals.*

**1.** ........... you like to have tea or coffee?
(a) Could (b) Would
(c) Can (d) Will

**2.** If Ram had money he ........... have helped you.
(a) will (b) can
(c) may (d) would

**3.** If you are not feeling well, you ........... consult a doctor.
(a) must (b) should (c) ought to (d) can

**4.** We ........... respect our parents.
(a) must (b) should
(c) ought to (d) will

**5.** She advised that I ........ curtail my expenditure.
(a) should (b) shall
(c) should have (d) will

**Directions** *(Q. Nos. 6-10) What does the modal used in the sentence suggest?*

**6.** My mother said, "Will you please help me in cooking dinner".
Here, the mother is
(a) asking a question (b) giving an instruction
(c) offering advice (d) making a request

**7.** You should serve your motherland.
Here the modal should shows
(a) love for the mother land (b) advice
(c) desire (d) suggestion

**8.** The doctor <u>must</u> be greedy, that's why he demanded so much money.
Here the word must shows
(a) certainty (b) possibility
(c) belief (d) suspicion

**9.** <u>Can</u> you speak more than two languages?
Here the word can shows
(a) capacity (b) ability
(c) skill (d) compliance

**10.** Tomorrow is Sunday. You need not go to school.
Here the words <u>need not</u> shows
(a) order (b) suggestion
(c) advice (d) possibility

**Directions** *(Q. Nos. 11-17) Fill in the blanks by Choosing appropriate Modals.*

**11.** There are dark clouds in the sky......
(a) it will rain (b) it shall rain
(c) it may rain (d) it must rain

**12.** I ....... buy an alarm clock today. I do not want to be late anymore.
(a) can (b) might
(c) must (d) may

**13.** Manjit said to Anisha, "Could you please open the window?"
In the above sentence Manjit is
(a) asking a question
(b) giving an instruction
(c) offering advice
(d) making request

**14.** Supply a model which expresses ability.

**All of them …… speak three language.**

(a) may (b) will
(c) must (d) can

**15.** We must come back by six.

**'Must' in the above sentence expresses**

(a) possibility
(b) advice
(c) desire
(d) necessity

**16.** Fill in the blanks with appropriate modal.

**One …… abide by the laws.**

(a) may (b) could
(c) need (d) should

**17.** He wished that she …… get well soon.

(a) may (b) might
(c) should (d) will

**Directions** *(Q. Nos. 18-22) What does the underlined modal auxiliary suggest in the following sentences?*

**18.** The conservatives should win the next election.

(a) Obligation (b) Probability
(c) Desirability (d) Conjecture

**19.** He must be at least sixty.

(a) Inference (b) Probability (c) Conjecture (d) Belief

**20.** Can you lift this box?

(a) Capacity (b) Competence (c) Ability (d) Skill

**21.** The game should be finished by now.

(a) Probability (b) Conjecture
(c) Deduction (d) Prediction

**22.** Choose the correct word to complete the given sentence.

**…… I speak to the principal for one day leave?**

(a) Can (b) May (c) Must (d) Should

## ANSWERS

| | | | | | | | | | | | | | | | | | | | |
|---|---|---|---|---|---|---|---|---|---|---|---|---|---|---|---|---|---|---|---|
| 1. | (b) | 2. | (d) | 3. | (a) | 4. | (c) | 5. | (a) | 6. | (d) | 7. | (d) | 8. | (b) | 9. | (b) | 10. | (c) |
| 11. | (c) | 12. | (c) | 13. | (d) | 14. | (d) | 15. | (d) | 16. | (d) | 17. | (c) | 18. | (c) | 19. | (b) | 20. | (c) |
| 21. | (c) | 22. | (d) | | | | | | | | | | | | | | | | |

Chapter 04

# Finite-Non Finite Clauses

A number of finite verbs in a sentence determine a number of clauses. Non-finite verbs are not considered for the purpose of clause analysis.

- In a **simple sentence,** there is one finite verb and hence only one clause.
  (a) She **is writing** a novel.
  (b) Parul **will examine** a patient.
- In a **complex sentence,** there are more than one clauses which are as follows
  (a) Principal/Main clause
  (b) Subordinate clauses
  (i) Noun clause (ii) Adjective clause
  (iii) Adverb clause

These subordinate clauses are joined by subordinating conjunctions.

- In a **compound sentence,** there are more than one Principal clause/Co-ordinate clause related to each other.
  (a) Principal clause (b) Co-ordinate clause

Co-ordinate clause is joined by co-ordinating conjunctions.

## Kinds of Clauses

*Kinds of clauses are explained below*

## Principal Clause

While analysing a sentence, a student is required to find out a Principal clause. It is easy to do so because the Principal clause is not introduced by any joining connective. Having found out the Principal clause, a student is expected to break up the rest of the sentence into Subordinate/Co-ordinate clauses.

*Study the following examples carefully*

- He told me that he would help my brother, who needed some money.
  — He told me. *(Principal clause)*
  — that he would help my brother. *(Noun clause, object of the verb 'told')*
  — who needed some money. *(Adjective clause, qualifying 'brother')*
- He gave money to the students, who were poor, whenever they asked for it.
  — He gave money to the students. *(Principal clause)*
  — who were poor. *(Adjective clause, qualifying the noun 'Students')*
  — whenever they asked for it *(Adverb clause of time, modifying verb 'gave')*

  So, a principal clause is identified by the subject and a finite verb of its own.

## Noun Clause

By now, it is clear that a Noun clause is one of the three subordinate clauses in a complex sentence. It does the work of a noun.

### Functions of a Noun Clause

*Study the following examples carefully*

- **The subject of a verb**
  (i) What he did is not desirable.
  (ii) That he will succeed is certain.

These sentences can also be written in the following manner to show that Noun clauses have been used in place of subject

(i) It is not desirable what he did.
(ii) It is certain that he will succeed.

Here, Noun clause is in apposition to Pronoun 'it'.

- **The object of a transitive verb**
  (i) He does not **know** when he will return.
  (ii) She **confessed** that she had met him.

In the above sentences, noun clauses explain the verb **know** and **confessed**.

- **The complement of a verb**
  - (i) The fact **is** that he is dishonest.
  - (ii) His hope **is** that his son will return.

  Noun clause following the verb 'to be' performs the function of a complement. *(in place of predicate)*

  'To be, become, seem, appear, grow, taste, smell, prove, come, go, feel' are some of the verbs followed by a Noun clause as a complement.
- **The object of a preposition/infinitive**
  - (i) There is no sense **in** what you say.
  - (ii) Pay heed **to** what your elders say.
  - (iii) I was pleased **to note** that he was recovering.
- **The apposition to a noun/pronoun**
  - (i) I have not heard the **news** that he has married her.
  - (ii) I do not believe in his **statement** that he was not present there.

## Adjective Clause

Adjective clause does the work of an adjective. It qualifies a noun or pronoun in the Principal or any other subordinate clause.

*Study the following examples carefully*

1. He is the man, **who is honest.** *(Qualifying the noun 'man')*
2. The time, **when he will come**, is not certain. *(Qualifying the noun 'time')*
3. Those, **who are honest**, succeed in life. *(Qualifying the pronoun 'those')*
4. I gave him the pen, **which I bought for myself**. *(Qualifying the noun 'pen')*

## Adverb Clause

As already described, an Adverb clause is a subordinate clause. It does the work of an adverb. It, therefore, modifies some adjective verb or an adverb.

*Adverb clauses are classified as follows*

- **Adverb Clause of Time** Time clause is introduced by conjunctions of time such as 'When, as, while, before, after, by the time, as soon as, until, till, whenever, since, as long as, ever since'. eg.

  – As he came into the room all rose to their feet.
- **Adverb clause of Condition**
  - (a) There are three types of Conditional clauses. Each kind contains a different pair of tenses.
    - (i) Present likely condition.
    - (ii) Present unlikely condition.
    - (iii) Past condition. eg.

  – It it rains we shall stay at home.
  - (b) Conditional clauses are introduced with connectives 'if, unless, would that suppose, on condition that, provided, in case.'

Sometimes, subordinate conjunction 'if' is omitted in Adverb clause of condition. ***(should, had, were** are used instead)* eg.

– Had I not seen **this** with my own eyes, I would not have believed

- **Adverb clause of Purpose** Adverb clause of Purpose is introduced by conjunctions 'That, so that, in order that and lest.'
- **Adverb clause of Place** Adverb clause of place is introduced by the conjunctions 'Where' and 'wherever' but Adverb clause of Place does not qualify any place given in the main clause. eg.

  – They can stay **where** they are.
- **Adverb clause of Result** Adverb clause of Result is expressed by 'that' in the adverb clause preceded by 'so', 'such' in the main clause. eg.

  – He is such a good man that all respect him.
- **Adverb clause of Reason** Adverb clause of Reason is introduced by 'Because, since, as'. However, *'so'* and *'therefore'* should be avoided in the Main clause. eg.

  – **Since** you are so clever, you will be able to explain this.
- **Adverb clause of Concession or Contrast** Adverb clause of contrast is introduced by 'Although, though, even if, however, whatever, no matter, notwithstanding that, as, whether, even though, much as, even as.' eg.

  – Although he is rich, he does not want to help the poor.

# Finite Clauses

Finite clauses must contain a verb which shows tense. They can be main clauses or subordinate clauses

(i) Is it raining? *(main: present)*
(ii) I spoke to Joanne last night. (main: past)
(iii) We didn't get any food because we didn't have enough time. *(main: past; subordinate: past)*

# Non-finite Clauses

Non-finite clauses contain a verb which does not show tense. We usually use non-finite verbs only in subordinate clauses. We often use a non-finite clause when the subject is the same as the subject in the main clause:

(i) I had something to eat before leaving.
(ii) He left the party and went home, not having anyone to talk to.

We often use non-finite clauses after some subordinating conjunctions like after, although, though and if

(i) By the end of the day, although exhausted, Rohan did not feel quite as tired as he had in the past.

We use non-finite clauses as the complements to verbs which take -ing or to-infinitive after them:

(i) I don't enjoy playing tennis in the rain.
(ii) I'd hate to travel to London every day.

# Practice Questions

**Directions** (Q. Nos. 1-15) ***Fill in the blanks in the given sentences with the correct use of clause.***

**1.** The professional .............. doesn't follow ethics cannot be considered a professional.
(a) which he (b) who
(c) who he (d) whose

**2.** What do you do when you are at a function .............. don't know people very well?
(a) where (b) that
(c) where you (d) who you

**3.** I always remember the times .............. my family and I spent summer holidays together.
(a) when (b) where
(c) who (d) that

**4.** Do you know where I can take the bus .............. goes to Chandigarh?
(a) which (b) when (c) who (d) that

**5.** Has Hema reviewed the latest sales report .............. gave us last week?
(a) who the sales manager (b) which the sales manager
(c) that the sales manager (d) whose the sales manager

**6.** There are a couple personality traits .............. would like to change about me. I am too moody and sometimes I am easily distracted.
(a) that (b) whose I
(c) that I (d) which

**7.** The man .............. received that recommendation letter works for the government.
(a) that she (b) who she
(c) from whom she (d) to whom she

**8.** The cougar has powerful legs, .............. it uses to climb and to jump into trees.
(a) whom (b) who (c) which (d) whose

**9.** When Jayant finishes weeding the garden, he .............. the grass in the front yard.
(a) cut (b) cuts
(c) has cut (d) will cut

**10.** Until my brother went to Brazil last year, he .............. outside the United States.
(a) has never been (b) wasn't
(c) had never been (d) won't be

**11.** By the time the police arrived at the bank, the robbers .............. with thousands of rupees in cash.
(a) escaped (b) had escaped
(c) will have escaped (d) escapes

**12.** I waited for my friend .............. .
(a) until he arrived (b) unless he arrived
(c) till he arrived (d) until he has arrived

**13.** I couldn't believe .............. it took them to process my application.
(a) how much (b) how many
(c) where (d) how long

**14.** My brother doesn't know .............. .
(a) how tall he is (b) he is tall
(c) how tall is he (d) how he is tall

**15.** I don't know .............. she will be admitted to the university.
(a) whether (b) what
(c) which (d) who

**Directions** (Q. Nos. 16-20) ***Determine the clause highlighted in underlined in the given sentences.***

**16.** Some people buy expensive cars simply because they can.
(a) Noun clause (b) Adjective clause
(c) Adverb clause (d) Either (a) or (c)

**17.** Many people hope that Canada can resolve its economic problems.
(a) Noun clause (b) Adjective clause
(c) Adverb clause (d) Either (a) or (c)

**18.** The bankers need to know what they should do.
(a) Noun clause (b) Adjective clause
(c) Adverb clause (d) Either (b) or (c)

**19.** Which one is the person who stole your car?
(a) Noun clause
(b) Adjective clause
(c) Adverb clause
(d) Either (a) or (b)

**20.** Wherever there is a large American city, there will be poverty.
(a) Noun clause (b) Adjective clause
(c) Adverb clause (d) Either (a) or (b)

## ANSWERS

| | | | | | | | | | | | | | | | | | | | |
|---|---|---|---|---|---|---|---|---|---|---|---|---|---|---|---|---|---|---|---|
| 1 | (b) | 2 | (c) | 3 | (a) | 4 | (d) | 5 | (c) | 6 | (c) | 7 | (c) | 8 | (c) | 9 | (d) | 10 | (c) |
| 11 | (b) | 12 | (a) | 13 | (d) | 14 | (a) | 15 | (a) | 16 | (c) | 17 | (a) | 18 | (a) | 19 | (b) | 20 | (c) |

Chapter 05

# Tense

Tense denotes time and action *or* tense is that form of verb which states the time and action of an event.

## Uses of Different Tenses

*Different types of tenses and their uses are as follows*

### The Present Indefinite Tense (Habitual Action)

- This tense is generally used to denote 'habit, custom, practice, repeated action, permanent activity, general truth' etc.
- These ideas are expressed by the adverbs of frequency such as 'often, seldom, usually, never, occasionally, sometimes, normally, generally, always, frequently, rarely, daily'.

  e.g.

  (i) The old lady **goes** for a walk in the morning.

  (ii) Parul usually **believes** everybody.
- This tense is also used to make a statement in the present showing permanent nature and activity of the subject and eternal principles.

  e.g.

  (i) I **know** him well.

  (ii) He **teaches** in St Xavier College.
- This tense is also used to denote historical present.

  e.g.

  (i) Now Netaji **enters** and **addresses** the Indian soldiers.

  (ii) Now Arjun **shoots** arrows at Bhishma.
- This tense is also used to denote future arrangement in the statement.

  e.g.

  (i) The Prime Minister **arrives** from New York tomorrow.

  (ii) He **leaves** his job next week.

### The Present Continuous Tense (Progressive Action)

- This tense is normally used for an action in progress that is temporary in nature (not for a permanent activity) in the present at the time of speaking.

  e.g.

  (i) She **is not working**. She **is swimming** in the river.

  (ii) It **is raining** outside.
- It also expresses future action or a definite arrangement in the near future.

  e.g.

  (i) **I am going** to the cinema tomorrow.

  (ii) She **is coming** next week.
- Continuous tense with 'always' may express an idea which is not to the liking of the speaker.

  e.g.

  (i) She is always **teaching** her children.

  (ii) He is always **praising** his friends.
- There are some of verbs which sometime don't admit of progressive action. Such verbs are called Non-progressive (Stative verbs).

  e.g.

  (i) **Verbs of Perception** See, taste, smell, hear, prefer, please.

  (ii) **Verbs of Thinking Process** Think, know, mean, mind.

  (iii) **Verbs Showing Possession** Own, have, belong, comprise, possess, contain.

  (iv) **Verbs Expressing Feelings or State of Mind** Believe, like, love, want, wish, desire, hate.

  (v) **Verbs in General** Look, seem, appear, affect, resemble, cost, require, stand, face, become.
- 'While, still, at the moment, presently (at present) and now' may help students to express progressive present.

### The Present Perfect Tense (Imperfect Past) (Preceding Action)

- This tense is a mixture of present and past. At the time of speaking, the action is already completed in the past. It always implies a strong connection with the present though action which took place in the past.
- Generally, the following adverbs and conjunctions are used to express the preceding action. 'Ever, just, recently, already, yet , till (time), so far, of late, lately, before, by the time, after' etc.

  e.g.

  (i) I have **just** seen that film.

  (ii) I have **already** had my breakfast.
- Present Perfect + Point of Time = Simple Past

  It should be noted that point of time in the past indicates that action took place at a point in the past. The point of time in the past is expressed by 'since, ever since'. e.g.

  – I have worked in Delhi **since** I left college.

### The Past Indefinite Tense (Habitual Action)

- This tense is used for a past habit, indicated generally by 'Often, seldom, usually, normally, generally, occasionally, sometimes, never, always, frequently, rarely, daily, used to, would' etc.

  e.g.

  (i) They **never drank** wine.

  (ii) He **always carried** an umbrella.
- This tense is also used for a single act completed in the past. Definite point of time is denoted by 'Since, ever since, earlier, ago, back, before, last, yesterday, the other day' (Any point of time in the past) etc.

  e.g.

  (i) I **met** your brother **yesterday**.

  (ii) She **bought** a car two years **ago**.

### The Past Continuous Tense (Progressive Action)

- This tense is chiefly used for past action in progress.

  e.g.

  (i) It **was** still **raining** when I reached there. *(Past action in progress)*

  (ii) He **was** busy in **packing** last evening. *(Past action in progress)*
- It is also used for a definite arrangement for future in the past.

  e.g.

  (i) He was **leaving** that night. *(Definite arrangement for future in the past)*

  (ii) I asked her what **she was doing next** Sunday. *(Definite arrangement for future in the past)*
- As mentioned in the case of the present continuous tense, certain verbs don't admit of progressive action. Please study such verbs carefully. Refer to such verbs under present continuous tense section.
- While, still, at that moment, and when may help the students to express progressive action in the past. e.g.

  – When the phone rang, she **was studying**.

### The Past Perfect Tense (Past Preceding)

- This tense is used when out of two actions it is necessary to emphasise that the preceding action was completely finished before the succeeding action started.

  e.g.

  (i) I **had gone to** Delhi last week before my father came. *(Correct)*

  (ii) I **had gone to** Delhi last week. *(Incorrect, because preceding action is not implied here)*
- Sometimes preceding action is implied and is indicated by the use of 'Ever, just, recently, already, yet, so far, till (time), by the time (by), before, after' etc.

  e.g.

  (i) I had **already** taken breakfast.

  (ii) I had finished the book **before** he came.
- This tense is also used as time expression with 'Since, for, how long, whole, all, throughout, all along' etc.

  e.g.

  (i) She had known him **for** two years.

  (ii) He had owned this plaza **for** five years.
- Past Perfect tense used with verbs such as, 'Want, hope, expect, think, suppose, mean, intend' indicate that the action mentioned did not take place.

  e.g.

  (i) I had wanted to help my brother. *(but could not help)*

  (ii) I had expected to pass. *(but did not pass)*

  (iii) My sister had hoped that I would send her money. *(unfulfilled hope)*

### The Future Indefinite Tense (Future Action)

- This tense expresses an action that is to take place in future. e.g. 'Soon, shortly, in a few moments, tomorrow, presently (soon), next year/month/week' etc indicate future action.

  e.g.

  (i) They **will** come here **shortly**.

  (ii) Ritu **will** take examination **next month**.
- It should be noted that there are several ways to express future action in English as given below

  (a) Future action is expressed in the present continuous tense. But it is more definite action than the action expressed in the future indefinite.

  e.g.

  (i) They **are coming** tomorrow. *(certain to come)*

  (ii) She **is marrying** soon. *(certain to marry)*

  (b) Future action is also expressed in the future continuous.

e.g.

(i) Sushant **will be arriving** soon. *(He will arrive)*

(ii) I **shall be going** tomorrow. *(I shall go)*

(c) Future action is also expressed in the present indefinite tense.

## The Future Continuous Tense
(Future Progressive)

- This tense is used to express an action that will be in progress with a point of time in future.

e.g.

(i) She **will be waiting** for me when I reach her home.

(ii) Rahul **will be watching** movie on television on Sunday.

- This tense is also used to express the future indefinite tense or definite future arrangement.

e.g.

(i) He **will be going to** Pune by car today.

(ii) She **will be arriving** tomorrow to meet her husband.

- As mentioned in the case of the present continuous tense certain verbs do not admit of progressive action. Refer to such verbs under Present Continuous tense section.

## The Future Perfect Tense
(Future Preceding)

- This tense is used when out of two actions it is necessary to emphasise that the preceding action will be completely finished before the succeeding action starts in future. Sometimes preceding action is implied and indicated by the use of 'Ever, just, already, recently, yet, so far, till (time), before, (by), by the time after.'

e.g.

(i) She **will have** already prepared food when I reach home.

(ii) He **will have** rung up his wife before he arrives.

- This tense is also used to express time expression. 'Since, for, how long, whole, all, throughout, all long' denote that action started sometime in the past and is continuing into the present.

e.g.

(i) He **will have known** her for two years next month.

(ii) He **will have suffered** a lot by now since his birth.

## Future Perfect Continuous Tense

- This tense is used for actions which will be in progress over a period of time that will end in future.

e.g.

– By next March we shall have been living here for four years.

## Perfect Continuous : Present, Past, Future
(Time Expression)

- Perfect continuous tense (Present, Past, Future) denotes an action continuing from the past into the present. It implies the duration of an action. (past to present)

The time expression is normally indicated by 'Since, for, how long, whole, all, throughout, all along.'

e.g.

(i) She **has been playing** since morning.

(ii) They have been building this bridge for several months.

**'For'** is used for a period of time from the past to present. **'Since'** is used for a particular point of time or some event in the past to present.

- Time expression can be used with both continuous and indefinite tenses as follows

(a) Continuous + Time expression
= Perfect continuous (Present, Past, Future)
*(Action is not yet complete)*

(b) Indefinite + Time expression
= Perfect (Present, Past and Future)
*(Action is completed)*

e.g.

(i) She goes to temple every Monday. *(Point of time)*

(ii) She has completed two letters since last night. *(Time expression)*

# Practice Questions

**Directions** (Q. Nos. 1-50) *The sentences given below, have three parts, indicated by (1), (2) and (3). Read each sentence to find out whether there is an error. If you find no error then mark (4) as the answer.*

***1.*** Each of these players (1)/have been warned (2)/ not to repeat the silly mistake. (3)/ No error (4)

***2.*** Lime and Soda (1)/ is (2)/ a digestive drink. (3)/ No error (4)

***3.*** The mother as well as her children (1)/ were brought (2)/ to the police station for interrogation. (3)/ No. error (4)

***4.*** His benevolence and kindness (1)/ are (2)/ admired by his friends. (3)/ No error (4)

***5.*** She never has and never will (1)/ allow her only son (2)/ to join politics. (3)/ No error (4)

***6.*** Intelligence, as well as knowledge of the subject (1)/ are required to grasp (2)/ the meaning of the book. (3)/ No error (4)

***7.*** Twenty officers have been dismissed and thirty left (1)/ on their own. (2)/ No error (3)

***8.*** Every word and every line (1)/ in the poems of Wordsworth (2)/ sings the blessings of nature. (3)/ No. error (4)

***9.*** So, honestly he worked (1)/ that he was rewarded (2)/ by the chairman of the company. (3)/ No error (4)

***10.*** Four miles (1)/ are not a long distance (2)/ for a young person like you. (3)/ No error (4)

***11.*** No sooner he was brought (1)/ here than he began (2)/ to feel uneasy. (3)/ No error (4)

***12.*** He, like the other members (1)/ of his family, were left shelterless (2)/ as a result of flood in the town. (3)/ No error (4)

***13.*** In old age none of the relatives (1)/ are prepared to come (2)/ to the help of the old and the sick. (3)/ No error (4)

***14.*** I don't think (1)/ five thousand rupees are a large sum (2)/ for the work you are going to undertake. (3)/ No error (4)

***15.*** It was the students (1)/ who wants the teacher (2)/ to declare holiday. (3)/ No error (4)

***16.*** So fast did he drive motor car (1)/ that even the best driver (2)/ could not overtake him. (3)/ No error (4)

***17.*** Everyone of the new Nursing Homes (1)/ coming up in the Urban areas (2)/ need a lot of improvement. (3)/ No error (4)

***18.*** Never I have come across (1)/ a man (2)/ who is foolish to such an extent. (3) No error (4)

***19.*** He will be likely (1)/ to take part in the ceremony (2)/ provided he is granted leave. (3)/ No error (4)

***20.*** Two thirds of the majority (1)/ are needed to pass (2)/ the resolution for the impeachment of the President. (3)/ No error (4)

***21.*** During freedom struggle (1)/ many a patriot (2)/ were filled with patriotism. (3)/ No error (4)

***22.*** There are a dozen (1)/ of Geography books lying in the shelf of my personal library (2)/ and you can use them whenever you like. (3)/ No error (4)

***23.*** The number of amendments to our constitution (1)/ have been very large (2)/ during the last fifty years of independence. (3)/ No error (4)

***24.*** Just to the North of India (1)/ is the Himalayas (2)/ that were once impregnable. (3)/ No error (4)

***25.*** She disappeared (1)/ and found dead (2)/ near a well outside the village. (3)/ No error (4)

***26.*** I had been (1)/ to Delhi last week (2)/ to visit my friend. (3)/ No error (4)

***27.*** This time tomorrow (1) I am lying (2) on the beach. (3) No error (4)

***28.*** It was the children (1)/ that caused a lot of problem to their parents (2)/ during long bus journey. (3)/ No error (4)

***29.*** He will be likely (1)/ to leave for the United States (2)/ last year to visit his brother. (3)/ No error (4)

***30.*** The soldiers along with the commander (1)/ was court-martialled (2)/ for defying the orders. (3)/ No error (4)

***31.*** The rest (1)/ of the students is (2)/ still working. (3)/ No error (4)

***32.*** No one in this world (1)/ can be able to do work (2)/ continuously for ten hours. (3)/ No error (4)

***33.*** The period of twenty-five years (1)/ have passed (2)/ and still he is without a job. (3)/ No error (4)

***34.*** People have a right to criticise (1)/ but at the same time each of them (2)/ have to remember his duty also. (3)/ No error (4)

***35.*** The child picked up (1)/ a burned paper (2)/ from the street. (3)/ No error (4)

***36.*** The teacher was angry (1)/ when he found that (2)/ you are not there. (3)/ No error (4)

***37.*** I would like you (1)/ to complete this assignment (2)/ before you will leave for Mumbai. (3)/ No error (4)

***38.*** One of his many (1)/ good traits that come to my mind (2)/ was his modesty. (3)/ No error (4)

**39.** When the dentist came in (1)/ my tooth was stopped aching (2)/ out of fear that I might lose my tooth. (3)/ No error (4)

**40.** The chief idea of very common type of traveller (1)/ is to see as many objects of interest (2)/ as he possibly could. (3)/ No error (4)

**41.** I took my children to watch (1)/ some children's films (2)/being screen in the city. (3)/No error (4)

**42.** The principal of the school (1)/does not believe that the teachers (2)/are working hard all these years. (3)/No error (4)

**43.** I remember in my youth I was used (1)/to go with my father to his shop and looked. (2)/ into his account books. (3)/No error (4)

**44.** I missed the last bus which I usually catch (1)/and have to stay back (2)/at the bus stop last night. (3)/No error (4)

**45.** Why does he worry (1)/ over petty matters and issues (2)/ is not known even to his parents. (3)/No error (4)

**46.** Leaders enable a group by imagining (1)/and create a future (2)/ which will fulfill the purpose of the group. (3)/No error (4)

**47.** Her goal is to win gold medal (1)/in the Asian games and (2)/made her country proud. (3)/No error (4)

**48.** He firmly belief that (1)/ if any disease is detected early then (2)/ it can be cured by yoga. (3)/No error (4)

**49.** Ramesh takes charge of (1)/ the project within a few days (2)/ of appointment. (3)/No error (4)

**50.** Economists have predicted that (1)/ the country's economic growth (2)/falls low to eight percent this year. (3)/No error (4)

## ANSWERS

**1.** (2) Replace 'have' by 'has'.

**2.** (4) No error.

**3.** (2) Replace 'were by 'was'.

**4.** (2) Replace 'are' by 'is'.

**5.** (1) Add 'allowed' after 'has'.

**6.** (2) Replace 'are' by 'is'.

**7.** (2) Add 'have' after 'thirty'.

**8.** (4) No error.

**9.** (1) Replace 'he worked' by 'did he work'.

**10.** (2) Replace 'are' by 'is'.

**11.** (1) Replace 'he was brought' by 'was he brought'.

**12.** (2) Replace 'were' by 'was'.

**13.** (2) Replace 'are' by 'is'.

**14.** (2) Replace 'are' by 'is'.

**15.** (2) Replace 'wants' by past tense 'wanted'.

**16.** (4) No error.

**17.** (3) Replace 'need' by 'needs'.

**18.** (1) Replace 'I have' by 'have I'.

**19.** (1) Replace 'will be' by 'is'.

**20.** (2) Replace 'are' by 'is'.

**21.** (3) Replace 'were' by 'was'.

**22.** (1) Replace 'are' by 'is'.

**23.** (2) Replace 'have' by 'has'.

**24.** (2) Replace 'is' by 'are'.

**25.** (2) Add 'was' after 'and'.

**26.** (1) Replace 'had been' by 'went'.

**27.** (2) am lying should be replaced with will be lying.

**28.** (1) Replace was by were.

**29.** (1) Replace 'will be' by 'was'.

**30.** (2) Replace 'was' by 'were'.

**31.** (2) Replace 'is' by 'are'.

**32.** (2) Replace 'can be' by 'is'.

**33.** (2) Replace 'have' by 'has'.

**34.** (3) Replace 'have' by 'has'.

**35.** (2) Replace 'burned' by 'burnt'.

**36.** (3) Replace 'are' by 'were'.

**37.** (3) Delete 'will'.

**38.** (3) Replace 'was' by 'is'.

**39.** (2) Replace 'was' by 'had'.

**40.** (3) Replace 'could' by 'can'.

**41.** (3) Replace 'screen' by 'screened'

**42.** (3) Replace 'are working' by 'have been contributing'. (The sentence is in present perfect continuous tense)

**43.** (1) Remove 'was'. 'Used to' is used for past habitual action.

**44.** (2) Replace 'have' by 'had'.

**45.** (1) Remove 'does'. The sentence is not in interrogative pattern. In interrogative pattern 'wh' word is followed by the helping verb. But in simple assertive sentences the subject is used before the Helping Verb. Use worries in place of does he worry.

**46.** (2) Replace 'create' by 'creating'.

**47.** (3) Replace 'made' by 'make'.

**48.** (1) Replace 'belief' by 'believes'.

**49.** (1) Replace 'takes' by 'took' as the sentence is in past tense.

**50.** (3) Replace 'falls' by 'will fall' as the sentence is in future tense.

Chapter 06

# Direct to Indirect Narration

Repoted Speech or Direct to Indirect Narration is the part of conversation in which events, incidents, data, detail etc are reported to another person or institution by the person responsible to report.
The actual words of the speaker undergo some important changes to suit the structure of the sentence.

When we report the actual words of the speaker or if we think those words are important or to create some dramatic effect, we call it Direct Speech. These words are put within Inverted Commas.

## Direct Narration

Direct narration is a kind of speech which is reported by some other person exactly in the words spoken by the speaker. This speech is placed within inverted commas. e.g.

– She said to him, "I shall give you money." *(Direct Narration)*

## Indirect Narration

Indirect narration is a speech which is reported by some other person by using certain conjunctions in place of commas and making necessary changes in the verbs and the pronouns of the reported speech.

– She told him that she would give him money. *(Indirect Narration)*

***For the purpose of changing narration, sentences are divided as follows***

1. **Assertive Sentences**
   Sentences denoting statements in affirmative and negative.
   e.g
   (i) You are playing. (ii) He did this work.
2. **Interrogative Sentences**
   (a) Sentences beginning with auxiliary verbs. (Yes or No answer type questions)
   e.g
   (i) Are you playing? (ii) They will not write to us.
   (b) Sentences beginning with question words such as 'when, where, why, who, which, what' etc.
   e.g.
   (i) When are you playing? (ii) Why did he do this work?
   (iii) Where was she sleeping?
3. **Imperative Sentences**
   Sentences denoting command, request and advice are called imperative sentences.
   e.g
   (i) She said, "Mohan, please bring me that book."
   (ii) Mother said to me, "Take umbrella with you when you go out."
4. **Exclamatory Sentences** (Expressing, joy, sorrow, wonder etc)
   e.g.
   (i) How nice of him!
   (ii) Ah! It is a beautiful locket
5. **Optative Sentences** (Expressing wish, prayer etc.)
   e.g.
   (i) May you live long!
   (ii) Good bye, my daughters!

### Some Hints to Change in Tenses

1. **Past Continuous**

Past continuous changes in speech when it refers to a complete action. e.g.

(i) She said to me, "I was thinking of helping him but changed my mind later on".
(ii) She told me that she had been thinking of helping him but had changed her mind later on.

2. **Past continuous does not change when it is used in time clause**

e.g

– He said to me, "While I was singing, she was dancing."*(Direct)*
He told me that while he was singing, she was dancing. *(Indirect)*

3. **Past indefinite does not change in the following cases**

- When it is used in time clause. e.g.
  – She said to me, "When I met him, he was playing." *(Direct)*
  She told me that when she met him he was playing. *(Indirect)*
- When it expresses two simultaneous actions. e.g.
  – She said, "I cooked vegetables and he fried rice." *(Direct)*
  She said that she cooked vegetables and he fried rice. *(Indirect)*

- When it expresses historical Past. e.g.
  - He said, "Netaji was born in Kolkata." *(Direct)*
  He said that Netaji was born in Kolkata. *(Indirect)*

**Change of 'Will'**

- 'Will' change into 'Should' when the speaker seeks advice or request. e.g.
  - The mother said, "What will I do with so much money, My son!" *(Direct)*
  The mother asked her son what she should do with so much money. *(Indirect)*

**Change of 'Could'**

- Could is changed in case of Permission. e.g.
  (i) She said to me. "When I was a student I could not go out alone." *(Direct)*
  (ii) She told me that when she was a student she was not allowed to go alone. *(Indirect)*

**Change of 'Must'**

- 'Must' normally does not change when it refers to duty or laws of nature. e.g.
  - Rahul said to her, "You must obey your parents." *(Direct)*
  Rahul said to her that she must obey her parents. *(Indirect)*
- 'Must' changes in the following cases. e.g.
  - She said, 'I must leave at once." *(Direct)*
  She said that she had to leave at once. *(Indirect)*

## Changes in Pronouns in the Reported Speech

- **First Person** (I, we) in the reported speech changes into the subject of the reporting verb.
  e.g.
  - She said to me, "I am unwell." *(Direct)*
  She told me that she was unwell. *(Indirect)*
- **Second Person** You in the Reported speech changes into the object of the Reporting verb.
  e.g.
  - He said to his mother, "Will you give me money." *(Direct)*
  He asked his mother if she would give him some money. *(Indirect)*
- **Third Person** (He, She, They, It) in the reported speech does not change. e.g.
  (i) I said to her, "He will not come." *(Direct)*
  (ii) I told her that he would not come. *(Indirect)*

**Change in Words**

*Some words expressing nearness in time or place are generally changed into words expressing distance*

| | |
|---|---|
| Now becomes | Then |
| Here becomes | There |
| Today becomes | That day |
| Tomorrow becomes | The next day |
| Yesterday becomes | The previous day |
| Ago becomes | before |
| Last night becomes | The night before |

# Practice Questions

**Directions** *(Q. Nos. 1-20) Change the following in Indirect speech.*

**1.** **I said to him, "I will not go there tomorrow."**
(a) I told him that I would not go there tomorrow.
(b) I told him that I would not go there the next day. (c) I said to him that I shall not go there tomorrow.
(d) I told him that he will not go there the next day.

**2.** **"There are ceremonies going on", he said to me.**
(a) He told me that there were ceremonies going on.
(b) He told that there had been ceremonies going on.
(c) He told that there had been ceremonies going on.
(d) He told that there had been ceremonies going on.

**3.** **She said, "When I was a child, I wasn't afraid of ghosts."**
(a) She said that when she was a child she wasn't afraid of ghosts.
(b) She said that when she was a child she hadn't been afraid of ghosts.
(c) She said that when she had been a child, she wasn't afraid of ghosts.
(d) She said that when she had been a child she hadn't been afraid of ghosts.

**4.** **He said, "Garima wants to take up a job while her husband wants her to look after the family."**
(a) He said that Garima wanted to take up a job while her husband wanted her to look after the family.
(b) He said that Garima wants to take up a job while her husband wanted her to look after.
(c) He told that Garima wanted to take up a job while her husband wants her to look after the family.
(d) He said to Garima that though she wanted to take up a job while her husband wanted her to look after the family.

**5.** **Kiran asked, "Did you see the cricket match on television last night?"**
(a) Kiran asked me whether I saw the cricket match on television the earlier night.
(b) Kiran asked me whether I had seen the cricket match on television the previous night .
(c) Kiran asked me did I see the cricket match on television last night.
(d) Kiran asked me whether I had seen the cricket match on television last night.

**6.** **"Would you mind taking off your shoes before entering the house?" He said to the foreigner.**
(a) He requested the foreigner to take off his shoes before entering the house.
(b) He told the foreigner that the must take off his shoes before entered the house.
(c) He said the foreigner that to take off his shoes before entered the house.
(d) Before entering the house he said that shoes must be taken off.

**7.** **He said, "Let Hari come with us, mother. I'll take care of him."**
(a) He requested his mother to let Hari come with them as he will take care of him.
(b) He informed his mother to let Hari come with them as he would take care of him.
(c) He told his mother to let Hari come of with them as he would take care of him.
(d) He told to his mother let Hari come with us as he would take care of him.

**8.** **He said, "I do not wish to see any of you, go away."**
(a) He said that he had not wished to see any of them and ordered them to go away.
(b) He said that he did not wish to see any of them and ordered them to go away.
(c) He told that he did not wish to see any of them and ordered them to go away.
(d) He said that he does not wish to see any of us and ordered us to go away.

**9.** **He said to her, "What a cold day!"**
(a) He told her that it was a cold day.
(b) He exclaimed that it was a cold day.
(c) He exclaimed sorrowfully that it was a cold day.
(d) He exclaimed that it was a very cold day.

**10.** **The tailor said to him, "Will you have the suit ready by tomorrow evening?"**
(a) The tailor asked him that he will have the suit ready by the next evening.
(b) The tailor asked him that he would had the suit ready by the next evening.
(c) The tailor asked him if he would have the suit ready by the next evening.
(d) The tailor asked him if he will like to have the suit ready by the next evening.

**11.** **The father said to his daughter, "When will you return?"**
**In reported speech the above sentence will be**
**The father asked his daughter**
(a) when will she return
(b) when would she return
(c) when she will return
(d) when she would return

**12.** **The teacher said to the students, "Be polite in your speech."**
**In reported speech the above sentence will be**
**The teacher asked the students**
(a) to be polite in their speech
(b) that be polite in their speech
(c) to be polite in your speech
(d) that be polite in your speech

**13.** My neighbour said to me, "I am going out for a few days."
In reported speech the above sentence will be
My neighbour told me that
(a) he was going out for a few days
(b) he is going out for a few days
(c) he will go out for a few days
(d) we are going out for a few days

**14.** Mohan said to Savita, "Can I borrow your book for a day?"
In reported speech the above sentence will be
Mohan asked Savita
(a) if he could borrow her book for a day
(b) if they could borrow her book for a day
(c) that could he borrow her book for a day
(d) if that he could borrow her book for a day

**15.** She said to her brother, "Do not buy mangoes."
In reported speech the above sentence will be
She asked her brother
(a) to not buy mangoes
(b) not to buy mangoes
(c) do not buy mangoes
(d) do not to buy mangoes

**16.** The students said, "We want to learn a foreign language."
In reported speech the above sentence will be
The students said that
(a) they want to learn a foreign language
(b) they wanted to learn a foreign language
(c) we want to learn a foreign language
(d) we wanted to learn a foreign language

**17.** Choose the correct indirect speech of the italicised sentence from the options given below.
"What are you doing old man?" said the king.
(a) The king told the old man that what he was doing.
(b) The king asked the old man what he was doing.
(c) The king asked what the old man is doing.
(d) The king told the old man what he was doing.

**18.** Identify the correct reported form of the given sentence.
My friend said, "You must accept this gift."
(a) My friend asked that I must accept that gift .
(b) My friend said that you must accept that gift.
(c) My friend requested that I must accept this gift.
(d) My friend insisted that I must accept that gift.

**19.** Choose the correct indirect form of the sentence.
The man said. "Let me have the first chance."
(a) The man proposed that he should have the first chance.
(b) The man proposed to have the first chance.
(c) The man desired that he had the first chance.
(d) The man claimed that he had the first chance.

**20.** Change the following into indirect speech by choosing correct alternative.
Our teacher said to us, "Sugar dissolves in water."
(a) Our teacher told us that sugar dissolved in water.
(b) Our teacher told us that sugar has dissolved in water.
(c) Our teacher said to us that sugar dissolves in water.
(d) Our teacher told us that sugar dissolves in water.

**Direction** *(Q. Nos. 21-26) In each of the following sentences a sentence has been given in Direct Speech. Out of four options suggested, select the one which best expresses the same sentence in Indirect Speech.*

**21.** He said to her, "Are you coming to the party?"
(a) He told her if she was coming to the party?
(b) He asked her if she was coming to the party.
(c) He asked her whether she would come to the party.
(d) He asked her if she will be coming to the party.

**22.** They said, " Mother, we are not hungry; we shall eat later."
(a) They told the mother they are not hungry, they will eat later.
(b) They told the mother that they were not hungry and would eat later.
(c) They said to the mother they shall eat later as they were not hungry.
(d) They informed the mother that they are not hungry and would eat later.

**23.** He said to his brother "The Earth moves round the Sun".
(a) He told his brother that the Earth moves round the Sun.
(b) He told his brother that the Earth would move round the Sun.
(c) He told his brother that the Earth moved round the Sun.
(d) He told his brother that the Earth had moved round the Sun.

**24.** He said to me "Are you going to Jaipur?"
(a) He told me if I am going to Jaipur?
(b) He said to me if I was going to Jaipur.
(c) He asked me if I was going to Jaipur.
(d) He asked me if I am going to Jaipur.

**25.** The boy said, "I saw him while I was running".
(a) The boy said that he had seen him while he (the boy) was running.
(b) The boy said that he saw him while he was running.
(c) The boy said that he had seen him while he was running.
(d) The boy said that he did see him while running.

**26.** She said, "I saw a lion there".
(a) She said that she saw a lion there.
(b) She said that she had seen a lion there.
(c) She told that she saw a lion there.
(d) She said that she saw a lion here.

**Direction** *(Q. Nos. 27-35) Change the following sentences into Direct narration. Choose from the options.*

**27.** John said that he loved that town.
(a) John said, "I will love this town".
(b) John said, "I love this town".
(c) John said, "I loved this town".
(d) John said, "I am loving this town".

**28.** He asked me if I was sure that I liked soccer.
(a) "Are you sure you like soccer?" He asked me.
(b) "Were you sure, you liked soccer?" He told me.
(c) "Are you sure", He asked me.
(d) "Are you sure you are liking soccer?" He asked.

**29. He said that he couldn't drive a lorry.**
(a) "I couldn't drive a lorry," he says.
(b) "I can't drive a lorry", he said.
(c) "I will not drive a lorry," he told me.
(d) "I cannot be driving a lorry," he said.

**30. She asked him what he had decided to do.**
(a) "What have you decided to do?" She asked him.
(b) "What do you want to do?" She asked him.
(c) "What did you want to do?" She asked him.
(d) "What will you do?" She asked.

**31. He advised the students to revise their lessons.**
(a) "You may revise your lessons," he said.
(b) "You should revise your lessons", he said.
(c) "You will revise your lessons"?, said he.
(d) "You can revise your lessons," he told.

**32. He wanted to know where I was born.**
(a) "Where was you born", he asked me.
(b) "Where is your birth from", he asked me.
(c) "Where were you born?" he asked me.
(d) "Where did you took birth?" he asked me.

**33. He asked/advised me to be nice to my brother.**
(a) He said, "Be nice to your brother".
(b) He told, "you should be nice to your brother".
(c) He said, "You have to be nice to your brother".
(d) He told, "you will have to be nice to your brother".

**34. Yesterday Nancy wanted to know why Namit hadn't gone to New York the summer before.**
(a) Nancy : "Why didn't Namit go to New York last summer?"
(b) Nancy : "Why do you Namit not go to New York last summer?"
(c) Nancy : "Namit, why didn't you visit New York last summer".
(d) Nancy : "Why did Namit refuse to go to New York?"

**35. She told the boys not to waste their money.**
(a) "Don't waste your money," she said.
(b) "Don't waste your money, boys", she said.
(c) "Don't you dare waste your money," she said.
(d) "Don't let your money be wasted," she said.

**Direction** ***(Q. Nos. 36-44) Change the following sentences into Direct Speech. Choose from the options given.***

**36. Dad asked where his clean shirt was.**
(a) "Where was my clean shirt", dad demanded.
(b) "Where's my clean shirt?" asked dad.
(c) "Where is my clean shirt lying?" dad asked.
(d) "Where would my clean shirt be?" dad said.

**37. Mom told him that it was hanging in the kitchen.**
(a) "It's hanging in the kitchen", answered mom.
(b) "It will be hanging in the kitchen", said mom.
(c) "It had been hanging in the kitchen," said mom.
(d) "It has been hanging in the kitchen," said mom.

**38. Sally observed that it was already eight o'clock.**
(a) "It's eight o'clock already", observed Sally.
(b) "It is eight o'clock already", said Sally.
(c) "It is eight o' clock already," said Sally.
(d) "It is eight now," said Sally.

**39. Dad agreed that it was time to leave.**
(a) "It will be time to leave" agreed Dad.
(b) "It is time to leave", agreed Dad.
(c) "Now is the time to leave", said Dad.
(d) "Now it is time to leave", agreed Dad.

**40. Mary told Peter it was his turn to make the dinner that night.**
(a) Mary said "It was your turn to make dinner tonight, Peter".
(b) "It is your turn to make dinner tonight, Peter", said to Mary.
(c) "It was your turn to make dinner this night", said Mary.
(d) "It is your turn to make dinner tonight Peter", said Mary.

**41. Peter reminded that he had made it only two days before.**
(a) "But, I made it only two days ago", Peter reminded Mary.
(b) "But I had made it only two days ago", Peter said to Mary.
(c) "But I had made it only two days in advance", Peter said to Mary.
(d) "But I made it only two days before", Peter said to Mary.

**42. Medha asked how much the tickets cost.**
(a) "How much did the tickets cost?" asked Medha.
(b) "How much do the tickets cost"? asked Medha.
(c) Medha asked, "How much the tickets cost?"
(d) Medha asked, 'How much do tickets cost?"

**43. Father asked how I had got there.**
(a) Father asked me "How did you get there?"
(b) Father asked me, "How do you get there?"
(c) Father asked me "How I had got there?"
(d) Father asked me, "How I had got there?"

**44. Jigna asked why I was not going to school that day.**
(a) Jigna asked "Why are you not going to school today"?
(b) Jigna asked, "Why I was not going to school today"?
(c) "Why are you not going to school today?" asked Jigna.
(d) "Why I am not going to school today?" asked Jigna.

## ANSWERS

| | | | | | | | | | | | | | | | | | | | |
|---|---|---|---|---|---|---|---|---|---|---|---|---|---|---|---|---|---|---|---|
| 1. | (b) | 2. | (a) | 3. | (a) | 4. | (a) | 5. | (b) | 6. | (a) | 7. | (b) | 8. | (b) | 9. | (d) | 10. | (c) |
| 11. | (d) | 12. | (a) | 13. | (a) | 14. | (a) | 15. | (b) | 16. | (b) | 17. | (b) | 18. | (d) | 19. | (a) | 20. | (d) |
| 21. | (b) | 22. | (b) | 23. | (c) | 24. | (c) | 25. | (a) | 26. | (b) | 27. | (b) | 28. | (a) | 29. | (b) | 30. | (a) |
| 31. | (b) | 32. | (c) | 33. | (a) | 34. | (a) | 35. | (b) | 36. | (b) | 37. | (a) | 38. | (a) | 39. | (b) | 40. | (b) |
| 41. | (b) | 42. | (a) | 43. | (a) | 44. | (c) | | | | | | | | | | | | |

Chapter 07

# Active and Passive Voice

Voice is the term used to describe whether a verb is active or passive. The voice of a verb tells us whether the subject of the said is acted upon or is acting.

The voice of a verb tells whether the subject of the sentence performs or receives the action.

- **Active Voice** In active voice, the subject performs the action expressed by the verb.
- **Passive Voice** In passive voice, the subject receives the action expressed by the verb.
  e.g.
  – He sings a song *(Active)*
  A song is sung by him. *(Passive)*

Active Verb A verb is 'active' when its form shows (as in sentence -a) that the subject does some work or subject is active.

Passive Verb A verb is 'passive' when its form shows (as in sentence -ii) that something is done to the subject (of sentence -i) or subject is not active, but passive.

## Active and Passive Voice

### Passive Voice is Used

- When subject is not known or it is not necessary to tell about the subject.
  e.g.
  (i) This temple was built five years ago.
  (ii) The mirror was broken yesterday.
- When it is necessary to give importance to the object.
  e.g.
  (i) The story was written by Rameez.
  (ii) The tiger was killed by the experienced hunter.
- The passive voice is especially helpful (and even regarded as mandatory) in scientific or technical writing or lab reports, where the subject is not really important but the process or principle being described is of ultimate importance.
  e.g.
  (i) Hydrochloric acid is produced when hydrogen and chlorine are mixed.
  (ii) Sewing machine was invented by Ilias.
- We use the passive voice to avoid responsibility for actions taken.
  e.g.
  – Wine ads are designed to appeal especially to students. (places the burden on the ads as opposed to burden on the designer/advertiser)
  – We designed the wine ads to appeal especially to students. ('we' accepts responsibility)

### General Rules to Change the Voice

If you want to change an active voice sentence to passive voice, consider carefully 'who' or 'what' (subject) is performing the action expressed by the verb, and then make that agent ('who' or 'what') the object of a 'by the...' phrase.

Make what is acted upon, the 'subject' of the sentence, and change the verb to a form of 'be + past participle'. Including an explicit 'by the...' phrase is optional. 'By' is used when the subject of active sentence is important.

*Read the following points carefully*

- Make the 'object' of the active sentence - 'subject' of the passive sentence.
  e.g.
  – I write a letter. *(Active)*
- Object of active sentence is 'a letter'. It becomes subject of the passive sentence as follows
  – A letter is written by me. *(Passive)*
- Make the 'subject' of the active sentence 'agent' of the passive sentence. The agent will be in objective form. Use 'by' before it. 'By' is used when the subject of active sentence is important to mention.
- In the above example, mentioned in point 1, subject of the sentence is 'I'; its objective form is 'me'. So we write 'by me'.
- Always use 'third form' of the verb (past participle) in passive structures. The past participle (V3) will be preceded by 'to be' form of verb, as per the tense of the sentence.
- Please take care that the 'to be' form of verb is governed by the new subject (subject of the passive sentence ).

e.g.

– She is helping the students. *(Active)*

The students are being helped by her. *(Passive)*

Here in the sentence, plural verb **are** is used as per the plural subject 'students'.

- Change of 'subject' of active sentence into 'object' of passive is done as per following table

| Active Voice | Passive Voice | Active Voice | Passive Voice |
|---|---|---|---|
| I | Me | She | Her |
| He | Him | They | Them |
| You | You | It | It |
| We | Us | Who | Whom |

- Only transitive verbs (those that take objects) can be transformed into passive constructions.
  Furthermore, active sentences containing certain verbs cannot be transformed into passive structures. 'To have' is the most important of these verbs. We can say "He has a new cycle," but we cannot say "A new cycle is had by him."
  Here is a brief list of such verbs : resemble, look, like, equal, agree with, mean, contain, hold, comprise, lack, suit, fit, become etc. These verbs are intransitive in nature.
- Sentences in present perfect continuous, past perfect continuous, future perfect continuous and future continuous can't be transformed into passive.
  The Passive voice is formed with the suitable tense of the verb 'be' followed by the past participle.

*The change of verbs (tensewise) takes place as per following table*

| Tense | **Verb** (Active) | **Verb** (Passive) 'To be' form + $V_3$ |
|---|---|---|
| Simple Present | go/goes | is/am/are gone |
| Simple Past | went | was/were gone |
| Simple Future | shall/will go | shall/will be gone |
| Present Continuous | is/am/are going | is/am/are being gone |
| Past Continuous | was/were/ going | was/were being gone |
| Present Perfect | has/have gone | has/have been gone |
| Past Perfect | had gone | had been gone |
| Future Perfect | shall/will have gone | shall/will have been gone |

**Types of Tense and their form of Active and Passive Voice**

| Tense (or Modal + base) | Active Voice | Passive Voice |
|---|---|---|
| Simple Present | take<br>take<br>takes | am taken<br>is taken<br>are taken |
| Present Continuous | am taking<br>is taking<br>are taking | am being taken<br>is being taken<br>are being taken |
| Present Perfect | has taken<br>have taken | has been taken<br>have been taken |
| Simple Past | took | was taken<br>were taken |
| Past Continuous | was taking<br>were taking | was being taken<br>were being taken |
| Past Perfect | had taken | had been taken |
| Simple Future | will take<br>shall take | will be taken<br>shall be taken |
| Can/May/Must, etc + base | can take<br>must take | can be taken<br>must be taken |

# Practice Questions

**Directions** *(Q. Nos. 1-5) Change the following into passive voice.*

**1.** **He handed her a cheque.**
(a) A cheque was handed over to her.
(b) A checue is handed over to her.
(c) A cheque has been handed over to her.
(d) A checue is being handed over to her.

**2.** **The waiter filled the glasses with water.**
(a) The glasses filled with water by the waiter.
(b) The glasses were filled with water by the waiter.
(c) The waiter was filled the glasses with water.
(d) The water were filled in the glasses by waiter.

**3.** **They have published all the details of the invention.**
(a) All the details of the invention have been published by them.
(b) The publication of the details of invention was done by them.
(c) All the details have been invented by the publishers.
(d) All the inventions have been detailed by them.

**4.** **He was driving the car so fast that it skidded on the snowy road.**
(a) The car was driven by him so fast that it skidded on the snowy road.
(b) The car was being driven by him so fast that it skidded on the snowy road.
(c) The car had been driven by him so fast that it skidded on the snowy road.
(d) The car has been driven by him so fast that it skidded on the snowy road.

**5.** **They will laugh at you.**
(a) You can be laughed at by them.
(b) You may be laughed at by them.
(c) You will be laughed at by them.
(d) You will have been laughed at by them.

**Directions** *(Q. Nos. 6-14) Change the voice of the following from passive to active.*

**6.** **Our task had been completed before sunset.**
(a) We completed our task before sunset.
(b) We have completed our task before sunset.
(c) We complete our task before sunset.
(d) We had completed our task before sunset.

**7.** **The most useful training of my career was given to me by my boss.**
(a) My boss has been giving me the most useful training of my career.
(b) My boss gives me the most useful training.
(c) My boss is giving me the most useful training.
(d) My boss gave me the most useful training of my career.

**8.** **It is being read by us.**
(a) We are reading it.
(b) It will be read by us.
(c) We can read it.
(d) We have to read.

**9.** **She was advised 15 days rest after her surgery.**
(a) The doctor was advised her 15 days rest after her surgery.
(b) The doctor has advised her 15 days rest after her surgery.
(c) The doctor advised her 15 days rest after her surgery.
(d) The doctor had advised her 15 days rest after her surgery.

**10.** **One's promises must be kept.**
(a) One's promises must keep.
(b) One's promises were kept.
(c) One's promises are kept.
(d) One must keep one's promises.

**11.** **Pick out the correct passive voice of the following.**
**They carried the injured player off the field.**
(a) Off the field was carried by the injured player.
(b) The injured player was carried off the field by them.
(c) The injured player be carried off the field by them.
(d) The injured player has been carried off the field.

**12.** **Select the active form of the following.**
**The wall is being built by the mason.**
(a) Mason has built the wall.
(b) The mason was building the wall.
(c) The mason is building the wall.
(d) The mason has been building the wall.

**13.** **Identify the correct passive voice of the sentence: Obey me.**
(a) I should be obeyed. (b) Let I be obeyed.
(c) Both (a) and (b) (d) None of these

**14.** **Change the following into passive voice. Rita writes a letter to him everyday.**
(a) To him a letter was written by Rita everyday.
(b) A letter was written to him by Rita everyday.
(c) A letter is written to him by Rita everyday.
(d) He is being written a letter by Rita everyday.

**15.** **Fill in the blank to complete sentence in passive voice. A number of plays were written .......... Shakespeare.**
(a) from (b) of
(c) in (d) by

**Directions** *(Q. Nos. 16-17) Identify the correct alternative from the given ones to fill in the blanks in the sentences given below.*

**16.** **Why should he ........ by me?**
(a) be suspected (b) being suspected
(c) have been suspected (d) is suspected

**17.** **The recitation ........... the audience.**
(a) was pleased (b) pleased
(c) have been pleased (d) will be pleased

**18.** **Point out the sentence in passive voice.**
(a) The striking students were throwing stones.
(b) Twenty lessons have been finished.
(c) The murderer hide the knife.
(d) The enemy will have sunk the ship by now.

**19.** Choose the correct active voice of the given sentence from the options given below.

Let your country be served.

(a) Serve your country.
(b) Do service your country.
(c) Service should be done to your country.
(d) Let serve your country.

**20.** Change the following into passive voice.

Do not insult your elder.

(a) Let not your elders be insulted.
(b) Your elders let not be insulted.
(c) Let your elders not be insulted by you.
(d) Let us not insult your elders.

**21.** Choose the correct passive construction of the sentence.

Someone sells tickets at the box office.

(a) Tickets are sold at the box office.
(b) Tickets are being sold at the box office.
(c) Tickets were sold at the box office by some body.
(d) At the box office tickets were sold by somebody.

**22.** Point out the active voice in the following sentence.

This notice has been altered.

(a) Alteration has been made is this notice.
(b) Some one has altered the notice.
(c) Already the notice has been altered.
(d) The notice has been altered previously.

**23.** Which of sentence will be in the passive voice?

She will write a letter.

(a) A letter written by her.
(b) A letter will be written by her.
(c) Written a letter will be by her.
(d) Will a letter be written by her.

**24.** The passive voice form of the sentence.

'Who will help you"? will be .........

(a) By whom will you be helped?
(b) Whom will you be helped?
(c) You will be helped?
(d) Whom will be you are helped?

**Directions** *(Q. Nos. 25-34) Change these sentences from active to passive voice. Fill in the blanks by choosing the correct option from the given choices.*

**25. Active** People speak Portuguese in Brazil.

**Passive** Portuguese .......... in Brazil.

(a) is speak (b) is spoke
(c) is spoken (d) speak

**26. Active** The staff cleans all the hotel rooms daily.

**Passive** The hotel rooms .......... daily.

(a) are clean (b) are cleaned
(c) is cleaned (d) is clean

**27. Active** We update the company website frequently.

**Passive** The company website .......... frequently.

(a) are updated (b) is updated
(c) was updated (d) will update

**28. Active** People see this beach as the most beautiful in the country.

**Passive** This beach .......... as the most beautiful in the country.

(a) is seen (b) is saw (c) is see (d) sees

**29. Active** Somebody ships the products via express mail.

**Passive** The products .......... via express mail.

(a) are shipped (b) is shipped
(c) were shipped (d) do shipped

**30. Active** A friend gave me this sweater.

**Passive** This sweater .......... to me by a friend.

(a) is given (b) was gave
(c) was given (d) gave

**31. Active** A famous author wrote these letters.

**Passive** These letters .......... by a famous author.

(a) is written (b) were written
(c) has been written (d) were wrote

**32. Active** We bake the biscuits over a charcoal fire.

**Passive** The biscuits .......... over a charcoal fire by us.

(a) were baked (b) is baked
(c) are baked (d) bakes

**33. Active** Who taught you how to write Hindi?

**Passive** By whom were .......... how to write Hindi?

(a) you teach (b) taught you
(c) you teach (d) you taught

**34. Active** The booking clerk will give you a ticket?

**Passive** A ticket .......... to you by the booking clerk.

(a) will be given (b) will give
(c) has given (d) would give

**Directions** *(Q. Nos. 35-44) Fill in the blanks and complete the sentences in passive voice by selecting the correct options.*

**35.** By the time the manager arrived, the problem ..........

(a) has already solved (b) had already been solved
(c) was already solved (d) were already being solved

**36.** Mr Green .......... for his commendable services to the university.

(a) has been awarded (b) was awarded
(c) awarded (d) have been awarded

**37.** Not much .......... about the accident since that time.

(a) has been said (b) has said
(c) have been said (d) said

**38.** A new book .......... by the company next year.

(a) will publish (b) will be published
(c) would publish (d) will have to publish

**39.** The secretary .......... to her new boss yesterday.

(a) introduced (b) was introduced
(c) is being introduced (d) were introduced

**40.** Stones .......... by those who live in glass houses.

(a) should not throw (b) should be not throw
(c) should not be thrown (d) should not be throwing

**41.** Our plan .......... by the members of the committee.
(a) being considered (b) is considered
(c) were considered (d) was to be considered

**42.** He .......... responsible for the accident.
(a) was holding (b) was held
(c) held (d) had held

**43.** A prize .......... to whoever solves this problem.
(a) is being given (b) will be given
(c) is given (d) was being given

**44.** Everybody .......... by the terrible news yesterday.
(a) shocked (b) was shocked
(c) were shocked (d) was being shocked

**Directions** (Q. Nos. 45-54) *Choose the correct options to complete the sentences.*

**45.** He dislikes .......... regarding his work.
(a) being criticise (b) being criticised
(c) for criticise (d) do criticised

**46.** The entertainment for Sunday's dinner party .......... by Mudit.
(a) is carefully being arranged
(b) careful is been arranged
(c) was been carefully arranged
(d) were being carefully arranged

**47.** The women on the committee .......... a fashion show.
(a) are going organising
(b) are going to organise
(c) are to be organised
(d) will be organise

**48.** The motorist wanted me .......... for the damage to his car.
(a) to be paid (b) to pay
(c) to be paying (d) to had paid

**49.** The little boys love .......... to ice creams and cookies.
(a) is treat (b) being treated
(c) to be treat (d) to have treated

**50.** We .......... by our neighbours to be more careful about fire hazards in the home.
(a) had being advised (b) were advised
(c) were to advised (d) had to be advised

**51.** Jill appreciates .......... about a possible promotion for her later in the year.
(a) being tell (b) being told
(c) to told (d) for told

**52.** We .......... Namit about the dangers of bungee jumping.
(a) have to warned (b) have to warn
(c) warn (d) was warn

**53.** She would like .......... for her mistakes rather than not being told about them.
(a) to penalise (b) to be penalised
(c) get penalise (d) have penalised

**54.** Meritorious students .......... scholarships by the University every year.
(a) are being awarded (b) are awarded
(c) do award (d) get award

## ANSWERS

| | | | | | | | | | | | | | | | | | | | |
|---|---|---|---|---|---|---|---|---|---|---|---|---|---|---|---|---|---|---|---|
| 1. | (a) | 2. | (b) | 3. | (a) | 4. | (b) | 5. | (c) | 6. | (d) | 7. | (d) | 8. | (a) | 9. | (d) | 10. | (d) |
| 11. | (b) | 12. | (c) | 13. | (c) | 14. | (c) | 15. | (d) | 16. | (d) | 17. | (b) | 18. | (b) | 19. | (c) | 20. | (c) |
| 21. | (a) | 22. | (b) | 23. | (b) | 24. | (a) | 25. | (c) | 26. | (b) | 27. | (b) | 28. | (a) | 29. | (a) | 30. | (c) |
| 31. | (b) | 32. | (c) | 33. | (d) | 34. | (a) | 35. | (b) | 36. | (a) | 37. | (a) | 38. | (b) | 39. | (b) | 40. | (c) |
| 41. | (d) | 42. | (b) | 43. | (b) | 44. | (b) | 45. | (b) | 46. | (a) | 47. | (b) | 48. | (b) | 49. | (b) | 50. | (b) |
| 51. | (b) | 52. | (b) | 53. | (b) | 54. | (b) | | | | | | | | | | | | |

Chapter 08

# Synonyms

A synonym is a word or phrase that means exactly or nearly the same as another word or phrase in the same language. Here is a list of some words along with their synonyms.

| Word | Synonyms |
|---|---|
| Admonish | Counsel, reprove, warn, chastise |
| Authentic | Genuine, reliable, valid, guaranteed |
| Beg | Implore, solicit, supplicate, beseech, request, plead |
| Bewilder | Confound, perplex, befuddle, befog, baffle, daze |
| Cajole | Persuade, flatter, wheedle, coax |
| Captious | Censorious, hypercritical, fault finding |
| Destitute | Needy, forsaken, orphan |
| Didactic | Teaching, instructive, perfecting |
| Elicit | Draw out, discover |
| Elude | Baffle, avoid, cheat, fool |
| Flagrant | Notorious, outrageous, disgraceful |
| Fortuitous | Chance, accidental, coincidental |
| Indignant | Angry, furious, irate, exasperated, outraged |
| Inanimate | Lifeless, dead, dormant, stagnant |
| Jolly | Jovial, merry, cheerful, affable |
| Jubilant | Elated, triumphant, cheerful |
| Knave | Fraud, cheat, scoundrel, rogue |
| Lament | Sorrow, mourn, grieve |
| Lethargy | Laziness, stupor, sluggishness |
| Misery | Sorrow, distress, affliction, grief |
| Morbid | Unhealthy, diseased, ghastly |

| Word | Synonyms |
|---|---|
| Malice | Bitterness, spite, ill-will, rancour |
| Notorious | Infamous, dishonourable |
| Obtrude | Impose, Impinge, Interfere, Intrude |
| Obliterate | Destroy, efface, demolish, erase |
| Pensive | Thoughtful, rational |
| Pathetic | Moving, touching, distressing |
| Quirk | Whim, caprice, fancy, peculiarity |
| Quip | Retort, repartee, remark, jest |
| Ricochet | Rebound, reflect, bounce, recoil |
| Rut | Groove, hollow, furrow, habit |
| Tirade | Outburst, denunciation |
| Tyrant | Autocrat, despot, dictator |
| Ulterior | Concealed, shrouded, obscured |
| Urchin | Waif, stray, foundling, orphan |
| Vindictive | Revengeful, malicious, resentful |
| Vehemence | Force, passion, emphasis |
| Vile | Trickery, artifice, ruse |
| Waive | Forgo, relinquish, defer |
| Yield | Surrender, submit, admit, agree |
| Yearn | Crave, desire, aspire, urge |
| Zeal | Zest, passion, enthusiasm |
| Zenith | Peak, apex, summit, acme |

# Practice Questions

**Directions** *(Q. Nos. 1-5) Choose the word which is most nearly the some in meaning as the words given below.*

**1.** Astute
(a) Shrewd (b) Unwise
(c) Dishonest (d) Inexplicable

**2.** disparate
(a) sim lar (b) encouraging
(c) strange (d) different

**3.** Self-possessed
(a) Shy (b) Confident
(c) Introvert (d) Extrovert

**4.** Lucid
(a) Arrogance (b) Clear
(c) Unconvincing (d) Long

**5.** Momentous
(a) Memorable (b) Melancholy
(c) Important (d) Hectic

**Directions** (Q. Nos. 6-13) *Given below are sentences with an underlined word in each. Find out the synonyms of underlined word.*

**6.** We were taken aback at the fulsome praise heaped upon our former enemy.
(a) elaborated (b) extravagant
(c) excessive (d) exorbitant

**7.** You may think at first that it is queer to talk of having too much paper money and that money is so nice and useful that you cannot have too much of it .
(a) ridiculous (b) absurd
(c) anomalous (d) odd

**8.** The government is under no obligation to offer contracts to companies which choose to flout guidelines.
(a) condemn (b) ignore
(c) defy (d) neglect

**9.** Soon he felt uncomfortable, for the coach was now moving over a rugged road.
(a) rough (b) narrow
(c) dusty (d) sturdy

**10.** The perpetual noise made it impossible for them to concentrate on the problems.
(a) irritating (b) constant
(c) unlimited (d) recurrent

**11.** Take care not to get hurt with the steam from the kettle.
(a) burnt (b) bruised
(c) scalded (d) cut

**12.** The sons take after their father.
(a) go behind (b) resemble
(c) irritate (d) respect

**13.** The synonym of Barbarian is
(a) Wild (b) Clever
(c) Bold (d) Damage

**Directions** (Q. Nos. 14-16) *Identify the closest meaning of the given word.*

**14.** Identify the closest meaning to the given word. 'perpetuate.'
(a) Abort (b) Ruin (c) Continue (d) Omit

**15.** Identify the closest n meaning to the word. 'Precise'
(a) Defined (b) permissive
(c) Mild (d) Diffused

**16.** Choose the synonym of the word 'malady' from the alternative given below.
(a) Disease (b) Melody
(c) Joy (d) Comedy

**Directions** (Q. Nos. 17-21) *Select the options which are the synonyms of the given words.*

**17.** Derogatory
(a) Resolution (b) Solace
(c) Humiliating (d) Forlorn

**18.** Cajole
(a) Coax (b) Evince
(c) Congratulate (d) Clarify

**19.** Treason
(a) Disloyalty (b) Passion
(c) Miserable (d) Disappear

**20.** Deceptive
(a) Opaque (b) Honest
(c) Transparent (d) Misleading

**21.** Consequence
(a) Proof
(b) Conclusion
(c) End
(d) Usucessfully

**Directions** (Q. Nos. 22-28) *Choose the synonym of underlined word.*

**22.** Mr. Jain is an affluent trader.
(a) wealthy (b) healthy
(c) rich (d) poor

**23.** Choose the correct synonym of the word 'Despise'.
(a) Affection (b) Hate
(c) Jealous (d) Love

**24.** Choose the correct synonym of the word 'Chaos'.
(a) Disorder (b) Blank
(c) Gap (d) Difference

**25.** Choose the synonym of the following word 'Inundate'.
(a) To flood (b) Sink
(c) Batter Down (d) Pass by

**26.** Mark the synonym of the given word.
'Carcass.
(a) Bulk (b) Federation
(c) Quality (d) Corpse

**27.** Choose the appropriate synonym of word.
'Opulent'.
(a) Greedy (b) Hungry
(c) Heavy (d) Wealthy

**28.** Select the appropriate synonym of word.
'Truncate'
(a) Cancel (b) Act cruelly
(c) Cut off (d) End swiftly

**Directions** (Q. Nos. 29-43) *Select the options which are the synonyms of the given words.*

**29.** Solitude
(a) Musical composition (b) Loneliness
(c) Single mindedness (d) True statement

**30.** Valour
(a) Wandering (b) Brightness
(c) Bravery (d) Affluence

**31.** Terminus
(a) Stop (b) Terminal
(c) Tenure (d) Junction

**32.** Impartial
(a) Optimistic (b) Enthusiastic
(c) Realistic (d) Unbiased

**33.** Remorse
(a) Despair (b) Regret
(c) Anger (d) Hatred

**34.** Amicable
(a) Just (b) Appropriate
(c) Durable (d) Friendly

**35.** Discreet
(a) Well-mannered (b) Mild
(c) Proud (d) Prudent

**36.** Misleading
(a) Illusory (b) Deceptive
(c) Misplaced (c) Informative

**37.** Momentous
(a) Memorable (b) Melancholy
(c) Important (d) Hectic

**38.** Reprimand
(a) Praise (b) Penalise
(c) Rebuke (d) Reward

**39.** Paucity
(a) Lack (b) Scarcity (c) Abundance (c) Excess

**40.** Pensive
(a) Sad (b) Thoughtful (c) Gloomy (d) Black

**41.** Tedious
(a) Tiring (b) Boring (c) Monotonous (d) Expensive

**42.** Disaster
(a) Auspicious (b) Mishap
(c) Accident (d) Unfortunate

**43.** Mentor
(a) Genius (b) Guide (c) Stylist (d) Philosopher

**Directions** (Q. Nos. 44-52) *In the following sentences a word is given in bold. For this four options are given. Choose the option nearest in meaning to the word in bold.*

**44.** He gave a **vivid** description of the movie he had seen a week before.
(a) Simple (b) Dull
(c) Clear (d) Confused

**45.** **Brevity** is suggested for expressing yourself.
(a) Conciseness (b) sharpness
(c) intelligence (d) confidence

**46.** Because of a family **feud**, the whole family was wiped out.
(a) Problem (b) Quarrel (c) Crisis (d) Trouble

**47.** His style is quite **transparent.**
(a) Witty (b) Funny
(c) Lucid (d) Involved

**48.** The merchant was **renowned** for his simple way of living.
(a) Notorious (b) Famous (c) Unknown (d) Notable

**49.** Since he promised to do so I **presume** he will come.
(a) think (b) guess
(c) Suppose (d) Believe

**50.** Different races follow different **modes** of living.
(a) Ways (b) Standards
(c) Customs (d) Attitudes

**51.** He is a man of **discreet** nature.
(a) obstinate (b) cunning
(c) prudent (d) Trust worthy

**52.** We must **eradicate** corruption.
(a) Minimise (b) Control
(c) Condemn (d) Remove totally

## ANSWERS

| | | | | | | | | | | | | | | | | | | | |
|---|---|---|---|---|---|---|---|---|---|---|---|---|---|---|---|---|---|---|---|
| 1. | (a) | 2. | (d) | 3. | (b) | 4. | (b) | 5. | (c) | 6. | (c) | 7. | (d) | 8. | (c) | 9. | (a) | 10. | (b) |
| 11. | (c) | 12. | (b) | 13. | (a) | 14. | (c) | 15. | (a) | 16. | (a) | 17. | (c) | 18. | (a) | 19. | (a) | 20. | (d) |
| 21. | (b) | 22. | (a) | 23. | (b) | 24. | (a) | 25. | (a) | 26. | (d) | 27. | (d) | 28. | (c) | 29. | (b) | 30. | (c) |
| 31. | (b) | 32. | (b) | 33. | (b) | 34. | (d) | 35. | (d) | 36. | (b) | 37. | (c) | 38. | (c) | 39. | (a) | 40. | (b) |
| 41. | (b) | 42. | (b) | 43. | (b) | 44. | (c) | 45. | (a) | 46. | (b) | 47. | (c) | 48. | (b) | 49. | (c) | 50. | (a) |
| 51. | (c) | 52. | (d) | | | | | | | | | | | | | | | | |

Chapter 09

# Antonyms

Antonyms are those words which provide just the opposite meaning of the given word. Here is a list of some words alongwith their Antonyms.

| Words | Antonyms |
|---|---|
| Accustomed | Unusual |
| Acquittal | Conviction |
| Active | Inert |
| Alert | Careless |
| Ample | Scanty or Meagre |
| Arrival | Departure |
| Arrogant | Humble |
| Attract | Repeal |
| Aches | Ecstasy |
| Activity | Passivity |
| Barbarism | Civilization |
| Blunt | Sharp |
| Bravery | Cowardice |
| Belief | Disbelief |
| Beauty | Ugliness |
| Beneficial | Injurious |
| Barren | Fertile |
| Bride | Bridegroom |
| Bless | Curse |
| Blustering | Gentle |
| Boon | Bane |
| Care | Neglect |
| Cheerfulness | Gravity |
| Comparison | Contrast |
| Classicism | Romanticism |
| Confidence | Diffidence |
| Consent | Dissent |
| Concord | Discord |
| Confession | Denial |
| Credit | Cash, Discredit |
| Continuity | Discontinuity |
| Conceited | Modest |
| Courage | Timidity |

| Words | Antonyms |
|---|---|
| Complication | Simplification |
| Converge | Diverge |
| Civilized | Savage |
| Creation | Destruction |
| Cause | Effect |
| Christian | Pagan |
| Celebrated | Obscure |
| Decrease | Increase |
| Deep | Independent |
| Destroy | Create |
| Discouragement | Encouragement |
| Economical | Extravagant |
| Elevation | Depression |
| Ease | Difficulty |
| Enthrone | Dethrone |
| Expedite | Impede |
| Entrance | Exit |
| Earning | Spending |
| Enjoy | Suffer |
| Enmity | Friendship |
| Fame | Infamy |
| Faith | Doubt |
| Faithful | Treacherous |
| Fail | Succeed |
| Frankness | Reserve |
| Fresh | Stale |
| Friendly | Hostile |
| Full | Empty |
| Firm | Infirm |
| Fortune | Misfortune |
| Fatigue | Refresh |
| Flexible | Rigid |
| Front | Rear |

| Words | Antonyms | Words | Antonyms |
|---|---|---|---|
| Fine | Coarse | Poverty | Affluence |
| Favour | Frown | Pursuit | Avoidance |
| Foreign | Native | Renounce | Denounce |
| Genuine | Spurious | Ruthless | Humane |
| Gain | Lose | Salubrious | Unhealthy |
| General | Particular | Tragedy | Comedy |
| Guest | Host | Town | Country |
| Gaiety | Gravity | Top | Bottom |
| Giant | Dwarf | Uniform | Varied |
| Lady | Lass | Uncle | Nephew |
| Legal | Illegal | Virtue | Vice |
| Optimist | Pessimist | Violent | Gentle |
| Obscure | Clear | Vivacious | Languid |
| Principal | Subordinate | Voluntary | Compulsory |
| Prodigality | Parsimony | Victor | Vanquished |
| Philanthropist | Misanthropist | Venturesome | Timid |
| Patriot | Traitor | Vague | Definite |
| Peace | War | Wild | Domestic |
| Plenty | Scarce | Worry | Comfort |
| Persuade | Dissuade | Wrap | Open |
| Plaintiff | Defendant | Written | Verbal |
| Pride | Humanity | Wrong | Right |
| Prohibition | Permission | Yesteryear | Modern |
| Pure | Adulterated | Yuppie | Approve |
| Polite | Impolite | | |

## Practice Questions

**Directions** (Q. Nos. 1-5) *Find out the correct antonym of the given word from four alternatives given below.*

**1.** Blemish
(a) Stigma (b) Strength
(c) Adornment (d) Bolt

**2.** Dismal
(a) Dreadful (b) Gloomy (c) Jovial (d) Cheerful

**3.** Modesty
(a) Reserve (b) Boldness
(c) Mildness (d) Humility

**4.** Precarious
(a) Comfortable (b) Senior (c) Privileged (d) Secure

**5.** Deliberate
(a) Negligible (b) Casual
(c) Unintentional (d) Legitimate

**Directions** (Q. Nos. 6-10) *Choose the word nearest opposite in meaning to that of the underlined word.*

**6.** The proposal was <u>denounced</u> by one and all.
(a) announced (b) pronounced
(c) appraised (d) commended

**7.** Where <u>ignorance</u> is sometimes bliss, illiteracy is always considered a curse.
(a) erudition (b) experience
(c) education (d) information

**8.** The news brought by the maidservants was <u>authentic</u>.
(a) authoritative (b) doubtful
(c) ridiculous (d) vacuous

**9.** The doctor said that there is no <u>improvement</u> in the condition of the patient.
(a) depression (b) deterioration
(c) change (d) degradation

**10.** He plunged into the <u>turbid</u> waters of the stream.
(a) deep (b) muddy
(c) clear (d) fresh

**Directions** (Q. Nos. 11-12 ) *In the following questions, select the opposites of the underlined given words in the sentences .*

**11.** We are <u>excited</u> about playing in the school team.
(a) serious (b) depressed
(c) bored (d) silent

**12.** A witness <u>concealed</u> the facts from the court.
(a) exaggerated (b) altered
(c) announced (d) revealed

**13.** The opposite of the word 'optimistic' is
(a) pessimistic (b) hopeful
(c) ideal (d) dull

**Directions** (Q. Nos. 14-15) *Choose the antonym for the words given below.*

**14.** Exterior
(a) Outer (b) Interior
(c) Internal (d) Insider

**15.** Pantheism
(a) Anti-social (b) Antitype
(c) Antithesis (d) Antitheism

**16.** Choose the word the meaning of which is opposite to 'refulgent'.
(a) Effortless (b) Dim
(c) Noisy (d) Snoring

**17.** Choose the word the meaning of which is opposite to 'Culpable'.
(a) Defendable (b) Careless
(c) Irresponsible (d) Blameless

**18.** Choose the word the meaning of which is opposite to 'Arrogant'.
(a) Humble (b) Cowardly
(c) Egoistic (d) Gentlemanly

**19.** Choose the correct/Antonym for the word given below. 'Debtor'
(a) Reluctant (b) Rigid (c) Static (d) Creditor

**20.** Choose the antonym of the given word. 'Brutal'
(a) Gentle (b) Inhuman
(c) Cruel (d) Barbarous

**Directions** (Q. Nos. 22-23) *Select the opposites of the italicised words in the given sentences.*

**21.** Please acknowledge receipt of this letter.
(a) deny (b) deliver
(c) agree (d) praise

**22.** This window-pane is *transparent*.
(a) solid (b) opaque
(c) translucent (d) fragile

**23.** His attitude is very *hostile*.
(a) kind (b) friendly (c) humane (d) helpful

**Directions** (Q. Nos. 24-25) *Choose of the word opposite in meaning of the following word.*

**24.** Atheist
(a) Rationalist (b) Theologist (c) Believer (d) Ritualist

**25.** Particularly
(a) Elaborately (b) Generally
(c) Entirely (d) Comprehensively

## ANSWERS

| | | | | | | | | | | | | | | | | | | | |
|---|---|---|---|---|---|---|---|---|---|---|---|---|---|---|---|---|---|---|---|
| 1. | (b) | 2. | (d) | 3. | (b) | 4. | (d) | 5. | (c) | 6. | (d) | 7. | (c) | 8. | (b) | 9. | (b) | 10. | (c) |
| 11. | (b) | 12. | (d) | 13. | (a) | 14. | (b) | 15. | (d) | 16. | (b) | 17. | (d) | 18. | (a) | 19. | (d) | 20. | (a) |
| 21. | (a) | 22. | (b) | 23. | (b) | 24. | (c) | 25. | (b) | | | | | | | | | | |

Chapter 10

# Homonyms

Word similar in sound or pronunciation, but different in meaning, are called Homonyms.

English में ऐसे बहुत से शब्द हैं जिनका उच्चारण लगभग एक जैसा होता है, लेकिन उनके अर्थ में अन्तर होता है, ऐसे शब्दों को Homonyms or Homophones कहा जाता है। जैसे : Access, Excess, Affect, Effect इन शब्दों का उचित ज्ञान न होने पर एक की जगह पर दूसरे शब्द को लिखने से सब कुछ गलत हो जाता है।

- **Affect** (*to act upon, to pretend* प्रभाव डालना) She affects too much innocence.
  The drought affected a large part of the district.
  **Effect** (*Result*–प्रभाव) Internet produces a bad effect on the young generation.
- **Adapt** (*accomodate*-व्यवहार) One should adapt oneself to the new circumstances.
  **Adept** (*expert*-निपुण) He is an adept in Folk dance.
  **Adopt** (*take up*-गृहण करना) One should not adopt unfair means to secure good marks.
- **Addition** (*putting more*–जोड़ना) I am to buy two more copies in addition to this one.
  **Edition** (*printing books*) The first edition of this book has sold like hot cakes.
- **Accede** (*Agree*–स्वीकार करना) He will not accede to your request.
  **Exceed** (*to be greater*–बढ़ना, बढ़ाना) Write an essay not exceeding three hundred words.
- **Access** (*approach*, reach–पहुँच) Now-a-days, every person has an easy access to the temples irrespective to his caste.
  **Excess** (*more than enough*–अधिकता) Excess of everything is bad.
- **Assent** (*agreement*–स्वीकारोक्ति)He gave his assent to the new proposal.
  **Ascent** (*going up*–ऊपर चढ़ना) He pushed the button and the elevator began its slow ascent.
- **Ail** (*to be ill*–बीमार होना) What ails the Industry is to be sorted out?
  **Ale** (*a drink*–शराब) He has gone to the ale-house.
- **Awed** (*in a state of wonder*–चकित) Awedly she was unable to recall his name.
  **Odd** (*not usual*) Find the odd word from the following passage.
- **Aye** (*Aye means yes*–हाँ) used in some dialects of British English.
- Do you remember your first day at school?' 'Oh aye. Yeah.'
  **Eye** (*ocular organ*–आँख) Her eyes are very beautiful.
- **Bale** (*package*–गाँठ) I received thirty bales of cotton last month.
  **Bail** (*security*–जमानत) The magistrate didn't grant him bail in theft case.
- **Berth** (*sleeping place in train*–ट्रेन में बर्थ) I have booked two berths in Shatabadi Express.
  **Birth** (*coming to life*–जन्म)This is not the birth place of Buddha.
- **Bare** (*uncovered*–नंगा, बिना ढका) He came here bare footed.
  **Bear** (*to tolerate*–सहन करना) I cannot bear your insulting remarks.
  (*an animal*–रीछ) There are three bears in that circus.
  **Beer** (*a kind of wine*–बीयर) I prefer to take beer.
- **Born** (*to take birth*–जन्म) My wife was born in 1960.
  **Borne** (*supported*–सहन किया) He is suffering from water borne disease.
- **By** (*assistance*–द्वारा) A snake was killed by Ram with a stick.
  **Buy** (*purchase*–खरीदना) I want to buy a car.

- **Beet** (*a vegetable*–चुकन्दर) I prefer mango to beet.
  **Beat** (*to thrash*–पीटना) It is wrong to beat the students with a stick.
- **Borrow** (*to take loan*–उधार लेना) I have borrowed some money from Bank.
  **Burrow** (*a hole in earth*–छेद) A mouse lives in this burrow.
- **Cell** (*a small cottage*–छोटी कोठरी) There are more than twenty cells in that prison.
  **Sell** (*to dispose off*–बेचना) He sells fruits and vegetables.
  **Sale** (*noun-act of selling*–बिक्री) I have purchased this dress from that shop.
  **Brake** (*lever*–ब्रेक) I am going to get the brake wire changed.
  **Break** (*to make a part*–तोड़ना) Can you break this stick with your hands?
- **Baron** (*a landlord*–जमींदार) There was a time when all powers rested in the hands of rich barons.
  **Barren** (*not fertile*–अनुपजाऊ) In barren land you can't cultivate any thing.
- **Blue** (*a colour*–नीला) I like blue colour.
  **Blew** (*whistled*–बजाई) The refree blew the whistle again and again.
- **Bait** (*food placed on a hook or in a trap to entice fish*) Let your bait falls gently upon the water.
  **Bate** (*to lessen*–कम करना) We listened with bated breath the stories of grandmother's travel.
- **Band** (*a group*–समूह) A band is a group of musician.
- **Banned** (*forbidden*–प्रतिबन्धित) Drinking is banned in Gujarat.
- **Bard** (*a poet*–कवि) People sometimes refer to William Shakespeare as the Bard.
  **Barred** (*enclosed by poles*–घेरना) The windows were closed and shuttered and the door was barred.
- **Basal** (*forming the base*–आधार बनाना) The basal layer of the skin was also torn.
  **Basil** (*an herb*–तुलसी) Basil is used in cooking also.
- **Bell** (*ding ding*–घंटी) Don't try to bell the cat.
  **Belle** (*beautiful woman*–सुन्दर स्त्री) She was the belle in last night party.
- **Better** (*superior*–अच्छा) It is always better to drive carefully.
  **Bettor** (*one who bets*–जुंआरी) The person who bets is called a bettor.
- **Bloc** (*an alliance*–मित्रगण) A bloc is a group of countries which have similar aims and interest and that generally act together over some issue.
  **Block** (*a block in a town is an area of land with streets on all its sides*–घरों की पंक्ति)
  She walked four blocks down High Street.
- **Bread** (*a loaf*–रोटी) Bread is necessary for the living.
  **Bred** (*past tense of breed*–नस्ल का भूतकाल) He is an ill bred fellow.
- **Brewed** (*fermented*–शराब बनाना) I like nicely brewed beer.
  **Brood** (*family*–परिवार, सोचना) A brood is a group of baby birds that were born at the same time to the same mother.
  If someone broods over something they think about it a lot seriously.
- **Brows** (*multiple foreheads*–भौंहें) Your brows on your forehead.
  **Browse** (*grazing*–चरना) Three red deer were browsing near my lodge.
- **Check** (*to verify, to stop*–जाँचना) He checked my passport. He checked me from leaving the function.
  **Cheque** (*bank document*–चेक) I issued a cheque favouring PNB.
- **Calendar** (*chart showing dates etc*–कलैण्डर) I have only one calendar in my office.
  **Calender** (*to press paper, cloth etc.*–प्रेस करना) Please calender my dress.
- **Canvas** (*a kind of rough cloth*–तिरपाल) My shoes are made of canvas.
  **Canvass** (*to solicit votes*–वोट माँगना) Now-a-days students are busy in canvassing for their friends.
- **Corpse** (*dead body*–लाश) The corpse was covered with a white bedsheet.
  **Corps** (*a body of troops*–सेना की टुकडी) I want to join National Cadet Corps.
- **Coma** (*state of senselessness*–बेहोशी) The patient has been in coma since Monday.
  **Comma** (*mark of punctuation*–कोमा) One should be careful about proper use of comma.
  **Censor** (*an official* examination–सेंसर) The Censor Board has awarded 'U' certificate to this film.
  **Censure** (*criticize adversely*–निन्दा) His conduct was censured by the Parliament.
- **Cease** (*discontinue*–छोड़ना) He resigned and thus, ceased to be the Chairman of our society.
  **Seize** (*to catch*–पकड़ना) Heroin worth 2 lacks rupees was seized from his office.
  **Siege** (*surrounded*–घेरना) Akbar's army sieged the castle of Chittorgarh.
- **Career** (*profession*–व्यवसाय) For better career opportunities, join computer courses.
  **Carrier** (*one who carries*–ले जाने वाला) Mosquitoes are carriers of virus.
- **Capital** (*centre of administration*–राजधानी) Delhi is the capital of India.

**Capitol** (*roman temple of Jupiter, US Congress House*–एक बिल्डिंग का नाम)
A meeting of US Congress be held in capitol tomorrow.

- **Complement** (*which completes*–पूरक) Husband and wife are complementary to each other.
**Compliment** (*regards*–अभिनन्दन) Please convey my best compliments to your parents.
- **Council** (*assembly*–सदन) He was nominated to the Council of State .
**Counsel** (*advice*–सलाह) He counsels in a right way.
- **Caste** (*Community*–जाति) He belongs to schedule caste.
**Cast** (*to give*–देना) Please cast your votes in favour of me.
- **Cattle** (*animal*–पशु) Cattle were grazing in the field.
**Kettle** (*vessel*–पतीली) Put the kettle on the gas burner.
- **Carat** (*unit of weight for precious stones, equal to 200 milligrams*)
**Caret** (*proofreader's insertion mark*–छुटा हुआ शब्द दिखाने का चिन्ह)
**Carrot** (*edible orange root*–गाजर) Carrot contains aburdent iron.
**Karat** (*one-24th part of otherwise pure gold*–24वाँ भाग या पूर्ण सोना)
- **Cent** (*one hundredth of a dollar*–डॉलर का सौवाँ हिस्सा)
**Scent** (*an aroma*–सुगन्ध) I like the aroma of freshly baked bread .
**Sent** (*dispatched*–भेजा) I have sent you a packet of wool.
- **Cents** (*hundredths of a dollar*–डॉलर का सौवाँ हिस्सा) A dollar has hundred cents.
**Scents** (*many things to smell*–सुगन्ध) Flowers are chosen for their scent as well as their look.
**Sense** (*physical abilities of sight, smell, hearing, touch and taste*–चेतना)
She has a good sense of humour.
- **Chard** (*spinach-like vegetable*–सब्जी) She is fond of chard.
**Charred** (*burnt*–जलकर खाक हो जाना) In the fire broke out yesterday seven persons were charred to ash.
- **Chile** (*a South American country*–एक देश) Keshav is living in Chile.
**Chilli** (*dried pod of red pepper*–मिर्ची) Chillies are used in cooking.
**Chilly** (*uncomfortably cool*–अत्यधिक ठण्डा) It was a chilly night.
- **Clack** (*a chattering sound*–आवाज) The windshield wipers clacked back and forth.
**Claque** (*a group hired to applaud, sycophants*–प्रशंसक) Whenever our team scored a goal the claque made a superb clappings which further boosted the spirit of the team.
- **Clause** (*clause is a group of words*–शब्द समूह) Containing a verb, contractual unit.
**Claws** (*big fingernails*–पंजा) The cat tried to cling to the edge by its claws.
- **Copes** (*gets along with adversity*–मुकाबला करना) It was amazing how my mother coped with bringing up three children on less than ₹ one thousand a month.
**Copse** (*a stand of trees*–पेड़ों की पंक्ति) A copse is a small group of trees growing very close to each other.
**Cops** (*police officers*–पुलिस अधिकारी) I do not like the cops standing near my house.
- **Desert** (*a waste track of land* –रेगिस्तान *noun, to forsked; verb* त्यागना) Churu is a desert area in Rajasthan. He has deserted his wife.
**Dessert** (*fruit served after dinner*–भोजन के बाद फल आहार) The dessert course after dinner was liked by all.
- **Dye** (*a verb-to colour*–रँगना) Dye my shirt in sky blue .
**Die** (*expire*–मरना) He died from cholera.
- **Dose** (*quantity of medicine*–दवा की खुराक) I have already taken four doses of this medicine by now.
**Doze** (*sleep*–ऊँघना) You were dozing in the class yesterday.
- **Draught** (*a quantity of liquid*–तरल की मात्रा) The patient was given a draught of medicine.
**Drought** (*want of rain*–सूखा) Due to scanty rain whole of the district is in the grip of drought.
- **Dam** (*surrounding area to stop flow of water*–बाँध) A dam is being built up here to storage the rainy water.
**Damn** (*condemn*–निन्दा) His behaviour is damned by all the members of the society.
- **Dear** (*loving*–प्रिय) He is my very dear friend.
**Deer** (*an animal*–हरिण) I saw many deer in that forest.
- **Decent** (*good*–बढ़िया) Because of his decent behaviour he was promoted to the post of General Manager.
**Descent** (*coming down*–नीचे उतरना) That hill has a steep descent to the south.
**Dissent** (*to differ*–मतभेद) He recorded his dissent on this proposal.
- **Device** (*noun-plan*–योजना) He used all devices to popularise the game.
**Devise** (*verb—to plan*–योजना बनाना) You are to devise a plan to increase the turn over.
- **Dam**(*holds back water*–बाँध) Government is building a dam on this river.
**Damn** (*a curse*–शाप देना) Don't be flippant , damn it! This is serious.
- **Eruption** (*bursting out*–फूटना) There was an eruption of Volcano near Gujarat border.

**Irruption** (*invasion*–आक्रमण) The irruption of Mughals destroyed the glory of Rajput empire.

- **Emerge** (*to come out*–बाहर आना) He emerged successfully out of the miserable circumstances.

  **Immerge** (*to plunge into*–डूबना) He is immerged in mythological thoughts.

- **Eligible** (*fit to be chosen*–योग्य) He is eligible for the post.

  **Illegible** (*that which cannot be read*–अपठनीय) His writing is illegible.

- **Earn** (*to come to deserve*–कमाना) Companies must earn a reputation for honesty.

  **Urn** (*a jar*–बर्तन) An urn is a container, in which a dead person's ashes are kept.

  An urn is a metal container used for making a large quantity of tea or coffee and keeping it hot.

- **Eyelet** (*small hole for laces*–छोटे छिद्र) My shoes have eight eyelets.

  **Islet** (*small island*–छोटा द्वीप) An islet is a small island.

- **Ere** (*before*) Take the water ere the clock strikes four.

  **Err** (*to make a mistake*) If you make a threat be sure to carry it out if he errs again.

- **Foul** (*unfair*–अनुचित) One can't achieve true success through foul means.

  **Fowl** (*a bird*–पक्षी) He is fond of fowl's meat.

- **Find** (*to get*–पाना) Go there you will find a tree near the river.

  **Fined** (*to charge*–जुर्माना) The court fined him ₹ 20000 for the offence.

- **Floor** (*surface*–फर्श) Clean the floor with dettol and water.

  **Flour** (*wheat meal*–आटा) He has a flour mill.

- **Forth** (*onward*–आगे आना) He alone came forth to assist that poor lady .

  **Fourth** (*third-fourth*–चौथा) April is the fourth month of the year.

- **Fain** (*gladly*–खुशी से) She would fain on seeing me.

  **Feign** (*pretend*–दिखावा) When his boss scolded him, he feigned as a deaf.

- **Fair** (*pure, a show*–पवित्र, मेला) I believe in using fair means to achieve the target.

  Let us go to the fair.

  **Fare** (*passage money*–किराया) A strike was called by the truckers demanding hike in minimum fare.

- **Feat** (*an exploit*–साहसिक कार्य) A racing car is an extraordinary feat of engineering.

  **Feet** (*plural of foot*–पाँव) Do not put your feet on the table.

- **Gage** (*security*–जमानत) I do not lend without sufficient gage.

  **Gaze** (*to look attentively*–एकटक देखना) She stood gazing at herself in the mirror.

- **Gait** (*manner of walk*–चाल) That model girl has a graceful and sexy gait.

  **Gate** (*large door*–दरवाजा) You should not enter through the main gate.

- **Goal**(*aim*–उद्देश्य) To achieve this goal you are to work hard.

  **Gaol** (*jail*–जेल) He has been to gaol earlier also.

- **Gilt** (*gold-plated*–धातु की परत चढ़ा हुआ) This is a gilt ornament.

  **Guilt** (*culpable*–दोषी) You aren't convinced of Mr. Charles guilt.

- **Guise** (*appearance*–दिखना) She presented her dance in the guise of a rabbit.

  **Guys** (*man*–व्यक्ति) Hi, guys! How are you doing?

- **Hail** (*frozen rain*–ओले) It is hailing. It hailed yesterday.

  **Hale** (*healthy*–स्वस्थ) May God keep you hale and healthy!

- **Horde** (*a gang*–समूह) A horde of mischievous students attacked the shop keepers.

  **Hoard** (*to store*–एकत्र करना) Hoarding of sugar beyond the prescribed limit is an offence.

- **Hair**(बाल) She has black hair.

  **Heir** (*successor*–उत्तराधिकारी) He is an heir apparent to the throne.

- **Hurt** (*injury*–चोट) Your comments can hurt her feelings.

  **Hart** (*a male deer*–हिरण) I have a beautiful pair of harts.

  **Heart** (*an organ in the body*–दिल) He is suffering from heart disease.

- **Heel** (*part of shoe*–जूते की एड़ी) The heels of my shoe are pinching.

  **Heal** (*to cure*–अच्छा होना) This medicine will help you in quick healing.

- **Hear** (*to listen*) I hear his voice.

  **Here** (*at this location*–यहाँ) Come here.

- **Idle** (*indolent*–निकम्मा) An idle man can't make any progress.

  **Ideal** (*visionary*–आदर्श) My teacher, Mr. Shrivastava, is an ideal for me.

  **Idol** (*an image of a deity*–मूर्ति) A section of the Hindus believe in idol worship.

- **Incite** (*to provoke*–उत्तेजित करना) His arrogant behaviour incited me a lot.

  **Insight** (*a clear vision*–स्पष्ट देखना) Do you know the insight story of this murder?

- **Indite** (*to compose*–रचना) Though he indited the letter carefully, yet it was not liked by the chairman.

  **Indict** (*to accuse*–दोषारोपण करना) He was indicted for theft and murder.

- **In** (*expressing inclusion*–में) He is in the room.

**Inn** (*hotel*–होटल) This is a well maintained inn.

- **Juggler** (*one who juggles* –जादूगर)He is a good juggler.

  **Jugular** (*artery to head*–सर की नस)

  (a) A jugular or jugular vein is one of the three important veins in your neck that carry blood from your head back to your heart.

  (b) If you say that someone went for the jugular, you mean that they strongly attacked another person's weakest points in order to harm him.

- **Knead** (*working bread dough*–गुंदना) He kneaded the mixture on a floured surface.

  She felt him knead the aching muscles.

  **Need** (*must have*–आवश्यकता) He needs your help.

- **Knight** (*chivalrous man*–बहादुर) He was knighted on the queen's birthday.

  **Night** (*darkness*–रात) Night comes after day.

- **Knot** (*fastening in cord*–गाँठ) He tied a knot at the end of the lace.

  **Naught** (*or nought is zero*–शून्य) Sales rose by naught point four percent last month.

  **Not** (*negation*–नहीं) He was not present in the party.

- **Know** (*to possess knowledge*–जानना) I know him.

  **No** (*negation*–नहीं) I have no pen.

- **Lightening** (*make lighter*–हल्का करना) We had appealed to the court for lightening the punishment, but of no avail.

  **Lightning** (*electric discharge in clouds*–बिजली चमकना) There was occasional lightning in the sky last night.

- **Loath** (*unwilling*–इच्छा के विरुद्ध) Nothing loath he did, as he was saying.

  **Loathe** (*to dislike greatly*–घृणा करना) I loathe her dressing pattern and arrogant way of talking.

- **Latter** (*antonym of former*–बाद में आने वाला) Between Ram and Shyam, the latter (Shyam) is a diligent student.

  **Later** (*comparative of late*–देरी से आने वाला) He came later than his friend.

- **Lose** (*to part with*–खोना) Where did you lose your briefcase?

  **Loose** (*to slack*–ढीला करना) He was wearing a loose cotton shirt.

- **Meat** (*flesh*–मांस) I don't like eating meat.

  **Meet** (*to assemble*–मिलना) She came here only to meet me.

- **Metal** (*iron, brass etc.*–धातु) Silver is a white metal.

  **Mettle** (*spirit, courage*–साहस) Our leaders have no mettle to fight against corruption.

- **Metre** (*poetic rhythm*–छन्द) Can you tell me in what metre Shelley's 'Skylark' is written?

  **Meter** (*a measuring instrument =100 cm.*, –मीटर) One meter is equal to hundred centimetres.

- **Minor** (*underage*–छोटा) Minors are not allowed to open current account in Banks.

  **Miner** (*one who works in mine*–खान पर काम करने वाला) He is a miner, works in a coal mine.

- **Marshal** (*a military officer*–मार्शल) He is a marshal of the court.

  **Martial** (*war like*–युद्ध जैसा) He has martial spirit and courage to fight in odd circumstances.

- **Maize** (*corn*–मक्का) I like to eat maize cake.

  **Maze** (labyrinth–घुमाव) This castle has many hidden mazes.

- **Made** (*accomplished*–बनाया) The table is made of wood.

  **Maid** (*young woman*–नौकरानी) She is our maid-servant.

- **Mall** (*a large shopping area*–शापिंग की जगह)

  **Maul** (*savage*–क्रूर) He had been mauled by a tiger.

  **Moll** (*gangster's girlfriend*–लड़की मित्र) She is the moll of the don.

- **Manner** (*method*–तरीका) I am a professional and I have to conduct myself in a professional manner. She smiled in a friendly manner.

- **Manor** (*lord's house or a large private house*–बड़ा व्यैक्तिक घराना) The thieves broke into the manor at night.

- **Naval** (*pertaining to ships and the sea*–जहाज से सम्बन्धित) He is captain in naval forces.

  **Navel** (*pertaining to the belly button*–नाभिक) There is a black mole near her navel.

- **Nay** (*no*–नहीं) The Rajya Sabha can merely say yea or nay to such a bill.

  **Neigh** (*a horse's cry*–हिनहिनाना) The horse gave a loud neigh.

- **Our** (*plural of 'my'*–हमारा) This is our house.

  **Hour** (*a period of time*–घण्टा) I have been waiting for you for half an hour.

- **Oar** (*used for rowing a boat*–नाव का डण्डा Life without aim is like a boat without an oar.

  **Ore** (*mineral from which metal can be extracted*–खनिज) Iron is extracted from its ore by melting.

- **Overdo** (*carried to excess*–अधिक) It is important never to overdo new exercises.

  **Overdue** (*past time for payment or some action*–देर) The meeting is long overdue.

- **Pray** (*entreat*–प्रार्थना) I pray to God everyday.

  **Prey** (*hunt*–शिकार) Do not prey upon the innocent animals.

- **Peace** (*tranquility*–शान्ति) Peace of mind is more precious than the materialistic richness.

  **Piece** (*fragment*–टुकड़ा) The dog found a piece of meat .

- **Price** (*value*–कीमत) What is the price of this shirt?

  **Prize** (*reward*–ईनाम) She could not win any prize this time.

- **Patrol** (*going round*–गश्त लगाना) A chowkidar was patrolling at the main gate.
  **Petrol** (*oil*–पकठ-पेट्रोल) Petrol is required to run vehicles.
  **Pail** (*Bucket*–बाल्टी) I have two pails full of water.
  **Pale** (*Yellowish appearance*–पीला) On seeing a lion , his face turned pale.
- **Presence** (*the state of being present*–उपस्थिति) The meeting took place in the presence of the Judge.
  **Presents** (*gifts*–उपहार) He gave a nice present to his friend on his wedding anniversary.
- **Pride** (*ego*–गर्व) We take pride in offering you the best services.
  **Pried** (*opened*–खोला) I pried the top off a can of chilli.
- **Quite** (*altogether*–पूरी तरह से) I am quite well now.
  **Quiet** (*silent*–शान्त) Please keep quiet.
- **Rein**(*bridle*–लगाम) Keep the rein tight, otherwise you may be thrown out by the horse.
  **Reign** (*rule*–शासन करना) The reign of Akbar is known for communal harmony.
- **Rap** (*a sharp blow*–थप्पड़) He rapped her on the cheek.
  **Rape** (*to ravish*–बलात्कार) He raped a college girl.
  **Wrap** (*to enclose*–बन्द करना) The book was wrapped in a piece of white paper.
- **Sooth** (*truth* सच) Sooth to speak, he is not a good boy.
  **Soothe** (*to calm*–शान्त करना) You can't soothe his anger with lame excuses.
- **Stationary** (*Fixed*–स्थिर) Earth is not stationary, it moves round the sun.
- **Stationery** (*Writing material*–स्टेशनरी) I am going to market to purchase several stationery items for the office.
- **Straight** (*opposed to curved*–सीधा) I believe in straight talks.
  **Strait** (*narrow*–तंग) The lane is too strait to pass through for an elephant.
- **Sore** (*painful*–दर्दकारक) I can't sing as my throat is sore.
  **Soar** (*to fly high*–ऊंचा उड़ना) Birds soar in sky.
  **Sour** (*not sweet*–खट्टा) The grapes were sour.
- **Story** (*a tale*–कहानी) My grandmother told me a story of an oldman.
  **Storey** (*floor of a building*–मंजिल) I have taken a room at first storey.
- **Seal** (*to close*–बन्द करना) He sealed the envelope and put on a stamp.
  **Seel** (*to close someone's eyes*–आँखे बन्द करना) Close the eyes of (a hawk etc.) by stitching up the eyelids·
- **Sign** (*displayed board bearing information*–निशान) Equations are generally written with a two bar equals sign.
  **Sine** (*reciprocal of the cosecant*) Find the sine value of this angle.
- **Some** (*a few*–कुछ) Please give me some money.
  **Sum** (*result of addition*–फेड़) The sum of all the angles of a triangle is 180 degree.
- **Soot** (*black residue of burning*–काजल) Soot is black powder which rises in the smoke from a fire and collects on the inside of chimneys.
  This wall is blackened by soot.
  **Suit** (*clothes*–पहनने का सूट) I have a blue suit.
  **Suite** (*a set of rooms*–कमरों का समूह) We enjoyed our time during the week in a suite at London.
- **Team** (*a group of players*–टीम) Our college team has won the trophy.
  **Teem** (*to be full of*–बहुतायात) Rajasthan is a state teeming with natural resources.
- **Toe** (*a part of foot*–पैर का अँगूठा) She hurt her left toe in an accident.
  **Tow** (*to draw by a rope*–बाँधना) The boat was towed with a tree near the shore.
- **Tail** (*part of body*–पूँछ) Cow has a long tail.
  **Tale** (*story*–कहानी) My grandmother told me an interesting tale.
- **Their** (*belong to they*–उनका) They have learnt their lessons.
  **There** (*at that place*–वहाँ) I am to go there now.
- **Throne** (*royal seat*–सिंहासन) All the brothers are fighting for the throne.
  **Thrown** (*third form of throw*–फेंक दिया) She has thrown her certificates into the river.
  **Thorn** (*impediment*–काँटा) You need a needle to get the thorn out.
- **Tare**(*the seed of a vetch used in refence to its small size*–एक प्रकार की घास) When the harvest is gleaned the evil tares will be separated from the good wheat.
  **Tear** (*salty drops from eyes*–आँसू) Her eyes are filled with tears.
  **Tier** (*a horizontal row*–पंक्ति) I have booked your seats in two tier compartment.
- **Taught** (*past tense of teach*–पढ़ाया) Who taught you English?
  **Taut** (*stretched tight*–तना हुआ) The clothes line is pulled taut and secured.
- **Tea** (*herbal infusion*–चाय) I am fond of tea.
  **Tee** (*golfball prop*–गोल्फ से सम्बन्धित) The tee was broken accidentally.
- **Tenner** (*english slang for a ten pound note*–दस का) I have only a tenner in my pocket.

**Tenor** (*tendency*–तात्पर्य) The whole tenor of discussion has changed.

- **Told** (*what was spoken*–बोला) He told me how to do it.

  **Tolled** (*a bell was rung*–घण्टी बजाना) The pilgrims tolled the bell.

- **Troop** (*a company of soldiers*–सिपाहियों का समूह) Twenty thousands troops were deployed on the border.

  **Troup** (*a company of actors*–एक्टर्स का समूह) She belongs to an acrobatic performing troup.

- **Umpire** (*a referee*–अम्पायर) You must not disobey the umpire.

  **Empire** (*dominion*–राज्य) The king was unable to manage his empire properly.

- **Vein** (*a blood vessel*–शिरा) Veins take the blood to all parts of body.

  **Vane** (*weather cock*–मुर्गा) There is a vane at the top of the temple.

- **Vale** (*valley*–घाटी) The beautiful vale of Manali is worthseeing.

  **Veil** (*a cover*–पर्दा) Muslim ladies generally put a veil on her face.

  **Wail** (*to lament*–विलाप) Don't wail please, he is safe and sound.

- **Wave** (*unevenness*–लहर) The waves of ocean are rising higher and higher.

  **Wave** (*movement*–हिलाना) She waved her hand as the bus started.

  **Waive** (*relinquish*–छोड़ना) I request the officer to waive the punishment.

- **Waste** (*useless*–व्यर्थ करना) Don't waste your precious time.

  **Waist** (*part of body*–कमर) The boy had a chain round his waist.

- **Weather** (*atmosphere*–मौसम) It is cold weather today .

  **Whether** (*which of two*–यदि) I asked her whether she would come .

- **Vain** (*useless*–व्यर्थ) I made several request to our Principal but all in vain .

  **Wane** (*to decrease*–कम होना) I see the moon waning these nights.

- **Vary** (*to change*–बदलना) Your actions vary from the promise you made.

  **Very** (*more*–बहुत) She is a very beautiful girl.

  **Wary** (*cautious*–सतर्क) Because of his wary nature, he was saved.

- **Verses** (*paragraphs*–गद्य) This verse describes three reasons of his failure.

  **Versus** (*against*–विपरीत) India versus Pakistan is a greatly contesting cricket match.

- **Weight** (*weight*–वजन) He gained ten kg. of weight within a month.

  **Wait** (*to attend*–इन्तजार) Don't wait for me, I will go myself.

- **Week** (*period of seven days*–सप्ताह) Monday is the first day of a week.

  **Weak** (*feeble*–कमजोर) Ram is too weak to walk.

- **Ware** (*article*–समान) He has sold all his cook wares.

  **Wear** (*to put on*–पहनना) I like to wear silk sarees.

  **Wear** (*to diminish*–घिसना) My shirt has worn out.

- **Yearn** (*to long*–इच्छा करना) I am anxiously yearning to meet my wife.

  **Yarn** (*thread*–धागा) I have purchased three bundles of yarn.

- **Yoke** (*slavery*–दास बनाना) He is under the yoke of his master.

  **Yolk** (*yellow portion of an egg*–अण्डे की पीली जर्दी) Some people eat only the yolk of an egg.

  **You're** (*contraction of 'you are'*) You're a great writer.

  **Your** (*belonging to you*–तुम्हारा) Which is your house?

- **You'll** (*contraction of 'you will'*) You'll be asked to explain your conduct.

  **Yule** (*christmas*–क्रिसमस) Everyone makes enjoyment in his own way during yule time.

# Practice Questions

**1.** Because of his .......... behaviour, Rupal was promoted to the post of senior Manager.
(a) descent (b) dissent
(c) decent (d) None of these

**2.** It was amazing to see a sixty year old man .......... up with pressures of office work.
(a) copse (b) cope
(c) cops (d) None of these

**3.** Students should not ............ unfair means to secure good marks.
(a) adept (b) adapt
(c) adopt (d) None of these

**4.** After resigning from the post, he ............ to be the managing director of the company.
(a) seize (b) ceased
(c) siege (d) None of these

**5.** He is ............ poor to pay his fees.
(a) to (b) two
(c) toc (d) None of these

**6.** The girl ran very fast and vanished into thin
(a) here (b) hair
(c) air (d) None of these

**7.** The ............ of many astrologers about destruction of the world didn't come true.
(a) prophecy (b) prophesy
(c) prophezy (d) None of these

**8.** Our guest speaker this week is ............ writer Mr. Chetan Bhagat.
(a) eminent (b) imminent
(c) iminent (d) None of these

**9.** Our ............ concern is that the project may not be completed before the June dead line.
(a) principle (b) principal
(c) principel (d) None of these

**10.** We'll give you free ............ regarding design and pictures.
(a) rain (b) reign
(c) rein (d) None of these

**11.** I can not ............ your insulting remarks.
(a) bare (b) bear
(c) beer (d) None of these

**12.** I like the ............ of roses is my room.
(a) cent (b) sent
(c) scent (d) None of these

**13.** Your rude behaviour has really ............ me.
(a) heart (b) hurt
(c) hart (d) None of these

**14.** The judge was not convinced of Mr. Shekhar's ............ .
(a) guild (b) gilt
(c) guilt (d) None of these

**15.** A section of the Hindus believe in ............ worship.
(a) idle (b) ideal
(c) Idol (d) None of these

**16.** You need a needle to get the ............ out from your fingers.
(a) throne (b) thrown
(c) thorn (d) Nont of these

**17.** Due to drinking very cold water, I developed a ............ throat.
(a) soar (b) sore (c) sour (d) None of these

**18.** He presented me a book ............ in a beautiful cover.
(a) rap (b) wrapped (c) rape (d) None of these

**19.** Enjoy fully but don't let it take ............ over work.
(a) precedents (b) presidents
(c) precedence (d) None of these

**20.** He gave his T.V. to the landlord in ............ of rent.
(a) lie (b) Lieu
(c) Loo (d) None of these

## ANSWERS

| | | | | | | | | | | | | | | | | | | | |
|---|---|---|---|---|---|---|---|---|---|---|---|---|---|---|---|---|---|---|---|
| 1. | (c) | 2. | (b) | 3. | (c) | 4. | (b) | 5. | (c) | 6. | (c) | 7. | (a) | 8. | (a) | 9. | (b) | 10. | (c) |
| 11. | (b) | 12. | (c) | 13. | (b) | 14. | (c) | 15. | (c) | 16. | (c) | 17. | (b) | 18. | (b) | 19. | (c) | 20. | (b) |

Chapter 11

# One Word Substitutions

- Abdication — Voluntaily renouncing the throne.
- Aborigines — Original inhabitants of a country.
- Ablaut — A vowel change that accompanies a change in grammatical function. Same as 'gradation.' *Sing, sang,* and *sung.*
- Accismus — Pretended refusal of something desired.
- Acrolect — A variety of language that is closest to a standard main language, especially in an area where a creole is also spoken. *Standard Jamaican English,* where Jamaican Creole is also spoken.
- Adianoeta — An expression that carries both an obvious meaning and a second, subtler meaning.
- Adynaton — A declaration of impossibility, usually expressed as an exaggerated comparison with a more obvious impossibility.
- Alexia — Inability to read, usually caused by brain lesions; word blindness.
- Alliteration — The repetition of the same letter or sound at the begining of adjacent or closely connected words.
- Alphabetism — The expression of spoken sounds by an alphabet.
- Ambigram — A word, phrase, or sentence written in such a way that it reads the same way upside down as right.
- Anadiplosis — Rhetorical repetition of one or more words, particularly a word at the end of a clause. "*Men in great place are thrice servants: servants of the sovereign or state; servants of fame; and servants of business.*" — Francis Bacon
- Anagram — A rearrangement of a group of letters, especially a word that can be formed by rearranging the letters in another word.
- Accessible — Which can be approached.
- Acclimatize — To accustom oneself in a new climate.
- Aggressor — One who attacks first.
- Alimony — Allowance paid to wife on legal separation.
- Altruist — A person unselfishly concerned for or devoted to the welfare of others.
- Amateur — One who does thing for pleasure and not for money.
- Ambassador — Person representing a State in a foreign country.
- Ambidextrous — One who can use either hands without any problem.
- Ambiguous — That can be interpreted in more than one way.
- Amnesia — Loss of memory.
- Amphibian — Animals that live both on land and sea.
- Anarchy — Absence of rule or law and order.
- Annual — Which happens once a year.
- Anomaly — Deviation from common rule.
- Anonymous — Which does not bear the name of the writer.
- Antiseptic — Medicine used to save plant and animals from getting infected.
- Anaphora — Repetition of a word or phrase at the beginning of successive phrases, clauses or sentences.
- Antonym — Words which are opposite in meaning.
- Aphasia — A medical condition that makes a person unable to speak, write or understand speech or writing.
- Aquarium — Vessel in which fish and water plants are kept.
- Aquatic — Animals that live in water.
- Archeology — Study of Antiquities.
- Aristocracy — Government by the rich/aristocrats.
- Bachelorhood — State of being unmarried.
- Bankrupt — One who can't pay his debts.
- Bellicose — One who is fond of fighting .
- Belligerents — Nations engaged in war.
- Billingsgate — Coarsely abusive language.
- Bibliophile — One who loves or collects books.
- Biennial — Happening every second year.
- Bigamy — Having two husbands or two wives at a time.

- Biography — Life history of a person.
- Biped — Animal having two feet.
- Blasphemy — Speaking disrespectfully about sacred or religious things.
- Bookworm — One who devotes his full time in studying course books.
- Botany — Study of plants.
- Brigand — A member of a gang that ambushes and robs people in forests and mountains.
- Brittle — Which can be easily broken.
- Bullion — Gold or silver before using for manufacturing ornaments.
- Bureaucracy — Government run by officials.
- Caducity — The infirmity of old age, senility.
- Calligraphy — The art of beautiful handwriting; elegant penmanship.
- Cannibal — One who eats human flesh.
- Centrifugal — Anything tending to move away from centre.
- Centripetal — Anything tending to move towards centre.
- Century — One hundred years.
- Coprolalia — Uncontrolled, excessive use of obscene or scatological language, sometimes accompanying certain mental disorders.
- Colleagues — Persons working in the same office.
- Compatriot — Belonging to same country.
- Congenital — Present from birth.
- Convalescence — Period of gradual recovery after illness.
- Cosmopolitan — A citizen of the world.
- Credulous — One who easily believes others.
- Cryptography — Study of secret writing and coded words.
- Curable — Which can be cured.
- Cytology — Study of cell.
- Dead letter — An unclaimed letter.
- Deaf — One who cannot hear.
- Democracy — A country in which power is held by elected representatives.
- Dermatology — Study of skin and its diseases.
- Digestible — That which can be digested.
- Dilogy — An ambiguous speech.
- Dittograph — A letter or word repeated unintentionally in writing or copying.
- Dittology — Two distinct interpretations of the same text.
- Dipsomania — A strong desire to drink alcohol.
- Divisible — That which can be divided.
- Dotage — Extreme old age when one behaves like a child.
- Drawn — A game in which no party wins.
- Dumb — One who can't speak.
- Dysgraphia — Impairment of the ability to write, usually caused by brain dysfunction or disease.
- Dyslexia — A learning disorder distinguished by impaired ability to recognise and comprehend written words.
- Edible — A thing fit to be eaten.
- Effeminate — One who is womanish in habits.
- Eligible — One who is fit for the post.
- Elision — The omission of a letter or syllable. '*Don't*' instead of 'do not'
- Emigrant — One who goes to live in a foreign country.
- Employee — One who is paid to work for an organization or another person.
- Employer — One who employs.
- Endemic — A disease prevailing in a locality.
- Entomology — Study of insects.
- Endophoric — Characteristic of a reference to something outside the speech or text in which the reference occurs. See also: exophoric.
- Epic — A long narrative poem.
- Epanorthosis — Immediate rephrasing for emphasis, intensification or justification. "You, young lad, are most brave! Brave, did I say? No, heroic!"
- Epistrophe — Repetition of the same word or phrase at the end of successive phrases, clauses, or sentences.
- Epicure — One who is fond of sensual enjoyment.
- Epilogue — A speech given at the conclusion of a drama.
- Epitaph — Words inscribed on the tomb of the dead.
- Etymology — Science deals with formation of words.
- Eucrasia — A good or normal state of health.
- Etymon — An earlier form of a word in the same language or an ancestor language.
- Fanatic — One who is unreasonably enthusiastic for an extreme religious or political cause.
- Fastidious — Having very selective taste. Hard to please.
- Fatalist — One who believe in fate.
- Feminist — One devoted to the welfare of women.
- Foster child — Child brought by persons, who are not his biological parents.

- Franchise — Constitutional right to cast vote.
- Fratricide — Murder of brother.
- Garage — A shed for keeping motor car.
- Geology — Study of Earth's structure, surface and origins.
- Germicide — Which destroy germs.
- Glossolalia — Fabricated, nonmeaningful speech, especially such speech associated with a trance state or some schizophrenic syndromes.
- Glutton — One who is fond of eating too much.
- Gratis — Without any payment, free.
- Gregarious — Animals which live in flocks.
- Harangue — A noisy and loud speech before a large gathering.
- Haplology — The process by which a word is formed by removing one of two identical or similar adjacent syllables in an earlier word.
- Hearse — Vehicle to carry dead bodies.
- Herbivorous — Animals that live on herbs.
- Hendiadys — The use of a conjunction rather than the subordination of one word to another.
- Heterography — A method of spelling in which the same letters represent different sounds in different words, as in ordinary English orthography.
- Heterophemy — The unconscious saying, in speech or in writing, of some thing that one does not intend to say, especially when what is said is the reverse of what was intended.
- Histology — Study of microscopic structure of tissues.
- Holonym — A concept that has another concept as a part.
- Homicide — Murder of a human being.
- Homogeneous — Things of the same nature.
- Honeymoon — A holiday spent together by a newly married couple.
- Honorary — A post without any remuneration.
- Hydra — A serpent with many heads.
- Hydrophobia — A fear of water.
- Hygienist — One cares fully of his health.
- Hypothesis — A tentative assumption, made to drive a logical conclusion.
- Hypallage — Interchange of two elements in a phrase or clause from the order, in which they would normally appear. "A mind is a terrible thing to waste," instead of "To waste a mind is a terrible thing."
- Hypercorrect — Characteristic of an incorrect linguistic construction, in which the error is produced from a mistaken effort to be correct. "Between you and I," which should be 'between you and me.'
- Hyponym — A word that is more specific than a given word.
- Iconoclast — Breaker of art and literature.
- Idiosyncrasy — Peculiar behaviour of an individual.
- Idolatry — Worshipping of idols.
- Ignorant — A person who has no knowledge of any happening.
- Illegal — Unlawful.
- Illegible — That which cannot be read.
- Illiterate — One who can neither read nor write.
- Illeism — The practice of referring to oneself in the third person.
- Imitable — Which can be copied.
- Immigrant — A person from another country who comes to our country to settle.
- Immovable — Which can't be moved; fixed.
- Imposter — One who assumes name or title of someone else for deceiving others.
- Impregnable — A fort which can't be entered into.
- Incorrigible — That which cannot be corrected.
- Ingressive — Characteristic of a speech sound produced with an inhalation of breath.
- Incredible — Which cannot be believed.
- Inevitable — That cannot be avoided.
- Infallible — One who cannot make a mistake.
- Infanticide — Murder of an infant.
- Infection — A disease spread by contact.
- Inimitable — Cannot be copied.
- Insomnia — Loss of sleep.
- Interpolate — Inserting new matter in a book.
- Intraverous — Anything pushed inside veins.
- Invisible — That which cannot be seen.
- Invulnerable — Impossible to harm or damage.
- Irreparable — That which cannot be repaired.
- Irrevocable — A decision that can't be revoked.
- Isocolon — A sequence of parallel structures, having the same number of words and sometimes the same number of syllables.
- Itinerant — One who travels from place to place.
- Kindergarten — A school for small children.
- Kleptomania — An abnormal desire to steal.
- Linguist — One who knows many languages.
- Ligature — A character that consists of two or more joined letters, such as e.
- Lipogram — Writing composed of words not having a certain specific letter or letters.
- Litotes — Understatement by negating the opposite; a type of meiosis. *"I was not disappointed with the news."*
- Loquacious — Talkative.
- Lunar — of or relating to the Moon.
- Maiden speech — Speech made for the first time.

- Mammals — Animals which give milk.
- Manuscript — A book written by hand.
- Masochism — The condition or state of deriving (esp. sexual) gratification from one's own pain or humiliation.
- Materialistic — One for whom money is the most important thing.
- Matins — Morning prayer in church.
- Matricide — Murder of one's mother.
- Matrimony — State of being married.
- Maxim — A short statement of a general truth, principle or rule of behaviour.
- Meadow — A low level tract of uncultivated grassland.
- Meticulous — One who is very particular even about small details.
- Migratory — That moves from one place to another.
- Misogamist — One who hates the custom of marriage.
- Misogynist — Hater of women.
- Misologist — One who hates reasoning or debate.
- Mobocracy — Rule or domination by the masses.
- Monogamy — Marrying one person at a time.
- Morphology — Study of animal and plant structure.
- Narcotic — Medicine which induces sleep.
- Neologism — New word coined by an author.
- Neology — Study of formation of new words.
- Notorious — A man with bad reputation.
- Nosism — The practice of referring to oneself as we;
- Numismatics — Study or collection of Coins.
- Obsolete — No longer in practice.
- Oceanography — Study of oceans.
- Odontology — Study of teeth.
- Oligarchy — Government by a small group of powerful people.
- Omnipotent — One who is all powerful.
- Omniscient — One who knows everything.
- Omnivorous — One who eats both plants and flesh.
- Opaque — That which can't be seen through.
- Ophthalmology — Study of eye and its diseases.
- Optics — Study of light.
- Optimist — One who sees the bright side of things.
- Orthography — The study of correct spelling according to established usage.
- Ornithology — Study of birds.
- Orography — Study of mountains.
- Orphan — A child whose parents are dead.
- Orthodox — One who believes in traditional values.
- Ostracize — To exclude from a society or a group.
- Paleontology — Study of fossils.
- Panacea — A remedy for all ills.
- Pantisocracy — A form of utopian social organization in which all are equal in social position and responsibility.
- Pantomime — A dumb show.
- Palilogy — The repetition of a word or phrase in immediate succession, for emphasis.
- Parasite — One who depends on others.
- Parasol — A lady's umbrella.
- Pathology — Study of Disease.
- Patricide — Murder of one's one's father.
- Patrimony — Properties inherited from one's father.
- Patriot — One who loves one's country.
- Pedagogy — Study of the art of teaching.
- Pedantic — A style in which author displays his knowledge.
- Pedestrian — A person who is walking, especially in an area where vehicles go.
- Pessimist — One who sees the dark side of things.
- Philanderer — One who enjoys love making.
- Philanthropist — A lover of mankind.
- Philately — The collection or study of stamps.
- Philistine — One who does not care for art or literature.
- Philogynist — Lover of womankind.
- Philology — Study of words and their roots.
- Phonetics — The study of sounds made by human voice is speech.
- Phrenology — Study of skull with regard to human character.
- Physiology — Study of structure of human body.
- Pioneer — One who is one of the first people to do something.
- Plagiarism — Literary theft. Using ideas and words of another person and presenting them as own.
- Platitudes — Common place remarks.
- Plutocracy — Government by the rich.
- Polyandry — Marrying more than one husband at a time.
- Polygamy — Marrying more than one wife at a time.
- Post mortem — An examination of body after death.
- Primogeniture — Right of succession belonging to the first born.
- Pseudonym — An imaginary name of an author assumed to disguise himself.
- Pugnacity — Tendency to quarrel.
- Purist — One who is particular about the purity of one's language.
- Quadruped — An animal having four foot.
- Rebel — One who take up arms against government.
- Redtapism — Too much official formalities.

- Regicide — Murder of a king.
- Reticule — A lady's purse.
- Sadist — A person who derives (esp. sexual) pleasure from inflicting pain, suffering etc. on others.
- Simultaneous — Happening at the same time.
- Smuggle — Importing goods illegally without paying custom duties.
- Solar — Relating to Sun.
- Soliloquy — Speaking to one self when alone.
- Somniloquism — Talking in sleep.
- Spokesman — One who speaks on behalf of others.
- Stoic — One who is indifferent to pleasure and pain.
- Suicide — Killing of self.
- Snarl word — A word with negative connotations and therefore not desirable to use lest good public relations be undermined.
- Superordinate — A word that is more generic than a given word.
- Syllogism — Deductive reasoning in which a conclusion is derived from two premises.
- Synesis — Agreement of words to logic rather than grammatical form.
- Synchronize — Occurring of two or more events at a time.
- Teetotaller — One who does not take alcoholic drinks.
- Telltale — One who enjoys talking about others private affairs.
- Thearchy — Government by the God.
- Theist — One who believes in the existence of God.
- Theomania — A belief that one is God.
- Transparent — That which can be seen through.
- Truant — A student who leaves school or class without permission.
- Truism — An often repeated truth.
- Twins — Two child born together.
- Usurer — One who lends money at a higher rate of interest.
- Utopia — A state of highest perfection.
- Uxoricide — Murder of wife.
- Venial — An excusable fault.
- Verbatim — Using exactly the same words as were originally used.
- Verbicide — The destruction of the sense or value of a word.
- Verbose — Style full of words.
- Vesper — Evening prayer in a church.
- Veteran — A well and long experienced person in a particular occupation.
- Wardrobe — An almirah where clothes are kept.
- Widow — A woman whose husband has died.
- Widower — A man whose wife has died.
- Xenoepist — One with a foreign accent.
- Zoology — Study of animals.

# Practice Questions

**Directions** *(Q. 1-10) Give one word for each of the following expressions choosing from those given below each such expression.*

**1.** Life history of a man written by himself.
(a) Biography (b) Autobiography
(c) Calligraphy (d) Bibliography

**2.** A statement that can have a double meaning.
(a) Verbose (b) Ambivalent
(c) Epigraph (d) Ambiguous

**3.** Work inscribed on the tomb.
(a) Eulogy (b) Epitaph
(c) Epigraph (d) Eloquence

**4.** The intelligent and educated class.
(a) Literate (b) Aristocrat
(c) Educated (d) Intelligentsia

**5.** Science of plants.
(a) Zoology (b) Geology
(c) Anthropology (d) Botany

**6.** List of headings of the business to be transacted at a meeting.
(a) Minutes (b) Agenda
(c) Excerpts (d) Proceedings

**7.** One filled with excessive and mistaken enthusiasm in a cause.
(a) Pedant (b) Patriot
(c) Fanatic (d) Martyr

**8.** Regard for others as a principle of action.
(a) Altruism (b) Philanthropy
(c) Nepotism (d) Cynicism

**9.** One who promotes the idea of absence of government of any kind, when every man should be a law unto himself.
(a) Agnostic (b) Iconoclast
(c) Belligerent (d) Anarchist

**10.** Study of mankind.
(a) Pathology (b) Philology
(c) Physiology (d) Anthropology

**Directions** *(Q. Nos. 11-20) Give one word for each of the following expressions choosing from those given below each such expression.*

**11.** An office with no work, but high pay.
(a) Honorary (b) Sinecure
(c) Ex-officio (d) Reticent

**12.** One who deserts his religion.
(a) Deserter (b) Apostate
(c) Opportunist (d) Turn coat

**13.** The act of looking back upon past events.
(a) Introspection (b) Retrospection
(c) Extrospection (d) Circumspection

**14.** Very vigilant and cautious.
(a) Meticulous (b) Fastidious
(c) Anxious (d) Alert

**15.** Matter written by hand.
(a) Handwritten (b) Manuscript
(c) Amnesty (d) Proof

**16.** A small shop that sells fashionable clothes, cosmetics, etc.
(a) Store (b) Stall
(c) Boutique (d) Both

**17.** One who is honourably discharged from service.
(a) Retired (b) Emeritus
(c) Relieved (d) Emancipated

**18.** One who cannot be corrected.
(a) Incurable (b) Incorrigible
(c) Hardened (d) Invulnerable

**19.** One who is incharge of a museum.
(a) Curator (b) Supervisor
(c) Caretaker (d) Warden

**20.** The study of ancient societies.
(a) Anthropology (b) Archaeology
(c) History (d) Ethnology

**Directions** *(Q. Nos. 21-25) Give one word for each of the following expressions choosing from those given below each such expression.*

**21** Responsible according to law.
(a) Eligible (b) Legitimate
(c) Legalised (d) Liable
(e) Offensive

**22.** Constant effort to achieve something.
(a) Patience (b) Vigour
(c) Enthusiasm (d) Perseverance

**23.** Opposed to great or sudden change.
(a) Conservative (b) Revolutionary
(c) Evolutionary (d) Static
(e) Unalterable

**24.** Anything written in a letter after it is signed.
(a) Corrigendum (b) Manuscript
(c) Postscript (d) Post diction
(e) Posterity

**25.** That which cannot be done without.
(a) Impracticable (b) Indispensable
(c) Impossible (d) Unmanageable
(e) Irrevocable

**Directions** *(Q. Nos. 26-30) Give one word for each of the following expressions choosing from those given below each such expression.*

***26.*** **He could not give a good explanation for his extraordinary behaviour.**
(a) Be satisfied with (b) Account for
(c) Provide evidence for (d) Count for
(e) Readily dispense

***27.*** **Those who pass through this gate without permission will be prosecuted.**
(a) Bypassers
(b) Absconders
(c) Thoroughfares
(d) Trespassers
(e) Culprits

***28.*** **A careful preservation and protection of wildlife is the need of the hour.**
(a) Management (b) Embarkment
(c) Enhancement (d) Promotion
(e) Conservation

***29.*** **I could achieve success through conscious efforts.**
(a) Tremendous efforts
(b) Efforts made with critical awareness
(c) Efforts done after gaining consciousness
(d) Efforts done after being awakened
(e) Efforts done without any desire

***30.*** **We are looking forward to a good monsoon this year.**
(a) Getting (b) Predicting
(c) Hoping (d) Visualising
(e) Encouraging

**Directions** *(Q. Nos. 31-37) Substitute one word for each of the following sentences.*

***31.*** **The science of words and language is known as**
(a) philology (b) paleontology
(c) bibliography (d) entomology

***32.*** **One of the time-tested ways of remembering a series of items is known as a/an**
(a) recollection (b) schematizing
(c) mnemonic (d) ingenuity

***33.*** **Nations that do not trust each other look upon each other.**
(a) calmly (b) hopefully
(c) askance (d) retrospectively

***34.*** **If a person cannot be easily handled or dealt with, he will not be complimented for his**
(a) domesticity (b) knowledge
(c) tractability (d) eulogy

***35.*** **A person who constantly thinks he is sick is a**
(a) hypochondriac (b) misogynist
(c) misanthrope (d) hyperpituitary

***36.*** **But a person who is really sick and is unduly anxious about his health is a**
(a) valedictorian (b) vegetarian
(c) valetudinarian (d) dialectician

***37.*** **The order to stay in one's own bailiwick means that a person should remain in his own**
(a) room (b) district
(a) country (b) bed

## ANSWERS

| | | | | | | | | | | | | | | | | | | | |
|---|---|---|---|---|---|---|---|---|---|---|---|---|---|---|---|---|---|---|---|
| 1. | (b) | 2. | (d) | 3. | (b) | 4. | (d) | 5. | (d) | 6. | (b) | 7. | (c) | 8. | (a) | 9. | (d) | 10. | (d) |
| 11. | (b) | 12. | (b) | 13. | (b) | 14. | (a) | 15. | (b) | 16. | (c) | 17. | (b) | 18. | (b) | 19. | (a) | 20. | (a) |
| 21. | (d) | 22. | (a) | 23. | (a) | 24. | (c) | 25. | (b) | 26. | (b) | 27. | (d) | 28. | (e) | 29. | (b) | 30. | (d) |
| 31. | (a) | 32. | (c) | 33. | (c) | 34. | (c) | 35. | (a) | 36. | (c) | 37. | (b) | | | | | | |

Chapter 12

# Vocabulary

Vocabulary का अर्थ 'शब्द भण्डार' से है। अभ्यर्थी को अपनी Vocabulary को लगातार Enrich करना चाहिए। जिससे वह अंग्रेजी में बेहतर पकड़ बना सके। अंग्रेजी भाषा में अनेक ऐसे शब्द हैं जो परीक्षा की दृष्टिकोण से Learn करना चाहिए। ताकि आप परीक्षा में उत्तम अंक प्राप्त कर सकें।

## Some Famous Useful Words

| Word | Meaning | Word | Meaning |
|---|---|---|---|
| Incompetent | अक्षम | Ineligible | अपात्र |
| Advance | अग्रिम धन | Accused | अभियुक्त |
| Violation | अतिक्रमण | Accusation | अभियोग |
| Excess profit | अतिरिक्त लाभ | Invalid | अमान्य |
| Right | अधिकार | Fine | अर्थदण्ड |
| QuoWarranto | अधिकार पृच्छा | Qualification | अर्हता |
| Act | अधिनियम | Minority | अल्पसंख्यक |
| Notification | अधिसूचना | Minor | अव्यस्क |
| Speaker | अध्यक्ष | Joint family | अविभक्त परिवार |
| Ordinace | अध्यादेश | Motion of noconfidence | अविश्वास प्रस्ताव |
| Exclusive | अनन्य क्षेत्राधिकार | Illegal | अवैध |
| jurisdiction | अनुज्ञा | Incapacity | असमर्थता |
| Permit | अनुदान | Supreme Court | उच्चतम न्यायालय |
| Grant | अनुपात | High Court | उच्च न्यायालय |
| Proportion | अनुमति | Succession | उत्तराधिकार |
| Assent | अनमोदन | Successor | उत्तराधिकारी |
| Approve | प्रसन्न होना | Production | उत्पादन |
| Discipline | अनुशासन | Certiorari | उत्प्रेषण लेख |
| Disciplinary | अनुशासन सम्बन्धी | Proclamation | उद्घोषण |
| Ratification | अनुसमर्थन | Industry | उद्योग |
| Investigation | अनुसन्धान | Lunacy | उन्माद |
| International | अन्तर्राष्ट्रीय | Remedy | उपचार |
| Conscience | अन्तःकरण | Gratuity | उपदान |
| Libel | अपमान लेख | Consumption | उपभोग |
| Crime | अपराध | Vice President | उपराष्ट्रपति |
| Criminal | अपराधी | Appear | उपस्थित होना |

| Word | Meaning |
|---|---|
| Deputyspeaker | उपाध्यक्ष |
| Contravention | उल्लंघन |
| Debt | ऋण |
| Debenture | ऋणपत्र |
| Possession | कब्जा |
| Tax | कर |
| Duty | कर्त्तव्य |
| Staff | कर्मचारी वृन्द |
| Prison | कारागार |
| Imprisonment | कारावास |
| Trade union | कार्मिक संघ |
| Business | कार्य |
| Executive power | कार्यपालिका शक्ति |
| Executive | कार्यपालिका |
| Fare | किराया |
| Copyright | कृति स्वाम्य |
| Mineral | खनिज |
| Cost | खर्च |
| Clause | खण्ड |
| Account | गणना |
| Audit | गणना परीक्षा |
| Quorum | गणपूर्ति |
| Research | गवेषणा |
| Declaration | घोषणा |
| Discussion | चर्चा |
| Mark | चिह्न |
| Octroi | चुंगी |
| Cantonment | छावनी |
| Census | जनगणना |
| Tribal Area | जनजाति क्षेत्र |
| Inquire | जाँच करना |
| District | जिला |
| Gambling | जुआ |
| Coinage Typewriting | टंकण |
| Decree | डिग्री |
| Third Reading | तृतीय पठन |
| Triennial | त्रैवार्षिक |
| Police Station | थाना |
| Handicraft | दस्तकारी |
| Document | दस्तावेज |
| Punish | दण्ड देना |
| Criminal Court | दण्ड-न्यायालय |
| Magistrate | दण्डाधिकारी |
| Liability | दायित्व |
| Civil | दीवानी |

| Word | Meaning |
|---|---|
| Money | धन |
| Money Bill | धन धनविधेयक धंधा |
| Municipal Area | नगर क्षेत्र |
| Municipality | नगर पालिका |
| Committee | नगर पालिका |
| Citizenship | नागरिकता |
| Body | निकाय |
| Corporation | निगम |
| Direction | निर्देश |
| Fund | निधि |
| Control | नियन्त्रण |
| Rule | नियम |
| Appointment | नियुक्त |
| Judgemnent | निर्णय |
| Casting Vote | निणायकमत |
| Assessment | निर्धारण |
| Manufacture | निर्माण |
| Export | निर्यात |
| Export Duty | निर्यात शुल्क |
| Discharge | निर्वाहन |
| Election | निर्वाचन |
| Constituency | निर्वाचन क्षेत्र |
| Supension | निलम्बन |
| Retirement | निवृत्ति |
| Pension | निवृत्ति वेतन |
| Forbid | निषेध |
| Allegiance | निष्ठा |
| Cheif minister | मुख्य मन्त्री |
| Capital | मूलधन |
| Petition | याचिका |
| Traffic | यातायात |
| Reservation | रक्षण |
| Receipt | रसीद |
| Revenue | राजस्व |
| Revenue Court | राजस्व न्यायालय |
| State | राज्य |
| State Fund | राज्यनिधि |
| Council of States | राज्य परिषद् |
| Governor | राज्यपाल |
| Opinion | राय |
| Amount | राशि |
| Nation | राष्ट्र |
| President | राष्ट्रपति |
| Vacancy | रिक्त स्थान |
| Bar | रुकावट |

| Word | Meaning | Word | Meaning |
| --- | --- | --- | --- |
| Rent | लगान | Session court | सत्र न्यायालय |
| Impose | लगाना | House | सदन |
| Cost | लागत | Member | सदस्य |
| Profit | लाभ | Morality | सदाचार |
| Writ | लेख | Association | संस्था |
| House of the people | लोक सभा | Treaty | सन्धि |
| Community | लोक समाज | Assembly | सभा |
| Plead | वकालत करना | Chairman | सभापति |
| Major | वयस्क | Equality | समता |
| Will | वसीयत | Dedication | समर्पण |
| Freight | वस्तु भाड़ा | Intercourse | समागम |
| Consul | वाणिज्य दूत | Newspaper | समाचार पत्र |
| Cause | वाद | Committee | समिति |
| Cause of action | वाद मूल | Community | समुदाय |
| Debate | वाद विवाद | Estate duty | सम्पदा शुल्क |
| Annual | वार्षिक | Conference | सम्मेलन |
| Sale | विक्रय | Government | सरकार |
| Sales Tax | विक्रय कर | Concurrence | सहमति |
| Consideration | विचार | Grants-in-aid | सहायक अनुदान |
| Distribution | वितरण | Resolution | संकल्प |
| Finance | वित्त | Union | संघ |
| Financial | वित्तीय | Organization | संगठन |
| Finance Minister | वित्त मन्त्री | Communication | संचार |
| Foreign Affairs | विदेशीय कार्य | Message | सन्देश |
| Legislative Council | विधान परिषद् | Property | सम्पत्ति |
| Legislature | विधान मण्डल | Contact | सम्पर्क |
| Legislative Assembly | विधान सभा | Consent | सम्मति |
| Law | विधि | Guardian | संरक्षक |
| Bill | विधेयक | Constitution | संविधान |
| Appropriation | विनियोग | Inflation | मुद्रास्फीति |
| Section | विभाग | Order cheque | आदेशी चेक |
| Distribution | विभाजन | Recurring deposit | आवृर्ती जमा |
| Respite | विराम | Bill of collection | उगाही बिल |
| Repugnant | विरुद्ध | Credit deposit | उधार जमा |
| Dispute | विवाह | Letter of credit | उधार पत्र |
| Divorce | विवाह-विच्छेद | Sale on credit | उधार बिक्री |
| Privilege | विशेषाधिकार | Rough Day book | कच्ची बही |
| motion of confidence | विश्वास प्रस्ताव | Paper scale | कागज पैमाना |
| Subject | विषय | Paper currency | कागजी मुद्रा |
| Extension | विस्तार | Time money | कालिक ऋण |
| Pay | वेतन | Gross earning | कुल मकाई |
| Deprive | वंचित करना | Gross loss | कुल हानि |
| Expenditure | व्यय | Standing credit | खड़ी जमा |
| Labour | श्रम | Bill of costs | खर्चे का बिल |
| Labour union | श्रमिक संघ | Credit book | उधार बही |

| Word | Meaning | Word | Meaning |
|---|---|---|---|
| Book deposit | खाता ऋण | Capital sums | पूँजीगत राशि |
| Book debt | खाता कर्ज | Capital profit | पूँजीगत लाभ |
| Balance cheque | खुला चेक | Capitalist | पूँजीपति |
| Sales ledger | ग्राहक खाता | Capital assest | पूँजी परिसम्पत्ति |
| Fluctuation | घटत-बढ़त | Capital account | पूँजी लेखा |
| Running credit | चालू उधार | Floating money | फालतू रुपया |
| Current deposit | चालू जमा | Retail Price | फुटकर कीमत |
| Chartered accountant | चार्टर लेखाकार | Arrears | बकाया |
| Crediting | जमा करना | Call in arrears | बकाया माल |
| Paying book | जमा कापी | Saving deposit | बचत खाता |
| Creditnote | जमा पत्र | Discount amount | बट्टा (खाता) |
| Forged note | जाली नोट | Balancing | शेष निकालना |
| Mint par | टकसाल | Stock in trade | बिक्री का माल |
| Wear and tear | टूट-फूट | Commodity market | बाजार उपयोगी वस्तु |
| Bad debt | डूबी रकम | Out station cheque | बाहरी चेक |
| Bankruptcy | दिवाला | Sale account | बिक्री खाता |
| Tight money | दुलर्भ रुपया | Bill of sale | बिक्री बिल |
| Indigenous bank | देशी बैंक | Free of charge | बिना मूल्य |
| Draft | धनादेश | Expired loan | बीता कर्जा |
| Cash credit | नकद जमा | Endorser | प्रचारक |
| Cash memo | नकद पर्ची | Clean loan | बेजमानती कर्जा |
| Cashvalue | नकद मूल्य | Morning loan | बेजमानती कर्जा |
| Debit account | नाम खाता | Bankrate | बेमियादी कर्जा |
| Withdrawn amount | निकाली की रकम | Bank rate | बैंक दर |
| Alloted fund | नियत निधि | Bank charge | बैंक प्रभार |
| Maker's brand | निर्माता की छाप | Bank cash | बैंक रोकड़ |
| Export duty | निर्यात कर | Bank account | बैंक लेखा |
| Net production | निबल उत्पादन | Bank call | बैंक लेखा माँग |
| Check register | पड़ताल खाता | Firm market | मजबूत बाजार |
| Charge | प्रभार, खर्च व्यय | Arbitrator | मध्यस्थ |
| Bill received | प्राप्त हुण्डी | Demand loan | माँग कर्जा |
| Receipts | प्राप्तियाँ | Demand draft | माँग धनादेश |
| Accounts rendered | पिछला हिसाब | Call notice | माँग सूचना |
| State cheque | पुराना चेक | Goods | माल |
| Capital reserve fund | पूँजी आरक्षित निधि | Freight | भाड़ा |
| Capitalised | पूँजीकृत | Stock limit | माल रखने की सीमा |
| Capitalised Value | पूँजीकृत लाभ | Stock account | माल लेखा |
| Capital out flow | पूँजी का निर्गम | | |

# Practice Questions

**Directions** *(Q. No- 1-20) Fill in the blank with suitable words to make sentence meaningful.*

**1.** If you don't like the soup, why don't you ......... to the manager of the restaurant.
(a) úomplain (b) protest
(c) criticise (d) insult

**2.** If you were a more ......... person, you would have not left me alone.
(a) polite (b) considerate
(c) kind (d) humorous

**3.** Oh I am so .......... Let's go and do some shopping and watch a movie.
(a) boring (b) fed up
(c) tired (d) henhappy

**4.** I don't think shweta is ......... at home. Her friends are with her.
(a) lonely (b) solitary
(c) hensociable (d) alone

**5.** His Uncle owns four computer companies and lives in a big ......... out in the country.
(a) mansion (b) bungalow
(c) apartment (d) fut

**6.** The company could not make any ......... and closed down many outlets.
(a) profit (b) success
(c) victory (d) winnings

**7.** I am feeling really ......... today. The weather is terrible and I got some bad news this morning too.
(a) lazy (b) punctual
(c) miserable (d) starving

**8.** By turning off electricity switches when not required, you can ......... a lot of money.
(a) earn (b) save
(c) win (d) gain

**9.** You can ......... my surprise when I heard the news.
(a) suppose (b) think
(c) imagine (d) believe

**10.** I cut my finger on a rusty tin and it became bodly ......... .
(a) affected (b) Infected
(c) effected (d) diseased

**11.** Violent programes on television may have a bad ......... on children.
(a) Influence (b) control
(c) pressure (d) affection

**12.** The local tourist bureau will send you .........about hotels in the area.
(a) knowledge (b) news
(c) Information (d) notice

**13.** Where do you ......... going for your holidays this year?
(a) intend (b) expect
(c) pretend (d) guess

**14.** Be quiet. It is rude to ......... people when they are speaking.
(a) Interfere (b) interrupt
(c) prevent (d) introduce

**15.** The boy's allergy to dust caused his skin to .......... .
(a) itch (b) rub
(c) blemish (d) flush

**16.** When he makes a ......... by car, he takes his family along with him.
(a) voyage (b) cause
(c) journey (d) passage

**17.** Because of the poor harvest, wheat prices have ......... in the last six months.
(a) added (b) soared
(c) amounted (d) gathered

**18.** I would like to ......... touch with my friends but I have so little time.
(a) be in (b) be out
(c) lose (d) keep in

**19.** There was total silence in the room and she could hear the ......... of her heart.
(a) beating
(b) knocking
(c) striking
(d) tapping

**20.** ......... of money prevented us from taking a holiday this year.
(a) Limit (b) Freeze
(c) Emptiness (d) Lack

## ANSWERS

| | | | | | | | | | | | | | | | | | | | |
|---|---|---|---|---|---|---|---|---|---|---|---|---|---|---|---|---|---|---|---|
| 1. | (a) | 2. | (b) | 3. | (b) | 4. | (d) | 5. | (a) | 6. | (a) | 7. | (c) | 8. | (b) | 9. | (c) | 10. | (b) |
| 11. | (a) | 12. | (c) | 13. | (a) | 14. | (b) | 15. | (a) | 16. | (c) | 17. | (b) | 18. | (d) | 19. | (a) | 20. | (d) |

# Chapter 13

# Prefix and Suffix

**Prefix** It is kind of syllable placed before the root of a word. For example Unhappy conists of prefix 'Un' which means not and root word is happy.

**Suffix** A suffix is a group of letters placed after the end of a word to form a new word.

**For example Improvement** Here the root word is improve and we have added suffix ment. To the addition of a suffix often changes a word from one part of speech to another.

## Suffixes Used to Form Nouns

| | | |
|---|---|---|
| ee | — | Payee, examiness, employee |
| sion | — | submission, recession, discussion |
| al | — | survival, revival |
| ion | — | action, selection, attraction |
| ance | — | brilliance, acceptance, appearance |
| ment | — | improvement, payment |
| ar, er, or | — | beggar, actor, preacher, spectator |
| ery, ary, ory | — | victory, misery, missionary |
| ence | — | excellence, innence, difference |
| ure | — | pleasure, treasure |
| mony | — | patrimony, harmony, testimony |
| dom | — | freedom |
| ship | — | friendship, studentship, hardship |
| ness | — | bitterness, sweetness |
| th | — | death, dearth, worth, growth |
| hood | — | manhood, womanhood, childhood |
| ty | — | cruelty, enemity, entity |
| ism | — | rationalism, communism |
| ing | — | riding, waiting, sleeping, gardening |

## Suffixes Used to Form Verbs

| | | |
|---|---|---|
| se | — | cleanse |
| ise/ize | — | memorise, fertilize, advertise |
| er | — | weaker, harder, quicker, broader, faster |
| fy | — | simplify, falsify, purify |
| ate | — | rotate, captivate, activate |

## Suffixes Used to Form Adjectives

| | | |
|---|---|---|
| ful | — | beautiful, hopeful, playful |
| some | — | winsome, wholesome, quarrelsome |
| less | — | fearless, cashless, jouless, cheerless |
| al | — | multinational, bilateral, loyal |
| ine | — | bovine, canine, feline |
| ate | — | fortunate, temperate, sedate |
| ary | — | necessary, customary |
| ly | — | cowardly, manly, glutlemanly, likely |
| en | — | woollen, golden, rotten |
| y | — | sundry, needy, sandy, ready |
| like | — | childlike, womanlike, slatelike |
| ish | — | womanish, childish, prudish |
| ic | — | phonetic, organic, cyclic, heroic |
| que | — | picturesque, grotesque, unique |

## Suffix 'ly' is Used with Adjective to make adverb

| | | |
|---|---|---|
| beautiful | — | beautifully |
| innocent | — | innocently |
| pleasant | — | pleasantly |
| hard | — | hardly |
| violent | — | violently |

## Prefixes Used to Form Verbs

| | | |
|---|---|---|
| em | — | empower, embody, embolden |
| be | — | bemoan, befriend, besiege, |
| en | — | enable, enlarge, entail, enslave, endanger |
| de | — | decode, defame, devalue, degrade |
| hyper | — | hyper active, hyper sensitive |
| ex | — | export, excessive, exonerate |

Re — Return, Refund, Refuse, Reconsider, Rewrite
mis — misuse, misrepresent, mistook
dis — disappear, disappointment, dislike, dis disembark, disagree

### Prefixes Used to Form Adjectives

Anti — Anticlockwise, anticlimax, antidote
Il — Illegal, Illegible, Illiterate, Ill-informed
Im — Impossible, Impatient, immobile, Impolite
In — Independent, incoherence, Incompatibility

### Prefixes Used to Form Nouns

Auto — autobiography, automobile, autocorrect
Anti — Anti government, antiracist, antiwar
dis — discomfort, dislike
Inter — Interaction, Interference
Mal — Matreatment, matrutition
Mis — Misconduct, misdeed, Mismanagement
Mono — Monosyllable, monograph, Monogamy

## Practice Questions

**1.** The Suffix in the word comfortable is
(a) for (b) table (c) able (d) ible

**2.** The Prefix in the word Irreligious is
(a) ar (b) Irr (c) Ir (d) Irre

**3.** What is the prefix in the word dissociate?
(a) Ate (b) Dis (c) Sociale (d) As

**4.** Which word below contains a suffix?
(a) Beauty (b) Empower (c) Attraction (d) Export

**5.** Which word below contains a prefix?
(a) Uncle (b) Unhappy
(c) Under (d) Understand

**6.** Which suffix will form a word from 'dent' which means a person who fixes teeth.
(a) ic (b) ist (c) tion (d) atiou

**7.** What is the suffix in the word Reformation?
(a) on (b) mation
(c) ation (d) ion

**8.** Add the correct suffix to form a word from 'journal which means the writing and publishing of newspaper and magazine'.
(a) ist (b) ism (c) ly (d) ic

**9.** What suffix you will add in the noun Memory to make it a verb?
(a) able (b) ation (c) ize (d) ion

**10.** What prefix you will use to make the opposite of word 'credible?
(a) Un (b) em (c) In (d) Ir

**11.** What suffix you will use in the noun 'miser' to make it an adjective?
(a) able (b) y (c) ary (d) ent

**12.** What is the suffix which will be used to make noun 'captive' into a verb?
(a) se (b) ate (c) en (d) ize

**13.** What prefix you will add to the word 'active' to mean extremely energetic and active?
(a) de (b) un (c) hyper (d) re

**14.** The word missionary has a suffix. Find it out.
(a) nary (b) ary (c) ry (d) onary

**15.** The adjective 'beautiful' contain which suffix?
(a) iful (b) ul (c) tiful (d) ful

**Directions** *(Q. Nos.16-20) complete the sentences by using a prefix or suffix.*

**16.** In many countries it is ........ legal to keep a gun in your house.
(a) un (b) il (c) in (d) is

**17.** She is thinking of going back to university and taking a ........graduate course.
(a) post (b) under
(c) pro (d) for

**18.** You should not eat any food which is ........ cooked.
(a) anti (b) under
(c) mis (d) up

**19.** She works in a/an ........ national company which is headquartered in US
(a) in (b) inter
(c) multi (d) bi

**20.** Everyone was watching me and I felt very ........ conscious.
(a) un (b) over
(c) self (d) pi

## ANSWERS

| | | | | | | | | | | | | | | | | | | | |
|---|---|---|---|---|---|---|---|---|---|---|---|---|---|---|---|---|---|---|---|
| 1. | (c) | 2. | (c) | 3. | (b) | 4. | (c) | 5. | (b) | 6. | (b) | 7. | (c) | 8. | (b) | 9. | (c) | 10. | (c) |
| 11. | (a) | 12. | (b) | 13. | (c) | 14. | (b) | 15. | (d) | 16. | (b) | 17. | (a) | 18. | (b) | 19. | (b) | 20. | (c) |

Chapter 14

# Reading Comprehension (Unseen Passage)

Reading Comprehension is an integral part of any competitive examination. A reading comprehension test is designed to assess your knowledge of grammar, vocabulary and your ability to understand and analyse the written passage. Therefore, an aspirant is required to read the passage carefully and choose the correct answer out of the alternatives given below the question. However, the questions are challenging and they all require an appreciation of more than just the superficial understanding of the passage. Therefore, it is very important that due attention should be paid to comprehension exercises.

## Tips for Solving Comprehension

1. Read the passage quickly at the first go to get the general idea of the passage.
2. At the second go, read the passage slowly so as to know the details.
3. Now, study the questions thoroughly. Turn to the relevant part of the passage to get the answer of the questions.
4. If you are asked to give the meaning of any phrase or word from the passage, the answer should be based on the context of the passage.

Here, one passage has been given for better understanding of reading comprehension.

**Direction** *Read the passage and answer the questions given below.*

A newly appointed teacher with a good academic record has come to take up English classes of class VII. He is sincere enough and has sound knowledge of the new trends and approach of teaching English Language, whether through, functional communicative method or the direct method. He tries to follow his professional skills acquired from the handbook or the teacher's manual and advice from linguists. In the classroom, he uses only English as the medium of his instruction. He advises his learners to guess the meanings. He sincerely tries to improve the standard of teaching by means of interaction. As a man, he is a sociable one and within a few days he becomes popular among his students. But, unfortunately, after a few days he comes to know from one of his students outside the classroom that they could understand very little of what he taught. The teacher asks politely,
"Why did you not confess your problem in the classroom?" The student replies modestly but hesitatingly, "We could not say anything as you were not speaking our mother tongue and we cannot speak English".

***1.*** The teacher is a sociable one, which means he is
(a) friendly (b) gets easily influenced
(c) does not like society (d) very popular

***Ans*** (a) As per the given passage, sociable means 'friendly'.

***2.*** As a result of his teachings, the students
(a) were able to understand everything
(b) could understand only little of what was taught
(c) found everything very interesting and pleasing
(d) got bored and stressed

***Ans*** (b) After reading the complete passage, we come to know that the students could understand very little of what was taught to them as they could not speak English.

***3.*** Modestly means
(a) rudely
(b) bashfully
(c) Politely and genuinely
(d) ashamedly

***Ans*** (c) Modestly means 'politely and genuinely'. So, option (c) is the correct answer.

**4.** **If Hindi is our mother tongue, then English is our**
(a) first language
(b) third language
(c) second language
(d) None of the above

***Ans*** (c) If Hindi is our mother tongue, English would be our second language.

**5.** **His teaching skills are aided by**
(a) teacher's manual (b) advice from linguists
(c) website (d) Both (a) and (b)

***Ans*** (d) Here, teacher's manual and advice from linguists is the correct answer.

**6.** **What is his method of teaching?**
(a) Functional communicative method
(b) Direct method
(c) Both (a) and (b)
(d) Descriptive and elaborate

***Ans*** (c) The passage clearly states that his method of teaching is functional, communicative and direct method.

# Practice Questions

## Passage 1

**Directions** (Passages 1-20) *Read the following passages carefully and answer the questions that follow.*

The forces that generate conditions conducive to crime and riots are stronger in urban communities than in rural areas. Urban living is more anonymous living. It often releases the individual from community restraints more common in tradition-oriented societies. But more freedom from constraints and controls also provides greater freedom to deviate. And living in the more impersonalised, formally controlled urban society means that regulatory orders of conduct are often directed by distant bureaucrats. The police are strangers executing these prescriptions on an anonymous set of subjects. Minor offences in small town or village are often handled without resort to official police action. As disputable as such action may seem to be, it results in fewer recorded violations of the law compared to the big cities. Although, perhaps causing some decision-difficulties for the police in small town, formal and objective law enforcement is not always acceptable to villagers.

Urban areas with mass population, greater wealth, more commercial establishments and more products of our technology also provide more frequent opportunities for theft. Victims are impersonalised, property is insured, consumer goods in more abundance are vividly displayed and are more portable. The crime-rate increases despite formal moral education given in schools.

**1.** **According to the passage, which of the following contribute to higher crime-rates in urban areas except**
(a) higher standard of living (b) urban impersonalised living
(c) increasing population (d) inadequate police force

**2.** **Which of the following is a characteristic of an urban setting?**
(a) Unreported minor crimes
(b) Deviation from freedom
(c) Less forceful social control
(d) Minimal opportunities of crime due to better law enforcement

**3.** **The author's view of 'Traditional Societies' is best expressed by which of the following?**
(a) They provide less freedom for the individual in many circumstances
(b) They have lower crime-rates because of the moral teachings in schools
(c) They provide inadequate freedom for personal movements and travel
(d) They are ruled and controlled by distant bureaucrats

**4.** **People live under more social control in**
(a) formally controlled urban societies
(b) an anonymous form of living
(c) non-traditional societies
(d) None of the above

**5.** **It can be inferred from the passage that urban crime can be controlled by**
(a) enforcement of law by distant bureaucrats
(b) vivid display of expensive consumer goods
(c) making the expensive consumer goods less portable
(d) None of the above

**6.** **Which of the following statements is true in the context of the passage?**
(a) The display of consumer goods is the main cause of crime
(b) Lack of personal contacts increases crimes in urban areas
(c) Small communities have more minor crimes than in urban centres
(d) Police in urban areas settle minor disputes without official action

## Passage 2

A close look at the facts relating to political interference in administration shows that it is not a one-way process. There is often a nexus between power-hungry and corrupt politicians and civil servants with convenient principles. Many civil servants are only too anxious to oblige the politicians, and then cash the obligation when they need some special favour. So, the attitude of self-righteousness adopted by the civil service is sometimes only a way of covering their own flaws by blaming others.

Every now and then some retired civil servants come out with his memoirs, painting a glorious picture of the heights of administrative efficiency reached during his reign. There is often the suggestion that had there not been so much political interference, things would have been even more fantastic. It is not unusual for the self-styled hero to blame not only interfering politicians but also fellow civil servants who were idiots or crooks, for his failures.

This attitude of smug self-satisfaction is, unfortunately, developed during the years of service. Self-preservation rather than service is encouraged by our whole system of rules and procedures. The remedy has to be drastic and quickly effective. The over-protection now granted of civil servants must end. Today to remove an erring civil servant is just not possible. And the only thing that the highest authority in the Government, both in the State and at the Centre, can do is to transfer an official from one job to another.

The rules for taking disciplinary action are so complicated that, in the end, the defaulting civil servant gets away, and gets his full emoluments even for the period of the disciplinary proceedings, thus making it a paid holiday for him. The result is that the administration has become rule-oriented and not result oriented. Action is possible against the official who takes some interest in his work, but no action is ever taken against a person who does not deliver the goods. If the country is to adopt a result-oriented approach, it is necessary to link job performance with job retention.

**1.** The facts relating to the problem of political interference indicate that
(a) honest bureaucrats are always being troubled by politician
(b) politicians are often misled and trapped by civil servants
(c) politicians and civil servants co-operate to gain mutual advantages
(d) politicians and civil servants use interference as an excuse for victimising the common man

**2.** The attitude of self-righteousness adopted by the civil service, according to the writer
(a) is not welcomed and supported by politicians
(b) is dishonest and conceals the facts
(c) is very difficult to maintain because of opposition
(d) does not really help the public get fair treatment

**3.** Civil servants who write their memoirs after retiring
(a) claim that they would have achieved outstanding success if interference had not come in the way
(b) prove that constant political interference made it impossible for them to do anything properly
(c) complain that the credit for their achievements goes to dishonest politicians
(d) prove that people of inferior quality in the civil service bring about interference

**4.** The existing system of administration seems to encourage civil servants
(a) to become self-styled heroes and boss over others
(b) to present a glorious picture of the administration
(c) to become self-centred and concerned mainly about their own gain
(d) to become self-righteous and fight back against corrupt politicians

**5.** The problem with the present set-up needing urgent action is
(a) a lack of accountability on the part of civil servants
(b) a lack of control over the power of politicians
(c) a neglect of the ideals of self-righteousness
(d) complicated rules and procedures that greatly reduce efficiency

**6.** The main principle of the remedy proposed by the writer is, that
(a) the politicians should be made accountable for all their decisions
(b) the high level of protection enjoyed by civil servants should be reduced
(c) the common man's right to efficient and fair administration must be protected
(d) rules should be simplified so that there is less scope for misuse

## Passage 3

True, it is the function of the army to maintain law and order in abnormal times. But in normal times there is another force that compels citizens to obey the laws and to act with due regard to the rights of others. The force also protects the lives and the properties of law abiding men. Laws are made to secure the personal safety of its subjects and to prevent murder and crimes of violence.

They are made to secure the property of the citizens against theft and damage to protect the rights of communities and castes to carry out their customs and ceremonies, so long as they do not conflict with the rights of others. Now the good citizen, of his own free will obey these laws and he takes care that everything he does is done with due regard to the rights and well-being of others.

But the bad citizen is only restrained from breaking these laws by fear of the consequence of his actions. And the necessary steps to compel the bad citizen to act as a good citizen are taken by this force. The supreme control of law and order in a State is in the hands of a Minister who is responsible to the State Assembly and acts through the Inspector General of Police.

**1.** The expression 'customs and ceremonies' means
(a) fairs and festivals
(b) habits and traditions
(c) usual practices and religious rites
(d) superstitions and formalities

**2.** A suitable title for the passage would be
(a) The Function of the Army
(b) Laws and the People's Rights
(c) The Fear of the Law and Citizen's Security
(d) The Functions of The Police

**3.** Which of the following is not implied in the passage?
(a) Law protects those who respect it
(b) Law ensures people's religious and social rights absolutely and unconditionally
(c) A criminal is deterred from committing crimes only for fear of the law
(d) The forces of law help to transform irresponsible citizens into responsible ones

**4.** According to the writer, which one of the following is not the responsibility of the police?
(a) To protect the privileges of all citizens
(b) To check violent activities of citizens
(c) To ensure peace among citizens by safeguarding individual rights
(d) To maintain peace during extra-ordinary circumstances

**5.** Which of the following reflects the main thrust of the passage?
(a) It deals with the importance of the army in maintaining law and order
(b) It highlights role of the police as superior to that of the army
(c) It discusses the roles of the army and the police in different circumstances
(d) It points to the responsibility of the Minister and the Inspector General of Police

**6.** "They are made to secure the property of citizens against theft and damage", means that the law
(a) helps in recovering the stolen property of the citizens
(b) assist the citizens whose property has been stolen or destroyed
(c) initiate process against offenders of law
(d) safeguard people's possessions against being stolen or lost

# Passage 4

On attending a conference which focused on the role of the services sector in Indian economy, I was amazed. The conference gave a very interesting **perspective** on the role of the service sector in the growth of Indian economy in relation to growth rates in agriculture and industry.

The current situation in India is that the growth rate of services has overtaken both agriculture and industry and is now contributing to more than 50% of GDP. The service sector has the highest growth rate and is the least **volatile** sector, Growth is particularly marked in public services, IT and financial services. In some areas, the growth rate of the service sector is 40-50% due to increased use of mobile technologies. India, therefore has, a service-oriented economy. It hasn't followed traditional growth models as in China. However, in the process of doing so it has skipped the manufacturing stage and has jumped straight from the agriculture stage to service stage, which is also the main reason for the expansion of the service sector.

In fact, the situation now is such that the growth in the service sector can and will support in the agriculture and industrial sectors.

However, the only setback for Indian economy is the lack of growth in the manufacturing sector which causes dependence on other countries, which is not so desirable in terms of job creation and increased prosperity.

Population is also a major concern of the Indian economy. As the population of India grows so also does the number of dependents in the population in both the lower and higher age groups. In such a scenario of increasing population, especially in an economy which still recovering from crisis, growth becomes difficult. For such an economy to grow it has to invest. Currently, the public sector invests more than it saves. The household sector saves in surplus, but it is not increasing so it cannot continue to support private and public sectors. There is a **massive** need to spend on agriculture and infrastructure development of the country, Apart from that health and education should also be the priority of the government particularly the education of women in order to reduce the birth rate.

**1.** Choose the word which is most opposite in meaning to word given in bold as used in the passage.
Volatile
(a) Erratic (b) Impatient (c) Stable (d) Solid

**2.** According to the passage, which of the following is/are true about the impact of increasing population on Indian economy?
A. If India attempts to absorb all the labour force, it will impact the growth of service sector negatively and in turn hamper the economic growth of the country.
B. As the population of the country increases, the number of dependants in the country also increase which in turn increases the pressure on the economy.
C. An increasing population can never lead the economy of the country towards prosperity; in fact it can only put strain on the economy of a country.

**Codes**
(a) Only B (b) Only C (c) B and C (d) A and C

**3.** According to the passage, which of the following can be said about the agriculture and industry sectors in India?
A. Looking at the growth of the services sector in India it can be safely said that the service sector will soon be in a position to support both agriculture and industry sector.
B. The agriculture and the industrial sector of the country have reached their threshold and there would be no use of further investment in these sectors.
C. Currently, the agriculture and industry sectors contribute lesser as compared to service sector to the GDP of the country.

**Codes**
(a) Only A (b) Only C
(c) A and C (d) B and C

**4.** What does the author mean by the statement, ..... a 'growth window' for India will open?

(a) In the coming years, the Indian economy will grow as the service sector of the country would be booming due to the focus of the government in that sector

(b) In the next two decades, Indian economy will have an opportunity to grow as the working population of India will be high as compared to the dependant population

(c) There would be only a small period of time in which the economy of India has to grow and if it fails to do so it will never be able to recover from the economic downfall

(d) Only upto the next two decades would Indian people interested in finding jobs in the country beyond which they would search for jobs abroad thus, hampering the growth of Indian economy

**5.** Choose the word which is most similar in meaning to the word given in bold as used in the passage.

Massive

(a) Huge (b) Bulky (c) Solid (d) Grand

**6.** Choose the word which is most similar in meaning to the word given in bold as used in the passage.

Perspective

(a) Viewpoint (b) Prospect (c) Attitude (d) Agreement

## Passage 5

The great recession hasn't been great for free trade. As unemployment has risen throughout the world, governments have become more focused on protecting their own industries than on promoting international commerce. The US, though typically an enthusiastic supporter of open markets, included failing 'buy American' clauses in its stimulus package and propped up its falling auto industry with handouts. But according to the Asian Development Bank (ADB), in the part of the world that was hit hardest by the trade crash -Asia the number of Free-Trade Agreements (FTAs) signed by Asian countries has grown from just three in 2000 to 56 by the end of August 2009. Nineteen of those FTAs are among 16 Asian economies, a trend that could help the region become a powerful trading bloc.

The drive to lower trade barriers has taken on fresh urgency amid the recession. As Asian manufacturing networks become more intertwined - and as Asian consumers become wealthier - regional commerce is becoming critical to future economic expansion. Intra-regional trade last year made up 57% of total Asian trade, up from 37% in 1930. In the past Asia produced for America and Europe, now Asia is producing for Asia. Of course, Asia is still dependent on sales to the West. But FTAs could reduce the region's exposure to the United States by giving Asian companies preferential treatment in selling to Asian companies and consumers. However, these benefits could come with downsides. According to experts, FTAs create a 'non-level playing field with advantages for Asian countries.'

If the most dynamically growing part of the global economy gives the US restricted access, it will impact global balance. Companies in countries like the United States left out of the trade pacts could face disadvantages when trying to tap fast-growing Asian markets. This, in turn, could have a negative impact of efforts to rebalance excessive debt in the US and excessive savings in Asia. Still, the benefits of greater regional integration could prove powerful enough to overcome the roadblocks. In Asia, the only thing everyone agrees upon is business. If it does, the world economy may never be the same.

**1.** What do the Asian Development Bank (ADB) statistics indicate?

(a) Asian economies are financially more sound than those of the developed world

(b) The financial crisis impacted the West far more than it did Asia

(c) Asian countries have aligned themselves on lines similar to the European Union

(d) Asian countries have been actively opening their markets to one another

**2.** What has given rise to the large number of trade agreements between Asian countries?

(a) The need to insulate Asian economies from over exposure to the American economy

(b) Angry reaction among Asian countries owing to America's protectionist policy

(c) The aim of empowering the poorer Asian economies and being them on par with Western economies

(d) The desire to achieve conditions conducive to global consensus on trade regulations and tariffs

**3.** Which of the following is/ are not true in the context of the passage?

I. Political and economic rivalries between Asian countries are non-existent today.

II. Asian countries hold America responsible for the recession and have imposed economic sanctions against the US.

III. America has adopted a protectionist strategy after the recession.

**Codes**

(a) Only I (b) II and III
(c) I and II (d) Only III

**4.** Which of the following describes expert predictions about trade pacts between Asian countries?

(a) These will be beneficial and are likely to give rise to a common Asian currency

(b) Tariffs will be lowered and bureaucratic regulations will become transparent

(c) Widening of differences between participant and non-participant countries will hamper global stability

(d) Regional conflicts will increase as competition and inequities between Asian nations will intensify

**5.** Which of the following has/have not been (an) impact(s) of the recession?

I. Various trade agreements signed between developed and Asian countries have not been honoured.

II. The US Government has restructured the automobile industry.

III. Regional conflicts in Asia have substantially reduced.

**Codes**

(a) Only IIII (b) Only I

(c) I and II (d) All of the above

**6.** According to the author, what danger does creating an Asian trading bloc pose?

(a) Political instability in Asia will rise as some countries are wealthier than others

(b) American consumers have ceased their demands for Asian goods

(c) Unemployment in Asian countries will rise as many plants will be forced to close down

(d) None of the above

# Passage 6

The small village of Somnathpur contains an extraordinary temple, built around AD 1268 by the Hoyasalas of Karnataka- one of the most prolific temple builders. Belur and Helebid are among their better known works. While these suffered during the invasion of the 14th century, the Somnathpur temple stands more or less intact in near-original condition.

This small temple captivates the beauty and vitality of its detailed sculpture, covering almost every inch of the walls, pillars and even ceilings. It has three shikharas and stands on a star shaped platform with 24 edges. The outer walls have a profusion of detailed carvings: the entire surface runs over by a carved plaque of stone.

There were vertical panels covered by exquisite figures of Gods and Goddesses. Vishnu seemed the most popular, with many of his incarnations being depicted. Shiv, Brahma and Indra weren't left out and there were plenty of female deities too like Durga and Saraswati. There were shapely nymphs too, some carrying an ear of maize.

The elaborate ornamentation, very characteristic of Hoyasalas sculptures, was a remarkable feature.

On closer look and it is worth it- the series of friezes on the outer walls revealed intricately carved caparisoned elephants, charging horsemen, stylised flowers, warriors, musicians, crocodiles and swans.

The temple was actually commissioned by Soma Dandanayaka or ( Somnath), he named the temple after him, the minister of the Hoyasalas king, Narsimha the Third. The temple was built to house three versions of Krishna. The inner center of the temple was Kalyana Mandapa.

Leading from here were three corridors, each ending in a shrine, one for each kind of Krishna-Venugopala, Janardana and Prasanna Keshava, though only two remain in their original form. In the darkness of the sanctum, I tried to discern the different images. The temple's sculptural perfection is amazing and it includes the doors of the temple and the three elegantly carved towers.

**1.** After whom was the temple named?

(a) Kalyana Mandapa (b) Lord Shiva

(c) Minister of the Hoyasalas King (d) Lord Krishna

**2.** What would the word 'maize' mean here?

(a) Grain (b) Deer

(c) Symbol of prosperity (d) Symbol of weakness

**3.** The most remarkable feature of Hoyasalas sculptures was

(a) elaborate ornamentation (b) beautiful clothing

(c) sharply cut sculptures (d) real expression

**4.** What stands on the 24 edges star shaped raised platform?

(a) Shrines (b) Temple (c) Shikharas (d) Pillars

**5.** What will be the most suitable antonym of 'reveal'?

(a) Impart (b) Disclose (c) Conceal (d) Refuse

**6.** The word 'intricately' can also mean

(a) easy (b) complicated (c) tangled (d) simple

# Passage 7

There was a time when the aged were revered in India as symbols of tradition, respect, wisdom and experience. They controlled and guided the destinies of all the members of joint families. Urbanisation and industrialisation has led to the breaking up of the joint family system. The disintegration of joint families has had an adverse impact on the elderly people. Many elderly people get neglected because of the nuclear set up of families. The aged are now viewed as a useless and non-productive entity. Modernisation has led to the degradation of their status and authority. Their existence as integral part of the family is now uprooted. With the decline in their functional position as the head of the family, they have lost their authority, respect and prestige they used to command earlier.

The changing values and the dependence of the aged on their sons and daughters-in-law has complicated the problems. The aged are marginalised, alienated and left out of mainstream. Neglect, lack of respect, verbal taunts, inter-actional stress and increasing gap in communication make the aged feel unwanted and unpleasant entities. The only peaceful place for these weak, sad and depressed people in the evening of their life are the homes of the aged. Under the existing circumstances, the need for old age homes has certainly increased and they have become a must for the elderly to lead a peaceful and happy life among those who share and care for them.

**1.** Urbanisation and industrialisation has led to

(a) neglect and stress (b) degradation of the families

(c) breakup of joint family set up (d) non-productive entity

**2.** The elderly people are getting neglected because of

(a) the joint family system (b) nuclear set up

(c) their age (d) their ailing health

**3.** We should behave more responsibly and revise our
(a) past (b) moral values
(c) behaviour and conduct (d) strengths and weakness

**4.** The only peaceful place left for the aged is
(a) their native place (b) their parents home
(c) old age home (d) orphanage

**5.** Who were seen as symbols of tradition, respect and experience?
(a) The palatial buildings (b) The aged
(c) The new generation (d) Joint families

**6.** Neglect, lack of respect, verbal taunts, communication gap make the aged feel
(a) unwanted and unpleasant (b) cared and concerned
(c) stressed and strained (d) unavailable and outdated

## Passage 8

In spite of all the honours that we heaped upon him, Pasteur, as has been said, remained simple at heart. Perhaps the imagery of his boyhood days, when he drew the familiar scenes of his birthplace and the longing to be a great artist, never wholly left him. In truth he did become a great artist, though after his sixteenth year he abandoned the brush forever.

Like every artist of worth, he put his whole soul and energy into his work and it was this very energy that in the end wore him out. For to him, each sufferer was more than just a case that was to be cured. He looked upon the fight against hydrophobia as a battle and he was absorbed in his determination to win. The sight of injured children, particularly, moved him to an indescribable extent. He suffered with his patients and yet he would not deny himself a share in that suffering. His greatest grief was when sheer physical exhaustion made him give up his active work. He retired to the estate of Villeneuve Etang, where he had his Kennels for the study of rabies and there he passed his last summer, as his great biographer, Vallery Robot, has said, 'practicing the gospel virtues'.

The attitude of this man to the science, he had done so much to perfect, can be best summed up in a sentence that he is reputed once to have uttered, concerning the materialism of many of his contemporaries in similar branches of learning to his own: "the more I contemplate the mysteries of nature, the more my faith becomes like that of a peasant."

But even then, in retirement he loved to see his former pupils, and it was then he would reiterate his life's principles: 'Work,' he would say, 'never cease to work'.

He passed as simply as a child, the greatest man France had ever produced, derived from a plebiscite among the French people. Napoleon, the idol of France was placed fifth. No greater tribute could have been given to Louis Pasteur, the tanner's son, the scientist, the man of peace and the patient worker for humanity.

**1.** What advice Pasteur always gave to his pupils?
(a) Never to stop working
(b) To work according to one's health
(c) Work and rest at the same time
(d) Work to earn money

**2.** How did Pasteur engage himself in the estate?
(a) He took enough rest as he was very exhausted
(b) Conducted study on rabies
(c) Practiced the Gospel Virtues (d) Both (b) and (c)

**3.** How did Pasteur view those who suffered from diseases?
(a) He gave them best treatment
(b) As subjects of pity
(c) The sufferer was more than just a case for him
(d) He dealt carefully not to give pain in wounded areas

**4.** Give one word for the phrase- Vote by the people of the country to decide a matter of national importance.
(a) Election (b) Plebiscite
(c) Hydrophobia (d) Contemporaries

**5.** Who was ranked fifth after the achievements of Louis Pasteur?
(a) Napoleon (b) Hitler
(c) Nelson Mandela (d) Thomas Addison

**6.** Even accolades and honours did not change the simple man that Pasteur was
(a) because he did not like false praises
(b) he was very simple and child like at heart
(c) he wanted more than what he had achieved
(d) he was very egoistic

**7.** Opposite word for 'humanity' is
(a) callousness (b) early man
(c) homogeneous (d) people

## Passage 9

The modern youth are more intelligent and hardworking than the previous generations. They have more facilities for education and they do utilise them. But they lack proper direction. In the absence of proper guidance, young boys and girls go on increasing their academic qualifications. Some of them secure high percentage of marks whereas most of them get average or below average marks. Since the number of aspirants for a job is much higher than the number of vacancies, most of the young boys and girls do not get any employment. This causes the problem of the educated unemployment and depression among the youth.

The problem of the educated unemployed can be solved partly through proper guidance and counselling and partly through grooming. Young students often disregard the advice of their parents and go on imitating their peers. This sets in the chain of the blind leading the blind. Uneducated or semi-educated parents think of academic qualification as achievement. Young students must seek the advice of the school counsellors and select a course of studies that suit their aptitude. Instead of pursuit of academic excellence, they must go in for proficiency in technical field of information technology, computers, biotechnology, biochemistry and consumer services. In this way, their youthful energy will get directed in the proper channel and they may get fruitful employment or become competent enough to launch their own project and give employment to others.

1. What is the positive aspect of today's generation?
   (a) They are more intelligent and hardworking
   (b) They are more into fashion and time pass
   (c) They have the power to work less and get more
   (d) The youth now knows what he has to do
2. Academic qualification is seen as an achievement, which adds to the problem due to
   (a) uneducated or semi-educated parents
   (b) increase in the urge of getting higher remunerations
   (c) lack of focus and attention
   (d) disillusionment and depression
3. Frustration, irritation, anger, indiscipline, arrogance, disillusionment and depression are all the result of
   (a) growing modernisation
   (b) educated unemployment
   (c) aspirations not meeting goals
   (d) lack of grooming and counselling
4. Suggest a suitable title for this extract.
   (a) Educated Unemployed (b) Education- A Revolution
   (c) Fight for Power (d) Professionalism
5. The synonym for 'cautioned' is
   (a) ignorance (b) negligence
   (c) prudence (d) discretion
6. Identify the correct statement.
   (a) Young students must seek the advice of the school counsellors to select a course.
   (b) Young students must take a course which their friends are opting for.
   (c) Young students must take a course as suggested by their parents.
   (d) Young students get the employment easily.
7. Opposite word for 'proficiency' is
   (a) incompetence (b) expertise (c) skill (d) formula

## Passage 10

'Why did you keep away yesterday? Asked the head master, looking up. Swaminathan's first impulse was to protest that he had never been absent. But the attendance register was there. 'No-No-I was stoned. I tried to come, but they took away my cap and burnt it. Many strong men held me down when I tried to come ... When a great man is sent to gaol ... I am surprised to see you a slave of the Englishmen ... Didn't they cut off - Dacca Muslin - Slaves of Slaves ....'

These were some of the disjoined explanations which streamed into his head and which, even at that moment, he was discreet enough not to express. He wanted to mention a headache, but he found to his distress that others beside him had one. The headmaster shouted, 'won't you open your mouth?' He brought the cane sharply down on Swaminathan's right shoulder. Swaminathan kept staring at the headmaster with tearful eyes, massaging with his left hand the spot, where the cane was laid. 'I will kill you if you keep on staring without answering my question,' cried the headmaster.

'I-I- couldn't come', stammered Swaminathan.

"Is that so? Asked the headmaster and turning to a boy said, bring the peon".

Swaminathan thought What ! is he going to ask the peon to thrash me? If he does any such thing, 'I will bite everybody dead'. The peon came. The headmaster said to him, 'now say what you know about this rascal on the desk.'

The peon eyed Swaminathan with a sinister look, grunted and demanded, 'Didn't I see you break the panes?'

Of the ventilators in my room? added the headmaster with zest.

Here, there was no chance of escape. Swaminathan kept staring foolishly till he received another whack on the back. The headmaster demanded what the young brigand had to say about it. The brigand had nothing to say. It was a fact that he had broken the panes.

They had seen it. There was nothing more to it. He had unconsciously become defiant and did not care to deny the charge. When another whack came on his back, he ejaculated, 'don't beat me, Sir. It pains.' This was an invitation to the head master to bring down the cane four times again. He said, "keep standing here, on this desk , staring like an idiot, till I announce your dismissal".

1. The headmaster's reaction to Swami's pleading is
   (a) to beat Swami more (b) to forgive Swami
   (c) to allow him to go (d) not to allow him to go
2. The title of the passage can be
   (a) The Peon's Evidence (b) Swami's Punishment
   (c) Swami's Excuses (d) Swami at School
3. In the end, Swami is
   (a) defiant (b) submissive
   (c) calm (d) indifferent
4. According to the peon, Swami had
   (a) broken the panes (b) bitten someone
   (c) been rude (d) been absent from school
5. If Swami is not 'discreet', he would be
   (a) careless (b) intelligent
   (c) wise (d) smart
6. The headmaster's attitude towards Swami is one of
   (a) kindness for Swami (b) pleasure in punishing him
   (c) pleasure in asking questions (d) hatred for Swami

## Passage 11

Your attitudes are the perspectives from which you view life. Some people seem to have a good attitude towards most things. Some people seem to have a bad attitude towards everything. But when you look closer, you will find that most of us have a combination of attitudes, some good, some not so good. Whatever attitude we have towards anything will affect how we feel about it, which in turn determines whether or not we will do well. So our right attitudes play a very important part in helping us become successful.

In fact, as we can see, a good attitude is essential for achievement of any kind! We so often hear of someone who is said to have a 'bad attitude'. The term is often applied to young people, especially to teenagers who frequently get into trouble, but we often hear it about adults, too .The implication is always that the individual in question is not going to make it if he doesn't change his attitude.

I would agree, without a good attitude it is not possible to see the opportunities ahead and set one's sights to reach them. But even more important is the fact that in order to possess the kind of feelings which work for us we've got to have the right attitude to start with. But where do we get our attitudes from? Are we born with them or do they just appear out of nowhere? Our attitudes are no accident: They don't just happen. Our attitudes are created and influenced entirely by our beliefs.

**1.** Which one of the following statements is correct?
(a) Our attitudes are influenced by our parents only
(b) Our attitudes are created and controlled by our beliefs
(c) Our attitudes are the results of own personal experience
(d) We are born with our attitudes

**2.** The word 'determine' most nearly means
(a) influence (b) overcome (c) engage (d) govern

**3.** Which part of speech is the underlined word in the sentence given below?
'Some people seem to have a <u>good</u> attitude towards most things.'
(a) Preposition (b) Adjective (c) Conjunction (d) Adverb

**4.** A/An ................ attitude is absolutely necessary for attainment of any kind.
(a) cheerful (b) optimistic (c) good (d) virtuous

**5.** The term 'bad attitude' is used for young people because they
(a) behave irresponsibly (b) often get into difficulty
(c) are unpredictable (d) defy all kinds of authority

## Passage 12

Your body is made up of sixty per cent water and you lose the essential fluid every minute of every day as you breathe, digest and hopefully work up a sweat. It is important that you put back every drop. Starting now, drink eight 230 ml glasses of water every single day—that's the minimum, your body needs daily. That is the non-negotiable sugar savvy hydration mantra. Many times when you think you're hungry, sleepy, depressed and/or irritated, you're actually just dehydrated. Drinking enough water actually helps you combat water retention. Sounds counterintuitive, but think about it. If you are running around in a semi-dehydrated state all the time, your body is going to hang on to every single drop, giving you that puffy, unhealthy appearance. When you are properly hydrated, your body gets the message that all systems are operating smoothly and it continues its work of flushing out your system and ridding itself of the excess fluids.

If your goal is to lose weight, water is a must. When you're dehydrated, your body sends out signals that you need assistance. Many people mistake those thirsty SOS signals for hunger and take in hundreds of extra calories. They also don't solve the real problem—thirst! Drinking water can be a powerful appetite suppressant and allows you to cue into your real hunger. Your body also needs plenty of water for proper digestion, so you can get the most from the foods you eat. You are less susceptible to food cravings when your stomach is full and you're getting all the nutrients you need. Drink two glasses of water before every meal— you'll eat less ! Your body uses water for fat.

**1.** ....... helps fight water retention.
(a) Having a balanced diet (b) Drinking enough water
(c) Exercising regularly (d) A regular morning walk

**2.** Our systems operate satisfactorily
(a) if excess fat is reduced
(b) when we enjoy a sound sleep
(c) when we are properly hydrated
(d) if we consume lots of fruits and vegetables

**3.** The best way to lose weight is to
(a) eat less starchy food (b) take weight-reducing pills
(c) exercise at least twice a day (d) drink plenty of water

**4.** When we are dehydrated, we think we
(a) are about to collapse (b) want to vomit
(c) are tired (d) need food

**5.** The word 'irritated' most nearly means
(a) annoyed (b) troubled (c) uneasy (d) frustrated

**6.** The word which is opposite in meaning to 'assistance' is
(a) fragrance (b) hinderance
(c) persistence (d) existence

## Passage 13

Raja Ram Mohan Roy is considered the pioneer of modern Indian Renaissance for the remarkable reforms he brought about in the 18th century India. Among his efforts, the abolition of the *Sati-pratha*—a practice in which the widow was compelled to sacrifice herself on the funeral pyre of her husband—was prominent. His efforts were also instrumental in eradicating the *Purdah* System and child marriage. In 1828, Ram Mohan Roy formed the Brahmo Samaj, a group of people, who had no faith in idol-worship and were against the caste restrictions.

Raja Ram Mohan Roy's father was a wealthy Brahmin and strictly performed the duties set by the religion. Ram Mohan himself was also devoted to Lord Vishnu and in his 14th year, he wanted to become a monk but his mother, Tarini Devi objected to his desire.

Ram Mohan viewed education as a medium to implement the social reforms. So, in 1815, Ram Mohan came to Calcutta and the very next year, started an English College by putting in his own savings. He was well aware that the students should learn the English language and scientific subjects and that's why he criticised the government's policy of opening only Sanskrit schools. According to him, Indians would lag behind if they do not get to study modern subjects like Mathematics, Geography and Latin. The government accepted this idea of Ram Mohan and also implemented it but not before his death. Ram Mohan was also the first to give importance to the development of mother tongue. His Gaudiya Byakaran in Bengali is the best of his prose works.

Rabindranath Tagore and Bankimchandra also followed in the footsteps of Ram Mohan Roy. Ram Mohan Roy was a staunch supporter of free speech and expression and fought for the rights of Vernacular Press. He also brought out a newspaper in Persian called Miratul-Akhbar (the Mirror of News) and a Bengali weekly called Sambad Kaumudi (the Moon of Intelligence). In those days, items of news and articles had to be approved by the government before being published. Ram Mohan protested against this control by arguing that newspapers should be free and that the truth should not be suppressed simply because the government did not like it.

***1.*** Raja Ram Mohan Roy is known for his

(a) economic reforms (b) literary reforms
(c) political reforms (d) social reforms

***2.*** When he was a teenager, Raja Ram Mohan Roy expressed his desire to become a

(a) journalist (b) monk
(c) teacher (d) businessman

***3.*** Raja Ram Mohan Roy believed that Indians would lag behind if they

(a) forgot their cultural roots (b) did not learn traditional skills
(c) gave up study of Sanskrit (d) did not study modern subjects

***4.*** Raja Ram Mohan Roy strongly supported

(a) rituals and observances
(b) physical education
(c) freedom of speech and expression
(d) moral education

***5.*** The word 'eliminating' most nearly means

(a) banishing (b) eradicating
(c) banning (d) dismissing

***6.*** The word which is opposite in meaning to 'encouraged' is

(a) crushed (b) misled
(c) disheartened (d) suppressed

***7.*** Which 'part of speech' is the underlined word in the sentence given below?
"He was a staunch supporter of free <u>speech</u> and expression."

(a) Adjective (b) Conjunction
(c) Noun (d) Adverb

***8.*** 'Raja Ram Mohan Roy viewed education ... .' The 'voice' in the above sentence has been correctly changed in

(a) education was viewed
(b) education is viewed
(c) education has been viewed
(d) education had been viewed

# Passage 14

A remarkable feature of Edison's inventions was their basic simplicity. There were innumerable scientists possessing deep knowledge of electricity, chemistry etc. but it was this unschooled genius who succeeded where they failed. What were his unique qualities? *Firstly*, he had an uncanny ability to judge the practical use of any scientific fact.

*Secondly*, he was blessed with patience and perseverance. He would try out countless ideas till he found the right one. *Third* was his business acumen, which enabled him to earn the large sums of money necessary to conduct experimental work. Edison's enthusiasm for work and optimistic attitude ensured a long and productive life. Only after crossing the age of seventy-five did he start slowing down. During his final illness, his curiosity about his condition, medicines and treatment, made the doctors think that possibly he was taking this too as one of his scientific investigations! He passed away on 18th October, 1931, at the ripe old age of eight-four.

During his lifetime itself Edison became one of the most famous men in the world. Honours were showered on him. Among them was the Congressional Gold Medal in 1928 for his contributions to human welfare. In 1960, he was posthumously elected to the Hall of Fame for Great Americans at New York University. But the tribute that was most eloquent was quite unintended. The authorities contemplated switching off the power supply in New York, the scene of his triumph in 1882, for two minutes as a mark of respect on his death. But 1931 was not 1882. Since normal life would have come to a standstill by the two minutes power cutoff, the idea was given up. There could be no greater tribute to the man than this negative tribute!

***1.*** The most remarkable feature of Edison's inventions was their

(a) low cost (b) aesthetic aspect
(c) fundamental simplicity (d) multiple usefulness

***2.*** According to the author, Edison became prosperous because he

(a) had great business sense (b) had luck on his side
(c) worked very hard
(d) made the best use of his time

**3.** To conduct experimental work, Edison needed
(a) calm and quiet atmosphere (b) sophisticated gadgets
(c) support of generous patrons (d) huge amounts of money

**4.** Edison's long and productive life can be attributed to
(a) his positive attitude
(b) his immensely good health
(c) a large circle of friends
(d) his involvement in charitable work

**5.** The word 'uncanny' as used in the passage means
(a) astonishing (b) weird (c) great (d) terrific

**6.** The opposite of 'famous' is
(a) negligible (b) unnoticeable
(c) unpopular (d) unknown

**7.** Which 'part of speech' is the underlined word?
"He had an uncanny ability to judge the practical use of any scientific fact."
(a) Adverb (b) Preposition
(c) Noun (d) Adjective

# Passage 15

The art of Madhubani painting is the traditional style developed in the Mithila region, in the villages around Madhubani, Bihar. Madhubani literally means a forest of honey. This style of painting has been traditionally used by the women of the region, though today men are also involved to meet the demand. The work is done on freshly plastered mud walls. For commercial purposes, it is now being done on paper, cloth etc.

The paintings are basically of religious nature. They are done in the special rooms of their homes (in the Pooja room, ritual area, bridal room), on the main village walls, etc. for ceremonial or ritualistic purposes. The women offer prayers to the deity before starting the work. Figures from nature and mythology are adapted to suit their style. The themes and designs widely painted are the worship of Hindu deities such as Krishna, Rama, Shiva, Durga, Lakshmi, Saraswati, Sun and Moon, Tulsi plant, court scenes, wedding scenes and other social events taking place around them.

Floral, animal and bird motifs, geometrical designs are used to fill up all the gaps. There is hardly any empty space in this style. Cotton wrapped around a bamboo stick forms the brush. The colours applied are prepared by the artists. The skill is handed down the generations, and hence the traditional design and patterns are widely maintained. It is believed that genesis of Madhubani paintings came about when King Janaka asked for paintings to be developed for his daughter Sita's wedding.

**1.** Madhubani paintings are no longer done exclusively by women on walls
(a) as paper is cheaper
(b) because cloth is more durable
(c) to meet their widespread demand
(d) as men are better painters

**2.** Madhubani paintings are essentially of religious nature when they are done
(a) using figures from nature (b) in the Pooja room
(c) in the bridal room (d) on the village walls

**3.** These paintings become secular when they depict
(a) wedding scenes (b) court scenes
(c) worship of Saraswati (d) Tulsi plant

**4.** A Madhubani painting shows only
(a) geometrical designs
(b) a balanced portrayal of all of them
(c) Hindu deities
(d) flowers and plants

**5.** The art of Madhubani painting is learnt in the
(a) homes of renowned artists (b) Ashrams of Madhubani
(c) schools of art (d) families at home

**6.** 'Floral' is an adjective derived from the noun, 'flower'. 'Aural' is derived from the noun
(a) eye (b) mouth
(c) morning (d) ear

**7.** The word 'genesis' means the same as
(a) spirit (b) growth
(c) birth (d) original

# Passage 16

World Animal Day has been observed on 4th October since 1931, as a way of highlighting the plight of endangered species. Since then, it has become a day for remembering and paying tribute to all animals and the people who love and respect them. It's celebrated in different ways in every country, with no regard to nationality, religion, faith or political ideology.

Since the official World Animal Day website was launched by Naturewatch Foundation, the number of events taking place throughout the world has increased and the trend continues. And, that is the aim of the World Animal Day initiative to encourage everybody to use this special day to highlight their importance in the world; celebrate animal life in all its forms; celebrate humankind's relationship with the animal kingdom; acknowledge the diverse roles that animals play in our lives- from being our companions, supporting and helping us, to bringing a sense of wonder into our lives; and acknowledge and be thankful for the way in which animals enrich our lives.

Increased awareness will lead the way to improved standards of animal welfare throughout the world. Building the initiative is a way to unite the animal welfare movement with something that everyone can join in, whether they are part of an organisation, group or as an individual. Through education, we can help to create a new culture of respect and sensitivity, to make this world a fairer place for all living creatures.

On the website, people will find everything they need to make World Animal Day a reality in their area. If we care about animals, we should not miss this special day to help make animal welfare issues front page news around the globe- a vital catalyst for change.

1. In reading this passage, we learn that the World Animal Day is an/a ............ celebration.
   (a) monthly on the 4th
   (b) year long
   (c) annual
   (d) commemoration held in 1931
2. The writer points out that animals are important because they
   (a) can replace people by being more resourceful
   (b) will outlive human beings in the years to come
   (c) be put to work in many ways
   (d) make us appreciate the diversity of life
3. The launch of the website is to
   (a) promote social networking by animal lovers
   (b) provide guidelines to celebrate Animal Day
   (c) information about endangered animals species
   (d) serve as a source of reference about animals
4. The writer implies that animals are
   (a) treated cruelly by human beings
   (b) given due protection
   (c) ignored altogether
   (d) subject to mistreatment
5. Identify the correct statement.
   (a) often pose a danger to people
   (b) People tend to forget to celebrate Animal Day
   (c) Animal Day reminds us to care for other species
   (d) The new website was started by the writer
6. The expression : 'a sense of wonder' means
   (a) a critical reaction (b) a sympathetic attitude
   (c) an emotional response (d) a deep understanding
7. A closest synonym for the word 'sensitivity' as used here is
   (a) passivity (b) affection
   (c) awareness (d) tolerance
8. The antonym of the word 'initiative' is
   (a) enterprise (b) idleness
   (c) ambition (d) advance

# Passage 17

Meditating can have an almost instant effect on reducing stress, researchers have found. They say three consecutive days of 25-minute sessions can have a dramatic effect. Researchers studied 'mindful meditation'- the guiding principle is to live more 'in the moment,' spending less time going over past stresses and worrying about future problems. Techniques include moving the focus of attention around the body and observing sensations that arise- the so-called 'body scan'. A secular practice, it is said to help people recognise and overcome negative thoughts. For the study, the research team had 66 healthy individuals aged 18-30 years old participate in a three-day experiment. Some participants went through a brief mindfulness meditation training programme for 25 minutes for three consecutive days, the individuals were given breathing exercises to help them monitor their breath and pay attention to their present moment experiences. A second group of participants completed a matched three day cognitive training programme in which they were asked to critically analyse poetry in an effort to enhance problem-solving skills. Following the fined training activity, all participants were asked to complete stressful speech and mathematical tasks in front of stern-faced evaluators. Each individual reported their stress levels in response to **stressful** speech and mathematical performance stress tasks and provided saliva samples for measurement of cortisol, commonly referred to as the stress hormone. The participants who received the brief mindfulness meditation training reported reduced stress **perceptions** to the speech and mathematical tasks, indicating that the mindfulness meditation fostered psychological stress resilience.

1. The text is a .............. piece of writing.
   (a) factual (b) descriptive
   (c) biographical (d) reflective
2. The writer's attitude to mediation is
   (a) indifferent (b) different
   (c) suspicious sometimes (d) supportive
3. The writer, by referring to the experiment, suggests that, it is
   (a) stress that cannot be controlled
   (b) possible for us to control stress
   (c) mathematics that is a stressful subject
   (d) poetry analysis is easier than solving Mathematical problems
4. The 'body scan' is a reference to
   (a) an experiment in a lab
   (b) a form of meditation
   (c) a research experiment
   (d) a problem solving activity
5. An antonym for the word 'stressful' would be
   (a) annoying (b) calming
   (c) challenging (d) erasing
6. The word that can replace 'perception' in the text is
   (a) belief (b) attention
   (c) conceptualisation (d) trust

# Passage 18

As District Employment Officer, my father was given a jeep by the government. There was no garage in the office, so the jeep was parked in our house. My father refused to use it to commute to the office. He told us that the jeep is an expensive resource given by the government-he reiterated to us that it was not 'his jeep' but the government's jeep. Insisting that he would use it only to tour the interiors, he would walk to his office on normal days. He also made sure that we never sat in the government jeep-we could sit in it only when it was stationary. That was our early childhood lesson in governance-a lesson that corporate managers learn the hard way, some never do.

The driver of the jeep was treated with respect due to any other member of my father's office. As small children, we were taught not to call him by his name. We had to use the suffix 'dada' whenever we were to refer to him in public or private. When I grew up to own a car and a driver by the name of Raju was appointed, I repeated the lesson to my two small daughters. They have, as a result, grown up calling him 'Raju Uncle'—very different from many of their friends who refer to their family drivers as 'my driver.' When I hear that term from a school or college going person, I cringe, to me the lesson was significant—you treat small people with more respect than you treat big people. It is more important to respect your subordinates than your superiors.

**1.** The author's father would not allow his family to use the jeep because
(a) it was not their private vehicle
(b) the roads were full of potholes
(c) he was afraid of accidents
(d) the jeep was in a bad condition

**2.** The author taught his children to
(a) be firm with servants
(b) treat small people with respect
(c) maintain a discreet distance from servants
(d) be kind to small people

**3.** The author was critical of his children's friends because their attitude to servants smacked of
(a) weakness (b) coarseness
(c) arrogance (d) loftiness

**4.** The author's attitude towards servants can be described as
(a) respectful (b) indifferent
(c) rational (d) affectionate

**5.** The opposite of the word 'refused' is
(a) accepted
(b) received
(c) justified
(d) admired

**6.** The word that can replace 'reiterated' is
(a) revised (b) repeated
(c) recalled (d) reconsidered

## ANSWERS

**Passage 1** 1. *(c)*, 2. *(c)*, 3. *(a)*, 4. *(d)*, 5. *(d)*, 6. *(b)*

**Passage 2** 1. *(c)*, 2. *(b)*, 3. *(a)*, 4. *(c)*, 5. *(c)*, 6. *(b)*

**Passage 3** 1. *(c)*, 2. *(d)*, 3. *(b)*, 4. *(d)*, 5. *(c)*, 6. *(d)*

**Passage 4** 1. *(c)*, 2. *(a)*, 3. *(c)*, 4. *(b)*, 5. *(a)*, 6. *(a)*

**Passage 5** 1. *(d)*, 2. *(a)*, 3. *(c)*, 4. *(c)*, 5. *(d)*, 6. *(d)*

**Passage 6** 1. *(c)*, 2. *(c)*, 3. *(a)*, 4. *(b)*, 5. *(c)*, 6. *(b)*

**Passage 7** 1. *(c)*, 2. *(b)*, 3. *(b)*, 4. *(c)*, 5. *(b)*, 6. *(a)*

**Passage 8** 1. *(a)*, 2. *(d)*, 3. *(c)*, 4. *(b)*, 5. *(a)*, 6. *(b)*, 7. *(a)*

**Passage 9** 1. *(a)*, 2. *(a)*, 3. *(b)*, 4. *(a)*, 5. *(c)*, 6. *(a)*, 7. *(a)*

**Passage 10** 1. *(a)*, 2. *(d)*, 3. *(b)*, 4. *(a)*, 5. *(a)*, 6. *(b)*

**Passage 11** 1. *(b)*, 2. *(a)*, 3. *(b)*, 4. *(b)*, 5. *(b)*

**Passage 12** 1. *(b)*, 2. *(c)*, 3. *(d)*, 4. *(d)*, 5. *(a)*, 6. *(b)*

**Passage 13** 1. *(d)*, 2. *(b)*, 3. *(d)*, 4. *(c)*, 5. *(b)*, 6. *(c)*, 7. *(c)*, 8. *(a)*

**Passage 14** 1. *(c)*, 2. *(a)*, 3. *(d)*, 4. *(a)*, 5. *(b)*, 6. *(d)*, 7. *(c)*

**Passage 15** 1. *(c)*, 2. *(b)*, 3. *(b)*, 4. *(b)*, 5. *(d)*, 6. *(d)*, 7. *(c)*

**Passage 16** 1. *(c)*, 2. *(d)*, 3. *(b)*, 4. *(d)*, 5. *(c)*, 6. *(c)*, 7. *(c)*, 8. *(b)*

**Passage 17** 1. *(b)*, 2. *(d)*, 3. *(b)*, 4. *(c)*, 5. *(b)*, 6. *(c)*

**Passage 18** 1. *(a)*, 2. *(b)*, 3. *(c)*, 4. *(a)*, 5. *(a)*, 6. *(b)*

# Chapter 15

# Note-Making

Note-making and abstraction (i.e. summarising) is an advanced writing skill which is acquiring increasing importance due to the knowledge explosion. There is a need to remember at least the main points on any given topic. Making notes is an activity which combines several skills.

## How to Make Notes

1. **Careful Reading of Passage** Read the passage carefully, underlining the key sentences and phrases. This will help you in giving a title to the notes and also help in making the main points.
2. **Logical Sequence** Make rough notes of the main points and give them a logical sequence.
3. **Format** Use any convenient format (see sample format given later on in this chapter) but it should depend on the theme of the passage.
4. **Headings** You have to find out the main idea of the passage. Frame a heading based on the central idea and write it in the middle above the notes.
5. **Sub-headings** Understand how the main idea has been presented and developed. There may be two or three subordinate/associated ideas. You can frame sub-headings based on these.
6. **Sub-sub-headings** There will be further details or sub-sub-headings of the sub-headings that you want to mention in these notes. Mention them below the relevant sub-headings.
7. **Indenting** All sub-headings and sub-sub-headings at the same level should be written at the same distance from the margin.

## Points to be Kept in Mind

Some points which should be kept in mind while making notes are

- Notes should be short and to the point.
- They should be written in points only, not full sentences. They should be put one below the other and numbered properly.
- They should have all the important and relevant information contained in the passage.
- The information should be systematically divided and subdivided.
- Use universally recognised symbols and abbreviations wherever required and provide a key to the abbreviations used.
- The Title to the passage should be short (not more than 3–4 words) and should reflect the spirit of the passage

## Using Abbreviations

1. Use standard abbreviations and symbols as far as possible:
   (a) Capitalise first letters of a combination of words USA, UK, ATM, MBA etc.
   (b) Common abbreviations used in newspapers and magazines Sc. (for Science), Mr., Ms., Dr., Govt. etc.
   (c) Common symbols \, ∴ , +ve, -ve, ↑ (rising), ↓ (falling), =, < (less than), > (more than) etc.
   (d) Measurements and Figures 100', 100", 100 kg, 1000 mm, 100 ml etc.
2. Make your own abbreviations:
   (a) Keep the main sounds of the word. For example, edn. (education), progm. (programme). Remove all vowels except the one starting the word.
   (b) Retain the suffix so that later when you are going over the notes you may recall the full form of the word. For example, ednl (educational), prgsv (progressive).
   (c) A minimum of four abbreviations should be used.

*Your notes should look like this*

**Heading**

**1. Subheading 1**

1. a Point 1
1. b Sub-Sub heading        1. b. 1 Sub Point 1
1. b. 2 Sub Point 2
1. c Point 1

**2. Subheading 2**

2. a Point 1        2. b Sub-Sub heading
2. b. 1 Point 1

**Key**

abbr - abbreviation        avt - aviation        fmly - family
pnt - point        engr - engineer

You will observe that indenting, i.e., shifting from the margin, has been used to clearly indicate sub-headings and sub-sub-headings. Sub-headings, though separated by points, occur below one another. Such use of indenting gives your notes a visual character. At a glance you can see the main idea and its aspects.

## Abstraction or Summarising

Here you have to write a paragraph summarising the passage using the points listed in the notes as a guide. Complete and grammatically correct sentences must be used. They should be logically and cohesively linked using suitable linking words. Abbreviations and symbols are not to be used. Usually the summary should be about 80 words, unless otherwise mentioned in the question.

### Points to be Kept in Mind

*Some points which should be kept in mind while summarising are*

- Summary is made out of the notes, not the passage. No point should be mentioned in the summary which is not included in the notes.
- Do not divide the summary into different paragraphs. Only one paragraph should be used.
- The summary should be attempted immediately after the note making is completed.
- Do not start the summary like 'The passage talks about .......'.
- Try to follow the order of the notes as far as possible.
- Do not exceed the word limit given in the question.

## Sample Passage for Note-Making

Resistance to suggestion can be built up in two ways. First, children can be taught to rely on their own internal resources and not to depend on incessant stimulation from without. This is doubly important. Reliance on external stimulation is bad for the character. Moreover, such stimulation is the stuff with which propagandists bait their hooks, the jam in which dictators conceal their ideological pills. An individual who relies on external stimulations thereby exposes himself to the full force of whatever propaganda is being made in his neighbourhood. For a majority of people in the West, purposeless reading, purposeless listening-in, purposeless listening to radios, purposeless looking at films have become addictions, psychological equivalents of alcoholism and morphinism.

Things have come to such a pitch that there are many millions of men and women who suffer real distress if they are cut off for a few days or even a few hours from newspaper, radio, music or moving pictures. Like the addict to a drug, they have to indulge their vice, not because the indulgence gives them any real pleasure, but because, unless they indulge, they feel painfully subnormal and incomplete. Even by intelligent people, it is now taken for granted that such psychological addictions are inevitable and even desirable, that there is nothing to be alarmed at in the fact that the majority of civilised men and women are now incapable of living on their own spiritual resources, but have become abjectly dependent on incessant stimulation from without. How can children be taught to rely upon their own spiritual resources and resist the temptation to become reading addicts, hearing addicts, seeing addicts?

First of all, they can be taught how to entertain themselves by making things, by playing musical instruments, by purposeful study, by scientific observation, by the practice of some art and so on. But such education of the hand and the intellect is not enough.

Along with the necessary knowledge and skill must be given the will to use them even under the pressure of incessant temptation to take the line of least resistance and become an addict to psychological drugs. Most people will not wish to resist these temptations unless they have a coherent philosophy of life, which makes it reasonable and right for them to do so. The other method of heightening resistance to suggestion is purely intellectual and consists in training young people to subject the diverse devices of the propagandists to critical analysis. The first thing that educators must do is to analyse the words currently used in newspapers, on platforms by preachers and broadcasters. Their critical analysis and constructive criticism should reach out to the children and the youth with such a clarity that they learn to react to forceful suggestions the right way at the right time.

**Qns.** On the basis of your reading of the above passage, make notes on it using headings and sub-headings. Use recognisable abbreviations wherever necessary. Also supply an appropriate title to it.

***Ans.***

**Title** Developing Resistance to Suggestion

**Notes**

**I.** Resistance to suggestion can be built up in two ways
- (*i*) chldrn shd rely on themselves
- (*ii*) not on external stmltn
  - (a) bad for character
  - (b) propagandists & dictators use it
  - (c) gets addictive
  - (d) dpdc on ext stmltn inevitable
- (*iii*) Ext stmltn

**II.** Chldrn shd be taught to rely on their spiritual resources by self-entertainment
- (*i*) making things
- (*ii*) playing musical instruments
- (*iii*) purposeful study
- (*iv*) scientific observation
- (*v*) practising art

III. Edn not to take line of least resistance
(*i*) critically analyse (*ii*) react to suggestions right way - right time

Key to Abbreviations

| Abbreviations | Words |
|---|---|
| chldrn | *children* |
| shd | *should* |
| stmltn | *stimulation* |
| ext | *external* |
| dpdc | *dependence* |
| edn | *education* |

# Practice Questions*

## PASSAGE 1

There are two problems that cause great worry to our educationists – the problem of religious and moral destruction in the land of many faiths and the problems arising out of the large variety of languages.

Taking up the education of the children, we see that they should be trained to love one another, to be kind and helpful to all, to be tender to the lower animals and to observe and think right. The task of teaching them how to read, to count and to calculate is important, but it should not make us lose sight of the primary aim of moulding personality in the right way.

For this, it is necessary to call into aid culture, tradition and religion. But in our country we have, in the same school, to look after boys and girls born in different faiths and belonging to families that live diverse ways of life, no easy path of evading the difficulty by attending solely to physical culture and intellectual education. We have to evolve a suitable technique and method for serving the spiritual needs of school children professing different faiths. We should thereby promote an atmosphere of mutual respect, a fuller understanding and helpful co-operation among the different communities in our society. Again, we must remain one people and we have, therefore, to give basic training to our schools to speak and understand more languages than one and to appreciate and respect the different religions prevailing in India. It is not right for us to be overtaking the young mind. What is necessary must be done. And it is not in fact that great a burden.

Any attempt to do away the differences with a steamroll of governmental coercion and indirect pressure would be as futile as it would be unwise. Any imposition of a single way of life and form of worship on all children or neglect of a section of the pupils in this respect, or barren secularisation will lead to conflict between school and home life, which is harmful. On the other hand, if we give due recognition to the different prevailing faiths in educational institutions by organising suitable facilities for religious teaching for boys and girls of all communities, our problem will be solved to a large extent. This may itself serve as a broadening influence of great national values.

**Qns.** ***On the basis of your reading of the above passage, make notes on it using headings and sub-headings. Use recognisable abbreviations, wherever necessary (minimum 4).***

## PASSAGE 2

The most alarming of man's assaults upon the environment is the contamination of air, earth, rivers and sea with lethal materials. This pollution is for the most part irrevocable; the chain of evil it initiates is for the most part irreversible. In this contamination of the environment, chemicals are the sinister partners of radiation in changing the very nature of the world; radiation released through nuclear explosions into the air comes to the earth in rain, lodges into the soil, enters the grass, or corn or wheat grown there, and reaches the bones of a human being, there to remain until his death. Similarly, chemicals sprayed on crops lie long in soil, entering living organisms, passing from one to another in a chain of poisoning and death. Or they pass by underground streams until they emerge and combine into new forms that kill vegetation, sicken cattle, and harm those who drink from once pure wells. It took hundreds of millions of years to produce the life that now inhabits the earth and reached a state of adjustment and balance with its surroundings. The environment contains elements that were hostile as well as supporting. Even within the light of the sun there

* *Here questions on Note-Making are given for the basic understanding about Note-Making. In the examination questions can be asked in different format.*

are short-wave radiations with power to injure. Given time, life has adjusted and a balance reached . For time is the essential ingredient, but in the modern world there is no time. The rapidity of change and the speed with which new situations are created follow the heedless pace of man rather than the deliberate pace of nature. Radiation is no longer the bombardment of cosmic rays; it is now the unnatural creation of man's tampering with the atom. The chemicals to which life is asked to make adjustments are no longer merely calcium and silica and copper and all the rest of the minerals washed out of the rocks and carried in the rivers to the sea; they are the synthetic creations of man's inventive mind, brewed in his laboratories, and having no counterparts in nature.

**Qns.** *On the basis of your understanding of the above passage, make notes on it using headings and sub-headings. Use recognisable abbreviations. Also supply a title to it*

## PASSAGE 3

It is not easy to write a familiar style. Many people mistake a familiar for a vulgar style, and suppose that to write without affectation is to write at random. On the contrary, there is nothing that requires more precision, and, if I may so say, purity of expression, than the style I am speaking of. It utterly rejects not only all unmeaning pomp, but all low, cant phrases, and loose, unconnected, slipshod allusions. It is not to take the first word that offers, but the best word in common use; it is not to throw words together in any combinations we please, but to follow and avail ourselves of the true idiom of the language.

To write a genuine familiar or truly English style is to write as anyone would speak in common conversation who had a thorough command and choice of words, or who could discourse with ease, force, and perspicuity, setting aside all pedantic and oratorical flourishes. Or, to give another illustration, to write naturally is the same thing in regard to common conversation as to read naturally is in regard to common speech.

It does not follow that it is an easy thing to give the true accent and inflection to the words you utter, because you do not attempt to rise above the level of ordinary life and colloquial speaking. You do not assume, indeed, the solemnity of the pulpit, or the tone of stage-declamation; neither are you at liberty to gabble on at a venture, without emphasis or discretion, or to resort to vulgar dialect or clownish pronunciation. You must steer a middle course. You are tied down to a given and appropriate articulation, which is determined by the habitual associations between sense and sound, and which you can only hit by entering into the author's meaning, as you must find the proper words and style to express yourself by fixing your thoughts on the subject you have to write about.

Anyone may mouth out a passage with a theatrical cadence, or get upon stilts to tell his thoughts; but to write or speak with propriety and simplicity is a more difficult task. Thus, it is easy to affect a pompous style, to use a word twice as big as the thing you want to express: it is not so to pitch upon the very word that exactly fits out of eight or ten words equally common, equally intelligible, with nearly equal pretensions; it is a matter of some nicety and discrimination to pick out the very one the preferableness of which is scarcely perceptible, but decisive. A word may be a fine-sounding word, of an unusual length, and very imposing from its learning and novelty, and yet in the connection in which it is introduced, may be quite pointless and irrelevant.

**Qns.** On the basis of your reading of the above passage, make notes on it using headings and sub-headings. Use recognisable abbreviations wherever necessary. Also supply an appropriate title to it.

## PASSAGE 4

The Great Wall of China was built to link existing fortifications into a united defense system and better keep invading Mongol tribes out of China. It is the largest man-made monument ever to have been built and it is reputed that it is the only one visible from space. Many thousands of people must have given their lives to build this huge construction.

The Great Wall of China is a series of towers made of stone, brick, earth, wood, and other materials, generally built along an East-to-West line across the historical northern borders of China to protect the Chinese states and empires against the raids and invasions of the various nomadic groups of the Eurasian Steppe. Several walls were being built as early as the 7th century BCE; these, later joined together and made bigger and stronger, are now collectively referred to as the Great Wall. Especially famous is the wall built (220-206 BCE) by Qin Shi Huang, the first Emperor of China. Little of that wall remains. Since then the Great Wall has on and off been rebuilt, maintained, and enhanced; the majority of the existing wall is from the Ming Dynasty (1368-1644). Other purposes of the Great Wall have included border controls, allowing the imposition of duties on good transported along the Silk Road, regulation or encouragement of trade and the control of immigration and emigration. Furthermore, the defensive characteristics of the Great Wall were enhanced by the construction of watch towers, troop barracks, garrison stations, signalling capabilities through the means of smoke or fire, and the fact that the path of the Great Wall also served as a transportation corridor. The Great Wall stretches from Dandong in the East to Lop Lake in the West, along an arc that roughly delineates the southern edge of Inner

Mongolia. A comprehensive archaeological survey, using advanced technologies, has concluded that the Ming walls measure 8,850 km. This is made up of 6,259 km sections of actual wall, 359 km of trenches and 2,232 km of natural defensive barriers such as hills and rivers. Another archaeological survey found that the entire wall with all of its branches measures out to be 21,196 km.

King Zheng of Qin conquered the last of his opponents and unified China as the First Emperor of the Qin dynasty (Qin Shi Huang) in 221 BCE. Intending to impose centralised rule and prevent the resurgence of feudal lords, he ordered the destruction of the sections of the walls, however, he ordered the building of new walls to connect the remaining fortifications along the empire's northern frontier. Transporting the large quantity of materials required for construction was difficult, so builders always tried to use local resources. Stones from the mountains were used over mountain ranges, while rammed earth was used for construction in the plains.

The Great Wall concept was revived again under the Ming dynasty in the 14th century, to gain a clear upper hand over the Mongolian tribes.

**Qns.** *On the basis of your reading of the above passage make notes on it, using headings and subheadings. Use recognisable abbreviations. Also supply an appropriate title to it.*

## PASSAGE 5

Petty corruption can be checked, but not the sophisticated variety. It is incorrect to suppose that corruption is best fought through investigation and punishment. Our experience with law enforcement and the judiciary suggests otherwise. Corruption is better addressed through transparency, clear rules for decision-making and e-governance. The RTI Act is probably an answer to corruption.

Limiting the role of government does not limit corruption. Most people associate corruption with government. They believe that if the role of government is restricted, it will limit the scope of corruption.

This is astonishingly naive. Corruption thrives in the corporate sector as well. And some of the biggest opportunities for graft relate to the sale of government land and natural resources to the private sector. A state that mishandles ownership of public assets is also likely to mishandle their transfer to private hands.

Privatisation is no answer to corruption. It only creates another avenue for graft.

Corruption has more to do with the economic structure of society than with individuals being good or bad. The crucial point is that corruption is a manifestation of an underlying malaise, namely, an iniquitous economic structure.

"The surest way to corrupt a youth is to instruct him to hold in higher esteem those who think alike than those who think differently", said Friedrich Nietzsche, German philosopher, poet and composer.

In such a structure, those at the top will benefit from both legal and illegal corruption. Any answer to corruption must attack the economic structure itself. Addressing inequalities in society may be a more sensible way of tackling corruption than bringing in tough anti-corruption laws or appealing to our values. Yet people who profess revulsion at corruption have no qualms about supporting economic measures that widen inequalities or criticising measures aimed at reducing these.

Corruption is not just about bad guys who give or take bribes; the greater corruption involves nice guys who are comfortably ensconced in a predatory economic structure. That structure is as old as mankind; it only keeps changing its forms. Anti-graft crusades can slow down the wheels of the economy in the short-run, as decision making in government is paralysed. In the long run, such crusades end up delegitimising the institutions of democracy and pave the way for dictatorship, which makes corruption even worse.

**Qns.** *On the basis of your reading of the above passage, make notes on it using headings and sub-headings. Use recognisable abbreviations wherever necessary. Also supply an appropriate title to it.*

## PASSAGE 6

People tend to amass possessions, sometimes without being aware of doing so. They can have a delightful surprise when they find something useful which they did not know they owned. Those who never have to change house become indiscriminate collectors of what can only be described as clutter. They leave unwanted objects in drawers, cupboards and attics for years in the belief that they may one day need them. Old people also accumulate belongings for two other reasons, lack of physical and mental energy, and sentiment. Things owned for a long time are full of associations with the past, perhaps with the relatives who are dead, and so they gradually acquire a sentimental value.

Some things are collected deliberately in an attempt to avoid wastage. Among these are string and brown paper, kept by thrifty people when a parcel has been opened. Collecting small items can be a mania. A lady cuts out from newspapers sketches of model clothes that she would like to buy if she had money. As she is not rich, the chances are that she will never be able to afford such purchases. It is a harmless habit, but it litters up her desk. Collecting as a serious hobby is quite different and has many advantages.

It provides relaxation for leisure hours, as just looking at one's treasure is always a joy. One doesn't have to go out for amusement as the collection is housed at home. Whatever it consists of - stamps, records, first editions of books, China – there is always something to do in connection with it, from finding the right place for the latest addition to verifying facts in reference books. This hobby educates one not only in the chosen subject, but also in general matters which have some bearing on it.

There are other benefits also. One gets to meet like-minded collectors to get advice, compare notes, exchange articles, to show off one's latest find etc. So one's circle of friends grows. Soon the hobby leads to travelling, perhaps a meeting in another town, possibly a trip abroad in search of a rare specimen, for collectors are not confined to one country. Over the years one may well become an authority on one's hobby and will probably be asked to give informal talks to little gatherings and then, if successful, to larger audiences.

**Qns.** *On the basis of your understanding of the above passage make notes on it using headings and sub-headings. Use recognisable abbreviations. Also supply an appropriate title to it.*

## PASSAGE 7

I had called upon my friend Sherlock Holmes upon the second morning after Christmas, with the intention of wishing him the compliments of the season. He was lounging upon the sofa in a purple dressing-gown, a pipe-rack within his reach upon the right, and a pile of crumpled morning papers, evidently newly studied, near at hand. Beside the couch was a wooden chair, and on the angle of the back hung a very shabby and disreputable hard felt hat, much the worse for wear, and cracked in several places. A lens and a forceps lying upon the seat of the chair suggested that the hat had been suspended in this manner for the purpose of examination.

"You are engaged", said I; "perhaps I interrupt you."

"Not at all. I am glad to have a friend with whom I can discuss my results. The matter is a perfectly trivial one" — he jerked his thumb in the direction of the old hat — "but there are points in connection with it which are not entirely devoid of interest and even instruction."

I seated myself in his armchair and warmed my hands before his crackling fire, for a sharp frost had set in, and the windows were thick with the ice crystals. "I suppose", I remarked, "that, homely as it looks, this thing has some deadly story linked on to it — that it is the clue which will guide you in the solution of some mystery, and the punishment of some crime."

"No, no. No crime", said Sherlock Holmes, laughing. "Only one of those whimsical little incidents which will happen when you have four million human beings all jostling each other within the space of a few square miles. Amid the action and reaction of so dense a swarm of humanity, every possible combination of events may be expected to take place, and many a little problem will be presented which may be striking and bizarre without being criminal, we have already had experience of such."

"So much so", I remarked, "that of the last six cases which I have added to my notes, three have been entirely free of any legal crime."

"Precisely. You allude to my attempt to recover the Irene Adler papers, to the singular case of Miss Sutherland, and to the adventure of the man with the twisted lip. Well, I have no doubt that this small matter will fall into the same innocent category. You know Peterson, the Commissionaire?"

"Yes"

"It is to him that this trophy belongs."

"It is his hat."

"No, no; he found it. Its owner is unknown. I beg that you will look upon it, not as a battered billycock, but as an intellectual problem. And, first, as to how it came here. It arrived upon Christmas morning in company with a good fat goose, which is, I have no doubt, roasting at this moment in front of Peterson's fire."

**Qns.** *On the basis of your reading of the above passage, make notes on it using headings and sub-headings. Use recognisable abbreviations wherever necessary. Also supply an appropriate title to it.*

## PASSAGE 8

Research has shown that the human mind can process words at the rate of about 500 per minute, whereas a speaker speaks at the rate of about 150 words a minute. The difference between the two, at 350, is quite large.

So, a speaker must make every effort to retain the attention of the audience and the listener should also be careful not to let his mind wander. Good communication calls for good listening skills. A good speaker must necessarily be a good listener. Listening starts with hearing but goes beyond. Hearing, in other words, is necessary, but is not a sufficient condition for listening. Listening involves hearing with attention. Listening is a process that calls for concentration. While listening, one should also be observant. In other words, listening has to do with the ears, as well as with the eyes and the mind. Listening is to be understood as the total process that involves hearing with attention, being observant and making interpretations. Good communication is essentially an interactive process. It calls for participation and involvement. It is quite often a dialogue rather than a monologue. It is necessary to be interested and also show or make it abundantly clear that one is interested in knowing what the other person has to say.

Good listening is an art that can be cultivated. It relates to skills that can be developed. A good listener knows the art of getting much more than what the speaker is trying to convey. He knows how to prompt, persuade but not to cut off or interrupt what the other person has to say. At times the speaker may or may not be coherent, articulate and well-organised in his thoughts and expressions. He may have it in his mind and yet he may fail to marshal the right words while communicating his thoughts. Nevertheless a good listener puts him at ease, helps him articulate and facilitates him to get across the message that he wants to convey. For listening to be effective, it is also necessary that barriers to listening are removed. Such barriers can be both physical and psychological. Physical barriers generally relate to hindrances to proper hearing, whereas psychological barriers are more fundamental and relate to the interpretation and evaluation of the speaker and the message.

**Qns.** *On the basis of your reading of the above passage, make notes on it using headings and sub-headings. Use recognisable abbreviations, wherever necessary. Also supply an appropriate title to it.*

## PASSAGE 9

The International Labour Organisation (ILO) has estimated that 218 million children between the ages of five and seventeen work in developing countries. Of these, 122.3 million children work in the Asia-Pacific region, 49.3 million work in sub-Saharan Africa, and 5.7 million work in Latin America and the Caribbean. Most working children in rural areas are found in agriculture; many children work as domestic help; urban children work in trade and services, with fewer in manufacturing and construction.

Child labour ranges from four year olds tied to rug looms to keep them from running away, to seventeen year olds helping out on the family farm. In some cases, a child's work can be helpful to him or her and to the family; working and earning can be a positive experience in a child's growing up. This depends largely on the age of the child, the conditions in which the child works, and whether work prevents the child from going to school.

The Children's Rights Division at Human Rights Watch has focused its effort on the worst forms of child labour, those prohibited by the ILO's Worst Form of Child Labour Covention. Children who work long hours, often in dangerous and unhealthy conditions, are exposed to lasting physical and psychological harm, working at rug looms, for instance, has left children disabled with eye damage, lung disease, stunted growth, and susceptibility to arthritis as they grow older. Children making silk thread in India dip their hands into boiling water that burns and blisters them, breathe smoke and fumes from machinery, handle dead worms that cause infections, and guide twisting thread that cuts their fingers. Children harvesting sugarcane in El Salvador use machetes to cut cane for upto nine hours a day in the hot sun; injuries to their hands and legs are common and medical care is often not available. Denied an education and a normal childhood, some children are confined and beaten, reduced to slavery. Some are denied freedom of movement—the right to leave the workplace and go home to their families. Some are abducted and forced to work. The human rights abuses in these practices are clear and acute. We have found similar problems in Asia, the Middle East, Latin America, and the United States. Children who work for too many hours and too many days for too little, or sometimes no pay, are subjected to physical abuse, exposed to dangerous pesticides and made to work with dangerous tools. The need of the hour is to start a debate on child rights and work issues.

**Qns.** *On the basis of your reading of the above passage, make notes on it using headings and sub-headings. Use recognisable abbreviations wherever necessary. Also supply an appropriate title to it.*

## PASSAGE 10

Although stupidity is commonly defined as 'a lack of normal intelligence,' stupid behaviour is not the behaviour of a person lacking in intelligence but the behaviour of a person not using good judgement or sense. In fact, stupidity comes from the Latin word that means 'senseless.' Therefore, stupidity can be defined as the behaviour of a person of normal intelligence who acts in a particular situation as if he or she isn't very bright. Stupidity exists at three levels of seriousness.

First is the simple, relatively harmless level. Behaviour at this level is often amusing. It is humorous when someone places the food from a fast food restaurant on the roof of the car while unlocking the door and then drives away with the food still on the roof. We call this absent-minded. The person's good sense or intelligence was temporarily absent. At this level, other than passing inconvenience or embarrassment, no one is injured by the stupid behaviour.

The next type-serious stupidity-is more dangerous. Practical jokes such as putting sugar in the salt shakers are at this level. The intention is humorous, but there is a chance of harm. Irresponsible advice given to others is also serious stupidity. An example is the person who plays psychiatrist on the basis of an introductory psychology course or doing a TV program on psychiatry. The intention may be to help, but if the victim really needs psychiatric help an amateur will only worsen the situation. Even worse is the third kind of stupidity. Kind people, who would never injure another living being, stupidly throw away a box of six-week-old kittens along a country road. Lacking the heart to kill the poor things, they sentence them to almost certain death from wild animals, infections, exposure or the wheels of a passing vehicle. Yet they are able to tell themselves that they will find nice homes or 'animals can get along wild.' Another example of this kind of stupidity is the successful local businessman who tries to have as many office affairs as he can get away with. He risks the loss of his business and his home. He fails to see that what he is doing is wrong. His is the true moral stupidity of a person not willing to think about the results of his actions or take responsibility for them. The common defence of a person guilty of stupidity is – 'But I didn't think.......' This, however, is not a proper excuse, especially when serious or harmful stupidity is involved.

**Qns.** *On the basis of your reading of the above passage, make notes on it using headings and sub-headings. Use recognisable abbreviations wherever necessary.*

# ANSWERS

## Passage 1

**Notes**

I. Worry of our educationists
   (*i*) problem of rlgs & moral edn
   (*ii*) innmbl faiths & variety of lngs
II. Task of teaching
   (*i*) moulding right personality
   (*ii*) loving one another
   (*iii*) being kind & helpful
   (*iv*) tender to lower animals
   (*v*) observe & think right
III. Spiritual needs of school children
   (*i*) teaching mutual respect
   (*ii*) co-operation among diff communities
   (*iii*) speaking & understanding more lngs that one

### Key to Abbreviations

| Abbreviations | Words |
|---|---|
| rlgs | *religious* |
| & | *and* |
| edn | *education* |
| innmbl | *innumerable* |
| lngs | *languages* |
| diff | *different* |

## Passage 2

**Title** Man's Assault on Environment

**Notes**

I. Earth's adjustment and balance in disarray
   (*i*) humans respl for disbalancing nature
   (*ii*) envn full of hostile as well as supptg elements
   (*iii*) natural sunlight full of short-wave radiation
   (*iv*) can cause injury
   (*v*) time, an essential element to maintain balance, missing
   (*vi*) rapidity of change – main cause of disturbing nature
II. Pollution/ contamination of earth
   (*i*) pltn irreversible and irrevocable
   (*ii*) chemicals evil partners of radtn
   (*iii*) nuclear explsns cause radiation
   (*iv*) it affects grass, crop
   (*v*) mixes with rain, goes inside soil
   (*vi*) consumption of such food affects humans
III. Pollution of water
   (*i*) chemical sprayed on crops – cause poisoning and death
   (*ii*) pollute underground streams
   (*iii*) combine in new forms, spoil vegetation, cattles and humans
   (*iv*) well water gets poisoned
IV. Natural chemicals replaced by synthetic chemicals
   (*i*) man-made chemicals more deadly
   (*ii*) adjustment possible with natural chemicals
   (*iii*) with synthetic chemicals– no balancing act possible
   (*iv*) cause mass destruction

### Key to Abbreviations

| Abbreviations | Words |
|---|---|
| respl | *responsible* |
| envn | *environment* |
| supptg | *supporting* |
| pltn | *pollution* |
| radtn | *radiation* |
| explsns | *explosions* |

## Passage 3

**Title** Writing and Speaking English

**Notes**

I. Essentials of this style
   (*i*) rqrs precision
   (*ii*) avoids all antecedents & allusions
   (*iii*) use best words
II. True English style is spoken English
   (*i*) Has cnvrstnl tone
   (*ii*) Speaker must have good dctn
   (*iii*) Must have good accent and articulation
   (*iv*) Express well
   (*v*) Speak in lucid & simple language
III. Use logical and rlvt words
   (*i*) Avoid fine-sounding and bombastic words
   (*ii*) Make value jgmnt
   (*iii*) Select words rlvt to the topic

### Key to Abbreviations

| Abbreviations | Words |
|---|---|
| rqrs | *requires* |
| & | *and* |
| cnvrstnl | *conversational* |
| dctn | *diction* |
| rlvt | *relevant* |
| jgmnt | *judgement* |

## Passage 4

**Title** The Great Wall of China

I. ntroduction
   (*i*) lgst man made monument
   (*ii*) only one visible from outer space
   (*iii*) many gave their lives for its cnstrtn

II. Physical description
   (*i*) series of towers
   (*ii*) made of local materials like
      (a) stones (b) bricks
      (c) earth (d) wood
   (*iii*) blt from Dandong in East to Lop Lake in West
   (*iv*) svrl walls being built in 7th century BC

III. Purpose of Great Wall
   (*i*) prtcd Chinese states and empire against raids
   (*ii*) cntrld border
   (*iii*) imposition of duties on goods
   (*iv*) rgltn and encrgmt of trade
   (*v*) cntrld
      (a) immigration (b) emigration

### Key to Abbreviations

| Abbreviations | Words |
|---|---|
| lgst | *largest* |
| cnstrtn | *construction* |
| blt | *built* |
| svrl | *several* |
| prtcd | *protected* |
| cntrld | *controlled* |
| rgltn | regulation |
| encrgmt | |

## Passage 5

**Title** Dealing with Corruption

**Notes**

I. Transparency and clear rules for decision
   (*i*) Transparency helps fight crrptn
   (*ii*) RTI
   (*iii*) Pvtsn - no answer to crrptn

II. Crrptn has to do with ecnmc structure
   (*i*) legal and illegal crrptn
   (*ii*) iniquitious ecnmc structure
   (*iii*) anti-crrptn laws to be enforced

III. Great crrptn involves nice guys
   (*i*) crrptn not only about bad boys
   (*ii*) predatory ecnmc structure
   (*iii*) Anti-graft crusades
   (*iv*) Short-run paralyses decision making
   (*v*) Long-run de-legitimises instns

### Key to Abbreviations

| Abbreviations | Words |
|---|---|
| crrptn | *corruption* |
| RTI | *Right to Information* |
| pvtsn | *privatisation* |
| ecnmc | *economic* |
| instns | *institutions* |

## Passage 6

**Title** Collecting as a Hobby or for Other Reasons

**Notes**

I. Collecting odds and ends - unaware
   (*i*) rsns
      (a) no change of house
      (b) need of unwanted objects some day
      (c) stmtl value
      (d) avoid wstg
   (*ii*) dsdvtgs
      (a) it becomes a mania (b) causes messiness

II. Collecting as a hobby – stamps, records, books etc
   (*i*) advtgs
      (a) provides rlxtn
      (b) becomes own treasure
      (c) amsmt or something to do at home
      (d) educates us in the chosen subject and related matters
      (e) enbls meeting other like-minded collectors
      (f) can lead to travel
      (g) enbls us to become authority in subject

### Key to Abbreviations

| Abbreviations | Words |
|---|---|
| rsns | *reasons* |
| stmtl | *sentimental* |
| wstg | *wastage* |
| dsdvtgs | *disadvantages* |
| advtgs | *adventages* |
| rlxtn | *relaxation* |
| amsmt | *amusement* |
| enbls | *enables* |

## Passage 7

**Title** Sherlock Holmes With a Trophy

**Notes**

I. Nrtr meets Sherlock Holmes at home after Christmas
   (*i*) holmes rlxg after examining peculiar hat
   (*ii*) wants discuss matter with narrator
   (*iii*) hat indctd something peculiar
   (*iv*) not ncsrly related crime

II. Discussion with nrtr
   (*i*) holmes says earlier cases not always crimes
   (*ii*) hat not likely has crime behind it
   (*iii*) found by Cmsr with fat goose
   (*iv*) owner unknown

### Key to Abbreviations

| Abbreviations | Words |
|---|---|
| nrtr | *narrator* |
| rlxg | *relaxing* |
| indctd | *indicated* |
| ncsrly | *necessarily* |
| Cmsr | *Commissionaire* |

## Passage 8

**Title** The Art of Good Listening

**Notes**

I. Human mind processes words much faster than spkr can speak
   (*i*) mind 500 wpm (*ii*) speak 150 wpm
   (*iii*) spkr must retain audience attn
   (*iv*) lstnr not allow mind to wander

II. Dfrnc btwn hrng & lstng
   (*i*) hrng involves only ears
   (*ii*) lstng involves ears, eyes and mind

III. Gd lstng skill can be developed
   (*i*) prompt, persuade spkr but not interrupt
   (*ii*) sometimes spkr not articulate
   (*iii*) gd lstnr helps, facilitates him

IV. Barriers to lstng
   (*i*) physical – hindrances to hearing
   (*ii*) psychological – relate to interpretation, evaluation

### Key to Abbreviations

| Abbreviations | Words |
|---|---|
| spkr | *speaker* |
| wpm | *words per minute* |
| attn | *attention* |
| lstnr | *listener* |

### Key to Abbreviations

| | |
|---|---|
| dfrnc | *difference* |
| hrng | *hearing* |
| lstng | *listening* |
| btwn | *between* |
| gd | *good* |

## Passage 9

**Title** Child Rights and Work Issues

**Notes**

I. Child labour btwn the age of five & seventeen
   (*i*) According to ILO, underage chldrn work
   (*ii*) Most found in agriculture
   (*iii*) Employed in dfrt types work according to age structure

II. Worst form of child labour
   (*i*) Chldrn wrkng for long hrs suffer
   (*ii*) Long hrs wrk deforms children
   (*iii*) Insufficient medical care

III. Child rights denied
   (*i*) Chldrn not given edn
   (*ii*) Chldrn physically & mentally tortured
   (*iii*) Many examples (*iv*) Debate need of the hour

### Key to Abbreviations

| Abbreviations | Words |
|---|---|
| btwn | *between* |
| & | *and* |
| ILO | *International Labour Organisation* |
| chldrn | *children* |
| dfrt | *different* |
| wrkng | *working* |
| hrs | *hours* |
| wrk | *work* |
| edn | *education* |

## Passage 10

**Title** Levels of Stupidity

I. Stupidity
   (*i*) bhvr not using good judgement or sense
   (*ii*) not bhvr of person w/o intlgc
   (*iii*) three levels of seriousness

II. First level
   (*i*) simple
   (*ii*) relatively harmless
   (*iii*) hmrs

(*iv*) also called absent-minded
(*v*) causes incvnc or embrsmt

III. Second level
(*i*) practical jokes
(a) intn hmrs (b) can cause harm
(*ii*) irspbl advice
(a) intn to help
(b) amateurs worsen situation

IV. Third level
(*i*) moral stupidity (*ii*) harmful
(*iii*) not taking rspblty for action
(*iv*) defence – "did not think"
(*v*) e.g.'s
(a) release animal babies in open
(b) morally bad bhvr of businessman in office

### Key to Abbreviations

| Abbreviations | Words |
|---|---|
| bhvr | *behaviour* |
| w/o | *without* |
| intlgc | *intelligence* |
| hmrs | *humorous* |
| incvnc | *inconvenience* |
| embrsmt | *embarrassment* |
| intn | *intention* |
| irspbl | *irresponsible* |
| rspblty | *responsibility* |
| e.g.'s | *examples* |

# PART B

- Fiction
- Drama
- Poetry
- Prose
- Figures of Speech and Forms of Poetry
- Short Story
- Novel

# Chapter 16

# Pride and Prejudice

*Jane Austen*

## About the Author

### Austen's Early Life

Born on 16th, December 1775, Jane Austen was the seventh of eight children born to George and Cassandra Austen. The family lived in Steventon, a small Hampshire town in South-Central England, where her father was a Priest.

Jane Austen's life resembles her novels - at first glance they seem to be composed of a series of quiet, unexceptional events. The fact that Austen's life lacked the drama that other authors may have experienced in no way detracted her skill as a writer. Out of her seven siblings, Austen was closest to her only sister, Cassandra. From 1783 to 1785, the two girls attended schools in Oxford and Southampton and the Abbey School of Reading. When the Austens could no longer afford the tuition, Jane and Cassandra returned home to read extensively and learn from their family how to speak French and Italian and play the piano.

When Austen was 20, she met Tom an Irish and they were close enough. Their affair was on a high note but Tom's parents were not willing to this as they couldn't accept Austen being a daughter of a clergyman. Most accounts agree that the Austen daughters were pretty and enjoyed the slightly limited but interesting round of country parties described in Austen's novels.

### Works and Last Phase of Life

From 1796-1798, Austen wrote her first three novels-Northanger Abbey (originally titled Susan), Sense and Sensibility (originally titled Elinor and Marianne), and Pride and Prejudice (originally titled First Impressions) - but none was published until later.

Austen lived the last eight years of her life in Chawton. Her personal life continued to be limited to family and close friends, and she prized herself on being a warm and loving aunt as much as being a successful novelist. A sudden illness, possibly Addison's disease, made her stop work on the novel Sandition, and she died in 1817.

## Summary

### Mr Bennet and his Daughters

Mr Bennet of the Longbourne Estate has 5 daughters, but his property is entailed meaning that none of the girls can inherit it. Having married a woman who had no fortune, it is imperative that one of the girls marries well in order to support the others on his death. However, Jane Austen's opening line 'It is a truth universally acknowledged that a single man in possession of a good fortune must be in want of a wife is a sentence filled with irony and playfulness'.

The novel revolves around the necessity of marrying for love, not simply for mercenary reasons despite the social pressures to make a good wealthy match. The Bennet Family consists of five daughters. The elder of the girls, Jane and Elizabeth, are intelligent, rational young women; The younger daughters, Mary, Kitty, and Lydia, are thoughtless and silly. Mr Bennet himself is an aloof father watching rather than guiding his daughters. Mrs Bennet is as foolish as her younger children.

### New Tenant at Manor of Netherfield Park

The news that a wealthy young gentleman named Charles Bingley has rented the manor of Netherfield Park causes a great stir in the nearby village of Longbourn, especially in the Bennet household.

### Mrs. Bennet's Pursuit to Talk to Mr Bingley

The novel opens with Mrs Bennet trying to persuade Mr Bennet to visit an eligible bachelor, Mr Bingley, who has arrived in the neighbourhood. The visit is proceeded by an invitation to a ball at the local assembly rooms that the whole neighbourhood will attend.

### The Ball Party and Darcy's Refusal to Dance with Elizabeth

At the ball, Mr Bingley is open and cheerful, popular with all the guests, and appears to be very attracted to the beautiful Miss Bennet. His friend, Mr Darcy, is reputed to be twice as wealthy, however is haughty and aloof. He declines to dance with Elizabeth suggesting that she is not pretty enough to tempt him. She finds this amusing and jokes about the statement with her friends. Miss Jane Bennet also attracts the attention of Mr Bingley's sister Caroline, who invites her to visit.

### A Turn in Relationship of Darcy and Elizabeth

Mr Darcy finds himself increasingly attracted to Elizabeth's charm and intelligence. Jane's friendship with Mr Bingley also continues to burgeon, and Jane pays a visit to the Bingley mansion.

Mr Collins, a cousin of Mr Bennet and heir to the Longbo, visits the Bennet family. He is a pompous and obsequious clergyman because he expects each of the Bennet girls to wish to marry him due to his inheritance.

### Wickham's Story to Elizabeth

Elizabeth and her family meet the dashing and charming Mr Wickham who singles out Elizabeth and tells her a story of the hardship that Mr Darcy has caused him by depriving him of a living promised to him by Mr Darcy's late father. Elizabeth's dislike of Mr Darcy is confirmed.

### Another Affinity between Darcy and Elizabeth

At a ball, at which Mr Wickham is not present, Elizabeth dances with Mr Darcy rather against her will. Other than Jane and Elizabeth, all the members of the Bennet family show their lack of decorum. Mr Darcy and his cousin, Colonel Fitzwilliam, visit Lady Catherine. Colonel Fitzwilliam tells Elizabeth how Mr Darcy managed to save a friend from a bad match by convincing the friend of the lady's indifference.

Elizabeth is horrified at Darcy's involvement in an affair which has caused her sister so much pain. Mr Darcy, however has fallen in love with Elizabeth and proposes to her. She rejects him in a dazzling display of independence.

The following morning Mr Darcy gives Elizabeth a letter that explains his treatment of Mr Wickham. Darcy apologices for hurting Jane and Elizabeth begins to rejudge Mr Darcy on a clearer basis.

### Elizabeth Visits Darcy's Estate with her Uncle and Aunt

Some months later, Elizabeth and her Aunt and Uncle Gardiner visit Mr Darcy's estate in Derbyshire, Pemberly. While she was there, Elizabeth hears an account of him from the housekeeper as being kind and generous.

After an agonising wait, Mr Wickham is persuaded to marry Lydia with only the payment of debts required. With some degree of decency restored, Lydia visits Elizabeth and tells her that Mr Darcy was at the wedding. Mrs Gardiner informs Elizabeth that it is Mr Darcy who has made the match and hints that he may have a motive for doing so.

### The Happy Ending

At this point Mr Bingley and Mr Darcy return to Netherfield. Bingley proposes to Jane and is accepted, much to the delight of all.

Lady Catherine visits Elizabeth under the impression that she is going to marry Mr Darcy. Elizabeth refuses to deny this claim and Lady Catherine leaves outraged by her perceived insolence.

Darcy and Elizabeth go for a walk together and at this point Elizabeth thanks him for all he has done for her family.

Darcy replies that he thought only of her. In the course of this walk, they become engaged. Elizabeth then has to convince her father that she is not marrying for money. He is very concerned and it is only after she speaks about Mr Darcy's true worth that he is happy about the wedding.

## Practice Questions

**1.** When was Jane Austen born?
(a) 16th, December 1775 (b) 16th, October 1775
(c) 16th, December 1776 (d) None of these

**2.** Jane Austen was the ...............of eight children.
(a) 5th (b) 7th
(c) 8th (d) None of these

**3.** Parents of Jane Austen were
(a) George and Cassandra Austen
(b) Rubert and Elizebth Austen
(c) Darcy and Jane Austen (d) None of these

**4.** The family of Jane Austen lived in
(a) Steventon (b) Manchester
(c) Southampton (d) None of these

**5.** What probably made Austen's writing possible by freeing her time to work on her books?
(a) Lack of extraordinary experience
(b) Lack of a spouse and children
(c) Both (a) and (b)
(d) None of the above

**6.** Austen never achieved personal recognition for her works outside her sphere of family and friends. Why?
(a) Because her books were published anonymously
(b) Her book were not published at all
(c) Both (a) and (b)
(d) None of the above

**7.** Out of her seven siblings, who was closest to Austen?
(a) Jane (b) Cassandra
(c) Lydia (d) None of these

**8.** When did Austen meet Tom?
(a) When she was 17 (b) When she was 20
(c) When she was 30 (d) None of these

**9.** Who was Tom Lefroy?
(a) An Irish (b) A British
(c) An American (d) None of these

**10.** Why Lefroy's family sent him home?
(a) Because Austen and Tom were on the verge of engagement
(b) Because Austen was a Clergyman's daughter
(c) Both (a) and (b)
(d) None of the above

**11.** When did Austen's second brush with marriage occur?
(a) At 27 age (b) At 23 age
(c) At 26 age (d) None of these

**12.** Where did Austen lived her last eight years of her life?
(a) Chawton (b) Steventon
(c) Southampton (d) None of these

**13.** What stopped her from her work on the novel Sandition?
(a) Addison's disease (b) Leprosy
(c) Malaria (d) None of these

**14.** When did Jane Austen die?
(a) 1818 (b) 1819 (c) 1820 (d) 1817

**15.** Who learns the error of making hasty judgements and comes to appreciate the difference between the superficial and the essential?
(a) Bingley (b) Darcy (c) Elizabeth (d) Jane

**16.** Mr Bennet of the Longbourne Estate has
(a) 4 daughters (b) 5 daughters
(c) 6 daughters (d) 3 daughters

**17.** Where do the Bennets live?
(a) London (b) Meryton (c) Kent (d) Hertfordshire

**18.** What is the name of the Bennet estate?
*Or* The Bennet family lives in the village of .......
(a) Longbourn (b) Netherfield
(c) Pemberley (d) Rosings

**19.** With whom does Lydia go to Brighton?
(a) Mrs Bennet (b) Mrs Philips
(c) Mrs Forster (d) Wickham

**20.** Who is the governess who betrays Georgiana Darcy?
(a) Miss Price (b) Mrs Williams
(c) Miss Denny (d) Miss Younge

**21.** Mrs Bennet's reaction to Lydia's marriage is best described as
(a) indifferent (b) condemnatory
(c) cautiously pleased (d) unreservedly jubilant

**22.** Why does Mr Collins come to Longbourn?
(a) He wants to redecorate it
(b) He wants to become acquainted with his relatives
(c) He is looking for a wife
(d) He is passing through town

**23.** Who is Mr Collins's patroness?
(a) Mrs Lucas (b) Mrs Hurst
(c) Lady Catherine (d) Lady Anne

**24.** What is Mr Gardiner's profession?
(a) Clergyman (b) Lawyer (c) Army officer (d) Merchant

**25.** What feature initially attracts Darcy to Elizabeth?
(a) Her smile (b) Her cheerfulness
(c) Her intelligence (d) Her eyes

**26.** Why doesn't Bingley visit Jane while she is in London?
(a) He doesn't know that she's there
(b) Lady Catherine forbids him from going
(c) He thinks that Jane does not like him
(d) Darcy advises him against it

**27.** What is the name of the Estate that Bingley rents?
(a) Longbourne (b) Fox Hall
(c) Netherfield (d) Rosings

**28.** Why does Elizabeth reject Darcy's initial proposal?
(a) He is too poor
(b) She does not like him
(c) It was customary for women at that time to reject the first proposal
(d) She is in love with someone else

**29.** What event interrupts Elizabeth's vacation with the Gardiners?
(a) The death of Mr Collins
(b) Darcy's second proposal
(c) Lydia's elopement with Wickham
(d) The news of Jane's engagement to Bingley

**30.** Which of the Bennet sisters dislikes social events?
(a) Lydia (b) Mary (c) Kitty (d) Jane

**31.** Where do Lydia and Wickham go when they run off from Brighton together?
(a) Gloucester (b) London (c) Scotland (d) Kent

**32.** Why does Wickham flee from Brighton?
(a) He has been fired from his post on account of misconduct.
(b) He has accumulated over 1,000 pounds gaming debts.
(c) He wants to leave the militia and become a clergyman.
(d) He has fallen madly in love with Lydia.

**33.** Mr Bennet responds to the news of Elizabeth's engagement with
(a) resignation (b) skepticism
(c) anger (d) unreserved joy

**34.** Who finds Lydia and Wickham in London?
(a) Mr Darcy (b) Mr Gardiner
(c) Mrs Gardiner (d) Mr Bennet

**35.** What is the name of Darcy's Estate?
(a) Mansfield Park (b) Netherfield
(c) Northgate (d) Pemberley

**36.** Why does Charlotte marry Mr Collins?
(a) She wants financial security
(b) She enjoys conversing with him
(c) Elizabeth advises her to do so
(d) She is flattered by his affection

**37.** Whom does Caroline want Mr Bingley to marry?
(a) Jane (b) Miss De Bourgh
(c) Georgiana Darcy (d) Miss Hurst

**38.** How many children do the Gardiners have?
(a) Five (b) Two (c) Four (d) No Children

**39.** After finding out about Lydia's elopement, Elizabeth runs into
(a) Mrs Gardiner (b) Mr Gardiner
(c) Darcy (d) Charlotte Lucas

**40.** Which of the Bennet sisters is the youngest?
(a) Mary (b) Elizabeth (c) Lydia (d) Kitty

**41.** Which daughter is Mrs Bennet's favorite?
(a) Elizabeth (b) Kitty
(c) Lydia (d) Jane

**42.** Elizabeth initially believes Wickham's charges against Darcy.
(a) True (b) False
(c) Partially true (d) Partially false

**43.** Who supports Elizabeth in her rejection of Collins's marriage proposal?
(a) Lydia (b) Mr Bennet (c) Jane (d) Mrs Bennet

**44.** Why does Lizzy go to Netherfield?
(a) To ask them to attend a ball at Longbourne
(b) To nurse Jane back to health
(c) To confront Darcy for his rudeness
(d) To apologise for Lizzy's behavior

**45.** After the Meryton ball, what does Elizabeth ironically accuse Jane of ?
(a) Of being coy (b) Of being reticent
(c) Of being blind (d) Of being over chatty

**46.** Why is Elizabeth so sure Wickham will not marry Lydia?
(a) Because he will tire of her in a fortnight
(b) Because he will never get Mr Bennet's consent
(c) Because Lydia is too young to be legally married
(d) Because of her lack of family fortune

**47.** In whom is Jane interested at the Meryton ball?
(a) Bingley (b) Colonel Fitzwilliam
(c) Collins (d) Darcy

**48.** Elizabeth thinks that ......... is the woman whom Darcy saved a friend from marrying.
(a) Herself (b) Charlotte (c) Lydia (d) Jane

**49.** Elizabeth readily agrees to Darcy's second marriage proposal. The statement is
(a) False (b) True (c) Partially true
(d) Partially false

**50.** Why does Collins select Elizabeth rather than Jane as his potential wife?
(a) He thinks Elizabeth is better looking
(b) He thinks Elizabeth will be an interesting challenge
(c) He is told that Jane already has a suitor
(d) He thinks Jane is too timid

**51.** Which of the following is not one of the reasons Elizabeth rejects Darcy's first marriage proposal?
(a) For his arrogance
(b) For his refusal to apologise
(c) For Jane and Bingley's separation
(d) For the way he treated Wickham

**52.** How does Darcy feel about Elizabeth's nursing of her ill sister, Jane?
(a) He thinks she is being ridiculous
(b) He thinks Elizabeth is trying to make him feel sorry for her
(c) He thinks it's another sign of her being 'common'
(d) He is impressed by her devotion

**53.** Which of the following does Darcy do after locating Wickham and Lydia?
(a) Pays off Wickham's debts
(b) Puts Wickham on a steamer headed for America
(c) Makes Wickham publicly apologise
(d) Has the marriage annulled

**54.** Darcy resolves Wickham's problems because he feels guilty about his treatment of the man. The statement is
(a) True (b) False
(c) Partially true (d) Partially false

**55.** Whom does Darcy prevent from marrying Wickham?
(a) Elizabeth (b) Charlotte
(c) Georgiana (d) Lydia

**56.** What transgression against Wickham is Darcy falsely accused of ?
(a) Of speaking ill of Wickham to a potential employer
(b) Of stealing Wickham's girlfriend
(c) Of excluding Wickham from an important society function
(d) Of cutting Wickham out of Darcy's father's will

**57.** What did Darcy lose when Elizabeth refused his first proposal?
(a) His prejudice (b) His self-respect
(c) His vanity (d) His heart

**58.** How does Darcy describe the guests at the Meryton ball?
(a) Rude (b) Unfashionable
(c) Common (d) Uncouth

**59.** Who tries to prevent Darcy from proposing Elizabeth for the second time?
(a) Colonel Fitzwilliam (b) Bingley
(c) Lady De Bourgh (d) Georgiana Darcy

**60.** Who buys an Estate near Darcy and Elizabeth?
(a) Colonel Fitzwilliam and Georgiana
(b) Lydia and Wickham
(c) Bingley and Jane
(d) Collin and Charlotte

**61.** What is Collins' job?
(a) Parson (b) Estate lawyer
(c) Doctor (d) Shopkeeper

**62.** Why is Collins going to inherit Longbourn?
(a) Mr Bennet owes a debt to Collins father
(b) He holds the note on the property
(c) Only men can inherit property
(d) Mr Bennet believes he deserves it as a man

**63.** How is Collins related to Mr Bennet?
(a) Nephew (b) Cousin
(c) Grandfather (d) Godfather

**64.** The novel, Pride and Prejudice, ends with
(a) Darcy marrying Elizabeth and Bingley marrying Jane
(b) Darcy marrying Elizabeth and Bingley marrying Miss Darcy
(c) Bingley marrying Jane and Elizabeth marrying Wickham
(d) Darcy marrying Elizabeth and Wickham marrying Jane

**65.** Which of the following best describes Collins?
(a) Sincere (b) Down-to-earth
(c) Well-meaning (d) Pompous

**66.** What did Wickham take in exchange of his parsonage?
(a) An Estate in America
(b) A sailing vessel
(c) A gold watch
(d) Three thousand pounds

**67.** How does Wickham know Darcy?
(a) They had served in the military together
(b) They grew up together
(c) Wickham used to date Darcy's sister
(d) They had been college room-mate

**68.** With whom did Wickham elope?
(a) Mary (b) Kitty
(c) Georgiana (d) Lydia

**69.** What had the elder Mr Darcy bequeathed to Wickham?
(a) A cottage (b) A parsonage
(c) A sailing vessel (d) Pemberley

**70.** For what does Darcy mistake Jane's mild-mannered nature?
(a) Snobbery (b) Timidity (c) Contempt (d) Indifference

**71.** Jane is younger than Elizabeth.
(a) False (b) True
(c) Not mentioned in the novel (d) Both are twins

**72.** Whom does Jane wed?
(a) Collins (b) Wickham
(c) Bingley (d) Colonel Fitzwilliam

**73.** Who nurses Jane back to health when she falls ill at Netherfield?
(a) Mrs Bennet (b) Georgiana
(c) Elizabeth (d) Charlotte

**74.** Which of the following best characterises Lady Catherine De Bourgh's manner of speaking?
(a) Tricky (b) Shy
(c) Frank (d) Falsely cheerful

**75.** Lady Catherine De Bourgh wants..........to marry her daughter.
(a) Bingley (b) Colonel Fitzwilliam
(c) Collins (d) Darcy

**76.** To whom does Lady Catherine De Bourgh acts as benefactor?
(a) Bingley (b) Wickham (c) Darcy (d) Collins

**77.** Who speaks frankly to Lady Catherine De Bourgh?
(a) Jane (b) Miss De Bourgh
(c) Elizabeth (d) Lydia

**78.** How is Lady Catherine De Bourgh related to Darcy?
***Or*** Lady Catherine De Bourgh is Darcy's :
(a) Aunt (b) Sister
(c) Mother (d) First wife

**79.** Mr Bennet married for love. The statement is
(a) True (b) False
(c) Partially true (d) Partially false

**80.** How does Mr Bennet make a living?
(a) He lives off the interest from a large inheritance
(b) He is a doctor
(c) He is a lawyer
(d) The revenue generated from his Estate

**81.** Who is Mr Bennet's favorite child?
(a) Jane (b) Elizabeth (c) Lydia (d) Mary

**82.** Why must Mr Bennet let Mr Collins inherit Longbourn?
(a) Collins actually holds the note on the property
(b) Only males can inherit property
(c) Mr Bennet does not think any of his daughters capable of running the Estate
(d) Mr Bennet owes a huge debt to Collins' father

**83.** How is Mr Bennet related to Collins?
(a) Grandfather (b) Nephew (c) Brother (d) Uncle

**84.** Lydia is the middle child. The statement is
(a) True (b) False
(c) Not mentioned in novel (d) Irrelevant

**85.** Which of the following best describes Lydia?
(a) Serious (b) Grounded (c) Thoughtful (d) Flighty

**86.** Who resolves Lydia and Wickham's financial difficulties?
(a) Darcy (b) Colonel Fitzwilliam
(c) Bingley (d) Lady Catherine

**87.** How old is Lydia?
(a) 15 (b) 20 (c) 16 (d) 18

**88.** With whom does Lydia elope?
(a) Colonel Fitzwilliam (b) Bingley
(c) Collins (d) Wickham

**89.** Mrs Bennet is generally ................. by her husband.
(a) ignored (b) ridiculed
(c) defended (d) abused

**90.** What is Mrs Bennet's main goal in life?
(a) To make her husband look foolish
(b) To remain wealthy
(c) To attend posh balls
(d) To see her daughters got married

**91.** Mrs Bennet's chief criteria is that her daughters marry for love. The statement is
(a) False (b) True
(c) Partially true (d) Partially false

**92.** Which of the following best describes Mrs Bennet?
(a) Shallow (b) Intellectual
(c) Cruel (d) Fair-minded

**93.** How do Elizabeth and Jane generally feel about their mother?
(a) They want to protect her
(b) They are usually angry with her
(c) They think she is doing her best
(d) They are embarrassed by her

**94.** Which couple does Bingley introduce to one another?
(a) Colonel Fitzwilliam and Kitty (b) Collins and Charlotte
(c) Lydia and Wickham (d) Darcy and Elizabeth

**95.** Whose Estate is near Bingley's own property?
(a) Colonel Fitzwilliam's (b) Lady Catherine's
(c) Darcy's (d) The Bennet's

**96.** Who does Bingley marry?
(a) Mary (b) Lydia (c) Georgiana (d) Jane

**97.** How are Bingley and Darcy related?
(a) Cousins (b) They are friends
(c) Nephew and uncle (d) Brothers

**98.** Lizzy agrees with Charlotte Lucas' advice for Jane. The statement is
(a) True (b) False (c) Partially true
(d) Partially false

**99.** Which Bennet(s) do the Bingley sisters favor?
(a) Kitty and Lydia (b) Elizabeth and Jane
(c) Mr Bennet (d) Mrs Bennet

**100.** What does Charlotte Lucas say Jane should alter about her conduct toward Mr Bingley?
(a) Jane should stop leading him on since she does not have feelings for him
(b) Jane should learn to conceal her emotions
(c) Jane should pull him aside and announce her love for him
(d) Jane should be more openly affectionate

**101.** Who does Sir William Lucas attempt to convince to dance with Mr Darcy?
(a) Mary Bennet (b) Charlotte Lucas
(c) Elizabeth Bennet (d) Lydia Bennet

**102.** Despite disliking her at first, Darcy comes to regard which young lady as his favourite?
(a) Jane Bennet (b) Charlotte Lucas
(c) Elizabeth Bennet
(d) Darcy says he has found no tolerable woman

**103.** What occupies the younger Bennet sisters during this chapter?
(a) Studying for their Latin examinations
(b) Preparing for the ball at Netherfield
(c) The girls found no occupation to amuse them; they continually complained about their boredom
(d) A militia regiment came to Meryton

**104.** Rain was coming, so why does Jane not take a carriage to Netherfield?
(a) The carriage had a leak was currently being repaired
(b) Mr Bennet refused to allow Jane to go to the party, so she secretly snuck out of the house
(c) Mrs Bennet wanted Jane to get caught in the rain and be unable to return home immediately; she hoped Mr Bingley would return to Netherfield before Jane left
(d) Lizzy had taken the carriage to Meryton

**105.** Why does Lizzy decide to go to Netherfield?
(a) Caroline Bingley invited her to join the party
(b) She wanted to see Darcy
(c) Jane was sick
(d) She had left her coat there on her last visit

**106.** Who invited Jane to a small gathering at Netherfield?
(a) Charles Bingley
(b) Fitzwilliam Darcy
(c) Caroline Bingley
(d) Charlotte Lucas

**107.** How did Mr Bennet punish Lydia and Kitty for their 'silly' conduct?
(a) He assigned them extra chores on the Estate
(b) He refused to let them go to the upcoming ball
(c) He did not punish them
(d) He grounded them for two weeks

**108.** Who did the Netherfield party send for?
(a) Charlotte Lucas (b) Mrs Bennet
(c) Elizabeth Bennet (d) Mr Jones

**109.** Elizabeth believes that she knows at least a dozen women who meet Darcy's characterisation of an accomplished woman. This statement is
(a) True (b) False
(c) Ambiguous (d) Hackened

**110.** According to Darcy, what is the mark of a truly accomplished woman?
(a) Proficiency in Latin phaedra
(b) The ability to play multiple musical instruments
(c) The improvement of her mind by extensive reading
(d) The ability to converse on a variety of topics, including culture, politics and economics

**111.** What do the Bingley sisters say about Lizzy behind her back?
(a) She had been rude to Mr Bingley at the ball
(b) She was a lovely woman
(c) She was fairer than Jane
(d) She had bad manners

**112.** Of the Netherfield party, who appears to show the most genuine regard for Jane's recovery?
(a) Charles Bingley
(b) Caroline Bingley
(c) No one at Netherfield shows any regard for Jane
(d) Mr Hurst

**113.** Which woman exposes her poor manners and lack of social grace?
(a) Elizabeth Bennet (b) Mrs Bennet
(c) Mrs Hurst (d) Caroline Bingley

**114.** Who does Mrs Bennet say is the prettiest Bennet daughter?
(a) Jane (b) Elizabeth (c) Lydia (d) Mary

**115.** What prompts Mr Bingley to promise to hold a ball at Netherfield?
(a) Mrs Bennet impolitely asks him whether he does not plan to keep his earlier promise to hold the ball
(b) Darcy mentions that he regrets not dancing more at the earlier ball
(c) Jane tells him she thinks it would cheer her spirits and help her recovery
(d) Lydia abruptly reminds him of his earlier promise

**116.** How did Mrs Bennet react to Jane's illness upon seeing her at Netherfield?
(a) Upon seeing how serious Jane's illness was, she immediately regretted forcing Jane to travel to Netherfield on horseback in the rain
(b) Upon realising she was not deathly ill, she hoped her recovery would be prolonged so Jane could extend her stay at Netherfield
(c) Mrs Bennet was angry with Jane not being careful about her own health
(d) Mrs Bennet became angry with Mr Bennet for ignoring the demand of a carriage by Jane

**117.** According to Austen, Lydia had .......... spirits.
(a) refined (b) angelic (c) animal (d) subdued

**118.** Why does Elizabeth think Darcy keeps staring at her?
(a) She had sauce on her face
(b) He found her more reprehensible than any person present
(c) He is annoyed at her for interrupting him
(d) He was in love with her

**119.** Who continually interrupts Darcy while he tries to write a letter to his sister?
(a) Elizabeth (b) Mr Bingley (c) Mrs Bennet (d) Miss Bingley

**120.** What does Darcy believe saves him from being in danger due to his crush on Elizabeth?
(a) His nearing departure from Netherfield
(b) The inferiority of her connections
(c) He believes Elizabeth hates him
(d) He is engaged to Caroline

**121.** What does Darcy say about humility?
(a) It has no purpose
(b) It is the principle virtue of a prudent woman
(c) It is Mr Bingley's highest virtue
(d) It is deceitful

**122.** What does Caroline tease Darcy about?
(a) His hatred of dancing
(b) Marrying Elizabeth
(c) His sober manner
(d) His relationship with his sister

**123.** Select the character who makes the following observation: "There is, I believe, in every disposition a tendency to some particular evil, a natural defect, which not even the best education can overcome".
(a) Darcy (b) Charles
(c) Jane (d) Elizabeth

**124.** What is Mr Hurst's sole source of entertainment?
(a) Writing letters to his mistress (b) Pheasant hunting
(c) Playing cards (d) Reading

**125.** What does Darcy say is Lizzy's defect?
(a) To ignore the virtues in others
(b) To wilfully misunderstand other people
(c) To ignore the vices in others
(d) To hate others with undue cause

**126.** What does Lizzy say is Darcy's defect?
(a) A propensity to talk badly about others behind their backs
(b) A propensity to think himself greater than he ought to
(c) A propensity to hate everybody
(d) A propensity to trust others too easily

**127.** Who invites Lizzy to walk about the room?
(a) Darcy (b) Mrs Hurst
(c) Caroline (d) Jane

**128.** How did Darcy behave toward Elizabeth during her final day at Netherfield?
(a) He talked to her constantly and scarcely left her side
(b) He ignored her
(c) Both (a) and (b)
(d) None of the above

**129.** Of the Bennet family members, who was the most happy to see Jane and Elizabeth return?
(a) Mary (b) Lydia
(c) Mr Bennet (d) Mrs Bennet

**130.** Who does Mr. Bennet announce will attend dinner?
(a) Mr Collins (b) Mr Darcy
(c) Sir William Lucas (d) Mr Bingley

**131.** In what denomination was Collins recently ordained?
(a) Methodist
(b) Presbyterian
(c) Church of England
(d) Roman Catholic Church

**132.** Why does Mrs Bennet show such contempt for Mr Collins?
(a) He feigned attraction for her when they were children.
(b) He is a drunkard
(c) She thinks that he stole a silver candlestick during his last visit to Longbourn
(d) He is heir to the Bennet Estate

**133.** What event interrupts Elizabeth's vacation with Gardiners ?
(a) the death of Mr. Collins
(b) Lydia's elopment with Wickham
(c) Darcy's second proposal
(d) the news of Jane's engagement to Bingley

**134.** How does Collins feel about his Patron/Patroness?
(a) He has not yet met his Patron/Patroness
(b) He cannot stand him/her
(c) He is enamoured with him/her
(d) None of the above

**135.** Who interrupts Collins while he is reading?
(a) Jane (b) Elizabeth (c) Lydia (d) Mr Bennet

**136.** What type of book does Collins choose to read aloud to the Bennets?
(a) A book of sermons
(b) A history of the Roman Empire
(c) A scandalous romance
(d) A science fiction novel

**137.** After learning the prospects of marriage with his desired choice were dim, which Bennet daughter did Collins turn his attentions to?
(a) Mary (b) Jane (c) Elizabeth (d) Lydia

**138.** How had Mr Collins acquired his position as a parson?
(a) Merit
(b) An elaborate interview process
(c) Chance
(d) Family connections

**139.** The Bennets met both Mr Wickham and Mr Darcy in town. How did the two men react when they bumped into one another?
(a) They embraced each other
(b) They laughed at an inside joke from their childhood
(c) They had never met before, so they introduced themselves
(d) They appeared awkward and uncomfortable

**140.** How did Collins intend to 'make amends' to the Bennets for being the heir to Mr Bennet's Estate?
(a) Relinquishing his claim to the Bennet Estate
(b) Marrying one of the Bennet daughters
(c) Providing the Bennet daughters with a large income
(d) Purchasing the Bennet Estate from Mr Bennet before his death

**141.** Which Bennet daughter did Collins first desire to marry?
(a) Lydia (b) Kitty
(c) Jane (d) Elizabeth

**142.** What was the name of Darcy's sister?
(a) Jane (b) Lydia
(c) Georgiana (d) Elizabeth

**143.** What vice does Wickham accuse Darcy of?
(a) Something else (b) Prejudice
(c) Pride (d) None of these

**144.** According to Wickham, who had stolen his inheritance?
(a) Wickham's drunken father (b) Darcy
(c) His accountant (d) Bingley

**145.** What was Wickham's relationship to the late Mr Darcy (Fitzwilliam Darcy's father)?
(a) Nephew (b) Godson
(c) Adopted son (d) Illegitimate child

**146.** What profession did Wickham say he had been brought up for?
(a) Lawyer (b) Soldier
(c) Doctor (d) Clergyman

**147.** With whom did Elizabeth converse at length while visiting her aunt and uncle Philips?
(a) Mr Bingley
(b) Mr Jones
(c) Mr Darcy
(d) Mr Wickham

**148.** What did Elizabeth realise about Collins towards the end of the chapter?
(a) He opposed all amusements such as dancing and gambling
(b) He was gravely ill
(c) He intended to ask her to marry him
(d) He had lied about his position and wealth

**149.** What was the Bennet family making preparations for?
(a) A fair in Meryton
(b) An important dinner at Longbourn
(c) A ball at Netherfield
(d) A trip to London

**150.** What was Elizabeth's opinion about Darcy and Wickham?
(a) She sided with Wickham (b) She defended both men
(c) She condemned both the men (d) She sided with Darcy

**151.** Which man did Jane side with after Elizabeth related what Wickham had said about his history with the Darcy family?
(a) She sided with Wickham
(b) She sided with Darcy
(c) She defended both the men
(d) She condemned both the men

**152.** Why was Elizabeth ashamed of her mother?
(a) She tripped and ripped her dress while dancing with Mr Bennet
(b) She invited herself to dinner at Netherfield
(c) She told Mr Bingley that Jane was in love with him
(d) She spoke loudly of Jane's inevitable marriage to Mr Bingley while standing in front of Darcy

**153.** Why did Elizabeth accept Darcy's request to dance with her?
(a) She had previously promised to dance with him at the next ball
(b) She was caught off guard and spoke without thinking
(c) It was impolite to refuse an invitation to dance from a man of a higher class
(d) She had begun to develop feelings for him

**154.** Why was Mrs Bennet so pleased at the end of the chapter?
(a) Mr Bingley had asked Mr Bennet for permission to marry Jane
(b) She thought Kitty had been the most graceful dancer at the ball
(c) She believed that she would soon have two daughters married
(d) Darcy had invited the Bennets to Pemberley

**155.** Although, she immediately regretted it, how did Elizabeth purposely wound Darcy?
(a) She refused to talk to him while they were dancing
(b) She brought up Wickham in conversation
(c) She purposely stepped on Darcy's foot while they were dancing
(d) She refused his offer for another dance

**156.** Why didn't Wickham attend the Netherfield ball?
(a) He had a family emergency
(b) He knew Darcy would be there
(c) His militia unit moved to another part of England
(d) He was not invited

**157.** Why was Elizabeth ashamed of Mary?
(a) She was rude to Sir William Lucas
(b) She presumed to play music in public without first being asked
(c) She spoke back to her father in front of Mr Darcy
(d) She engaged in a loud argument with Miss Bingley

**158.** Which bachelor favours Jane?
(a) Collins (b) Charles (c) Pemberley (d) Darcy

**159.** What did Wickham do with the money Darcy had given him?
(a) Invested it
(b) Gave it to Lydia
(c) Lost it is gambling
(d) Refused to take it

**160.** When Darcy first proposes, Elizabeth
(a) Asks for a long engagement (b) Declines
(c) Wants to elope right away
(d) Accepts and sets a date

## ANSWERS

| | | | | | | | | | | | | | | | | | | | |
|---|---|---|---|---|---|---|---|---|---|---|---|---|---|---|---|---|---|---|---|
| 1. | (a) | 2. | (b) | 3. | (a) | 4. | (a) | 5. | (c) | 6. | (a) | 7. | (b) | 8. | (b) | 9. | (a) | 10. | (c) |
| 11. | (a) | 12. | (a) | 13. | (a) | 14. | (d) | 15. | (c) | 16. | (b) | 17. | (d) | 18. | (a) | 19. | (c) | 20. | (d) |
| 21. | (d) | 22. | (c) | 23. | (c) | 24. | (a) | 25. | (c) | 26. | (a) | 27. | (c) | 28. | (b) | 29. | (c) | 30. | (b) |
| 31. | (b) | 32. | (b) | 33. | (b) | 34. | (a) | 35. | (d) | 36. | (a) | 37. | (c) | 38. | (c) | 39. | (c) | 40. | (c) |
| 41. | (c) | 42. | (a) | 43. | (b) | 44. | (b) | 45. | (c) | 46. | (d) | 47. | (a) | 48. | (d) | 49. | (b) | 50. | (c) |
| 51. | (b) | 52. | (c) | 53. | (a) | 54. | (b) | 55. | (c) | 56. | (d) | 57. | (c) | 58. | (c) | 59. | (c) | 60. | (c) |
| 61. | (a) | 62. | (c) | 63. | (b) | 64. | (a) | 65. | (d) | 66. | (d) | 67. | (b) | 68. | (d) | 69. | (b) | 70. | (d) |
| 71. | (a) | 72. | (c) | 73. | (c) | 74. | (c) | 75. | (c) | 76. | (d) | 77. | (c) | 78. | (b) | 79. | (a) | 80. | (d) |
| 81. | (b) | 82. | (b) | 83. | (d) | 84. | (b) | 85. | (d) | 86. | (a) | 87. | (a) | 88. | (d) | 89. | (b) | 90. | (d) |
| 91. | (b) | 92. | (a) | 93. | (d) | 94. | (d) | 95. | (d) | 96. | (d) | 97. | (b) | 98. | (a) | 99. | (b) | 100. | (d) |
| 101. | (d) | 102. | (c) | 103. | (d) | 104. | (c) | 105. | (c) | 106. | (c) | 107. | (c) | 108. | (d) | 109. | (a) | 110. | (c) |
| 111. | (d) | 112. | (a) | 113. | (b) | 114. | (a) | 115. | (d) | 116. | (b) | 117 | .(c) | 118. | (b) | 119. | (d) | 120. | (b) |
| 121. | (d) | 122. | (b) | 123. | (a) | 124. | (c) | 125. | (b) | 126. | (c) | 127. | (c) | 128. | (b) | 129. | (c) | 130. | (a) |
| 131. | (c) | 132. | (d) | 133. | (d) | 134. | (c) | 135. | (c) | 136. | (a) | 137. | (c) | 138. | (c) | 139. | (d) | 140. | (d) |
| 141. | (d) | 142. | (c) | 143. | (c) | 144. | (b) | 145. | (d) | 146. | (d) | 147. | (d) | 148. | (c) | 149. | (d) | 150. | (a) |
| 151. | (c) | 152. | (d) | 153. | (b) | 154. | (c) | 155. | (b) | 156. | (d) | 157. | (b) | 158. | (b) | 159. | (c) | 160. | (b) |

Chapter 17

# A Tale of Two Cities

*Charles Dickens*

## About the Author

### Early life

Charles Dickens is a Victorian novelist who created some of the most memorable characters in English Literature, while also criticising the worst excesses of Victorian society. Charles Dickens was born in Portsmouth on 7th February 1812, to John and Elizabeth Dickens. As a child, Charles experienced the fickle hands of fate; he was first taught at a private school before being removed because of his family's financial hardship. Charles managed to escape the grind of factory work, by training to be a shorthand writer and gaining employment as a journalist and reporting on court cases.

### Literary Career

In 1833, he became a parliamentary journalist for the Morning Chronicle. The young Dickens was fascinated with the Houses of Parliament, though he was often left with a lowly impression of the MPs. Shortly after this, he began writing his first serialised stories, published under a pseudonym – Boz. In 1836, he married Catherine Hogarth. That year, he saw the first publication of 'The Pickwick Papers'. His first book proved to be a great seller, and this enabled him to become a full-time writer.

There are various themes which run throughout his writings, which often reflect a degree of autobiography. He frequently highlighted the worst excesses of Victorian society and made a passionate case for a more caring and moral society. Dickens was a noted philanthropist helping to raise funds for charities, such as Great Ormond Street. He also helped to set up a home for fallen women. Redemption was an important aspect of Dickens' philosophy and he often criticised harsh and punitive punishments, such as solitary confinement. Dickens died on June 8th, 1870 after a stroke. He published well over a dozen major novels and novellas, a large number of short stories, including a number of Christmas-themed stories, a handful of plays, and several non-fiction books.

### Major works

- Oliver Twist (1839)
- A Christmas Carol (1843)
- The Chimes (1844)
- The Haunted Man (1848)
- David Copperfield (1850)
- Bleak House (1853)
- Hard Times (1854)
- A Tale of Two Cities (1859)
- Great Expectations (1861)

## Summary

### Jarvis Lorry Reunites Dr Manette with His Daughter

The year is 1775, and social ills plague both France and England.The early rumblings of the French Revolution are echoing across the English Channel when, in Paris, an old man waits in an attic for his first meeting with a daughter whom he has not seen since she was a baby. With the aid of Mr. Jarvis Lorry, an agent for the Franco-British banking house of Tellson & Co, the lovely Lucie Manette is brought to Paris to be reunited with her father, who was imprisoned for eighteen years in the Bastille.

Above the wine shop of Madame and Monsieur Defarge, Dr. Manette is kept secretly until his rescuers can take him safely back to England. Day after day, Madame Defarge sits outside her wine shop, knitting into a long scarf strange symbols that will later spell out a death list of hated aristocrats and enemies of the Revolution.Five years later, Lucie sits beside her father in the courtroom of the Old Bailey, where Charles Darnay, a teacher of languages, is on trial for treasonable activities that involve his passing between France and England on secret business. A man named John Barsad brings charges against him. Lucie and her father testify that they met Darnay on the boat when they travelled from France five years earlier. The prisoner was saved when Mr Stryver, the prisoner's counsel, pointed across the courtroom to another man, Sydney Carton, who so resembled the prisoner that legal identification of Darnay was shaken and Mr Stryver was able to secure an acquittal for the prisoner. Carton's relationship to Stryver is that of the jackal to the lion; the alcoholic, aimless Carton writes the cases that Stryver pleads in court. Lucie and her father live in a small tenement under the care of their maid, Miss Pross, and their kind friend, Mr. Lorry. Jerry Cruncher, the porter at Tellson & Co and a secret resurrectionist, is often helpful. Darnay and Carton become frequent callers in the Manette household, after the trial that brought them together.

## Charles Darnay's Family Commits Grave Injustices on Peasants in France

In France, the fury of the people grows. Monseigneur the Marquis St. Evrémonde is driving in his carriage through the countryside when he carelessly kills a child of a peasant named Gaspard. The nobleman returns to his castle to meet his nephew, Charles Darnay, who is visiting from England. Darnay's views differ from those of his uncle. Darnay knows that his family committed grave injustices, and he begs his uncle to make amends. Monseigneur the Marquis haughtily refuses. That night, the Marquis is murdered in his bed.

Darnay returns to England to seek Dr Manette's permission to court Lucie. In order to construct a bond of complete honesty, Darnay attempts to tell the doctor his true French name, but Manette fearfully asks him to wait until the morning of his marriage before revealing it. Carton also approaches Lucie with a proposal of marriage. When Lucie refuses, Carton asks her always to remember that there is a man who will give his own life to keep a life she loves beside her.

In France, Madame Defarge knits the story of the hated St Evrémondes into her scarf. Gaspard was hanged for the assassination of the Marquis; Monseigneur's house must be destroyed. Barsad, the spy, brings news that Lucie will marry Darnay, the nephew of the Marquis. This news disturbs Defarge, for Dr Manette, a former prisoner of the Bastille, holds a special honour in the eyes of the revolutionaries.

## The French Revolution Starts

Lucie and Darnay are married. Carton becomes a loyal friend of the family. Time passes, and tiny Lucie arrives. When the child is six years old, in the year 1789, the French people storm the Bastille. At the Bastille, Defarge goes to the cell where Dr Manette was a prisoner and extracts some papers hidden behind a stone in the wall.

One day, while Darnay is talking to Mr Lorry at Tellson & Co, a letter addressed to the Marquis St Evrémonde is placed on Mr Lorry's desk. Darnay offers to deliver it to the proper person. When he is alone, he reads the letter. It is from an old family servant who is imprisoned by the revolutionaries. He begs the Marquis St Evrémonde to save his life. Darnay realises that he must go to Paris. Only Dr Manette knows of Darnay's family name, and the doctor is sworn to secrecy.

## Darnay Returns to Paris to Save a Former Servant

Darnay and Mr Lorry go to Paris, the latter to look after the French branch of Tellson & Co Shortly after his arrival, Darnay is arrested as an undesirable immigrant after Defarge orders his arrest. Mr Lorry is considerably upset when Lucie and Dr Manette suddenly arrive in Paris. Some of the doctor's friends inform him of Darnay's arrest. The old man feels that his own imprisonment in the Bastille will win the sympathy of the revolutionaries and enable him to save his son-in-law.

## Darnay is Brought to Trial for His Uncle's Crimes

After fifteen months of waiting, Darnay is brought to trial. Because he is able to prove himself innocent of harming the French people, he is freed but forbidden to leave France. A short time later, he is again arrested, denounced by Defarge and one other person whose name the officer refuses to disclose. While shopping one day in the Paris market, Miss Pross and Jerry Cruncher, who are in Paris with Lucie and Mr Lorry, meet a man who causes Miss Pross to scream in amazement and Jerry to stare in silent astonishment. The man is Solomon, Miss Pross's lost brother. Jerry remembers him as Barsad, the man who was a spy-witness at the Old Bailey. Carton arrives on the scene at that moment, and he is able to force Barsad to come with him to the office of Tellson & Co for a private conference. Barsad fears detection of his duplicity, for he is now an employee of the Republican French Government. Carton and Jerry threaten to expose him as a former spy for the English government, the enemy of France. Carton makes a deal with Barsad.

## Darnay is Sentenced to Death at the Guillotine

When Darnay is once more brought before the tribunal, Defarge testifies against him and names Dr Manette as the other accuser. Defarge produces the papers that he found in Dr Manette's cell in the Bastille. Therein the doctor wrote the story of his arrest and imprisonment because he learned of a secret crime committed by a St Evrémonde against a woman of humble birth and her young brother. His account is enough to convict Darnay. Sentenced for the crimes of his ancestors, Darnay, the young St Evrémonde, is condemned by the tribunal to the guillotine.

## Sydney Carton, Who Resembles Darnay, Sacrifices His Life

Carton now begins to visit the Defarge wine shop, where he learns that Madame Defarge is the sister of the woman ruined by St Evrémonde years before. With the help of the false Barsad, he gains admittance to the prison where Darnay was taken. There he drugs the prisoner and, still aided by Barsad, has him carried from the cell, himself remaining behind. The resemblance between the two will allow him to pass as Darnay and prevent discovery of the aristocrat's escape.

Madame Defarge goes to the lodgings of Lucie and Dr Manette to denounce them. Only Miss Pross is there; the others, including Darnay, are already on their way to safety.

### Carton is Executed white Darnay Returns to London

To keep Madame Defarge from learning of their escape, Miss Pross struggles with the furious woman when she demands admittance to Lucie's apartment. Madame Defarge is killed when her pistol goes off. Miss Pross is deaf for the rest of her life. Lucie and Darnay return safely to England. Carton dies at the guillotine, giving up his own life for the happiness of those he loved.

## Practice Questions

**1. A Tale of Two Cities opens in 1775. Which of the following does not characterise this period?**
(a) The British colonies in America have just presented a list of grievances to the King of England.
(b) Crime and capital punishment plague the streets of London.
(c) The guillotine stands as a much-feared fixture on the streets of Paris.
(d) The French aristocracy causes great suffering among the lower classes.

**2. Why are the drivers of the Dover mail coach hesitant to stop for Jerry Cruncher's message?**
(a) They fear that he is a highwayman attempting to rob the passengers.
(b) They fear that stopping will put them behind schedule for delivering the mail in a timely fashion.
(c) They have been charged with the safety of Jarvis Lorry, one of the coach's passengers.
(d) Jerry Cruncher's troublesome reputation precedes him.

**3. What object does Doctor Manette keep during his imprisonment in order to escape "in spirit"?**
(a) A picture of his wife and daughter
(b) The Bible
(c) A keg of wine
(d) A lock of his wife's hair

**4. By what name do the men in Defarge's wine shop call their fellow revolutionaries?**
(a) Jacques (b) Pierre (c) Jasper (d) Xavier

**5. What skill did Doctor Manette develop in order to pass the time during his incarceration?**
(a) Drawing (b) Whittling
(c) Shoemaking (d) Storytelling

**6. What symbol does Dickens use to portend the bloodshed of the French Revolution?**
(a) The Dover mail coach
(b) The broken wine cask
(c) Tellson's Bank
(d) Madame Defarge's malevolent stare

**7. During her testimony, to whom does Lucie claim that Charles Darnay alluded on the boat ride from Calais to Dover?**
(a) Louis XVI (b) John Adams
(c) Napoleon Bonaparte
(d) George Washington

**8. After Darnay's acquittal, why does Sydney Carton claim to dislike him?**
(a) Darnay is unattractive and mean-spirited.
(b) Darnay abuses the love of Lucie Manette.
(c) Darnay reminds him of how far he has fallen and everything he might have been.
(d) Even though he has been acquitted, Darnay is a traitor.

**9. To which animal does Dickens compare Sydney Carton?**
(a) A jackal (b) A lion
(c) A weasel (d) A sloth

**10. A Tale of Two Cities was published in weekly installments from April to November of what year?**
(a) 1845 (b) 1859
(c) 1879 (d) 1890

**11. What image does Dickens frequently use to describe Lucie Manette?**
(a) An earth-bound angel (b) A golden thread
(c) A tiger lily (d) A calm in a storm

**12. What sound does Lucie often hear echoing off the street when she is in her home?**
(a) Footsteps (b) Brawling
(c) The yells of the crowd at public executions
(d) A choir singing

**13. Which of the following characters is related to the Marquis, whose carriage runs down a small child?**
(a) Doctor Manette (b) Sydney Carton
(c) Charles Darnay (d) Miss Pross

**14. Who does Miss Pross believe is the ideal suitor for Lucie Manette?**
(a) Sydney Carton (b) Charles Darnay
(c) Her brother, Solomon
(d) She believes that no man is good enough for Lucie.

**15. What does Mr Lorry try to persuade Mr Stryver not to do?**
(a) Propose to Lucie Manette
(b) Invest his money in Tellson's Bank
(c) Drop Sydney Carton as a business colleague
(d) Visit Paris at a time of political turmoil

**16. Who promises Lucie Manette that he would, if necessary, die for her?**
(a) Jarvis Lorry (b) Sydney Carton
(c) Charles Darnay (d) Monsieur Defarge

**17.** What does Jerry Cruncher frequently go out to do at night?
(a) Raid Tellson's Bank
(b) Deliver messages to prisoners in the Bastille
(c) Dig up bodies in the cemetery
(d) Meet with other revolutionaries to plan uprisings

**18.** Who informs the Defarges that Lucie Manette has married Charles Darnay?
(a) The mender of roads (b) Jarvis Lorry
(c) Gaspard (d) John Barsad

**19.** On the night after Lucie and Charles are married, what does Doctor Manette do?
(a) He prepares to join them on their honeymoon.
(b) He reverts to his prison pastime of making shoes.
(c) He confesses to Miss Pross that he thinks Lucie has made a terrible mistake.
(d) He writes a letter to Defarge, asking him to spare Darnay's life.

**20.** During the storming of the Bastille, who decapitates the fortress's guard?
(a) Madame Defarge
(b) Defarge
(c) John Barsad
(d) An anonymous Jacques

**21.** Why does the Paris mob kill Foulon?
(a) Because he is a spy
(b) Because he suggested that starving people should eat grass
(c) Because his carriage ran down a child in the street
(d) Because he collected high taxes from the peasants

**22.** What is the duration of Manette's psychological relapse after Lucie leaves for her honeymoon?
(a) Nine days
(b) Four days
(c) A fortnight
(d) A year and three months

**23.** Who develops a habit of watching and speaking to Lucie as she waits on a Paris street corner each day, hoping that Darnay will be able to see her from his prison window?
(a) Madame Defarge (b) Defarge
(c) A wood-sawyer (d) A seamstress

**24.** Who does the spy John Barsad turn out to be?
(a) Miss Pross' brother, Solomon
(b) A relation of the Marquis Evrémonde
(c) Madame Defarge's long-lost brother
(d) Roger Cly

**25.** Why was Doctor Manette imprisoned?
(a) He stole bread.
(b) He failed to save the life of an aristocrat's daughter.
(c) The Marquis Evrémonde feared that Manette would reveal one of the Marquis' dark secrets.
(d) He was an outspoken critic of the royal family.

**26.** Who is Miss Pross's brother, whose real name is Solomon, and a British spy?
(a) Monsieur Defarge (b) Roger Cly
(c) John Barsad (d) Mr. Lorry

**27.** What is Charles Darnay's real last name?
(a) Defarge (b) Marquis
(c) Gabelle (d) Evremonde

**28.** Whose side occupation is as a "Resurrection-Man"?
(a) Jerry Cruncher (b) Sydney Carton
(c) Doctor Manette (d) Charles Darnay

**29.** What saves Sydney Carton from his self-proclaimed wasted life?
(a) His love for Lucy (b) Giving up alcohol
(c) Finding God
(d) A near death experience

**30.** What did Monsieur Defarge do before he was a wine shop owner and revolutionary?
(a) He was a shoe maker.
(b) He was Doctor Manette's servant.
(c) He was a wood-sawyer.
(d) Nothing, he's actually an aristocrat.

**31.** Which characters go through profound transformations?
(a) Miss Pross and Jerry Cruncher
(b) Doctor Manette and Sydney Carton
(c) Monsieur and Madame Defarge
(d) Charles Darnay and Lucy

**32.** What helps explain Madame Defarge's vengefulness and bloodlust?
(a) Her hero is Lady Macbeth.
(b) Her need to prove that she's a good revolutionary
(c) Her family's suffering at the hands of oppression
(d) Her ambition to rule

**33.** What characterises Lucie?
(a) Love, purity, compassion, devotion
(b) Sensitivity, indecision, timidity
(c) Passion, drama, bold actions
(d) Anger, self-righteousness, defensiveness

**34.** Which character can be interpreted as being redeemed by actions?
(a) Mr. Lorry (b) Jerry Stryver
(c) Sydney Carton (d) Monsieur Defarge

**35.** Which characters have been singled out by critics as being too flat?
(a) Lucie and Charles Darnay
(b) Sydney Carton and Doctor Manette
(c) Jerry Cruncher and Mr. Lorry
(d) Lucy's daughter and Roger Cly

**36.** What does Carton's sacrifice suggest about France's fate?
(a) That all will be well
(b) That France is doomed
(c) That its violence may finally give way to a better society
(d) That the revolutionaries must be overthrown before the country can heal

**37.** What aspect of the revolution does the novel criticise?
(a) That the peasants are not vicious enough
(b) The way the peasants overthrow cruelty with cruelty
(c) The way money was redistributed
(d) That the British were not allowed to help restructure French society

**38.** Which one of these is not 'a double' in the narrative?
(a) England and France
(b) Lucy and Madame Defarge
(c) Monsieur Defarge and Doctor Manette
(d) Carton and Darnay

**39.** To whom is Carton often compared because of his sacrifice?
(a) Job (b) Christ
(c) Gandhi (d) The Buddha

**40.** What does the broken wine cask symbolise?
(a) The purity of the revolutionary dream
(b) Failings of the transport and agricultural ministries
(c) The inability to be washed free of sin
(d) Hunger and a bloodthirsty desire for change

**41.** Where does A Tale of Two Cities take place?
(a) In England and the United States
(b) In France and the United States
(c) In the United States only
(d) In England and France

**42.** What is Mr Lorry's occupation?
(a) Bodyguard
(b) He works for a bank called Tellson's.
(c) He runs a wine shop.
(d) Doctor

**43.** Where does Lucy Manette think her father has been?
(a) In the Americas (b) Missing
(c) Dead (d) In prison

**44.** How long did Doctor Manette spend in prison?
(a) 36 years
(b) Doctor Manette was a shoemaker, not a prisoner.
(c) About 7 years
(d) Almost 18 years

**45.** Where must Mr Lorry and Lucy go to get Doctor Manette?
(a) To the house of an old servant in Paris
(b) To Tellson's bank in London
(c) To the Royal George Hotel in Dover
(d) To the Bastille in Paris

**46.** What happens when a cask of wine spills along the street in Paris?
(a) People think it's blood and run screaming.
(b) A young boy slips and drowns in it.
(c) Monsieur Defarge is arrested for inciting a riot.
(d) Everyone rushes to drink some.

**47.** What is Jacques a codename for?
(a) Spies (b) Englishmen
(c) Revolutionaries (d) Aristocrats

**48.** Whom do the three Jacques watch through a hole in the wall in the fifth floor?
(a) Doctor Manette making shoes
(b) Lucy and Mr. Lorry talking about Doctor Manette
(c) Madame Defarge knitting
(d) John Barsad whom they've captured for spying

**49.** Whom does Doctor Manette think Lucy is at first?
(a) Madame Defarge (b) A ghost
(c) His mother (d) His late wife

**50.** What does Lucy want to do now that she's found her father?
(a) Take him back to London immediately
(b) Stay in Paris until he recovers
(c) Leave him and return home alone
(d) Put him in Mr Lorry's care

**51.** What does Jerry Cruncher do for a living?
(a) He's a banker.
(b) He works in a cemetery.
(c) Messenger and runner for Tellson's Bank
(d) He makes rust.

**52.** In what year do these chapters take place?
(a) 1492 (b) 1780 (c) 1917 (d) 1862

**53.** What is Charles Darnay on trial for?
(a) Being a revolutionary (b) Theft
(c) Treason (d) Murder

**54.** Why is Darnay acquitted?
(a) Because Sydney Carton looks just like him
(b) Because of Lucy's testimony
(c) Because of Doctor Manette's testimony
(d) Because the jury liked his impassioned speech

**55.** How does Carton describe himself to Darnay?
(a) Ambitious, vengeful, unforgiving
(b) Generous, devoted, friendly
(c) Disappointed, misanthropic, unloved
(d) Excitable, paranoid, fearful

**56.** How do Stryver and Carton know each other?
(a) Stryver defended Carton once.
(b) Carton saved Stryver's life.
(c) They went to school together.
(d) They are cousins.

**57.** What are Stryver's and Carton's nicknames, respectively?
(a) Lion and Hyena (b) Lion and Jackal
(c) Puffin and Grouse (d) Cheetah and Wolf

**58.** What does Miss Pross complain about?
(a) Doctor Manette making shoes
(b) All the suitors who visit Lucy
(c) How hard it is to keep the house clean
(d) The echo from the streets

**59.** What is Doctor Manette's occupation in London?
(a) Doctor (b) Shoemaker (c) Banker (d) Professor

**60.** What story does Darnay tell that makes Doctor Manette startle and look ill?
(a) About his conversation with Carton
(b) About a cask of wine breaking on the streets of Paris
(c) About a prisoner carving the word "dig" in his cell
(d) About his own experience in shoe making

**61.** What does Marquis Evremonde's carriage run over?
(a) A dog (b) A child
(c) A man who was riding under the carriage
(d) Madame Defarge's sister

**62.** What does the Marquis throw out of his carriage?
(a) A few coins for the man whose son he just killed
(b) Trash
(c) A cask of wine for the angry crowd
(d) A bag of apples

**63.** What does the road-mender tell the Marquis?
(a) That the Marquis killed a child
(b) That the Marquis is an evil aristocrat
(c) That someone was hanging off the back of the Marquis's carriage
(d) That someone was riding under the Marquis's carriage

**64.** What does Darnay tell the Marquis that their family legacy is?
(a) Fear, inhumanity, slavery
(b) Power, wealth, and success
(c) Good works and responsibility
(d) Engagement, philanthropy, and whimsy

**65.** What happens to the Marquis the next morning?
(a) He has four attendants serve him a soft-boiled egg.
(b) He receives a death threat and flees the estate.
(c) He is found stabbed to death by a 'Jacques'.
(d) The road-mender is imprisoned.

**66.** Who tells Doctor Manette of his love for Lucie?
(a) Darnay (b) Carton (c) Stryver (d) Defarge

**67.** Who goes to the bank to tell Mr. Lorry of his intention to propose to Lucie?
(a) Stryver (b) Carton (c) Darnay (d) Cruncher

**68.** What does Mr. Lorry find out about Stryver from Doctor Manette?
(a) Stryver is a revolutionary.
(b) Stryver is a spy.
(c) Stryver has no hope of Lucie marrying him.
(d) Lucie wants to marry him.

**69.** Who tells Lucie he loves her and would die for her?
(a) Carton (b) Darnay
(c) Stryver (d) Mr. Lorry

**70.** What does Carton say about his life?
(a) That he's destined for great things
(b) That he is determined to reform himself
(c) That he had a traumatic childhood
(d) That he's wasted it and he's beyond hope

**71.** Who is the dead man, Roger Cly?
(a) A chimney sweep
(b) A man who testified against Darnay
(c) Miss Pross's brother
(d) Charles Darnay's estate keeper

**72.** What does Jerry Cruncher's son see his father do?
(a) Dig up a corpse (b) Take a bribe
(c) Get in a fight
(d) Receive a reprimand from Mr. Lorry

**73.** What does the mender of roads tell the Jacques about?
(a) That a spy named Barsad is on his way
(b) That Darnay and Lucy are marrying
(c) That the authorities are coming to arrest the Defarges
(d) The execution of the Marquis's murderer

**74.** What is Madame Defarge knitting?
(a) A registry of names of who should be executed after the revolution
(b) She knits the same thing over and over as she spies on people.
(c) Shrouds for the victims of the upcoming revolution
(d) Baby shoes because she is pregnant

**75.** Whose name is added to the registry after the spy Barsad's visit to the wine shop?
(a) The Marquis (b) Doctor Manette
(c) Charles Darnay (d) Lucy Manette

**76.** What do Lucie and Darnay do?
(a) Get in a fight (b) Move to Paris
(c) Get married (d) Buy a house

**77.** What happens to Doctor Manette because of his talk with Darnay?
(a) He refuses to let Lucy marry Darnay.
(b) He leaves the house and Mr. Lorry can't find him for 10 days.
(c) He proposes to Miss Pross.
(d) He falls into a trance and makes shoes again for 10 days.

**78.** What do Mr. Lorry and Miss Pross get Doctor Manette to agree to when he recovers?
(a) To let them tell Lucy what happened to him
(b) To let them destroy his shoe-making bench and bury the tools
(c) To move out so Lucy and Darnay can have their own place
(d) To draw up a will and write them into it

**79.** What do Mr. Lorry and Miss Pross tell Lucy about her father's relapse?
(a) Nothing, but Doctor Manette tells Lucy everything
(b) Nothing
(c) They tell her about it when she and Darnay return from their honeymoon.
(d) They write to her immediately and she rushes home.

**80.** How does Lucy say Darnay should treat Carton?
(a) With sympathy and compassion
(b) With scorn and derision
(c) He should fight him if he ever tries to set foot in their house again.
(d) He should help him get a job.

**81.** Whom do the villagers hang?
(a) A wealthy man who said the starving should eat grass
(b) The Marquis
(c) A group of travelers they mistake for aristocrats
(d) Madame Defarge's sister

**82.** Whose castle do the revolutionaries burn down?
(a) Mr. Lorry's (b) The Defarges'
(c) Napoleon's (d) The late Marquis'

**83.** Who barely escapes from the fire?
(a) John Barsad, a spy
(b) Gabelle, a local tax collector
(c) The revolutionary who starts it (d) A small child

**84.** Why does Tellson's send Mr Lorry to France?
(a) To negotiate the release of a British prisoner
(b) To profit from the revolution
(c) To safeguard the bank's assets and papers
(d) For a holiday

**85. What does Gabelle's letter to Darnay say?**
(a) That he should not come to Paris or he will be executed
(b) He congratulates him on his marriage to Lucy.
(c) That he will be executed for overseeing Darnay's family estate
(d) That he stole from Darnay's family and wants forgiveness

**86. What happens to Darnay as soon as he gets to France?**
(a) He is declared a hero for renouncing his family.
(b) He is arrested and turned over to Defarge.
(c) He takes up the family name again and fights against the revolutionaries.
(d) He goes into hiding and rescues Gabelle.

**87. What form of execution has just been invented?**
(a) The guillotine (b) The electric chair
(c) The firing squad
(d) Drawing and quartering

**88. How does Doctor Manette help Darnay?**
(a) He becomes the Defarges' personal physician so he can get inside information
(b) He gets himself arrested so the two can find a way to escape together.
(c) He becomes a prison doctor so he can take care of Darnay's safety.
(d) He does favors for important revolutionaries in exchange for a promise of Darnay's safety.

**89. Why does Lucy stand in the same spot outside the prison every day for two hours?**
(a) So she can see Darnay in a prison window
(b) So she's out of the house while Doctor Manette makes shoes
(c) So that Darnay might see her from a prison window
(d) So she can send secret signals to the prisoners

**90. Who often talks to Lucie while she waits outside the prison?**
(a) Madame Defarge (b) Monsieur Defarge
(c) The wood-sawyer (d) John Barsad

**91. What happens at Darnay's first rowdy trial in France?**
(a) The crowd lynches him.
(b) He is found innocent and released.
(c) He is found guilty and sentenced to death.
(d) Doctor Manette makes a deal to take Darnay's place in prison.

**92. Who engineers Darnay's re-arrest the next day?**
(a) The Defarges (b) The wood-sawyer
(c) Sydney Carton (d) Louis XVI

**93. How does Carton convince Barsad to help him save Darnay?**
(a) He bribes him.
(b) He threatens to reveal to the revolutionaries that Barsad is an English spy.
(c) He starts to tell Miss Pross what her brother does for a living.
(d) He dangles him over a bridge until he agrees.

**94. What does the letter that Defarge reads reveal about Darnay's father and uncle?**
(a) That they tried to protect Darnay from arrest after he raped a woman
(b) That they tried to help get Doctor Manette released after he was imprisoned
(c) That Doctor Manette participated in the rape and murder of a woman and her family
(d) That they were resonsible for a rape, murders, and Doctor Manette's unjust arrest

**95. Why is Charles Darnay going to be executed?**
(a) Because of the sins committed by his family
(b) Because Madame Defarge overrules the court's decision
(c) Because he confesses
(d) Because he's an English spy

**96. What is revealed about Madame Defarge?**
(a) That she is Darnay's sister
(b) The she and Lucy are sisters
(c) That she is the sister of the woman raped by Darnay's uncle
(d) That she is an aristocrat by birth

**97. What does Carton do at the Manette's?**
(a) He gives them his traveling papers and instructs them to leave the next day.
(b) He gives Miss Pross a gun and says she will need it for protection.
(c) He tells them his plan to save Darnay.
(d) He begs Lucy to reconsider being with him or else he will kill himself.

**98. How does Carton get Darnay to switch places with him?**
(a) By saying his daughter is gravely ill
(b) By drugging him
(c) By pushing Darnay out of the cell and locking himself in
(d) By threatening Lucy's safety if he doesn't

## ANSWERS

| | | | | | | | | | | | | | | | | | | | |
|---|---|---|---|---|---|---|---|---|---|---|---|---|---|---|---|---|---|---|---|
| 1. | (c) | 2. | (a) | 3. | (b) | 4. | (a) | 5. | (c) | 6. | (b) | 7. | (d) | 8. | (c) | 9. | (a) | 10. | (b) |
| 11. | (b) | 12. | (a) | 13. | (c) | 14. | (c) | 15. | (a) | 16. | (b) | 17. | (c) | 18. | (d) | 19. | (b) | 20. | (a) |
| 21. | (b) | 22. | (a) | 23. | (c) | 24. | (a) | 25. | (c) | 26. | (c) | 27. | (d) | 28. | (a) | 29. | (a) | 30. | (b) |
| 31. | (b) | 32. | (c) | 33. | (a) | 34. | (c) | 35. | (a) | 36. | (c) | 37. | (b) | 38. | (c) | 39. | (b) | 40. | (d) |
| 41. | (d) | 42. | (b) | 43. | (c) | 44. | (d) | 45. | (a) | 46. | (d) | 47. | (c) | 48. | (a) | 49. | (d) | 50. | (a) |
| 51. | (c) | 52. | (b) | 53. | (c) | 54. | (a) | 55. | (c) | 56. | (c) | 57. | (b) | 58. | (b) | 59. | (a) | 60. | (c) |
| 61. | (b) | 62. | (a) | 63. | (d) | 64. | (a) | 65. | (c) | 66. | (a) | 67. | (a) | 68. | (c) | 69. | (a) | 70. | (d) |
| 71. | (b) | 72. | (a) | 73. | (d) | 74. | (a) | 75. | (c) | 76. | (c) | 77. | (d) | 78. | (b) | 79. | (b) | 80. | (a) |
| 81. | (a) | 82. | (d) | 83. | (b) | 84. | (c) | 85. | (a) | 86. | (b) | 87. | (a) | 88. | (c) | 89. | (c) | 90. | (c) |
| 91. | (b) | 92. | (a) | 93. | (b) | 94. | (d) | 95. | (a) | 96. | (c) | 97. | (a) | 98. | (b) | | | | |

Chapter 18

# Bye-Bye Blackbird

*Anita Desai*

## About the Author

Anita Desai was born on 24th June, 1937 in Mussoorie. She is an Indian novelist and the Professor of Humanities, at the Massachusetts Institute of Technology. She was born as Anita Mazumdar, the daughter of DN Mazumdar, a Bengali businessman and Toni Nime,who was a German. Anita received her earlier education at Queen Mary's Higher Secondary School. Anita was a precocious child, she started writing short stories at a very young age. Her first short story was published when she was mere nine.She joined 'Miranda House' for her bachelor's degree and completed her graduation in English literature in 1957 at the age of 20.

In 1958, Anita tied the nuptial knot with Ashvin Desai, a businessman. She ventured into the field of novel writing with her novel 'Cry, The Peacock', followed by 'The Voices of the City' and 'The Fire on the Mountain'. The Fire on the Mountain is based on the lives of three women residing in Kasauli and their different experiences of life.

In 1980, came her famous novel, 'The Clear Light of Day', which bears impressions of Anita Desai's own life. This novel set in old background is a story of a middle-class Hindu family around the time of partition of India . The story revolves around the central character Bim (Bimla). She lives in her house with her mentally retarded brother Baba. Her sister Tara and her elder brother go away with their respective families leaving her to bear all the problems and responsibilities of the household alone. The novel is partially a trip down memory lane.

Her other important works include 'Where Shall We Go This Summer?,' 'Games at Twilight' and 'other stories like 'Village by the Sea', 'In Custody', 'Baumgartner's Bombay,' 'In Journey to Ithaca,' 'Diamond Dust' and her booker prize nominated novel, 'Fasting Feasting'. 'The Zig Zag Way' published in 2004 is her recent novel. Anita Desai has been honoured with many literary awards including 'The Guardian Awards for Children's Fiction' for the novel 'The Village by the Sea' and in 1978, National Academy of Letter Award for her novel 'Fire on the Mountain'.

Anita Desai is a fellow of many prominent literary organisations such as 'The Royal Society of Literature', London and 'The American Academy of Arts and Letters'. Her daughter Kiran Desai has won the 2006 'Man Booker Prize' for her novel the 'Inheritance of Loss'.

## Summary

### Introduction

The background of the novel 'Bye-Bye Blackbird' is set in 1960s England which is written by Anita Desai. The story revolves around two friends Dev, and Adit in London. Adit has stayed for a longer period in London and married an English woman, Sarah. Dev comes to London for his higher studies and subsequent employment. The words of Adit show his disappointment when he says, All I could find was a ruddy clerking job in some Government of India tourist bureau. They were going to pay me two hundred and fifty rupees and after thirty years I could expect to have five hundred rupees. That is what depressed me. The thirty years I would have to spend in panting for two hundred and fifty rupees. This has compelled him to leave his mother country and settle in abroad for a decent income.

### Adit Adapts Himself as per the English

Adit adopted England as his home. He is able to withstand the insults hurled at him and humiliations. He admires the Western life and erstwhile masters. He says, I like the pubs, I like the freedom like a man has here-economic freedom! Social freedom! I like the Thames. I like old Ma Jenkins who cleans my rooms and I like weekend at the seaside. I even like the BBC.

He falls in love with an English girl and marries her. He becomes a 'spineless immigrant lover'. Sarah agrees to follow him like a typical Hindu wife.

Adit is overjoyed and remarks: You are like a Bengali girl. Bengali women are like that reserved, quiet. May be you were one in your previous life. But you are improving it, you are much prettier!

## Dev at Discomfortion in England

Dev, on the other hand, gets infuriated by being called as 'wog' by a school boy. When they are walking down the street, they hear Mrs Simpson muttering aloud, 'Littered with Asians! Must get Richard to move out of Clapham, it is impossible now'. These lines suggest how emigrants, especially Asians are looked down as others in England.

## Dev Insulting Adit

'Otherness' is defined by difference, typically difference marked by outward signs like race and gender. Dev understands that Adit is least bothered about insults he hurled at him and says, 'boot-licking' toady. Spineless imperialist lover....You would sell your soul, and your passport too, for a glimpse, at two shillings, of some draughty old stately home. But both have realised that they are opportunists after this juncture.

## Gathering of Emegrants is Planned

Few days later, they have planned a gathering with other coloured emigrants where they can eat and drink. 'Modern diasporas are ethnic minority groups of migrant origins residing and acting in host countries but maintaining strong sentimental and material links with their countries of origin, their homeland'. That gathering is a fusion of different migrants. One Pakistani claims, "My religion forbids me to drink or smoke or touch a woman. But here, in this country, what am I to do? I also do the things I see other men doing". Sarah and Adit enjoy Bhangra dance and the enjoyment has reached its peak with the high volume of radio.

## The Fun is Interrupted by a few English Men

All of a sudden they hear a voice saying, 'Wrap it up, you blighters, where d' you think you are, eh?' Next moment the scene has changed and the group is forced to reduce the intensity of its merry-making. Dev can't take this and says, "the trouble with you emigrants is that you go soft. If anyone in India told you to turn off your radio, you won't dream of doing it. You might even pull out a knife and blood would spill". Over here all you do is shut up and look sat upon, Samar recounts the day he was called a bloody Pakistani as he refused to close his umbrella at the order of an Englishman. These incidents leave a deep scar in Dev, who is divided between the opportunity he has got in England and the moments of bearing suppression and differences. The feelings of alienation and unidetification overwhelmed him. Desai expressed his agony.

Dev ventures into the city.... The menacing slighter of the escalators strikes panic in a speechless. Dev, as he swept down with an awful sensation of being taken where he does not want to go. Down, down and farther down – like Alice falling, falling down the rabbit hole, like a Kafka stranger wondering through the dark labyrinth of a prison....Dev is swamped inkily, with a great dread of being caught, step in the underground by some accident, some collapse, and being slowly suffocated to a worm's death, never to emerge into freshness and light.

## Dev at Peace After Passing of the Night

Dev's anguish disappears as he is ushered by the fresh morning. He himself is trying to meet the challenges of an immigrant. However, he tries to cope up with the arrogance of English people, the constant humiliations irked him. When Dev asks about the feelings of Adit, he says, "...the laziness of the clerks and the unpunctuality of the buses and trains and the beggars and the flies and the stench – and the boredom, the boredom of it... I live for the moment, I don't think, I don't worry".

## Adit and Sarah visit Adits's Former Landlady

One day, Adit insists to visit to his former land Lady where he stayed for three years. Strangely Sarah rejected and was reluctant to come. Adit says, "That's where I lived for three years, Dev".

That's the only landlady I stayed with for more than a fortnight. The others all threw me out but I stayed with them, with the Millers, for three years at the Millers". Adit is treated as an outsider and his visit gives him a feeling of unwelcome when he observes the treatment given by the landlady. When Adit sincerely enquired about their daughter, she wishes to reject the fact that Adit has lived there for three years. Mrs Miller expresses a feeling that she does not like any personal questions about her house or family. Though, Adit is taken back, he takes control of the situation and leaves the place. On their way back neighbours stare curiously from behind their techno-coloured rose trees and a dog barks. His visit is an unpleasant surprise to the white family and their neighbours.

## Adit Contemplates Changing his Decision to Staying England

Like any other Indian abroad he has been infected by schizophrenia. He cannot digest the experience he faced when he visited the landlady. His uncertainty is best described by Desai. In this growing uncertainty, he feels the divisions inside him divided further and then re-divided once more. Simple reactions and feeling lose their simplicity and develop complex angles, facets, shades and tints... there are days in which the life of an alien appears enthrallingly rich and beautiful to him and that of a homebody too dull, too stale to return to ever. Then he hears a word in the tube or notices an expression on an English face that overturns his latest decision and drawing himself together, he feels he can never bear to be unwanted immigrant but must return to his own land, however abject or dull, where he has, at least, a place in the Sun, security, status and freedom.

Again, they planned their visit to his mother-in-law's house and he expects that his mother-in-law rather treat him differently. But he is annoyed with the treatment he meted out. He says, "My mother-in-law hates and despises me. They make fun of the life I lead and the ideals I profess. Therefore, I am angry. I am hurt". These fleeting moods of anger are new to him and faced with one, he was unable to deal with it. He merely stood still and felt his leaden feet sink in as though in quick-sands. Adit has developed an extreme hatred for

England. He loses control of himself. He stood staring, not at one of the posters he so delighted in but at a piece of that Nigger, go home graffiti on the walls that had previously nearly skidded off the surface of his eyeballs without actually penetrating. Now he is screwed up his eyes and studied it as though it were a very pertinent sign board.

The eternal immigrants who can never accept their new home and continue to walk the streets like strangers in enemy territory, frozen, listless, but dutifully trying to be busy, unobtrusive and, however superficially, to belong.

Diaspora expresses the oscillated mind, suffering and agony of cultural change. He decides to leave England and says "Sarah, you know I've loved England more than you, I've often felt myself half-English, but it was only pretence, Silly. Now it has to be the real thing. I must go. You will come?".

## Sarah faces the Dilemma of Choosing between Her identity or Her Love

Though Sarah agrees to his proposal she faces an alienation that is internal. Desai remarkably stated that Sarah, "shed her name as she had shed her ancestry and identity and she sat there, staring, as though she watched them disappear". Sarah is brave enough to face the situations in life though she has gnawing fears in her mind. Sarah is alone and her friends are having a meeting. She recollects her emotions.

She felt all the pangs of saying goodbye to her past twenty-four years. It was her English self that was receding and fading and dying, she knew it, it was her English self to which she must say goodbye. That was what hurt – not saying goodbye to England would remain as it was, only at a greater distance from her but always within the scope of a return visit. England, she whispered but the word aroused no special longing or possessiveness in her. English, she whispered and then her instinctive reaction was to clutch at something and hold on to what was slipping through her fingers already.

## Sarah Finally Choose Her Love

She is in cross roads. Sarah can neither shed her native English culture nor accept the adopted Indian culture completely. At the time of farewell Christine asks her about baby, Sarah says, "You mean boy or girl? I don't mind either. Or do you mean who it will look like, Adit or me? I hope it will look like Adit, brown as brown, with black hair and black, black eyes". Christine replies, Well, in that case ...I suppose it will be better to have the child in India. Now she lost her identity as an English woman. She can be considered as a multicultured, Mrs Sen, the wife of an Asian, rather than Sarah, the English woman.

## Final Decision by Dev, Adit and Sarah

At the end of the story, Dev who always complains about the country and its people decides to settle in England to reap a rich harvest. He is successful to establish his roots in England. But Adit and Sarah bid goodbye to England. At the time of bidding goodbye, Dev calls out, 'Bye-Bye Blackbird'. This is how, Anita Desai describes the diasporic element to the eyes of readers.

# Practice Questions

**1.** What was the first lesson that Dev's first day in London taught him?
(a) One should not sleep with windows open
(b) Who wants tea must get up and make it
(c) One should not go to bed early in London
(d) One should have sufficient warm clothings

**2.** Who is Dev in the novel?
(a) He is the brother of Adit
(b) He is the husband of Sarah
(c) He is a friend of Adit who has come to London for higher studies
(d) He is the one who provides shelter to Adit in London

**3.** Who is Adit in the novel?
(a) He is the one who has recently come to London for studies
(b) He is a guest of Dev in London
(c) He is a business tycoon in London
(d) He is the husband of Sarah, who has stayed in London for a long period

**4.** Who is Sarah in the novel?
(a) She is a British who has married Adit Sen
(b) She is the wife of Dev
(c) She is an Indian who has gone to London for job
(d) She is the employer of Dev in London

**5.** Where does Adit Sen stay in London?
(a) Lambeth (b) Clapham (c) Fulham (d) Islington

**6.** Who has been termed as 'spineless immigrant lover in' the novel?
(a) Sarah (b) Dev
(c) Adit (d) None of these

**7.** Which road in London has the air of an Indian Bazaar ?
(a) 3 Valleys Crescent (b) Abbey Rise
(c) Abbot Street (d) Portobello Road

**8.** What does the novel 'Bye-Bye Blackbird' highlight?
(a) Susceptibility and vulnerability of Indian minds to English culture
(b) Magical Grace of England
(c) Tranquility of England
(d) Sophistication of England

**9.** Who has been denoted as 'black bird' in the novel?
(a) Dev (b) Immigrant Indians
(c) Sarah (d) Adit Sen

**10.** What does the novel expose about England ?
(a) Religious intolerance (b) Modernity of England
(c) Social disparity and discrimination prevalent in England
(d) Culture of openness in England

**11.** In the first part of the novel, Adit is full of ......... for England.
(a) hatred (b) criticism
(c) adoration (d) pescimism

**12.** Why does Adit Sen criticise India?
(a) For being cultural (b) For being religious
(c) For being a democratic nation
(d) For being somnolent and dull

**13.** What does Dev find in the alien surroundings of London in the beginning?
(a) Thrill (b) Emptiness
(c) Warmth (d) Liveliness

**14.** In which decade is the background of the novel 'Bye-Bye Blackbird' set?
(a) 1940s (b) 1950s (c) 1960s (d) 1980s

**15.** The story of the novel 'Bye-Bye Blackbird' revolves around
(a) Adit and Sarah (b) Dev and Sarah
(c) Dev and Adit (d) England

**16.** Who introduced Adit Sen to Sarah in the novel?
(a) Christine Langford (b) Mr Krishna Murthy
(c) Dev (d) Sarah herself

**17.** What does the river 'Thames' remind Adit of?
(a) Beauty of England
(b) Peace and serenity of England
(c) Liveliness of England
(d) Shameful little Jamuna, the slush and mud of Ganges.

**18.** What does Adit long to see?
(a) British night life (b) Indian sunset
(c) His family (d) Indian people

**19.** Why does Adit start behaving strangely with Sarah?
(a) The love between the two is gradually lost
(b) Adit has been involved in an affair with someone else
(c) Sarah has cheated him
(d) Fed up of English life, he yearns for India

**20.** What conflict does Adit undergo?
(a) Between illusion and reality
(b) Between Sarah and another unknown woman
(c) Between job and business
(d) Between right and wrong

**21.** How does Adit resolve his conflict?
(a) By deciding to separate from Sarah
(b) By deciding to return to India
(c) By deciding to embrace England permanently
(d) By deciding to quit job and take to business in London

**22.** What dilemma does Sarah face?
(a) Of choosing between Adit and Dev
(b) Of cheating Adit for a new man in life
(c) Of losing her identity i.e. uprootedness for her love
(d) None of the above

**23.** How does Sarah escape her dilemma?
(a) By separating from Adit
(b) By opting for the new man in life
(c) By deciding to go with Dev
(d) By creating a world of illusions of her own about India and embrace it

**24.** Sarah's love for India and its customs is revealed when
(a) she is with Miss Moffit, admiring everything Indian
(b) she criticises English culture
(c) she agrees to come to India
(d) None of the above

**25.** What prompts Sarah to leave England for India?
(a) Adit's love
(b) India's fascination
(c) The thought of their visit to the Millers of Clapham
(d) Dev's influence

**26.** What infuriates Dev while walking down the street in Clapham?
(a) The police interrupt his walk
(b) A school boy calls him 'wog'
(c) Thought of India
(d) Indifference of the British

**27.** Who mutters aloud 'Littered with Asians'?
(a) A school boy (b) Christine Langford
(c) Mr Miller (d) Mrs Simpson

**28.** Who says 'my religion forbids me to drink, smoke or touch a women'?
(a) A Pakistani immigrant living in England
(b) Dev
(c) Adit
(d) Sarah

**29.** Who was called a bloody Pakistani on refusing to close his umbrella at the order of an Englishman?
(a) Adit (b) Samar
(c) Dev (d) Mr Krishna Murthy

**30.** Who was Adit's landlady in his early days in England?
(a) Mrs Sympson (b) Sarah
(c) Mrs Miller (d) None of these

**31.** Who calls out 'Bye-Bye Blackbird'?
(a) Sara (b) Adit
(c) Christine (d) Dev

**32.** What does Dev finally decide to do ?
(a) To stay in England
(b) To come back to India
(c) To move to USA (d) None of the above

**33.** Who is the author of the novel 'Bye-Bye-Blackbird'?
(a) Kamla Das (b) Anita Desai
(c) Arundhati Roy (d) RK Narayan

## ANSWERS

| | | | | | | | | | | | | | | | | | | | |
|---|---|---|---|---|---|---|---|---|---|---|---|---|---|---|---|---|---|---|---|
| 1. | (b) | 2. | (c) | 3. | (d) | 4. | (a) | 5. | (b) | 6. | (c) | 7. | (d) | 8. | (a) | 9. | (b) | 10. | (c) |
| 11. | (c) | 12. | (d) | 13. | (b) | 14. | (c) | 15. | (c) | 16. | (a) | 17. | (d) | 18. | (b) | 19. | (d) | 20. | (a) |
| 21. | (b) | 22. | (c) | 23. | (d) | 24. | (a) | 25. | (c) | 26. | (b) | 27. | (d) | 28. | (a) | 29. | (b) | 30. | (c) |
| 31. | (d) | 32. | (a) | 33. | (b) | | | | | | | | | | | | | | |

Chapter 19

# The Portrait of a Lady

*Khushwant Singh*

## About the Author

Khushwant Singh, one of the best-known Indian writers of all times, was born in 1915 in Hadali (now in Pakistan). He was educated at the Government College, Lahore and at King's College, Cambridge University, and the Inner Temple in London. He practised law at the Lahore High Court for several years before joining the Indian Ministry of External Affairs in 1947. He began a distinguished career as a journalist with the All India Radio in 1951. He was the founder-editor of Yojana (1951-1953), editor of the Illustrated Weekly of India (1979- 1980), chief editor of New Delhi (1979-1980), and editor of the Hindustan Times (1980-1983). His Saturday column "With Malice Towards One and All" in the Hindustan Times was by far one of the most popular columns in India.

Among the several works he published are a classic two-volume history of the Sikhs, several novels (the best known of which are Delhi, Train to Pakistan, and The company of women), and a number of translations and non-fiction books on Delhi, Nature and Current Affairs. The Portrait of a Lady: Collected Stories was in the form of short story collection.Khushwant Singh was a member of the Rajya Sabha (upper house of the Indian Parliament) from 1980 to 1986. Among other honors, he was awarded the Padma Bhushan in 1974 and Padma Vibhushan in 2007.

Khushwant Singh died at the age of 99 on 20th March, 2014 because of a cardiac arrest.

## Summary

### The Author Remembers His Grandmother and Grandfather

The author recalls his grandmother as a very old lady. For the twenty years that the author had known his grandmother, he had found her old and wrinkled.

It was hard for him to believe that she had once been young and pretty and she had a husband. Khushwant Singh's grandfather's portrait hung on the wall of the drawing room. He wore a big turban. His clothes were loose. He looked at least a hundred years old. Looking at his portrait, one could not imagine him in his youth with his wife and children.

### The Author's Grandmother

The thought of the grandmother being young and pretty was almost revolting to him. She was short, fat and slightly bent in stature. Her face was a criss-cross of wrinkles. Her silvery white hair was scattered over her wrinkled face.

The author remembered her hobbling around the house in spotless white clothes with one hand resting on her waist to balance her stoop and the other hand busy counting the beads of her rosary. Her lips constantly moved in an inaudible prayer.

To the author, she could never have been pretty, but she reflected a divine beauty. She was like the winter landscape in the mountains.

### The Author's Childhood with His Grandmother

The author and his grandmother were good friends. His parents left him to stay with her when they shifted to the city. In the village, his grandmother took care of all his needs. She was quite active and agile. She used to wake him up in the morning and get him ready for school.

She said her morning prayers in a sing-song manner while she bathed and dressed him in the hope that her grandson would learn them by heart. The author listened to the prayers because he loved her voice, but never bothered to learn them.

Then she would fetch his wooden slate which, she had already washed, and plastered it with yellow chalk. She would take an earthen inkpot and a reed pen and tie them in a bundle and hand it to the author.

After having a thick, stale chapatti with a little butter and sugar spread on it for breakfast, they used to leave for school. The author's grandmother always accompanied him to the school as it was attached to the temple.

### The Author at School

The priest taught children the alphabet and the morning prayer. The children sat in two rows in the verandah. They would sing the alphabet or the prayer in a chorus. While the author learnt his lessons at school, the grandmother would read scriptures in the adjoining temple. On their way back, they would feed stale chapattis to the dogs.

### The Turning Point in the Relationship of Grandmother and the Author

The turning point came in their relationship when they moved to the city to stay with Khushwant Singh's parents. In the city, the author went to an English school in a motor bus. The grandmother could not accompany him to the school. As there were no dogs in the streets, the grandmother took to feeding the sparrows.

As the years rolled by, they saw less of each other. In spite of her immense interest in his studies, she could not help him in his lessons as he was learning English, the law of gravity, Archimedes' principle and many more such things which she could not understand, and this made her unhappy. Sometimes she would ask him what the teacher had taught him.

### Grandmother Distressed and Disturbed

Grandmother didn't believe in the things taught at the English school and was distressed to learn that there was no teaching about God and the scriptures in the school.

Moreover, she was very disturbed at the idea of music lessons being given at the English school. To her, music had lewd associations and she considered music to be unsuitable for gentle folk.

### The Common Link of Friendship gets Snapped

The common link of friendship between the author and the grandmother was broken when the author went to the University and was given a room of his own. The grandmother accepted her loneliness and rarely spoke to anyone. All day long, she sat spinning the wheel and reciting her prayers.

Only in the afternoon she relaxed for a while to feed the sparrows. They perched on her shoulders and some even on her head but she never shooed them away. It used to be the happiest half-hour of the day for her.

### The Author Leaves for Higher Studies

The author decided to go abroad for higher studies for five years. He was sure that his grandmother would be upset at his departure, but she was not even sentimental. She came to the railway station to see him off. She showed no emotion and was absorbed in praying and counting the beads of her rosary. Silently she kissed his forehead. The author thought that perhaps it was the last sign of physical contact between them.

### The Grandmother Celebrates the Author's Return and Falls Sick

After five years, the author found his grandmother at the station when he returned. She held him in her arms. He found her more religious and more self-contained. He could hear her reciting prayers. Even that day, the happiest moment for her was feeding the sparrows herself. However, something strange happened to her in the evening.

For the first time ever, she did not pray. Instead, she collected the women of the neighbourhood, got an old drum and started to sing songs of the homecoming of warriors. They tried to persuade her to stop to avoid overstraining herself. But she didn't listen. She fell ill the next morning.

### Grandmother's Death

The grandmother was diagnosed with a mild fever by the doctor but she insisted that her end was near. She told everyone that she did not want to talk to anyone and would rather spend her last moments praying. She ignored everyone's protests and started counting the beads in her rosary while praying. After a short while, the author noticed that his grandmother's lips stopped moving and the rosary fell from her lifeless fingers. She died a peaceful death. She was covered with a red shawl.

### The Sparrows Mourn Her Death

When the author and others came to take away the grandmother's body, they met a strange sight. To mourn her death, a lot of sparrows had surrounded the grandmother's body. They were all silent. When the author's mother offered the sparrows some bread, they refused to eat and quietly flew away after the grandmother's body was carried away for the last rites.

# Practice Questions

**1.** When was Khushwant Singh born?
(a) 1916 (b) 1918
(c) 1915 (d) 1917

**2.** Where was Khushwant Singh educated?
(a) Lahore (b) Lucknow
(c) London (d) Lahore and London

**3.** Before becoming a journalist, Khushwant Singh practised
(a) medicine (b) law
(c) dentistry (d) None of these

**4.** Khushwant Singh was also a member of ..........
(a) Rajya Sabha (b) Lok Sabha
(c) Municipal Council (d) Election Commission

**5.** When was Khushwant Singh awarded Padma Bhushan?
(a) 1974 (b) 2007
(c) 1984 (d) 1963

**6.** In 'Portrait of a Lady' Khushwant Singh describes about his
(a) mother (b) grand mother
(c) aunt (d) niece

**7.** Khushwant Singh could not believe that her grandmother once had been
(a) young (b) pretty
(c) married (d) All of these

**8.** Whose portrait hung in the drawing room of Khushwant Singh ?
(a) His father's (b) His grandmother's
(c) His grandfather's (d) His mother's

**9.** Khushwant Singh has compared her grandmother to
(a) summer landscape in the mountains
(b) the Moon
(c) the Sun
(d) winter landscape in the mountains

**10.** Grandmother always went to school with Khushwant Singh because
(a) she did not want to leave him alone
(b) she also studied in the same school
(c) the school was attached to a temple
(d) She taught in the same school

**11.** What was the turning point in Khushwant's friendship with his grandmother?
(a) When Khushwant Singh started practising law
(b) When Khushwant Singh went abroad
(c) When Khushwant Singh got married
(d) When they went to the city to live with their parents

**12.** Why was Khushwant Singh's grandmother unable to help him with his lessons when he joined an English school ?
(a) As she did not know English
(b) As she was illeterate
(c) As she had got very old
(d) As she did not get time

**13.** She rarely left her .......... to talk to anyone.
(a) rosary (b) prayers
(c) spectacles (d) spinning wheel

**14.** "She smiled and never shooed them away" In the above line, 'them' refers to
(a) school children (b) Khushwant's friends
(c) village dogs (d) birds

**15.** Khushwant went abroad for further studies for .......... years.
(a) two (b) five
(c) three (d) four

**16.** Grandmother's happiest moments was spent with her
(a) grandson
(b) husband
(c) dogs
(d) Sparrows

**17.** "In the evening a change came over her"
In the above lines 'the evening' refers to
(a) the evening when Khushwant went abroad
(b) the evening when Khushwant and her grandmother went to the city
(c) the last evening of grandmother's life
(d) the last evening of Khushwant's life

**18.** What was peculiar about 'the last evening'?
(a) Grandmother did not pray
(b) Grandmother did not speak
(c) Grandmother had fever
(d) Grandmother kept sleeping

**19.** What did grandmother sing on her last evening?
(a) homecoming of Khushwant
(b) homecoming of warriors
(c) a song that Khushwant liked
(d) a song in praise of Khushwant

**20.** The grandmother's body was covered in a ...........shroud.
(a) white (b) blue (c) red (d) yellow

## ANSWERS

| | | | | | | | | | | | | | | | | | | | |
|---|---|---|---|---|---|---|---|---|---|---|---|---|---|---|---|---|---|---|---|
| 1. | *(c)* | 2. | *(d)* | 3. | *(b)* | 4. | *(a)* | 5. | *(a)* | 6. | *(b)* | 7. | *(d)* | 8. | *(c)* | 9. | *(d)* | 10. | *(c)* |
| 11. | *(d)* | 12. | *(a)* | 13. | *(d)* | 14. | *(d)* | 15. | *(b)* | 16. | *(d)* | 17. | *(c)* | 18. | *(a)* | 19. | *(b)* | 20. | *(c)* |

Chapter 20

# Arms and the Man

*G.B. Shaw*

## About the Author

GB Shaw was born on 26th July, 1856, at Dublin, a city known for great dramatists. His parents were originally of English stock and he claimed descent from Macduff, the Thane of Fife, and from Oliver Cromwell, Lord Protector of the Commonwealth of England (1653-58). Preceded by two sisters, he was the only son of George Carr Shaw and Lucinda Elizabeth Gurley, daughter of Walter Bangenal Gurley, landed proprietor of county Carlow. Born of Protestant parents, Shaw was baptised in the faith of England in Ireland, believing that 'God was a Protestant and that Roman Catholics went to hell'.

### Student Life

At the age of ten, Shaw entered the Wesleyan Connexional School, afterwards Wesley College, but was never happy. In the preface to Misalliance he says, "My schooling did me a great deal of harm and no good whatever, it was simply dragging a child's soul through the dirt". He asserts, "It is evident that my schooling was a complete failure, and that the aesthetic education I received out of school was my salvation". As a formal student, Shaw's interest lays only in English composition and he often told his classmates stories from the Illiad and Odyssey with a Shavian slant. His general academic interests were literature, music and the graphic arts. By and large he was self-educated and at the age of fifteen he knew in music of least one important works by Handel, Mozart, Beethoven, Mendelssohn, Rossini, Bellini, Donizetti, Verdi and Gounod from cover to cover.

### Early Career

At the early age of fifteen, Shaw started working for an estate agent Charles Townsend and proved to be a highly accurate, efficient, industrious and excellent employee. Due to his efficiency he was soon promoted to the post of head cashier despite his young age. In 1872, however, his mother decided to sell the house and go to London with Lee because she thought that her career as a singing teacher and her elder daughter's as a singer demanded that they are be near Lee. GB Shaw soon understood that his father was not capable of being a good controlling head of the family and also realised that his mother was fully devoted to music to the exclusion of her children.

### Literary Career

The most notable incident in Shaw's life occurred on 2nd September, 1882, when he heard at the memorial hall in Farringdon Street, London, a lecture by Henry George, a great socialist and the author of immensely popular book 'Progress and Poverty'. Shaw's immediate reaction after listening to his forceful speaker was his historic conversion to socialism. Shaw was associated with many newspapers and magazines as a critic of art, literature, music and drama. He wrote for the scots observer and the daily chronicle. The Pall Mall Gazette, the star (with Pseudonym Carno di Bassetto, a musical instrument) and the Saturday Review.

### Achievements

For the sheer output of his work which embraces innumerable human problems, Shaw can be classed with the greatest creative writers of any age and time, one can safely predict that barring aside on occasional eclipse his reputation like that of Shakespeare will endure for ages to come. Shaw was awarded Noble Prize for literature in 1925. He died at Ayot St Lawrence in England, on 2nd November, 1950 deeply mourned by lots of friends and admirers in all parts of the world. Shaw's works include plays, novels and miscellaneous writings.

## Summary

### ACT-I

### Raina and Her Mother Catherine Talk Excitedly About a Successful Cavalry Charge

'Arms and Man' by GB Shaw is a play in three Acts. It is an anti-romantic comedy. He has blown off and ridiculed the old traditional views of love and chivalry in this play. The play has only seven characters. Major Petkoff, Major Sergius, Captain Bluntschli and Nicola are four male characters. Catherine, Raina and Louka are three female characters. Raina is the heroine of the play. She is the daughter of Major Petkoff and Catherine. She is in love with Sergius. The play opens' with the scene in Raina's bed-chamber in Bulgaria, in a small town near the Dragoman Pass, late in November, 1885. The bed-chamber is well-furnished. On the balcony a young lady (Raina), conscious of the romantic beauty of the night, is gazing at snowy Balkans. She is in her nightgown. Raina's mother, Catherine, enters the room.

She tells Raina that the Bulgarians have won the battle, and that entire credit of the victory goes to Sergius. She adds that Sergius is the hero of the hour, the idol of the regiment. She tells Raina about the Cavalry gauge led by Sergius over the Serbian unit of machine guns. This Sergius did even against the instruction of the Russian officers.

The Bulgarians had Russian officers with them, the Serbs had Austrian officers. Raina and her mother are interrupted by the entry of Louka, a handsome proud girl in a pretty Bulgarian peasant's dress. She is a maid-servant in the Petkoff family. She tells Raina to close all the window since there appear chances of shooting in the streets. The Serbs are being chased by the Bulgarians. Catherine and Louka have the room. Raina is left alone. She is happy over the victory of the Bulgarians suddenly in the darkness a man's voice is heard. Catherine at first expresses irritation against her daughter for exposing herself to the night air.

And then she, almost exulting in joy informs her daughter about the news she has received from the war-front. She tells Raina that her father Major Petkoff is safe and sound and the Bulgarians have won a great victory over the Serbs. In the battle of town, the allied forces of the Austrians and Serbs have been over thrown by the Bulgarians under the leadership of Major Sergius Saranoff. Raina is engaged to be married to Sergius.

He says Catherine, led a cavalry charge without the comments of the Russian officers and was the first man to sweep through the guns. He is, at present, the hero of the hour, the idol of the regiment. Raina feels proud of the heroism of her betrothed. She confesses that she has had doubts regarding the reality of the heroism of Sergius. But now on finding that Sergius is in reality as magnificient as he looks, she feels ecstatic. Her mother chides her for keeping Sergius waiting a year for betrothal and says that if Raina had any drop of Bulgarian blood in her veins she would now worship Sergius after his return from the battlefield.

## Louka Informs them that Street Fighting will Start Soon

At the moment, Louka a pretty young maid servant of the house comes in and informs them that the war-fugitives have entered the town seeking shelter to all the shutters and windows should be closed. The victorious Bulgarian cavalry soldiers are chasing the runaway Serbs so there is a possibility of some shooting in the streets. All the doors are fastened except one the belt of which is gone Louka and Catherine depart Raina retires to bed with the thoughts of her hero Sergius when on return would marry her. A gunfire breaks the silence of the night, Raina gets frightened. She puts out the candles and lies down on the bed again. In the darkness, she hears the sound of the shutters of the window being pulled open from outside. The shutters are then closed. Raina knows that some one has entered the room. She hears a gasping sound gathering up her courage. She inquires about the identity of the intruder.

## A Serbian Soldier Enters Raina's Bedroom

The man threatens her to school if she raised her voice. At his command, Raina lights a candle and sees a man of about thirty five and officer in Serbian uniform in a deplorable condition, all covered with snow, mud and blood. The man tells her that if he is discovered, his chasers will kill him and he does not want to die. Raina feels surprised to find a soldier afraid of death the man retorts that all the soldiers are like him. Actually, it is the duty of every human being to keep alive as long as possible, he says. During their conversation Raina becomes conscious of her half-naked state and runs to fetch her gown.

The man picks it up before her saying that her cloak can be better weapon for him than the revolver. Her condition would be really awkward if the Bulgarian soldiers came inside her bedroom and she is forced to meet them without her cloak. Raina will, therefore, not let anybody enter her room in her present state of undress and the fugitive will remain safe. The man justifies his unmannerly, ungentlemanly and unchivalrous act by saying that it may save his life and that is the most important thing. Just then a lot of noise is heard outside as the Bulgarian soldiers hammer the door of the Petkoff house. Catherine repeatedly warns them but they ignore her and force their entrance inside the house. They inform the mistress of the house that a Serbian military officer was seen climbing up the water pipe and they have come to search for him. The stranger in the bedroom of Raina prepares himself for the impending crisis feeling that his death is absolutely certain, he flings Raina's cloak back to her.

## Raina Agrees to Keep the Man Safe

Driven by an inexplicable sense of pity, Raina asks the fugitive to hide behind the curtains and assures him to save his life. When a Russian officer comes in followed by Bulgarian soldiers and searches the room, Raina opens the shutters standing with the back to curtains behind which the run away soldier is hiding. The Russian officer asks Raina whether anybody could have entered her room without her knowledge. Raina denies it vehemently and says that she had not gone to bed yet. A gunshot Shalters the glass-pane of the window during the inquiry. The Russian officer goes quickly to the balcony and orders his soldiers to cease fire. He begs their pardon, bids good night to both the ladies and leaves the room. Louka notice the pistol of the fugitive lying on the divan and casts a significant look towards the curtain with a suggestion of the presence of the man there and leaves the room behind her mistress Catherine.

As soon as they depart, the refugee soldier comes out from behind the curtain and expresses gratitude to Raina saying that it was a narrow escape for him. He informs Raina that he is not a native Serb. He is a Swiss mercenary who joined the Serbian army merely because he met them first on the road from Switzerland.

It is clear that the man is really frightened and nervous. He shies like a terrified horse when Raina jumps up with a shriek because she had my mistake sat on his revolver lying on the divan. The man tells her that he has become nervous and sensitive because he has been under fire for three days. If Raina just scolded him and he would start crying. The man also informs her that his revolver is unloaded and he has no bullets. Instead of cartridges he carries chocolate creams in his belt. He tells her that there are only two sorts of carry bullets with themselves and the latter food. Raina is really shocked to hear it. On Raina's request, the man describes the recent Bulgarian cavalry charge headed by Sergius. He compares Sergius with Don Quixote and says that this act of his was simply suicide. He won the battle due to a mere stroke of luck. Unfortunately the enemies were supplied wrong kind of ammunition and could not fire. Otherwise this cavalry charge was a stupid deed and the leader was the moddest soldier ever let loose on the war field. The man says that Sergius should have been court-martialled for charge.

The depiction threatens to shatter all the romantic notions cherished by Raina and so she feels disgusted and hurt. She shows him the photograph of her finance and the intruder quickly recognises him as the leader of the cavalry charge. When Raina informs him that the portrait is of the person to whom she is betrothed, the man accuses Raina and says that it was not fair on her part to lead him on. But even then he is hardly able to stifle his laugh. He says that perhaps he was wrong and Sergius has somehow received some hint of the wrong kind of ammunition somehow and know that the charge was safe. But Raina still feels hurt because such an explanation proves Sergius to be a pretender and coward. She asks the man to leave the room. But then she feel amazed to see him behave like a coward.

## Discussion of Raina and the Man

The man refuses to climb down the pipe and says that he would prefer to be caught. He is unable to exert himself and do anything. When, however, the man gets some hint of Raina's desperation he decides to climb down. Raina called him chocolate cream soldier because he behaved softly and cowardly and carried and ate chocolate creams. He wants to prove her wrong. But when he says that he is pining for sleep and does not care whether he dies or lives, she feels compassionate and assures him of safety and hospitable treatment. She tels him about her family being cultured and sophisticated, about their love of opera, about their possession of a personal library, about their social position, about their refined habits etc. After this she asks him to keep standing so that he does not fall asleep and goes to inform her mother about his presence in her bedroom. When she returns, she finds the man fast asleep in her bed. When Catherine shakes him hard to wake him up Raina requests her to let the poor darling rest. The epithet amazes her mother and she stares at her hard. The man sleeps profoundly and the first act comes to an end.

## ACT-II

## The War Ends and Sergius Lusts after Louka

The act takes place on the sixth of March, 1886 four months have elapsed. It is a fine spring morning. Major Petkoff's servant Nicola advises the maid servant Louka to behave respectfully with the mistress of the house. Nicola wants to marry Louka. He is planning to open a shop in Sofia. He is a middle-aged man. He is of quiet temperament. His head is shaved. His forehead is like that a Japanese. Louka knows many secret of the Petkoff's family, therefore, she is confident that Major Petkoff will not interfere into her private affairs, nor will he be dissatisfied with her work.

Nicola says that he is also in the know of family secrets of the Petkoff's, but he does not want to take any advantage out of it. In case he becomes uncivil he could be dismissed from service, and nobody world rely on him. His whispers into the ear of Louka that he has been in the service of the Petkoff's for the ten years. He knows so many secrets of Catherine's life which he will not reveal even if he were given a handsome amount for that. Even if he tells something Petkoff to Catherine, she would not talk to him at least for six months. He is aware of many secrets of Raina and Sergius and the proposed marriage between them would not materialise.

Louka flat heart at the last sentence of Nicola. She turns towards Nicola and asks him as to how he came to know of these secrets. She herself never told anything to him. Nicola tells Louka humorous way that she was feeling so proud of herself for knowing some little secrets of Raina's life. Nicola tells Louka that she should try to win the confidence of Petkoff which would benefit her. Louka comic way at Nicola and speaks to him with repugnance and indifference that slavery resides in his heart. Nicola tells Louka bluntly that there lies the secrets of success.

## Major Petkoff Return from the War

Somebody knocks the door from the side of the garden of the house. Major Petkoff has returned from the war. Nicola recognises his voice. He runs towards the door. He tells Louka to prepare hot coffee for the master. Major Petkoff is a man of about fifty. He is happy. He is the richest man of the town. It is on account of this that he has been given the rank of Major in the Bulgarian Army. Louka came with coffee. Nicola goes inside the house to inform the mistress of the house about the arrival of Major Petkoff. Petkoff cuts a joke with Louka that it is fortunate that the Serbians did not abduct away Louka with them. Louka push the bottle on the table and says that it could not have happened.

Catherine enters, her hair is bound up with a coloured handkerchief. She wears Turkish sleepers in her feet. She looks attractive in her dress. Louka enters the house. Petkoff tells Catherine that the war is over. The treaty has been signed three days back. The troops have been ordered accordingly a day before. Catherine complains of bad throat. Major Petkoff says that it is on account of the fact that under new fashion she keeps herself unduly engaged in clearing her throat and in taking bath. Catherine dismisses her husband remark and says that he is a brute of his time. She adds that the Russian officers should have given him proper warning. Petkoff tells Catherine that the Russian officers was impressed very much that they have their personal library. Catherine feels sorry that he did not tell his Russian officer about the electric bell which they have in their house. Had it been told to them their social status would have gone much higher in the eyes of the Russian officers. But the bell was put after the departure of Petkoff to the war. Catherine says that civilised people call their servants by ringing the bell. Major Petkoff points out to wants clothes hanging infront of them and says that civilised people do not dry up their clothes like this. Catharine acknowledge that civilised people do not take notice of such small things.

## Arrival of Sergius

The arrival of Sergius is announced. Major Petkoff is fed up with him because he keeps on bether him about his promotion. He therefore, urges his wife to keep him engaged until Raina comes there. Catherine requested that after the marriage of Raina with Sergius he must be given promotion. Major Petkoff says that as long as war continue he should not think of promotion. He can be rewarded only when there is no more battles to be fought. Sergius takes his seat. He speaks proudly that it was his unmatched strategy about warfare that brought victory to the Bulgarians. He complains that officers were too liberal towards ineffective soldiers, and that his abilities were not properly appreciated. He informs Petkoff about his resignation.

Raina enters, Major Petkoff affectionately put his hand upon Raina's head. The presence of Sergius makes no impact upon Raina. He is telling about his war experience. According to him, war is not an art, but a profession. He is in favour of leaving war in the hands of those that are expert in warfare. This is why he was examing the exchange of Swiss-guards Raina restrict. She asks about the number of Swiss officers. Petkoff replies that legally the Serbian officers are Austrians only one Swiss has been given the rank of an officer. Raina wants to know about the features of the Swiss officer. Catherine is afraid lest the matter be out therefore, she asks Raina to keep quiet.

## Petkoff Discuss about the Battle

Petkoff tells about the Swiss officer that had run away from the battle of town. Sergius says that the Swiss officer was an unprofessional soldier therefore, he could not face the cavalry charge and ran away. In order to save his life he climbed up the water pipe line and hide himself in the bed-chamber of a Bulgarian young lady. The young lady was defraud or cheat by the officer. He spent an hour there. Then the lady informed her mother. The aged lady was also duped by the officer. Before dawn, the officer was given the overcoat of the head of the family and helped to escape stealthily.

The head of the family was away from home at that time Raina and Catharine did not appreciate this account of Sergius. Raina told Sergius that by living in the camp, his life had become joyless and dry. Raina had never thought that he would narrate such a story before her. Catherine says that there be any such woman she does not know her. Sergius apologises. After this Major Petkoff and Catherine move inside. Raina and Petkoff get engaged in conversation. Raina proposes for a walk before lunch. She goes inside to take her hat. She is happy that she has had deep experience of love. Louka enters Sergius looks towards her stealthily. He behaves a bit stability with Louka. He hits the ground with his shoes. He turns towards Louka and asks her if the understand the meaning of the deepest type of love. Louka expresses her ignorance about it. Sergius says that the love of highest kind is untiring. Sergius wants to take some rest. He tries to embrace Louka. Louka disentangles herself and says that Sergius is humiliating her, Sergius says that he is surprised as to why he behaved as such.

Sergius is the embodiment of highest love. How would he feel if he notices this. Louka implores him to go to such a place as may keep them away from the eyes of Raina. Sergius cannot free himself from his own illusion and infatuation. He again takes Louka in his tight embrace. Louka says that all good men are alike. She says that Raina loves somebody else behind Sergius, and Sergius also does the samething. Sergius was enraged when he heard this from Louka. He wanted to know the name of the other lover of Raina. Louka says that she has only heard her voice, but she can say with certainly that Raina loves him. On hearing this, Sergius is more infuriated. In his excitement he presses Louka so hard that she cries out. It is at this time that Raina and Catherine enter. Raina says humorosly that Sergius was making love with Louka.

## Captain Bluntschli Arrives to Return the Coat He had Borrowed from Raina

Catherine says that Major Petkoff wants to talk to Sergius on some military matters. When Sergius goes away Catherine Choralists Raina for giving shelter to the Swiss officer. Both Sergius and Petkoff have come to know about it. Major Petkoff demands his old coat. If the truth could be known to all the proposed marriage between Raina and Sergius might be broken. Raina has faith in Sergius. She says that she herself will tell everything to Sergius. It is at this time that Louka informs that a Swiss officer, Captain Bluntschli, wants to meet Catherine. He has a bag in his hand. Catherine understand that the officer has come he returns the coat of Petkoff. She gets nervous lest Sergius and Petkoff may recognise him. She instructs Nicola to bring his bag and tells Louka to escort the guest inside.

Bluntschli comes in Catherine tells him to leave the place immediately since the antagonism between the two rivals has not yet ended. Raina enters the room. As soon as she sees Bluntschli, she cries out, 'chocolate and says that Raina had prepared bread of the shape of chocolate cream soldier which has been spoiled by Nicola. At the same time, Nicola enters in with the bag of Bluntschli. A new problem is created for Catherine. Both Petkoff and Catherine criticise Nicola for his impertinance. They speak ill of him for having spoiled the bread of Raina. Catherine does not want the say of Bluntschli there anymore but Petkoff and Sergius insist again and again on his staying there. Catherine keeps quite. Ultimately Bluntschli gives his consent to stay there.

## ACT-III

## Raina Falls in Love with Captain Bluntschli

It is afternoon captain Bluntschli is writing an order regarding the move of the regiment. Sergius is signing the papers. Major Petkoff is talking to his wife. Petkoff says that the people sitting at ease in homes cannot understand what pleasure one gets in wasting time. He demands his old coat because he was confident that the coat might not be there. He tells Bluntschli six times with stakes that he should give him back his coat. Sergius says that in returns of it he will bring an Arabian horse in place of a haunting horse for Raina. In the meantime, as per orders of Catherine, Nicola brings Petkoff's Coat and hands it over to him, Major Petkoff wears his coat merrily.

Raina and Bluntschli get in opportunity to talk to each other in a lonely place. Raina admires Bluntschli and says that he is looking handsome. Bluntschli says that it is an account of the fact that he takes bath regularly, washes his teeth with toothpaste and takes proper rest. Raina asks him if his colleagues consider him a culprit for his having run away from the battlefield. He says that they cannot say to because they also did the samething. Raina expresses her displeasure at the point that Bluntschli told his friends about his hiding himself in her bedroom. Raina tells further that this thing has become known to her father and Sergius both. She says that they do not know certainly that it was she (Raina) who gave him shelter. Raina says that she does not tell lies even then for his sake she spoke lies twice. One she told a lie to the Russian officer that he was not hiding in her room.

The second time she told of lie was when she connected a story about the bread to conceal the truth about the chocolate cream soldier. Bluntschli replies that this does not make any effection him since he consider telling lies quite ethical and secondly he does not want to remember the name of the person who saved his life. He says that whenever she talks in an hyperbolic manner; he wishes to embrace her. He cannot believe that she never tells lies. Raina asks Bluntschli how he can understand her inner feelings. Bluntschli replies that the knowledge of inner feeling and the worldly experience are his guides. Raina feels surprised that Bluntschli is the first man who does not wholly rely on her. Bluntschli tells her bluntly that he knows her reality very well. He admits this also that he is much impressed with Raina's Romantic temperament. Raina gets immensely attracted towards Bluntschli.

She asks him about her portrait. He is just stunned to hear this because he had never known that Raina had put her portrait into the pocket to her father's coat. Raina tells him that she had put her photograph, on which something was written, in the pocket of her father's coat. Bluntschli had gone out of her room wearing that coat Raina gets disturbed lest the photograph may fall into the hands of her father. Bluntschli says that he had mortgaged that coat. It could be possible that the person might have searched the pockets. Raina gets annoyed at her business mentality of lower type. Both keep quiet for a while.

## Louka and Sergius Confess Their Love for Each Other

Louka comes in. She brings some letters and a telegram for Bluntschli which convey the information about his father's death. His father had left behind a chain of hotels for management. On hearing the news of the death of Bluntschli's father, Raina expresses her condolences. Bluntschli goes out of give the near of his departure. Louka says that Bluntschli is a heartless fellow since he did not get disturbed the least on hearing the news of the death of his father. Contrary to it Sergius is emotional. Raina gets angry. She goes out of the room.

Nicola enters. He becomes happy to find Louka alone. He tells her what was reward Sergius and Bluntschli have given him thirty liva. He displays them proudly. Louka sits beside him and looks at them with greedy eyes and tried to snatch them. Nicola takes them in his lefthand so that Louka may not snatch them away. He says that Sergius is a fool, but Bluntschli is intelligent. He starts planning to spend the money. He will invest twenty liva in having Banks Account.

He will give the remaining ten livas to Louka for her expenses on condition that she talks to him lovingly. He says that being a servant he sometimes feels tired. Major Petkoff does not believe it, because Louka was already engaged to Nicola, and had already taken money from him for his marriage. But Nicola clarifies his position and says that his ambition higher than his actual position. He was helping Louka with a view getting the proper advantage from her in lier of it when she gets married in a high family.

Louka criticize Sergius. All humiliate her, but Sergius stands beside her and takes her in his arms. Seeing this right Catherine gets wonder struck. Petkoff declares that Sergius will marry Louka. Bluntschli congratulates Sergius on his practical wisdom. Catherine abuses Louka.

Bluntschli thinks that these difference be eliminated. The situation is somewhat complicated. He says that Raina is a naughty girl of seventeen. There is so much difference of age between him and Raina that the question of love between them does not arise at all, he adds that in this tender age Raina cannot know the depth of love. Raina says that she is not seventeen, she is twenty three. Bluntschli at once propose to Raina for marriage. Catharine rejects his proposal because she considers him much below the status of Petkoff family. Major Petkoff is prepared to ignore the questions of social status if he feels convinced that the person to whom Raina is married will keep her happy.

Bluntschli informs them that after the death of his father he has become the owner of several hotels, and that from the point of view of both social and economic status he is a suitable match for Raina. Raina's parents give their consent immediately. Raina says in a joke that she is not going to be sold away to the highest bidder. Bluntschli replies at once that for her he is a mere chocolate-cream soldier. Raina's behaviour clearly shows that she is also ready for the marriage and that she is fully prepared to accept Bluntschli as her husband. Bluntschli says that he will have to go to understand his business, but he will soon come back and then he will perform the marriage ceremony. He adds that it is his wish that the marriage of Sergius and Louka be also postponed till then.

# Practice Questions

**1.** GB Shaw was born in
(a) 1856 (b) 1858 (c) 1860 (d) None of these

**2.** GB Shaw was born in
(a) London (b) Scotland
(c) Dublin (d) None of these

**3.** GB Shaw died in
(a) 1945 (b) 1950 (c) 1956 (d) None of these

**4.** GB Shaw began his career as a
(a) Novelist (b) Poet (c) Dramatist (d) None of these

**5.** GB Shaw was
(a) a dramatist (b) a novelist
(c) a prosewriter (d) All of these

**6.** Which of the following novels is by Shaw?
(a) Immaturity (b) The Irrational knot
(c) Love Among the Artists (d) All of these

**7.** Which of the following plays is by Shaw?
(a) Arms and the Man (b) Candida
(c) Man and Superman (d) All of these

**8.** Which of the following is not by Shaw?
(a) The Apple Cart (b) Mrs Warren's profession
(c) As You Like IT (d) None of these

**9.** Shaw was awarded Noble Prize for Literature in
(a) 1925 (b) 1927 (c) 1930 (d) None of these

**10.** The themes of Shaw's works are
(a) Rationalism (b) Critical rebellion
(c) Realism (d) All of these

**11.** Bernard Shaw was a
(a) Realist (b) Fabian Socialist
(c) Great wit (d) None of these

**12.** Which of the following is a tragedy?
(a) St Joan (b) Man and Superman
(c) Arms and the Man (d) None of these

**13.** Who was the father of the theatre of ideas in England?
(a) Shaw (b) Galsworthy
(c) WB Yeats (d) None of these

**14.** Who is the author of 'Arms and the Man'?
(a) GB Shaw (b) WB Yeats (c) Galsworthy (d) None of these

**15.** Raina belongs to
(a) Italy (b) Bulgaria (c) Serbia (d) None of these

**16.** Louka is
(a) Raina's cousin (b) Raina's maid servant
(c) Raina's neighbour (d) None of these

**17.** Nicola is
(a) an old man (b) a youngman
(c) a middle-aged man (d) None of these

**18.** In the beginning of the play Raina seems to be a
(a) Romantic girl (b) Brave girl
(c) Sentimental girl (d) None of these

**19.** Louka finally
(a) marries Nicola (b) rejects Nicola
(c) marries Sergius (d) None of these

**20.** Who is chocolate-cream soldier?
(a) Bluntschli (b) Major Petkoff (c) Sergius (d) None of these

**21.** Major Petkoff
(a) likes bathing (b) dislikes bathing
(c) is silent about bathing (d) None of these

**22.** 'Arms and the Man' was first staged in London in
(a) 21st April, 1894 (b) 21st April, 1895
(c) 21st April, 1896 (d) None of these

**23.** In America 'Arms and the Man' was first staged in
(a) September, 1894 (b) September, 1895
(c) September, 1896 (d) None of these

**24.** The German production of 'Arms and the Man' took place in Berlin in
(a)1902 (b)1903 (c) 1904 (d) None of these

**25.** The French production of 'Arms and the Man' took place in Paris in
(a)1919 (b) 1920 (c) 1921 (d) None of these

**26.** Major Sergius was a officer in the
(a) Bulgarian Army (b) Serbian Army
(c) Swiss Army (d) None of these

**27.** Captain Bluntschli was an officer in the
(a) Bulgarian Army (b) Swiss Army
(c) Serbian Army (d) None of these

**28.** Major Petkoff was an officer in the
(a) Swiss Army (b) Serbians Army
(c) Bulgarian Army (d) None of these

**29.** The battle between Bulgarian and Serbia was fought in
(a) 1885 (b) 1886 (c) 1887 (d) None of these

**30.** The first scene of the play, 'Arms and the Man' opens late in November in the year
(a) 1885 (b) 1886 (c) 1887 (d) None of these

**31.** Who is Raina's mother?
(a) Catherine (b) Louka (c) Mary (d) None of these

**32.** Catherine is
(a) Major Petkoff's wife
(b) Raina's mother
(c) Both (a) and (b)
(d) None of these

**33.** Who gives the news of a battle at Slivnitza to Raina?
(a) Louka (b) Catherine (c) Nicola (d) None of these

**34.** Who tells Raina that Sergius is the hero of the hour, the Idol of the regiment?
(a) Catherine (b) Louka
(c) Nicola
(d) None of these

**35.** Sergius dified ......... commanders at the Cavalry charge.
(a) Russian (b) Bulgarian (c) Serbian (d) None of these

**36.** The Cavalry charge was made against the
(a) Swiss (b) Serbians (c) Bulgarians (d) None of these

**37.** The Serbs had ......... officers.
(a) Russian (b) Austrian (c) Swiss (d) None of these

**38.** Who enters Raina's bed-room in the night of November, 1885?
(a) Bluntschli (b) Sergius (c) Petkoff (d) None of these

**39.** Bluntschli was a man of
(a) 33 (b) 34 (c) 35 (d) None of these

**40.** Bluntschli was a
(a) Serbian artillery officer (b) Bulgarian officer
(c) Russian officer (d) None of these

**41.** By birth Bluntschli is
(a) a Swiss (b) a Serb (c) a Bulgarian (d) None of these

**42.** Nicola is a character who has no
(a) illusions about his rank (b) morals in his character
(c) love for Petkoff family (d) desire to marry Louka

**43.** The play 'Arms and the Man' was published in the year
(a) 1893 (b) 1894 (c) 1895 (d) 1896

**44.** The play 'Arms and the Man' was included in the volume
(a) Plays Pleasant (b) Play Unpleasant
(c) Plays Satirical (d) Plays for Actors

**45.** The terms Shavian is an adjective of the word
(a) Shave (b) Shaw (c) Save (d) Safe

**46.** Shaw's plays are the plays of
(a) realism (b) impressionism
(c) expressionism (d) surrealism

**47.** George Bernard Shaw's play are called
(a) Plays of action (b) Plays of inaction
(c) Plays of sentiment (d) Plays of ideas

**48.** George Bernard Shaw was most influenced by
(a) William Shakespeare (b) Ben Jonson
(c) Henrik Ibsen (d) William Congreve

**49.** The most romantic scene in 'Arms and the Man is the
(a) Louka and Sergius meeting scene
(b) Captain Bluntschli and Raina meeting
(c) Major Petkoff and Catherine meeting scene
(d) Raina and Sergius meeting scene

**50.** Which character is Shaw's mouthpiece
(a) Sergius (b) Raina (c) Louka (d) Bluntschli

**51.** 'Arms and the Man' can be categorised as
(a) Love play (b) Problem play
(c) Sentimental play (d) Romantic play

**52.** Shaw married Charlotte Frances in
(a) 1898
(b) 1899 (c) 1900
(d) None of these

**53.** Charlotte Frances was
(a) an English beauty (b) an Irish heiress
(c) a Welsh princess (d) None of these

**54.** Charlotte died in
(a) 1940 (b) 1941 (c) 1942 (d) 1943

**55.** Shaw died in
(a) 1950 (b) 1952 (c) 1953 (d) None of these

**56.** Shaw established his first direct connection with the theatre in
(a) 1885 (b) 1886 (c) 1887 (d) None of these

**57.** Shaw's dramatic career ran from
(a) 1892 to 1936 (b) 1892 to 1938
(c) 1892 to 1940 (d) None of these

**58.** Shaw wrote
(a) 58 plays (b) 59 plays
(c) 60 plays (d) None of these

**59.** 'Arms and the Man' was produced in
(a) 1892 (b) 1894 (c) 1896 (d) None of these

**60.** Shaw's famous play, 'Man and Superman' came out in
(a) 1903 (b) 1904 (c) 1905 (d) None of these

**61.** Which of the following plays is by Shaw?
(a) Arms and the Man (b) Saint Joan
(c) Caesar and Cleopatra (d) All of these

**62.** Bernard Shaw wrote
(a) Plays (b) Novels
(c) Miscellaneous prose (d) All of these

**63.** Which of the following play is by Shaw?
(a) Widower's House (b) Philanderer
(c) Mr Warren's Profession (d) All of these

**64.** Which of the following plays is by Shaw?
(a) Arms and the Man (b) Candida
(c) The Devil's Disciple (d) All of these

**65.** Whose speech is this, "Sergius is the hero of the hour, the idol of the regiment"?
(a) Petkoff (b) Bluntschli (c) Raina (d) Catherine

**66.** Whose Speech is this, "If you have a drop of Bulgarian blood in your veins, you will worship him when he comes back"?
(a) Catherine (b) Raina (c) Louka (d) None of these

**67.** Whose speech is this, "What faithless little creatures girls are"?
(a) Catherine (b) Raina (c) Louka (d) None of these

**68.** Whose speech is this, "The Serbs are being chased right back through the pass, and they say they may run into the town"?
(a) Catherine (b) Raina (c) Louka (d) None of these

**69.** Whose speech is this, "this is the happiest night of my life if there are no fugitives"?
(a) Raina (b) Catherine (c) Louka (d) None of these

**70.** Whose speech is this, "I hadn't even a revolver cartridge. Only Chocolate"?
(a) Sergius (b) Bluntschli (c) Petkoff (d) None of these

**71.** "And these was Don Quixote flourishing like a drum major." Who said this?
(a) Sergius (b) Petkoff (c) Bluntschli (d) None of these

**72.** Who said this, "He and his regiment simply committed suicide"?
(a) Bluntschli (b) Petkoff (c) Sergius (d) None of these

**73.** Whose speech is this, "You are my enemy, and you are at my mercy"?
(a) Catherine (b) Raina (c) Louka (d) None of these

**74.** Whose speech is this, "Oh you are a very poor soldier a chocolate cream soldier"?
(a) Catherine (b) Louka
(c) Raina (d) None of these

**75.** Whose speech is this, "Look at my father! He never had a bath in his life. I don't mind a good wash once a week to keep up my position"?
(a) Petkoff (b) Bluntschli (c) Sergius (d) None of these

**76.** Who said this, "It was the cradle and the grave of my military reputation"?
(a) Petkoff (b) Sergius (c) Bluntschli (d) None of these

**77.** Whose speech is this, "This hand is more accustomed to the sword than to the pen" ?
(a) Bluntschli (b) Petkoff (c) Sergius (d) None of these

**78.** Whose speech is this, "I'm your in fatuated admirer"?
(a) Bluntschli (b) Sergius (c) Petkoff (d) None of these

**79.** Who said this, "Our romance is broken. Life is a farce"?
(a) Bluntschli (b) Sergius (c) Louka (d) None of these

**80.** Whose speech is this, "Soldiering is the Coward's art of attacking mercilessly when you are strong and keeping out of harms way"?
(a) Sergius (b) Bluntschli (c) Petkoff (d) None of these

**81.** Who said this, "Get your enemy at a disadvantage and never, on any account, fight him on equal terms"?
(a) Petkoff (b) Sergius (c) Bluntschli (d) None of these

**82.** Whose speech is this, "People of high social status are all alike"?
(a) Raina (b) Bluntschli (c) Louka (d) None of these

**83.** Whose speech is this, "You said you had told only two lies in your whole life"?
(a) Bluntschli (b) Louka (c) Raina (d) None of these

**84.** Whose speech is this, "I would marry the man I loved, which no other queen in Europe has the courage to do"?
(a) Raina (b) Louka (c) Catherine (d) None of these

**85.** Whose speech is this, "If I loved you, and I were the Czar himself, I would set you on the throwne by my side"?
(a) Bluntschli (b) Nicola (c) Sergius (d) None of these

**86.** Whose speech is this, "You have deceived me, you are my rival. I brook no rivals"?
(a) Sergius (b) Bluntschli
(c) Nicola (d) None of these

**87.** Whose speech is this, "I have allowed you to call me a fool. "You may now call me a coward as well"?
(a) Bluntschli (b) Sergius (c) Nicola (d) None of these

**88.** Whose speech is this, "A man who has spoiled all his chances in life though an incurably romantic disposition a man"?
(a) Sergius (b) Petkoff (c) Bluntschli (d) None of these

**89.** Turkish Ottoman is
(a) a cushioned seat without back (b) a Turkish dog
(c) a Turkish scent (d) None of these

**90.** How old is Raina?
(a) 17 (b) 20 (c) 23 (d) None of these

**91.** How old is Bluntschli ?
(a) 30 (b) 32 (c) 34 (d) None of these

**92.** How old is Catherine?
(a) Over thirty (b) Over fifty (c) Over forty (d) None of these

**93.** Major Petkoff is affectionately called by Catherine
(a) Paul (b) Pat (c) Koff (d) None of these

**94.** How old is Major Petkoff ?
(a) About forty (b) About forty five
(c) About fifty (d) None of these

**95.** Dragoman is an imaginary
(a) River (b) Hill (c) Pass (d) None of these

**96.** Battle at Slivnitza was fought in
(a) 1885 (b) 1895 (c) 1983 (d) None of these

**97.** By birth Bluntschli was
(a) a Swiss (b) an Austrian
(c) a Serb (d) None of these

**98.** Don Quixote is a character created by
(a) Byron (b) Pushkin (c) Cervantes (d) None of these

**99.** Sergius is the hero of the battle of ..... according to Catherine.
(a) Slivnitza (b) Pirrot
(c) Philippopolis (d) Bucharest

**100.** The first name of Major Petkoff is ..... .
(a) Robert (b) Greg (c) Paul (d) Peter

**101.** The first act of the play takes place in November......... .
(a) 1881 (b) 1882 (c) 1884 (d) 1885

**102.** Raina and Sergius were very fond of reading
(a) Wordsworth and Keats (b) Shelley and Gorky
(c) Tolstoy and Scott (d) Byron and Pushkin

**103.** The Bulgarian army was commanded by
(a) Serbian officers (b) Austrian officers
(c) Russian officers (d) Bulgarian officers

**104.** In 'Arms and the Man' who is compared to Don Quixote charging at the windmills ?
(a) Bluntschli (b) Sergius Saranoff
(c) Major Petkoff (d) Nicola

**105.** Raina uses the epithet 'Chocolate Cream Soldier, for ......... .
(a) Bluntschli (b) Sergius Saranoff
(c) Major Petkoff (d) Nicola

**106.** Nicola is.......
(a) Shrewd and intelligent (b) Stupid and dumb
(c) Idle and worthless (d) Service and blunt

**107.** Sergius's cavalry charge on the Serbs was in fact.........
(a) unprofessional and foolhardy (b) heroic and valiant
(c) noble and professional (d) None of the above

**108.** Catherine's attitude to Sergius' cavalry charge is
(a) patriotic (b) romantic
(c) neutral (d) analytical

**109.** Bluntschli carries in his cartridge cases .........
(a) bullets (b) ammunition
(c) spices (d) chocolates

**110.** "He did it like an operatic tenor." Who speaks these words about whom?
(a) Sergius about Bluntschli (b) Bluntschli about Nicola
(c) Nicola and Major Petkoff (d) Bluntschli about Sergius

**111.** The serbs could not repel Sergius' cavalry charge because
(a) they were cowards
(b) they were taking rest
(c) they were supplied wrong kind of ammunition
(d) None of the above

**112.** "A regular handsome fellow, with flashing eyes and lovely moustache, shouting his war cry and charging like Don Quixote at the windmills". Who described whom in these words?
(a) Raina describes Bluntschli
(b) Bluntschli describes Sergius
(c) Sergius describes Major Petkoff (d) Catherine describes Sergius

**113.** While talking about the hospitality of 'The Petkoffs' Raina makes a reference to
(a) Pushkin (b) Byron
(c) Ernani (d) Virgil

**114.** Bluntschli is a
(a) French (b) Austrian
(c) Swiss (d) Russian

**115.** Raina utters the words 'The poor darling' for
(a) Sergius (b)Bluntschli
(c) Major Petkoff (d) None of these

**116.** Nicola dreams of opening a shop in
(a) Pirrot (b) Slivnitza
(c) Switzerland (d) Sofia

**117.** Catherine wants to make Prince........the Emperor of Balkans.
(a) George (b) Alexander
(c) Robert (d) Pushkin

**118.** Major Petkoff holds.....as responsible for Catherine's sore throats.
(a) daily washing (b) viral infection
(c) ice creams (d) cold drinks

**119.** What does Catherine get installed in her house when Major Petkoff is away fighting against the Serbs?
(a) A washing machine (b) An electric bell
(c) An electric lamp (d) None of these

**120.** "He was like a commercial traveller in uniform." Who utters these words about whom?
(a) Sergius about Nicola (b) Nicola about Bluntschli
(c) Bluntschli about Sergius (d) Sergius about Bluntschli

**121.** "You are an abominable little cold of common clay." Who abuses whom with these words?
(a) Louka abuses Sergius (b) Louka abuses Nicola
(c) Sergius abuses Louka (d) Nicola abuses Louka

**122.** The second Act begins on the 6th March,
(a) 1883 (b) 1994
(c) 1885 (d) 1886

**123.** The three regiments are to be sent to
(a) Pirrot (b) Pierpoint
(c) Philippines (d) Philippopolis

**124.** What is the designation of Bluntschli?
(a) Captain (b) Major
(c) Lieutenant (d) Colonel

**125.** To feel absolutely comfortable Major Petkoff only misses one thing. What is it?
(a) his pen (b) his shirt (c) his coat (d) his sword

**126.** "When you strike that noble attitude and speak in that thrilling voice, admire you but I find it impossible to believe a single word you say. Who is speaking to whom here?
(a) Sergius to Louka (b) Louka to Sergius
(c) Raina to Bluntschli (d) Bluntschli to Raina

**127.** Who claims to have made a woman of Louka ?
(a) Sergius (b) Nicola
(c) Bluntschli (d) Catherine

**128.** "The way to get on as a lady is the same as the way to get on as servant." Who speaks this sentence ?
(a) Bluntschli (b) Sergius
(c) Nicola (d) Louka

**129.** Sergius claims-"If I loved you and I were the ....... himself, I would set you on the throne by my side'.
(a) King (b) Emperor
(c) Czar (d) None of these

**130.** "Oh, War! War! the dream of patriots and heroes !" Who utters these words?
(a) Sergius (b) Bluntschli
(c) Major Petkoff (d) Nicola

**131.** 'Life is a farce'. Who says this in 'Arms and the Man'?
(a) Bluntschli (b) Sergius
(c) Major Petkoff (b) Nicola

**132.** Who, according to Nicola, "had a soul above her station."
(a) Raina (b) Catherine
(c) Louka (d) Sergius

**133.** Raina is ......... years of age.
(a) 17 (b) 19 (c) 21 (d) 23

**134.** Who says that he has got "an incurably romantic disposition?"
(a) Sergius (b) Bluntschli
(c) Major Petkoff (d) Nicola

**135.** Does Bluntschli own a tea garden also?

(a) Yes (b) No
(c) Cannct say (d) None of these

**136.** How many medals has Bluntschli won for distinguished services?

(a) Four (b) Five (c) Three (d) Two

**137.** "What-a man! Is he a man !" Whom do these words refer to

(a) Nicola (b) Major Petkoff
(c) Sergius (d) Bluntschli

**138.** Raina is

(a) an Indian (b) a Swiss
(c) a Bulgarian (d) a Serbian

**139.** Nicola is

(a) young (b) old
(c) small boy (d) middle aged

**140.** Louka finally

(a) marries Sergius (b) marries Bluntschli
(c) marries Nicola (d) marries Major Petkoff

**141.** The title of the play is lifted from a line by

(a) Homer (b) Virgil
(c) Horace (d) None of these

**142.** Catherine is a woman of about........ years of age.

(a) 30 (b) 40 (c) 50 (d) 60

**143.** Raina marries Bluntschli because he is a ......... man.

(a) rational (b) handsome
(c) witty (d) educated

**144.** The main theme of the play 'Arms and the Man' is

(a) war and love (b) love and marriage
(c) marriage and divorce (d) platonic love

**145.** 'Arms and the Man' is

(a) a historical play
(b) an anti-romantic comedy
(c) a romantic comedy
(d) None of the above

**146.** The marriage between Sergius and Louka is indicate of Shaw's

(a) nepotism (b) liberalism
(c) capitalism (d) socialism

**147.** The play 'Arms and the Man' was published in the year

(a) 1893 (b) 1894
(c) 1895 (d) 1896

**148.** The play 'Arms and the Man' was included in the volume:

(a) Plays pleasant (b) Plays unpleasant
(c) Plays satirical (d) None of these

**149.** Shaw's plays are the plays of

(a) Realism (b) Feminism
(c) Imagism (d) Expressionism

**150.** Shaw was most influenced by

(a) Wordsworth (b) Pinter
(c) Ibsen (d) Galsworthy

**151.** In the play 'Arms and the Man'........ is Shaw's mouthpiece.

(a) Sergius (b) Nicola
(c) Bluntschli (d) Major Petkoff

**152.** 'Arms and the Man' may be categorised as a

(a) romantic play (b) surrealistic play
(c) problem play (d) sentimental comedy

## ANSWERS

| | | | | | | | | | | | | | | | | | | | |
|---|---|---|---|---|---|---|---|---|---|---|---|---|---|---|---|---|---|---|---|
| 1. | (a) | 2. | (c) | 3. | (b) | 4. | (a) | 5. | (d) | 6. | (d) | 7. | (d) | 8. | (c) | 9. | (a) | 10. | (d) |
| 11. | (d) | 12. | (a) | 13. | (a) | 14. | (a) | 15. | (b) | 16. | (b) | 17. | (c) | 18. | (a) | 19. | (c) | 20. | (a) |
| 21. | (b) | 22. | (a) | 23. | (a) | 24. | (b) | 25. | (c) | 26. | (a) | 27. | (c) | 28. | (c) | 29. | (a) | 30. | (a) |
| 31. | (a) | 32. | (c) | 33. | (b) | 34. | (a) | 35. | (a) | 36. | (b) | 37. | (b) | 38. | (a) | 39. | (c) | 40. | (a) |
| 41. | (a) | 42. | (a) | 43. | (b) | 44. | (a) | 45. | (b) | 46. | (a) | 47. | (d) | 48. | (c) | 49. | (a) | 50. | (d) |
| 51. | (b) | 52. | (a) | 53. | (b) | 54. | (d) | 55. | (a) | 56. | (b) | 57. | (c) | 58. | (c) | 59. | (b) | 60. | (a) |
| 61. | (d) | 62. | (d) | 63. | (d) | 64. | (d) | 65. | (d) | 66. | (a) | 67. | (b) | 68. | (c) | 69. | (a) | 70. | (b) |
| 71. | (c) | 72. | (a) | 73. | (c) | 74. | (c) | 75. | (a) | 76. | (b) | 77. | (c) | 78. | (a) | 79. | (b) | 80. | (a) |
| 81. | (b) | 82. | (c) | 83. | (a) | 84. | (b) | 85. | (c) | 86. | (a) | 87. | (b) | 88. | (c) | 89. | (a) | 90. | (c) |
| 91. | (c) | 92. | (c) | 93. | (a) | 94. | (c) | 95. | (c) | 96. | (a) | 97. | (a) | 98. | (c) | 99. | (a) | 100. | (c) |
| 101 | (d) | 102. | (d) | 103. | (c) | 104. | (b) | 105. | (a) | 106. | (a) | 107. | (a) | 108. | (b) | 109. | (d) | 110. | (d) |
| 111. | (c) | 112. | (b) | 113. | (c) | 114. | (c) | 115. | (b) | 116. | (d) | 117. | (b) | 118. | (a) | 119. | (b) | 120. | (d) |
| 121. | (c) | 122. | (d) | 123. | (d) | 124. | (a) | 125. | (c) | 126. | (d) | 127. | (b) | 128. | (c) | 129. | (c) | 130. | (a) |
| 131. | (b) | 132. | (c) | 133. | (d) | 134. | (b) | 135. | (a) | 136. | (a) | 137. | (c) | 138. | (c) | 139. | (d) | 140. | (a) |
| 141. | (b) | 142. | (b) | 143. | (a) | 144. | (a) | 145. | (b) | 146. | (d) | 147. | (b) | 148. | (a) | 149. | (a) | 150. | (c) |
| 151. | (c) | 152. | (a) | | | | | | | | | | | | | | | | |

Chapter 21

# The Tempest

*William Shakespeare*

## About the Author

William Shakespeare was born on 26th April, 1564 in Stratford upon Avon, London. William Shakespeare was an English poet, playwright and actor, widely regarded as both the greatest writer in the English language and the world's pre-eminent dramatist. He is often called England's national poet and the 'Bard of Avon'.

His extant works including collaborations, consist of approximately 39 plays, 154 sonnets, two long narrative poems and a few other verses, some of uncertain authorship. His plays have been translated into every major living language and are performed more often than those of any other playwright. Shakespeare's first plays were written in the conventional style of the day. He wrote them in a stylised language that did not always spring naturally from the needs of the characters or the drama.

However, Shakespeare soon began to adapt the traditional styles to his own purposes. No single play marks a change from the traditional to the freestyle. Shakespeare combined the two throughout his career, with Romeo and Juliet perhaps the best example of the mixing of the styles.

The blank verse of his early plays is quite different from that of his later ones. Once Shakespeare mastered traditional blank verse, he began to interrupt and vary its flow. This technique releases the new power and flexibility of the poetry in plays such as Julius Caesar and Hamlet.

The first recorded works of Shakespeare are Richard III and the three parts of Henry VI, written in the early 1590s during a vogue for historical drama. 'Titus Andronicus', 'The Comedy of Errors', 'The Taming of the Shrew', and 'The Two Gentlemen of Verona' are also based on classical models.

### Comedy to Romanticism

Shakespeare's early classical and Italianate comedies, containing tight double plots and precise comic sequences, give way in the mid-1590s to the romantic atmosphere of his most acclaimed comedies. 'A Midsummer Night's Dream' is a witty mixture of romance, fairy magic and comic lowlife scenes. Shakespeare's next comedy, the equally romantic 'Merchant of Venice', contains a portrayal of the vengeful Jewish moneylender Shylock, which reflects Elizabethan views but may appear derogatory to modern audiences. The wit and wordplay of 'Much Ado About Nothing', the charming rural setting of 'As You Like It', and the lively merrymaking of 'Twelfth Night' complete Shakespeare's sequence of great comedies.

### Problem Plays

In the early 17th century, Shakespeare wrote so-called 'problem plays' 'Measure for Measure', 'Troilus and Cressida', and 'All's Well That Ends Well' and a number of his best known tragedies. The titular hero of one of Shakespeare's greatest tragedies, Hamlet, has probably been discussed more than any other Shakespearean character, especially for his famous soliloquy which begins 'To be or not to be; that is the question'. Unlike the introvert Hamlet, whose fatal flaw is hesitation, the heroes of the tragedies that followed, Othello and King Lear, are undone by hasty errors of judgement.

The plots of Shakespeare's tragedies often hinge on such fatal errors or flaws, which overturn order and destroy the hero and those he loves. In Othello, the villain Iago stokes Othello's sexual jealousy to the point where he murders the innocent wife who loves him.

In King Lear, the old king commits the tragic error of giving up his powers, initiating the events which lead to the torture and blinding of the Earl of Gloucester and the murder of Lear's youngest daughter Cordelia. In Macbeth, Shakespeare adds a supernatural element to the tragic structure.

### Romance to Tragicomedy

In his final period, Shakespeare turned to romance or tragicomedy and completed three more major plays: 'Cymbeline', 'The Winter's Tale', and 'The Tempest', as well as the 'Collaboration', 'Pericles', 'Prince of Tyre'.

He died on 23rd April, 1616.

## Summary

### Introduction

Although some scholars have speculated that Shakespeare wrote portions of The Tempest at an earlier stage in his career most literary historians assign the entire play a composition date of 1610 or 1611. And while Shakespeare may have had a hand in The Two Noble Kinsmen (written a decade or so after The Tempest and assigned to dual authorship), The Tempest is customarily identified as the Bard's last stage piece. These marginal issues aside, The Tempest is the fourth, final and the finest of Shakespeare's great and/or late romances. Along with Pericles, Cymbeline, and The Winter's Tale, The Tempest belongs to the genre of Elizabethan romance plays. It combines elements of tragedy (Prospero's revenge) with those of romantic comedy (the young lovers Miranda and Ferdinand) and like one of Shakespeare's problem plays, Measure for Measure, it poses deeper questions that are not completely resolved at the end. The romance genre is distinguished by the inclusion (and synthesis) of these tragic, comic and problematical ingredients and further marked by a happy ending (usually concluding with a masque or dance) in which all or most of the characters are brought into harmony.

### Theme

The richness of The Tempest as theater is matched by the extraordinary thematic complexity of its text. Recognising that all of the themes and accompanying figurative strands of the play cannot be discussed here, the play's topical highlights can still be approached by first noting the salience of two themes that arise from the very theatricality of the play: the opposition between reality and illusion and the tandem subject of the theater itself. The play challenges our senses and is self-consciously a performance orchestrated by Shakespeare's effigy in the master illusionist Prospero. In addition, there are numerous interpenetrating polarities in the play, most notably between nature and civilisation or art. These thematic strands come together at multiple points of intersection. Nevertheless, from one angle in the text, The Tempest asks a single question, one that Shakespeare had posed in many of his other plays: What is a human being? (or, in Elizabethan terms: What is man?)

When Shakespeare came to write The Tempest in 1610, the recent establishment of English colonies in the new world spurred interest among the dramatist's contemporaries in the differences among people in the two hemispheres. That led to philosophical speculations about human nature itself: Are all people the same, no matter where they live? How much does one's environment affect one's behaviour and more importantly, one's outlook on life? These are the questions that underlie Shakespeare's last drama, a play that transcends the traditional definitions of tragedy or comedy to encompass elements of both.

### Prespero with His Daughter, Miranda at Island

Prospero, the rightful Duke of Milan, has been living on a primitive island with his fifteen year old daughter, Miranda, for the past 12 years. His dukedom had been usurped by his own brother, Antonio, whom Prospero had entrusted to manage the affairs of government while he was concentrating on his study of the liberal arts.

### Conspiracy by Antonio

With the support of fernando Alonso, the King of Naples, Antonio conspired against his brother to become the new Duke of Milan. Prospero and his three year old daughter were put on 'a rotten carcass of a butt' without a sail. Gonzalo, a member of the king's council, took pity on them and stocked the leaky vessel with food, fresh water, clothing and Prospero's books. Providence has now brought his enemies to the shore of the island and Prospero must act quickly.

The action begins with a tempestuous storm at sea. Afraid for their lives, Alonso and Gonzalo urge the Boatswain to do all he can to save the ship, but he rudely orders the royal party to stay in their cabins and trouble him not. They are finally convinced to go below and pray for mercy.

### Ferdinand Meets Miranda

Ariel, an airy spirit, raised the tempest just as he was instructed by Prospero, his master, informing Prospero that all except the mariners plunged into the sea. Ariel reports that he has left the ship safely docked in the harbor with the mariners aboard. The rest of the passengers, with garments unblemished, have been dispersed around the island. Ariel then lures Ferdinand, Prince of Naples, onto the island with his songs, informing him of his father's supposed death by drowning. The young prince is led past Prospero's cave where he meets Miranda and they fall in love. To keep Ferdinand from winning his prize (Miranda) too quickly and easily, Prospero uses his magic to force Ferdinand to yield to the indignity of stacking logs.

### Alonso and Gonzalo Put to Sleep by Ariel

Elsewhere on the island, Ariel, with the help of Prospero's magic, puts Alonso and Gonzalo to sleep. While they sleep Antonio and Sebastian conspire to kill Alonso and Gonzalo and take over the throne. Just as they draw their swords, Ariel awakens Gonzalo and he in turn, rouses the king. The conspirators claim that they heard wild animals and drew their swords. The king readily accepts their excuse.

### Caliban Kneels to Stephano

Caliban enters, cursing his master, Prospero, for enslaving him. Trinculo, the king's jester, appears hiding under Caliban's cloak to escape a rainstorm. Stephano approaches them, thinking it is a monster with four legs.

He finally recognises Trinculo and is surprised to see him alive. Stephano, having drifted ashore on a barrel of wine, offers Caliban a drink. Unaccustomed to the effects of the alcohol, Caliban kneels to Stephano, taking him for a god who 'bears celestial liquor'. Determined that Stephano should be lord of the island, Caliban leads the pair to Prospero's cave where they plan to murder him.

## Royal Party Warned by Ariel

Prospero magically sets a banquet for the royal party but Ariel, disguised as a harpy, claps his wings over the table and it vanishes. Ariel warns the royal party that the storm was a punishment for their foul deeds and there is no way out except repentance.

## Ferdinand Relieved of His Duties

In another part of the island, Prospero relieves Ferdinand of his duties, telling him he has endured the difficult trial of love and has won Miranda's hand in marriage. Ariel arranges a masque in honour of the happy couple, but while the masque is in progress, Prospero suddenly remembers Caliban's plot to kill him and the masque vanishes.

## The Spirits in the Shape of Dogs Released by Ariel

Ariel has led the conspirators from the filthy-mantled pool to Prospero's 'glistering apparel' hanging on a lime tree in front of his cave. Though Caliban is annoyed, his companions are gleefully sidetracked, stealing the royal robes and forgetting their purpose at hand which is to murder Prospero. Finally, spirits in the shape of dogs are released, and the thieving trio are driven out.

## Prospero Gives up His Magical Powers

The king and his party are brought to Prospero where he charms them in his magic circle, praising Gonzalo for his kindness, but censuring Alonso for his cruelty and Antonio for his ambition. Removing his magician's robe, Prospero gives up his magical powers, presenting himself to Alonso as the 'wronged Duke of Milan', and the repentant king immediately restores his dukedom. In a sudden spirit of forgiveness, he pardons all of them for their crimes against him. He then leads Alonso to his cell where Ferdinand and Miranda are making a pretense of playing chess. Alonso is overjoyed to see his son alive.

Ariel enters with the master and boatswain of the ship. To the king's amazement the ship is undamaged and docked in the harbour.

## Conspirators Appeared before Prospero

The three conspirators, driven by Ariel, appear in their stolen royal apparel. Caliban calls himself a 'thrice-double ass' to have taken Stephano for a god. Prospero invites the king's entire party to spend the night in his cell where he will give them an account of his last 12 years on the island. In the morning, they will return to Naples where they will prepare for the marriage of the betrothed pair, Ferdinand and Miranda.

## Ariel Rewarded for His Services

Prospero rewards Ariel for his services by giving him his freedom and releasing him to the elements. In the epilogue Prospero tells the audience his magic powers are gone, his dukedom has been restored, and he has forgiven his enemies. He now asks them to praise his performance with their applause and thereby, release him from the illusory world of the island.

# Practice Questions

**1.** Who or what causes the shipwreck at the opening of the play?
(a) Poseidon
(b) A whirlpool
(c) Prospero
(d) The Boatswain's bad sailing

**2.** After the shipwreck, what does Prospero order Ariel to do?
(a) Become invisible
(b) Attack the lords
(c) Build a boat
(d) Make a feast

**3.** Who plots to murder the shipwrecked lords as they sleep?
(a) Caliban and Trinculo
(b) Stephano and Caliban
(c) Ferdinand and Miranda
(d) Stephano and Antonio

**4.** Who gets drunk and raucous?
(a) Ferdinand, Miranda and Prospero
(b) Stephano, Trinculo, and Caliban
(c) Alonso, Gonzalo and Sebastian
(d) Ariel, Caliban and Prospero

**5.** What are Ferdinand and Miranda doing when Prospero reveals them to the lords?
(a) Spying on the lords
(b) Playing chess
(c) Chopping wood
(d) Stealing clothing

**6.** Where was William Shakespeare born?
(a) Kingston-upon-Thames
(b) Berwick-upon-Tweed
(c) Shipston-on-Stour
(d) Stratford-upon-Avon

**7.** 'The Tempest' is probably the .......... play that Shakespeare wrote by himself.
(a) First (b) Last
(c) Longest (d) Most popular

**8.** What was the location of the real world tempest that Shakespeare drew upon when writing the play?
(a) Bermuda (b) South India
(c) Cypress (d) Micronesia

**9.** Some aspects of the play have the feeling of a highly stylised form of dramatic, musical entertainment called a
(a) carnivàle (b) fete
(c) masque (d) soiree

**10.** In 'The Tempest', the magical character that gives up his art has been broadly interpreted as referring to which real world figure?
(a) Queen Elizabeth (b) King James
(c) Christopher Marlowe (d) Shakespeare himself

**11.** Whom does Caliban mistake for one of Prospero's spirits sent to torment him?
(a) Stephano (b) Ferdinand
(c) Miranda (d) Trinculo

**12.** What was Prospero's title before his position was usurped and he was forced to flee Italy?
(a) Duke of Milan (b) King of Naples
(c) Duke of Naples (d) Pope of Rome

**13.** From which country is Alonso's ship returning when it is caught in the tempest?
(a) Naples (b) England
(c) Tunis (d) Bermudas

**14.** How long have Prospero and Miranda been on their island?
(a) Ten years (b) Fifteen years
(c) Twelve years (d) One day

**15.** What was the name of Caliban's mother?
(a) Ariel (b) Claribel
(c) Sycorax (d) Setebos

**16.** Over how many days does the action of 'The Tempest' take place?
(a) Two (b) One (c) Three (d) Four

**17.** Which mythical figures appear in the wedding masque Prospero stages for Miranda and Ferdinand?
(a) Cupid, Venus, and Mars (b) Jupiter and Saturn
(c) Ceres, Iris, and Juno (d) Isis and Osiris

**18.** Which character is Prospero's brother?
(a) Alonso (b) Sebastian
(c) Gonzalo (d) Antonio

**19.** Which character is Sebastian's brother?
(a) Prospero (b) Antonio
(c) Gonzalo (d) Alonso

**20.** What do we see Miranda and Ferdinand doing in the play's final scene?
(a) Playing cards (b) Carrying wood
(c) Playing chess (d) Playing tag

**21.** What shape does Ariel assume at the magical banquet in Act III, Scene III?
(a) Harpy (b) Eagle (c) Sea Nymph (d) Hound

**22.** What do Prospero and Ariel set out as bait for Caliban, Trinculo, and Stephano?
(a) butt of sack
(b) the nimble marmoset
(c) glistening apparel
(d) thousand twangling instruments

**23.** What does Caliban say must be done before Prospero can be killed?
(a) His magic cloak must be burnt
(b) His books must be seized
(c) Miranda must be killed
(d) A tempest must be raised

**24.** What is the name of Alonso's daughter?
(a) Claribel (b) Miranda (c) Sycorax (d) Alonsa

**25.** What does Prospero give as his reason for treating Caliban badly?
(a) Caliban tried to kill him
(b) Caliban tried to steal his books
(c) Caliban is merely a beast
(d) Caliban attempted to rape Miranda

**26.** Who helped Prospero and Miranda to flee Italy?
(a) Antonio (b) Gonzalo (c) Trinculo (d) Claribel

**27.** Where does Ariel put the mariners and Boatswain after the tempest?
(a) In a thicket
(b) Under Caliban's cloak
(c) Asleep in the ship in the harbor
(d) In Prospero's cell

**28.** Where did Sycorax imprison Ariel?
(a) On another island (b) In a cloven pine
(c) In a lion's den (d) Inside a stone

**29.** What task are both Caliban and Ferdinand forced to perform?
(a) Marrying Miranda (b) Singing drunkenly
(c) Collecting berries (d) Carrying wood

**30.** Who persuades Sebastian to try to kill Alonso?
(a) Antonio (b) Gonzalo
(c) Ariel (d) Alonso

**31.** What does Prospero intend to 'drown' after he has reconciled with his enemies?
(a) His magic garments (b) His book
(c) His staff (d) Caliban

**32.** What does Caliban say is his chief profit from learning language?
(a) He knows how to curse
(b) He can show Prospero the qualities of the isle
(c) He can woo Miranda
(d) He can sing with Trinculo and Stephano

**33.** Which characters do Stephano and Trinculo most clearly parody?
(a) Prospero and Miranda (b) Caliban and Sycorax
(c) Alonso and Gonzalo
(d) Antonio and Sebastian

**34.** What is the final task Prospero orders Ariel to perform?
(a) To release Sycorax
(b) To haul a load of wood
(c) To give the fleet calm seas on its return to Italy
(d) To take charge of Caliban

**35.** We are told that one of the following characters has visited England. Which one?
(a) Stephano (b) Prospero (c) Trinculo (d) Alonso

**36.** Who is the King of Naples?
(a) Prospero (b) Alonso
(c) Sebastian (d) Antonio

**37.** What has Prospero been doing on the island for twelve years?
(a) Building a boat (b) Hiding
(c) Plotting murder (d) Refining his magic

**38.** What did Prospero do for Ariel?
(a) Released him from imprisonment
(b) Taught him magic
(c) Gave him money
(d) Helped him to kill Sycorax

**39.** Who helped Prospero to escape to the island where the action of the play takes place?
(a) Ferdinand (b) Alonso (c) Ariel (d) Gonzalo

**40.** Who provides the main comic relief in the play?
(a) Antonio and Sebastian
(b) Ariel and Prospero
(c) Trinculo and Stephano
(d) Ferdinand and Miranda

**41.** What got Prospero into trouble before the play begins?
(a) His political ambition
(b) His pursuit of knowledge
(c) His boring nature
(d) His speeches

**42.** How have many critics and readers interpreted Prospero's role in the play?
(a) A political critique (b) A comic foil
(c) A parable
(d) As Shakespeare's surrogate

**43.** What does Miranda do in Act III, Scene I that is surprising?
(a) Proposes to Ferdinand (b) Attacks Caliban
(c) Fights with her father (d) Casts a spell

**44.** What is Caliban?
(a) The son of a witch-hag
(b) A complex figure
(c) A fool
(d) All of the above

**45.** What does Caliban do that contrasts with his savage demeanor and grotesque appearance?
(a) Rebels against Prospero
(b) Gives beautiful speeches
(c) Desires to impregnate Miranda
(d) Gets drunk

**46.** As the play progresses, what role does Prospero come to mirror more explicitly?
(a) Explorer (b) Teacher
(c) Dictator (d) Author

**47.** In the play, is Caliban a monster or a man?
(a) His nature is split
(b) He is monstrous
(c) He is made brutish by oppression
(d) The matter is left ambiguous

**48.** What kind of relationship does nearly every scene in the play depict?
(a) The relationship between lovers
(b) A power dynamic
(c) The father-daughter bond
(d) Business partnership

**49.** What does the parallel between Alonso's desire to drown himself and Prospero's promise to drown his book symbolise?
(a) Their depression
(b) Their need for sacrifice
(c) The power of water
(d) Unrequited love

**50.** What does 'The Tempest' that begins the play symbolise?
(a) Suffering and magical power
(b) Mother nature's anger
(c) A father's love
(d) The emptiness of revenge

**51.** In the opening of this scene, what are the nobles doing while the storm rages?
(a) Helping the boatswain
(b) Plotting their next action
(c) Running around in chaos
(d) Cursing the storm

**52.** What does Gonzalo suggest the mariners do?
(a) Leave the boat (b) Hang the boatswain
(c) Pray for the king (d) Sail for the shore

**53.** Where is the ship coming from?
(a) Naples (b) Tunis
(c) Milan
(d) Stratford-upon-Avon

**54.** Who do Sebastian and Antonio curse?
(a) Prospero (b) The Boatswain
(c) Gonzalo (d) The sea

**55.** Where do Antonio, Sebastian, and Gonzalo go when the mariners cry out?
(a) To look for the king (b) Overboard
(c) Back to Tunis (d) To the lifeboats

**56.** What does Miranda entreat Prospero to do with the men in the shipwreck?
(a) Kill them (b) Keep them safe
(c) Send a rescue boat (d) Let her help

**57.** As he tells his story, how many times does Prospero tell Miranda to listen?
(a) Three times (b) Eight times
(c) Never (d) Once

**58.** Who helped Antonio raise an army and usurp Prospero?
(a) Miranda (b) The King of Tunis
(c) The King of Naples (d) Caliban

**59.** Where was Ariel before Prospero set him free?
(a) Inside a cave (b) Inside a cage
(c) Inside a shell (d) Inside a tree

**60.** Who or what is Sycorax?
(a) A familiar spirit (b) A witch
(c) Prospero's wife
(d) Miranda's only friend

**61.** What does Caliban do after Prospero first summons him?
(a) Sings (b) Begins to chop wood
(c) Curses Prospero (d) Casts a spell

**62.** According to Caliban, what did Prospero do to anger him?
(a) Betrayed and enslaved him
(b) Taught him to speak
(c) Acted arrogantly
(d) Freed Ariel

**63.** What do Miranda and Ferdinand do when they first see each other?
(a) Curse each other (b) Fall in love
(c) Dance (d) Ignore each other

**64.** What does Prospero do with Ferdinand after Miranda and Ferdinand have fallen in love?
(a) Imprisons him (b) Makes him a feast
(c) Gives him new clothes (d) Cuts off his ear

**65.** How does Prospero feel about Miranda and Ferdinand falling in love?
(a) Disappointed (b) Indifferent
(c) Angry (d) Secretly pleased

**66.** Which of the lords expresses the belief that the island is a good place to be?
(a) Sebastian (b) Gonzalo
(c) Antonio (d) Francisco

**67.** Who doesn't fall asleep when Ariel enters playing 'solemn music'?
(a) Everyone present falls asleep
(b) Gonzalo
(c) Sebastian and Antonio
(d) Alonso and Francisco

**68.** What do Sebastian and Antonio plot while the others sleep?
(a) To build a utopia (b) To kill lions
(c) To run away (d) To kill Alonso

**69.** Who stops Alonso's murder?
(a) Ariel (b) Gonzalo
(c) Caliban (d) Ariel and Gonzalo

**70.** What does Sebastian do when everyone wakes up before he and Antonio can kill Alonso?
(a) Concocts a story (b) Admits the murder plot
(c) Runs away
(d) Laughs heartily

**71.** When Trinculo sees Caliban lying on the ground under a cloak, what does he do?
(a) Attacks Caliban
(b) Joins Caliban under it
(c) Runs away
(d) Starts drinking

**72.** When Stephano spots Trinculo and Caliban under the cloak, what does Stephano think he sees?
(a) A rock (b) A two-headed monster
(c) A magic trick
(d) Prospero

**73.** What does Caliban do after Stephano mistakes him for something else?
(a) He gets drunk (b) He fights the men
(c) He continues hiding (d) He falls ill

**74.** How do Stephano and Trinculo view Caliban when Caliban is drunk?
(a) As a threat
(b) As a new friend
(c) As a ridiculous monster
(d) As a sparring partner

**75.** What does Caliban offer the two men?
(a) To show them around (b) Food
(c) The means to escape (d) His cloak

**76.** What is Ferdinand doing at the beginning of this scene?
(a) Plotting to escape (b) Cursing Prospero
(c) Crying (d) Carrying wood

**77.** What word that Ferdinand uses to describe Miranda shares a Latin root word with her name?
(a) Miraculous (b) Admired
(c) Mire (d) Miracle

**78.** How does Miranda react to the news that Ferdinand is a prince?
(a) She is awed
(b) She is disgusted
(c) She is excited
(d) She seems unconcerned

**79.** What does Miranda ask when she finds out that Ferdinand is a prince?
(a) What time it is (b) If he loves her
(c) For news from Milan (d) If she's cursed

**80.** What does Miranda do when Ferdinand says that he loves her?
(a) Sneers (b) Proposes marriage
(c) Calls for Prospero (d) Says nothing

**81.** What title does Stephano assume in this scene?
(a) King of Naples (b) Lord of the Tempest
(c) Lord of the Island (d) King of the Island

**82.** What does the invisible Ariel do to cause trouble between Stephano and Trinculo?
(a) Ventriloquizes Trinculo
(b) Pinches Stephano
(c) Ventriloquizes Stephano
(d) Pinches Trinculo

**83.** What does Caliban say that himself, Stephano and Trinculo must do to take power from Prospero?
(a) Fight him physically (b) Steal his books
(c) Abduct Miranda (d) Use magic

**84.** What does Ariel do to lead the men astray and interrupt their plans?
(a) Brings Prospero to them (b) Becomes visible
(c) Beats them (d) Plays music

**85.** Why does Stephano relish the idea of becoming ruler of the island kingdom?
(a) It is beautiful (b) The music is free
(c) He likes islands (d) He will be rich

**86.** As the men are about to eat the banquet set before them, Ariel appears in what form?
(a) A giant bird (b) Disguised as Prospero
(c) Disguised as Ferdinand
(d) A harpy

**87.** Ariel tells the men that their shipwreck and the loss of Ferdinand are punishment for what?
(a) Endangering Prospero and Miranda
(b) Colonising the island
(c) Their classicism
(d) The sin of pride

**88.** When Ariel makes the banquet disappear, what do the men do?
(a) Laugh (b) Draw their swords
(c) Run away (d) Quietly watch him

**89.** Why can't the men attack Ariel with their swords?
(a) The swords become heavy
(b) Ariel is flying
(c) It seems rude
(d) Their swords disappear

**90.** What does Alonso do when reminded of the likely death of his son?
(a) Tries to drown himself (b) Attacks Prospero
(c) Gives a soliloquy
(d) Shrugs his shoulders

**91.** When the spirits perform the masque for Ferdinand and Miranda, they transform into which three mythological figures?
(a) Persephone, Venus, and Cupid
(b) Pluto, Persephone, and Venus
(c) Iris, Ceres, and Juno
(d) Ceres, Persephone, and Pluto

**92.** Why does Prospero suddenly end the masque?
(a) It was boring
(b) The wine runs out
(c) Ferdinand has upset him
(d) He remembers Caliban's plot

**93.** Where does Ariel led Trinculo, Stephano and Caliban to delay their attack?
(a) Into the sea (b) Into a swamp
(c) Straight to Prospero (d) Towards more alcohol

**94.** What do Prospero and Ariel use to distract Trinculo and Stephano from their scheme to murder Prospero?
(a) Bottles of alcohol
(b) Prospero's magic book
(c) Masks
(d) Fine clothing

**95.** What happens when Trinculo and Stephano touch the clothing?
(a) They are chased (b) Nothing
(c) Their skin burns (d) They feel guilty

**96.** After Prospero tells Ariel to release the men, he gives a soliloquy in which he gives up what?
(a) Magic (b) Scheming
(c) Wine (d) Public oration

**97.** What does Prospero promise to give Ariel at last?
(a) Ownership of the island
(b) His daughter's firstborn child
(c) His freedom
(d) Fine clothes

**98.** In this final scene, what does Prospero do to his enemies?
(a) Kills them (b) Enslaves them
(c) Curses them (d) Forgives them

**99.** What effect does the sight of more humans have on Miranda?
(a) She is disgusted (b) She is impressed
(c) She does not care (d) She laughs

**100.** Why does Prospero ask the audience to applaud him at the end of the play?
(a) To congratulate him
(b) To release him
(c) To give him power
(d) To unsettle the audience

## ANSWERS

| | | | | | | | | | | | | | | | | | | | |
|---|---|---|---|---|---|---|---|---|---|---|---|---|---|---|---|---|---|---|---|
| 1. | (c) | 2. | (a) | 3. | (d) | 4. | (b) | 5. | (b) | 6. | (d) | 7. | (b) | 8. | (a) | 9. | (c) | 10. | (d) |
| 11. | (d) | 12. | (a) | 13. | (c) | 14. | (c) | 15. | (c) | 16. | (b) | 17. | (c) | 18. | (d) | 19. | (d) | 20. | (c) |
| 21. | (a) | 22. | (c) | 23. | (b) | 24. | (a) | 25. | (d) | 26. | (b) | 27. | (c) | 28. | (b) | 29. | (d) | 30. | (a) |
| 31. | (b) | 32. | (a) | 33. | (d) | 34. | (c) | 35. | (c) | 36. | (b) | 37. | (d) | 38. | (a) | 39. | (d) | 40. | (c) |
| 41. | (b) | 42. | (d) | 43. | (a) | 44. | (d) | 45. | (b) | 46. | (d) | 47. | (d) | 48. | (b) | 49. | (b) | 50. | (a) |
| 51. | (c) | 52. | (c) | 53. | (b) | 54. | (b) | 55. | (a) | 56. | (b) | 57. | (a) | 58. | (c) | 59. | (d) | 60. | (b) |
| 61. | (c) | 62. | (a) | 63. | (b) | 64. | (b) | 65. | (d) | 66. | (a) | 67. | (c) | 68. | (d) | 69. | (d) | 70. | (a) |
| 71. | (b) | 72. | (b) | 73. | (a) | 74. | (c) | 75. | (a) | 76. | (d) | 77. | (b) | 78. | (b) | 79. | (b) | 80. | (b) |
| 81. | (c) | 82. | (a) | 83. | (b) | 84. | (d) | 85. | (b) | 86. | (d) | 87. | (a) | 88. | (b) | 89. | (a) | 90. | (a) |
| 91. | (c) | 92. | (d) | 93. | (b) | 94. | (d) | 95. | (a) | 96. | (a) | 97. | (c) | 98. | (d) | 99. | (b) | 100. | (b) |

# Chapter 22

# Hamlet

*William Shakespeare*

## Summary

### Hamlet mourning the Death of His Father

Hamlet, Prince of Denmark, is mourning the death of his father from home to school. King Hamlet, who has died two months earlier. Hamlet is disgusted by the marriage of his newly widowed mother, Queen Gertrude, to his Uncle, King Hamlet's brother, Claudius, who now has the throne.

### Appearance of Ghosts

Shortly thereafter, a ghost has appeared to guards on nightly watch as well as Hamlet's good friend, Horatio, who thinks the spirit has a likeness to the former King Hamlet.

### Murder Mystery of King Hamlet Revealed by Ghost

When prompted to speak by Horatio, the ghost will not. Horatio asks Hamlet to wait for the ghost and see if it will speak to him. The ghost of his father beckons Hamlet to follow him and reveals that his brother Claudius poisoned him in the ear. Hamlet vows to avenge his father's murder.

### Ophelia Warned to Stay Away from Young Hamlet

Meanwhile, Laertes, son to the King's advisor Polonius is set to return to France. Before he leaves, he tells Ophelia, his sister, to be weary of Hamlet's affections towards her. Polonius gives Laertes advice on how to act abroad and orders Ophelia to stay away from Hamlet.

Hamlet's sanity begins to be questioned by all. Claudius and Gertrude are both concerned; Polonius suggests it is Ophelia's rejection of his advances. Claudius and Polonius decide to spy on Hamlet and Ophelia. Claudius further employs Rosencrantz and Guildenstern, two childhood friends of Hamlet, to spy on him further. Hamlet quickly realises their intentions.

### Act of Murder Performed by a Troupe of Players

A troupe of players happens to be in town and Hamlet utilises the actors to determine the validity of his father's murder. He will have them perform the very act of murder, killing a king through poison in the ear, which the ghost has claimed. He asks Horatio to watch Claudius' reaction throughout the play. While the court is watching, Claudius is enraged and leaves the play convincing Hamlet that he is the murderer.

Hamlet comes upon Claudius in the chapel, kneeling down to pray. He considers killing him then and there but since Claudius is in mid-prayer and will therefore go to heaven if he dies, Hamlet decides to wait until Claudius is committing some sin, so that he will go to hell like Hamlet's father before him.

### Hamlet Argues with Gertrude

Hamlet meets Gertrude in her room and an argument ensues. When he hears Polonius who is hiding behind the curtain shout for help, he stabs him thinking it is Claudius. The ghost appears to Hamlet to refocus him on the task of killing Claudius.

### Claudius Conspires to Execute Hamlet

Fortinbras, Prince of Norway, whose father's lands were seized by the late King, decides to head to Denmark. Claudius demands that Hamlet, Rosencrantz and Guildenstern head for England. Claudius has sent a letter with them ordering Hamlet's execution during the trip. While at sea, however, Hamlet discovers his planned murder and switches the orders, causing Rosencrantz and Guildenstern to be executed. Hamlet returns to Denmark.

Meanwhile back at Elsinore, Ophelia has gone mad with grief. Laertes returns from France and learns it was Hamlet who has killed his father, Polonius. Claudius suggests that Laertes duel with Hamlet and poisons the tip of Laertes foil for a fatal blow.

If Laertes loses the duel, Claudius will put poison into a drink for Hamlet. Gertrude enters and announces that Ophelia has drowned.

In the graveyard, Hamlet reminisces on a friend of his, whose skull he has found. When the processional arrives with Ophelia's corpse, Laertes and Hamlet argue. A duel is scheduled.

### Laertes Confesses Claudius Plot

During the fight, Gertrude accidentally drinks from the poisoned chalice and dies. Hamlet is wounded with the poisoned sword, but in a scuffle, the foils are switched and Laertes is also wounded with the poisoned foil. In dying, Laertes confesses Claudius' plot to kill Hamlet. Hamlet stabs Claudius and Hamlet dies asking Horatio to tell his story. The Norwegian forces arrive at Elsinore, and Prince Fortinbras seizes control of Denmark.

Horatio, fulfilling Hamlet's last request, tells fotinbras Hamlet's tragic story. Fortinbras orders that Hamlet be carried away is a manner befitting a fallen solder.

## Practice Questions

**1.** Whom does Polonius send to France to spy on Laertes?
(a) Reynaldo (b) Ophelia
(c) Guido (d) Marcellus

**2.** Where does the ghost appear during the play?
(a) The castle ramparts and the great hall of Elsinore
(b) Fortinbras's tent and Hamlet's bedchamber
(c) The castle ramparts and Gertrude's bedchamber
(d) Gertrude's bedchamber and the great hall of Elsinore

**3.** How did Claudius murder King Hamlet?
(a) By stabbing him through an arras
(b) By pouring poison into his ear
(c) By ordering him to be hanged
(d) By poisoning his wineglass

**4.** Where is the university at which Horatio and Hamlet studied?
(a) Paris (b) Oxford
(c) Constantinople (d) Wittenberg

**5.** Whose skull does Hamlet discover in the churchyard?
(a) The former court jester's (b) Reynaldo's
(c) Ophelia's (d) His father's

**6.** Which of the following characters cannot see the ghost?
(a) Marcellus (b) Hamlet
(c) Gertrude (d) Horatio

**7.** Who escorts Hamlet on the voyage to England?
(a) Cornelius and Voltimand
(b) Rosencrantz and Guildenstern
(c) Marcellus and Bernardo
(d) Captain Vicissus and the one-eyed thief

**8.** Where do Hamlet and Laertes fight during Ophelia's funeral?
(a) In the nearby woods
(b) Beside Ophelia's grave
(c) Inside the church
(d) Inside the grave itself

**9.** Which of the following characters survive the play?
(a) Fortinbras, Horatio, and Osric
(b) Prince Hamlet, Polonius, and Gertrude
(c) Claudius, Rosencrantz, and Guildenstern
(d) Ophelia, Laertes, and King Hamlet

**10.** What does Hamlet claim to be able to tell the difference between when the wind is from the South?
(a) A flea and a fire log
(b) A nymph and a nihilist
(c) A hawk and a handsaw
(d) A shark and St. Timothy

**11.** In whose history of Denmark did Shakespeare find background material for his play?
(a) Oedipus of Thebes (b) Saxo Grammaticus
(c) Franz Guntherhaasen (d) Dionysus Finn

**12.** How does Ophelia die?
(a) Claudius stabs her
(b) Hamlet strangles her
(c) She slits her wrists
(d) She drowns in the river

**13.** Whose story does Hamlet ask the players to tell upon their arrival to Elsinore?
(a) Priam and Hecuba's
(b) Antony and Cleopatra's
(c) Gertrude and Claudius's
(d) Ophelia's

**14.** According to Polonius, why has Hamlet gone mad?
(a) He grieves too much for his father
(b) He despises Claudius for marrying Gertrude
(c) He is in love with Ophelia
(d) He is jealous of Laertes and longs to return to Wittenberg

**15.** Who is the last character to die in the play?
(a) Horatio (b) Hamlet
(c) Claudius (d) Fortinbras

**16.** How many characters die during the course of the play?
(a) Two (b) Five (c) Seven (d) Eight

**17.** Who speaks the famous 'To be, or not to be' soliloquy?
(a) Claudius (b) Hamlet
(c) The ghost (d) Laertes

**18.** In what country do Rosencrantz and Guildenstern die?
(a) Belgium (b) Denmark
(c) England (d) Poland

**19.** Why does Hamlet decide not to kill Claudius after the travelling players' play?
(a) Claudius is praying
(b) Claudius is asleep
(c) Claudius pleads for mercy
(d) Gertrude is in the next room

**20.** Who killed Fortinbras's father?
(a) Prince Hamlet (b) Laertes
(c) Fortinbras (d) Hamlet's father

**21.** Which character speaks the first line of the play?
(a) Bernardo (b) Francisco
(c) Hamlet (d) Horatio

**22.** In which of the following years was Hamlet most likely written?
(a) 1570 (b) 1601
(c) 1581 (d) 1610

**23.** Which of Claudius and Laertes' traps for Hamlet succeeds in killing him?
(a) The poisoned cup (b) The sharpened sword
(c) The poisoned dagger
(d) The poisoned sword

**24.** Which character speaks from beneath the stage toward the end of Act I?
(a) The ghost (b) Hamlet
(c) Claudius (d) Polonius

**25.** Who returns Hamlet to Denmark after his exile?
(a) Horatio (b) Claudius
(c) A group of pirates (d) A group of monks

**26.** Who joins Bernardo, the watchman, on his watch of the castle?
(a) Francisco and Horatio
(b) Marcellus and Horatio
(c) Prince Hamlet and Marcellus
(c) Francisco and Prince Hamlet

**27.** What do Marcellus and Bernardo want to show Horatio?
(a) Their wives (b) Prince Hamlet
(c) A ghost (d) Other watchmen

**28.** What proves to Horatio that the ghost is that of King Hamlet?
(a) His accent
(b) His resemblance to Prince Hamlet
(c) His armor
(d) His story

**29.** How does Horatio explain the appearance of King Hamlet's ghost?
(a) He says it's a warning sign
(b) He says it's a sign of peace
(c) He claims it's a sign of the King's wishes for his son
(d) He calls it a sign of the occult

**30.** Who is Fortinbras?
(a) Prince of Denmark (b) King of Denmark
(c) King of Norway (d) Prince of Norway

**31.** Who is now married to King Hamlet's wife?
(a) Polonius (b) Claudius
(c) Laertes (d) Cornelius

**32.** What does King Claudius say he is in mourning over?
(a) The death of his father
(b) The death of his son
(c) The death of his brother
(d) His recent marriage

**33.** What do Claudius and Gertrude want Prince Hamlet to do?
(a) Go back to school (b) Stay close to them
(c) Become the king (d) Get married

**34.** What does Prince Hamlet contemplate doing because he is so upset?
(a) Killing himself
(b) Running away
(c) Eloping
(d) Attacking Fortinbras

**35.** What does Fortinbras want from Claudius?
(a) A position in the Danish court
(b) Lands that once belonged to Norway
(c) A marriage to Ophelia
(d) A tax from the peasants

**36.** What does Laertes warn Ophelia about?
(a) Taking care of Polonius
(b) Falling in love with Hamlet
(c) Claudius's position as king
(d) Being responsible for their family property

**37.** What is Laertes' main objection to Ophelia's feelings?
(a) Hamlet is interested in other women
(b) Hamlet does not respect their father
(c) Hamlet has obligations to his country
(d) Hamlet fears the institution of marriage

**38.** **What does Polonius say about Ophelia's relationship with Hamlet?**
(a) He simply wants her to be happy
(b) He believes that Hamlet is a good match for her
(c) He does not believe that Hamlet has feelings for her
(d) He forbids her from seeing him anymore.

**39.** **What does Hamlet overhear while waiting for the ghost to appear?**
(a) The revelry of the King (b) The sounds of battle
(c) Ophelia crying (d) His own conscience

**40.** **Why do Horatio and Marcellus follow after Hamlet and the ghost?**
(a) To warn them of impending danger
(b) To protect Hamlet
(c) To overhear the ghost's secrets
(d) To bring him back to the King's party

**41.** **How did Hamlet's father die?**
(a) He was stabbed
(b) He was poisoned
(c) He died in battle
(d) He died in his sleep

**42.** **Who does the ghost of Hamlet's father say killed him?**
(a) Polonius (b) Fortinbras
(c) Laertes (d) Claudius

**43.** **What does the ghost of King Hamlet say about Gertrude, his wife?**
(a) He warns Hamlet to be afraid of her
(b) He tells Hamlet to get revenge
(c) He tells Hamlet to leave her alone
(d) He tells Hamlet to speak with her about Claudius

**44.** **What does Hamlet tell Horatio and Marcellus about his plan?**
(a) That he may pretend to be crazy
(b) That he intends on killing Claudius
(c) That he hopes to marry Ophelia
(d) That he plans to run away

**45.** **What does Hamlet do to upset Ophelia?**
(a) He tells her he doesn't love her
(b) He threatens to kill himself
(c) He tells her he loves her
(d) He acts frantic and chaotic

**46.** **Who are Rosencrantz and Guildenstern?**
(a) Hamlet's friends
(b) Hamlet's cousins
(c) Claudius's generals
(d) Gertrude's messengers

**47.** **Whom does Fortinbras swear he will not attack?**
(a) The Poles (b) The Italians
(c) The Danes (d) The Spanish

**48.** **How does Polonius plan to prove Hamlet's love for Ophelia?**
(a) Have him followed
(b) Spy on him personally
(c) Write a letter as Ophelia
(d) Challenge him to a duel

**49.** **What play does Hamlet want the players to perform?**
(a) The Murder of Gonzago (b) Oedipus Rex
(c) Beowulf (d) Faust

**50.** **How will Claudius react to the play, according to Hamlet?**
(a) He will laugh
(b) He will cry
(c) He will enjoy it
(d) He will appear guilty

**51.** **Why does Claudius want to be left alone?**
(a) So that he and Polonius can confer about Fortinbras
(b) So that he and Polonius can decide what to do about Hamlet's moodiness
(c) So that he and Polonius can watch Hamlet and Ophelia interact
(d) So that he and Polonius can discuss the upcoming play

**52.** **What do Polonius and Claudius overhear Hamlet discussing?**
(a) The life he led at school
(b) His feelings of mourning
(c) Whether or not to marry Ophelia
(d) Whether or not to commit suicide

**53.** **What does Ophelia give Hamlet?**
(a) Her love (b) A letter
(c) The gifts he has given her (d) A rejection

**54.** **Why does Hamlet call women dishonest?**
(a) Because they only care about money
(b) Because they wear make-up and deceive men
(c) Because he does not trust his mother
(d) Because he believes that women are inferior to men

**55.** **What does Claudius say he will do about Hamlet?**
(a) Send him to England
(b) Marry him off to Ophelia
(c) Monitor his behavior closely
(d) Kill him

**56.** **What does Hamlet ask Horatio to do during the play?**
(a) Monitor Ophelia's behavior
(b) Keep an eye on Gertrude
(c) Pay attention to Polonius's movements
(d) Watch Claudius's reactions

**57.** **How does Hamlet tease Ophelia?**
(a) He makes inappropriate sexual jokes
(b) He touches her
(c) He makes fun of her family
(d) He tells her he doesn't love her

**58.** **What does Hamlet do during the performance?**
(a) He sneaks out.
(b) He explains everyone's behavior.
(c) He tries to make up with Ophelia.
(d) He tries to kill Claudius.

**59.** **What is Claudius's reaction to the play?**
(a) He admires the performances
(b) He doesn't pay attention
(c) He yells and leaves
(d) He demands an encore

**60.** Who sends for Hamlet after the play?
(a) Claudius (b) Ophelia
(c) Horatio (d) Gertrude

**61.** What does Claudius want Rosencrantz and Guildenstern to do with Hamlet?
(a) Kill him (b) Find out what's wrong
(c) Take him to England (d) Help him win back Ophelia

**62.** Who plans to spy on Gertrude and Hamlet?
(a) Claudius (b) Horatio
(c) Ophelia (d) Polonius

**63.** What does Claudius feel guilty for?
(a) Killing his brother (b) Marrying the queen
(c) Sending Hamlet away (d) Running out of the play

**64.** Why does Hamlet refrain from killing Claudius when he has the opportunity?
(a) He does not want to be king
(b) Claudius is still his uncle
(c) Claudius is praying
(d) He does not want to hurt his mother

**65.** When does Hamlet plan to kill Claudius?
(a) When Claudius is sleeping
(b) When there is a diversion
(c) When his mother is away
(d) When Claudius behaves badly

**66.** Why does Polonius want to eavesdrop on Hamlet?
(a) Because he promised Claudius he would
(b) So that he can find out how Hamlet feels about Ophelia
(c) Because Gertrude is scared for her own safety
(d) So that he can find out why Hamlet is angry and upset

**67.** What does Hamlet accuse his mother?
(a) Betraying Claudius (b) Betraying him (Hamlet)
(c) Betraying his father (d) Betraying herself

**68.** Why does Hamlet kill Polonius?
(a) Because he believes his mother is having an affair
(b) Because Polonius does not believe that Ophelia and Hamlet should marry
(c) Because he is going crazy
(d) Because he mistakes Polonius for Claudius

**69.** Why does Gertrude think Hamlet is mad?
(a) Because he killed Polonius
(b) Because he is making accusations against Claudius
(c) Because he appears to be talking to himself
(d) Because he attacks her

**70.** What message does the ghost bring Hamlet?
(a) To leave his mother alone
(b) To remember that he has not yet gotten revenge
(c) To hide Polonius's body
(d) To give up

**71.** Whom does Gertrude rush to see after Polonius is killed?
(a) Claudius (b) Hamlet
(c) Rosencrantz and Guildenstern (d) Ophelia

**72.** What does Gertrude compare herself to?
(a) A wilting flower (b) A bruised fruit
(c) The violent ocean (d) A hurt child

**73.** What is Claudius's main concern?
(a) Gertrude's emotional state
(b) Hamlet's sanity
(c) His own conscience
(d) Keeping his power

**74.** Why does Hamlet accuse Rosencrantz and Guildenstern of?
(a) Not caring about him (b) Being spies for Claudius
(c) Courting Ophelia (d) Revealing his secrets

**75.** What does Hamlet allow Rosencrantz and Guildenstern to do?
(a) Explain their allegiances to Claudius
(b) Leave Denmark
(c) Accompany him back to Claudius
(d) Kill him

**76.** Who reveals the location of Polonius's body?
(a) Rosencrantz and Guildenstern
(b) Gertrude
(c) Horatio (d) Hamlet

**77.** What orders does Claudius send to England with Rosencrantz and Guildenstern?
(a) That Hamlet be institutionalised
(b) That Hamlet be killed
(c) That Hamlet be imprisoned
(d) That Hamlet be set free

**78.** What is Fortinbras doing when he comes across Hamlet, Rosencrantz, and Guildenstern?
(a) He is on his way to attack Poland
(b) He is on his way to avenge the death of his father
(c) He is on his way to find Hamlet
(d) He is on his way to attack Denmark

**79.** Why is Hamlet surprised by the nature of the conflict between Poland and Norway?
(a) Because he is surprised it hasn't escalated faster
(b) Because Fortinbras cannot explain his own motivations
(c) Because the conflict seems so insignificant
(d) Because he has never thought about the military before

**80.** What does Hamlet resolve to do after meeting Fortinbras?
(a) Achieve his revenge
(b) Help Fortinbras in his conquest
(c) Betray Rosencrantz and Guildenstern
(d) Nothing

**81.** How does Ophelia handle the news of Polonius's death?
(a) She demands revenge (b) She runs away
(c) She is relieved (d) She goes crazy

**82.** What does Horatio urge Gertrude to do?
(a) Punish Ophelia (b) Punish Hamlet
(c) Console Ophelia (d) Console Hamlet

**83.** How do the peasants feel about Laertes upon his return?
(a) They feel that he ought to be king
(b) They feel that he abandoned them when he left
(c) They want him to kill Hamlet
(d) They want him to take Ophelia away

**84.** What advice does Claudius give to Laertes?
(a) That his first priority should be taking care of Ophelia
(b) That he should seek revenge on whoever is responsible for Polonius's death
(c) That he should return to France
(d) That he should prepare to take over his father's duties

**85.** What does Hamlet's letter to Horatio say?
(a) That he leaves the kingdom of Denmark in Horatio's hands
(b) That he finally feels at peace with his father's death
(c) That he is returning to Denmark with news
(d) That he is being held against his will by pirates

**86.** Why doesn't Claudius punish Hamlet?
(a) Because he doesn't believe that Hamlet killed Polonius
(b) Because he is not upset that Polonius is dead
(c) Because too many people adore Hamlet
(d) Because he doesn't have the power to

**87.** Why is Laertes happy about Hamlet's return to Denmark?
(a) Because he plans to kill him
(b) Because he hopes to help Hamlet with his plan for revenge
(c) Because he wants Hamlet to take care of Ophelia
(d) Because he hopes that Hamlet will help him become king

**88.** When does Laertes plan to kill Hamlet?
(a) While he sleeps
(b) During the king's upcoming ball
(c) At a fencing match
(d) At dinner

**89.** What do Laertes and Claudius plan to do if Hamlet wins the duel?
(a) Forgive him and let him live
(b) Give up the throne
(c) Poison him with a cup of wine
(d) Have someone else stab him

**90.** How does Ophelia die?
(a) She drowns in a river
(b) She poisons herself
(c) She throws herself off a bridge
(d) She catches a fever

**91.** Why are the gravediggers arguing about Ophelia?
(a) Because they remember her being beautiful
(b) Because they hear that she has killed herself
(c) Because they feel pity for Laertes
(d) Because they do not believe that Ophelia has died

**92.** What does the gravedigger say to Hamlet when he asks whose grave he is digging?
(a) He says that it's Opheilia's grave
(b) He says that it's Polonius's grave
(c) He says that it's Hamlet's grave
(d) He says that it's his own grave

**93.** What does Hamlet notice about the funeral procession?
(a) That the procession seems irregular and suggests a suicide
(b) That those who are mourning seem excessively upset
(c) That Laertes has returned to take part in the funeral
(d) That the funeral does not seem particularly sad

**94.** What does Hamlet say to Laertes upon realising that it is Ophelia's funeral?
(a) That Laertes is a terrible brother
(b) That he loved Ophelia in ways that no one could understand
(c) That he vows to take his own life now that Ophelia is dead
(d) That he feels Ophelia's death is a punishment for his own bad deeds

**95.** What finally appeases Laertes at Ophelia's funeral?
(a) Hamlet expresses his true feelings for Ophelia
(b) Gertrude and Claudius say that Hamlet is insane
(c) Claudius reminds Laertes that they have a plan to kill Hamlet
(d) Hamlet makes a fool of himself.

**96.** What does Hamlet tell Horatio about death?
(a) That it is inevitable
(b) That it should be fought at all costs
(c) That he fears it
(d) That thinking about it comforts him

**97.** How does Gertrude die?
(a) Hamlet forces her to drink a cup of poisoned wine
(b) She accidentally drinks wine that Claudius poisoned
(c) She kills herself with a sword
(d) Horatio kills her with a fencing foil

**98.** How does Hamlet find out about Claudius's plan?
(a) He overhears Claudius discussing it.
(b) Gertrude tells him what she knows.
(c) Laertes makes a dying declaration.
(d) Horatio finds the poison.

**99.** What does the dying Hamlet tell Horatio to do?
(a) Avenge his death
(b) Become king
(c) Mourn for him
(d) Live and pass along his story

**100.** Who rules Denmark at the end of the play?
(a) Rosencrantz (b) Horatio
(c) Guildenstern (d) Fortinbras

**101.** Who initially calls for Rosencrantz and Guildenstern?
(a) Claudius and Polonius (b) Gertrude and Claudius
(c) Gertrude and Hamlet (d) Polonius and Hamlet

**102.** Who first sees the ghost of Hamlet's father?
(a) Hamlet (b) Laertes
(c) Marcellus and Bernardo (d) Bernardo and Hamlet

**103.** Who are Ophelia's blood relatives?
(a) Polonius and Laertes (b) Polonius and Gertrude
(c) Polonius and Horatio (d) Polonius and Hamlet

**104.** Why does Fortinbras want to attack Denmark?
(a) To marry Ophelia
(b) To seek revenge for his father's death
(c) For fame and glory
(d) Because he is told to

**105.** How is Hamlet related to Claudius?
(a) Claudius is his father (b) Claudius is his cousin
(c) Claudius is his brother (d) Claudius is his uncle

**106.** What words best describe Hamlet's character throughout the play?

(a) Mysterious, thoughtful, morose
(b) Brave, sociable, fun
(c) Easy-going, smooth, charismatic
(d) Sensual, caring, effeminate

**107.** What is Claudius's most powerful weapon?

(a) H s money
(b) His sex appeal
(c) H s way with words
(d) His aggressiveness

**108.** Why is Hamlet sometimes considered to be a play about inaction?

(a) Because Hamlet never hesitates when it comes to acting against Claudius
(b) Because Hamlet spends the play trying to figure out if the ghost is real
(c) Because Hamlet needs to know Claudius is guilty before acting
(d) Because Gertrude and Ophelia are passive and inactive heroines

## ANSWERS

| | | | | | | | | | | | | | | | | | | | |
|---|---|---|---|---|---|---|---|---|---|---|---|---|---|---|---|---|---|---|---|
| 1. | (a) | 2. | (c) | 3. | (b) | 4. | (d) | 5. | (a) | 6. | (c) | 7. | (b) | 8. | (d) | 9. | (a) | 10. | (c) |
| 11. | (b) | 12. | (d) | 13. | (a) | 14. | (c) | 15. | (b) | 16. | (d) | 17. | (b) | 18. | (c) | 19. | (a) | 20. | (d) |
| 21. | (a) | 22. | (b) | 23. | (d) | 24. | (a) | 25. | (c) | 26. | (b) | 27. | (c) | 28. | (c) | 29. | (a) | 30. | (d) |
| 31. | (b) | 32. | (c) | 33. | (b) | 34. | (a) | 35. | (b) | 36. | (b) | 37. | (c) | 38. | (d) | 39. | (a) | 40. | (b) |
| 41. | (b) | 42. | (d) | 43. | (c) | 44. | (a) | 45. | (d) | 46. | (a) | 47. | (c) | 48. | (b) | 49. | (a) | 50. | (d) |
| 51. | (c) | 52. | (d) | 53. | (c) | 54. | (b) | 55. | (a) | 56. | (d) | 57. | (a) | 58. | (b) | 59. | (c) | 60. | (d) |
| 61. | (c) | 62. | (d) | 63. | (a) | 64. | (c) | 65. | (d) | 66. | (d) | 67. | (c) | 68. | (d) | 69. | (c) | 70. | (b) |
| 71. | (a) | 72. | (c) | 73. | (d) | 74. | (b) | 75. | (c) | 76. | (d) | 77. | (b) | 78. | (a) | 79. | (c) | 80. | (a) |
| 81. | (d) | 82. | (c) | 83. | (a) | 84. | (b) | 85. | (c) | 86. | (c) | 87. | (a) | 88. | (c) | 89. | (c) | 90. | (a) |
| 91. | (b) | 92. | (d) | 93. | (a) | 94. | (b) | 95. | (c) | 96. | (a) | 97. | (b) | 98. | (c) | 99. | (d) | 100. | (d) |
| 101. | (b) | 102. | (c) | 103. | (a) | 104 | (b) | 105. | (d) | 106. | (a) | 107. | (c) | 108. | (c) | | | | |

Chapter 23

# True Worship

*Rabindranath Tagore*

## About the Author

Rabindranath Tagore was born on 7th, May, 1861 in Calcutta. Rabindranath Tagore is a Bengali poet, short-story writer, song composer, playwright, essayist and painter who introduced new prose and verse forms and the use of colloquial language into Bengali literature, thereby freeing it from traditional models based on classical Sanskrit. He was highly influential in introducing Indian culture to the West and vice versa and he is generally regarded as the outstanding creative artist of early 20th century India. In 1913, he became the first non-European to receive the Nobel Prize for Literature.

He is the son of the religious reformer Debendranath Tagore. He began to write verses early and after incomplete studies in England in the late 1870s, he returned to India. There, he published several books of poetry in the 1880s and completed Manasi (1890), a collection that marks the maturing of his genius. It contains some of his best-known poems including many in verse forms new to Bengali as well as some social and political satire that was critical of his fellow Bengalis.

In 1891, Tagore went to East Bengal (now in Bangladesh) to manage his family's estates at Shilaidaah and Shahzadpur for 10 years. Most of his finest short stories, which examine 'humble lives and their small miseries', date from the 1890s and have a poignancy laced with gentle irony, that is unique to him.

In 1901 Tagore founded an experimental school in rural West Bengal at Shantiniketan (Abode of Peace), where he sought to blend the best in the Indian and Western traditions. He settled permanently at the school, which became Visva-Bharati University in 1921. Years of sadness arising from the deaths of his wife and two children between 1902 and 1907 are reflected in his later poetry, which was introduced to the West in Gitanjali (1912). This book containing Tagore's English prose translations of religious poems from several of his Bengali verse collections including Gitanjali (1910), was hailed by WB Yeats and André Gide and won him the Nobel Prize in 1913. Tagore was awarded a knighthood in 1915, but he repudiated it in 1919 as a protest against the Amritsar (Jallianwalla Bagh) Massacre.

From 1912, Tagore spent long periods out of India, lecturing and reading from his work in Europe, the Americas, and East Asia and becoming an eloquent spokesperson for the cause of Indian independence.

In the late 1920s, when he was in his 60s, Tagore took up painting and produced works that won him a place among India's foremost contemporary artists. His famous works include:

Novels like 'Nastanirh' (1901) 'Chokher Bali' (1902-1903) 'Noukadubi' (1906) 'Gora' (1909) 'Ghare-Baire' (1916) 'Chaturanga' (1916) 'Jogajog' (1929) 'Shesher Kabita' (1929), Stories such as 'Hungry Stones' Kabuliwala List of stories, Poetry like 'Bhanusimha Thakurer Padabali' (1884), 'Gitanjali' (1910), Songs such as Rabindra Sangeet Gitabitan, 'Amar Sonar Bangla', 'Birpurush', 'Chitto Jetha Bhayshunyo', 'Ekla Chalo Re', 'Jana Gana Mana', 'Vocation' and Plays like 'Valmiki-Pratibha' (1888), 'Raja' (1910), 'The Post Office' (1912) and 'Chitra' (1913).

## Summary

### God's wish is True Worship

The poem 'True Worship' written by Rabindranath Tagore shows us the real path of true worship. According to the poet, true worship is not when one blindly performs rituals, but it is the practice to know God's wish. God wants us to offer our true love that is in the heart instead of the flowers that we offer upon the feet of God.

### Love for Fellow beings is True Love

True love is the love for our fellow human beings and nature as God is in everything. God will not accept the rituals of placing the lighted candles before Him unless the worshipper purifies himself first by removing the dark shadows of sin from his heart.

## God has no regard for Superiority Complex

God has no regard for those who think themselves better and superior to others. We should try to get rid of the feeling of arrogance before bowing our heads before God.

The people who have been oppressed by the rich and the powerful people require our love, care, sympathy and affection.

## Respecting fellow beings is True Worship

The poet says that we should first give respect our fellow beings before bending in front of God to taste the sweetness of true worship.

First forgive the fellow human beings for their bad deeds they have done against you and then pray to God to forgive your sins and God will definitely forgive you.

# Practice Questions

**1.** **When was Rabindranath Tagore born?**
(a) 7th May, 1861 (b) 12th June, 1858
(c) 22nd March, 1865 (d) 31st August, 1871

**2.** **Which university was founded by Rabindranath Tagore?**
(a) Benaras Hindu University (b) Calcutta University
(c) Visvabharati (d) Bombay University

**3.** **In which year was Rabindranath Tagore awarded Nobel Prize for Literature?**
(a) 1901 (b) 1913 (c) 1928 (d) 1930

**4.** **In which year did Rabindranath Tagore surrender the knighthood as a protest against Jallianwalla Bagh massacre?**
(a) 1919 (b) 1924 (c) 1935 (d) 1939

**5.** **When did Rabindranath Tagore die?**
(a) 7th August, 1941 (b) 21st June, 1947
(c) 8th April, 1936 (d) 18th August, 1945

**6.** **What does the poet want us to do before putting flowers upon the feet of God?**
(a) to take a bath
(b) to pluck the flowers to offer
(c) to bend before Him
(d) to fill our house with the fragrance of love

**7.** **What should we do with our hearts first?**
(a) remove the darkness of sin from our hearts
(b) a regular health check up
(c) fill with the fragrance of flowers
(d) None of the above

**8.** **Who are the 'downtrodden' as mentioned in the poem?**
(a) people who are hungry and poor
(b) people who are treated so badly by rich and powerful people
(c) people who do not worship God
(d) People who never treat anyone with love and affection

**9.** **How should we treat the down–trodden people?**
(a) We should punish them
(b) They should be forced to worship God
(c) They should be neglected
(d) We should give them support, love and care

**10.** **What should we learn before bowing our heads in prayer?**
(a) to bow in humility
(b) to offer flowers upon the feet of God
(c) to bow against the priest
(d) to ligts the candles

**11.** **The word 'alter' means ______ here.**
(a) A statue of God (b) A holy table
(c) A building (d) None of these

**12.** **What does the word 'humility' refer in the poem?**
(a) Devotion
(b) Humanity
(c) Humbleness (d) Love

**13.** **What is true worship according tothe poet?**
(a) To follow what God wants
(b) TO offer flowers to God
(c) To recite prayers for God
(d) To devote one self in the service of God

**14.** **What, according to the poet, God wants us to do?**
(a) To sing God's praise
(b) To serve the mankind with love and equality
(c) To bow down to God
(d) To renounce the world for God

## ANSWERS

| | | | | | | | | | | | | | | | | | | | |
|---|---|---|---|---|---|---|---|---|---|---|---|---|---|---|---|---|---|---|---|
| 1. | (c) | 2. | (c) | 3. | (b) | 4. | (a) | 5. | (a) | 6. | (d) | 7. | (a) | 8. | (b) | 9. | (d) | 10. | (a) |
| 11. | (b) | 12. | (c) | 13. | (a) | 14. | (b) | | | | | | | | | | | | |

Chapter 24

# Ode to a Skylark

*PB Shelley*

## About the Poet

Percy Bysshe Shelley was born 4th August, 1792, at Field Place, near Horsham, Sussex, England. He was one of the major English Romantic poets, and is regarded by some as among the finer lyric and philosophical poets in the English language, and one of the more influential. A radical in his poetry as well as in his political and social views, Shelley did not see fame during his lifetime, but recognition of his achievements in poetry grew steadily following his death. Shelley was a key member of a close circle of visionary poets and writers that included Lord Byron, Leigh Hunt, Thomas Love Peacock, and his own second wife, Mary Shelley, the author of Frankenstein.

In 1811, Shelley anonymously published a pamphlet called 'The Necessity of Atheism', which resulted in his expulsion from Oxford University. Shelley is perhaps best known for classic poems such as 'Ozymandias', 'Ode to the West Wind', 'To a Skylark' (also known as 'Ode to a skylark'), 'Music', 'When Soft Voices Die', 'The Cloud' and 'The Masque of Anarchy'. On 8th, July 1822, shortly before his thirtieth birthday, Shelley was drowned in a storm while attempting to sail from Livorno to La Spezia, Italy, in his schooner, the Don Juan.

## Summary

### The Poet Addresses the Skylark as a Spirit, Not a Mortal Living

The speaker, addressing a skylark, says that it is a 'blithe spirit' rather than a bird, for its song comes from heaven, and from its full heart pours 'profuse strains of unpremeditated art'.

### The Bird flies up into the Sky at Evening Time

The skylark flies higher and higher, 'like a cloud of fire' in the blue sky, singing as it flies. In the 'golden lightning' of the Sun, it floats and runs, like 'an un-bodied joy'. As the skylark flies higher and higher, the speaker loses sight of it, but is still able to hear its 'shrill delight', which comes down as keenly as moonbeams in the 'white dawn,' which can be felt even when they are not seen.

The Earth and air ring with the skylark's voice, just as heaven overflows with moonbeams when the moon shines out from behind 'a lonely cloud'.

### The Poet Compares the Skylark to Various Things

The speaker says that no one knows what the skylark is, for it is unique: even 'rainbow clouds' do not rain as brightly as the shower of melody that pours from the skylark. The bird is 'like a poet hidden in the light of thought', able to make the world experience 'sympathy with hopes and fears it heeded not'. It is like a lonely maiden in a palace tower, who uses her song to soothe her lovelorn soul.

It is like a golden glow-worm, scattering light among the flowers and grass in which it is hidden. It is like a rose embowered in its own green leaves, whose scent is blown by the wind until the bees are faint with 'too much sweet'. The skylark's song surpasses 'all that ever was, joyous and clear and fresh', whether the rain falling on the 'twinkling grass' or the flowers the rain awakens.

### Beautiful Things Created by Humans Cannot Match the Beauty of the Bird's Singing

Calling the skylark 'Spirit or Bird'. the speaker asks it to tell him its 'sweet thoughts', for he has never heard anyone or anything call up 'a flood of rapture so divine'. Compared to the skylark's, any music would seem lacking. What objects, the speaker asks, are 'the fountains of thy happy strain?' Is it fields, waves, mountains, the sky, the plain, or 'love of thine own kind' or 'ignorance or pain'?

Pain and languor, the speaker says, 'never came near' the skylark: it loves, but has never known 'love's sad satiety'. Of death, the skylark must know 'things more true and deep' than mortals could dream; otherwise, the poet asks, 'how could thy notes flow in such a crystal stream?'

## Human Songs are Tinged with Sadness, but the Bird's Song is Pure Joy

For mortals, the experience of happiness is bound inextricably with the experience of sadness: dwelling upon memories and hopes for the future, mortal men 'pine for what is not'; their laughter is 'fraught' with 'some pain'; their 'sweetest songs are those that tell of saddest thought'.

But, the poet says, even if men could 'hate and pride and fear', and were born without the capacity to weep, they still do not know how they could ever approximate the joy expressed by the skylark.

## The Poet Dreams of Being Able to Sing Joyfully Like

Calling the bird a 'scorner of the ground', he says that its music is better than all music and all poetry. He asks the bird to teach him 'half the gladness that thy brain must know', for then he would overflow with 'harmonious madness,' and his song would be so beautiful that the world would listen to him, even as he is now listening to the skylark.

## Form

The eccentric, songlike, five-line stanzas of 'To a Skylark'—all twenty-one of them—follow the same pattern. The first four lines are metered in trochaic tri-meter, the fifth in iambic hexameter. The rhyme scheme of each stanza is 'ABABB'.

# Practice Questions

**1.** When was Percy Bysshe Shelley born?
(a) 31st January, 1786 (b) 4th August, 1792
(c) 4th May, 1794 (d) 19th December, 1784

**2.** The writing of which pamphlet caused Percy Bysshe Shelley's expulsion?
(a) Common Sense (b) The Necessity of Atheism
(c) A Declaration of Rights (d) Pride and Prejudice

**3.** When did Percy Bysshe Shelley die?
(a) 3rd December, 1832 (b) 11th November, 1846
(c) 7th August, 1834 (d) 8th July, 1822

**4.** How did Percy Bysshe Shelley die?
(a) Drowned (b) Natural death
(c) Died of fever (d) Shot

**5.** In his poem 'To a Skylark', Shelley viewed the skylark as ............
(a) an annoyance (b) a small, brown bird
(c) a good singer (d) a spirit

**6.** In his poem 'To a Skylark', Shelley compared the skylark to ............
(a) a glow worm (b) a princess in a tower
(c) a rose flower (d) All of these

**7.** 'Pourest thy full heart' In profuse strains of unpremeditated art.'
To which bird are these lines addressed by Shelley?
(a) Raven (b) Nightingale
(c) Skylark (d) Cuckoo

**8.** From which university was Shelley expelled?
(a) Harvard (b) Columbia
(c) Oxford (d) Cambridge

**9.** What does the speaker appear to envy about the Skylark?
(a) The bird's song (b) The easy life of a bird
(c) The ability to fly (d) The freedom the bird has

**10.** During the poem, Shelley begins using what literary device for five straight stanzas?
(a) Assonance (b) Metaphor
(c) Alliteration (d) Repetition

**11.** How does the speaker compare the Skylark to a 'high born maiden'?
(a) The Maiden has beauty like the bird's song
(b) They both are up high where they are out of sight
(c) The Maiden gives her heart as a Skylark sings with their heart
(d) The poet does not make this comparison

**12.** Shelley wrote with what artistic drive?
(a) Impulse (b) Deep thought
(c) Life experience (d) Love for literature

**13.** What is the speaker's request to the Skylark in the last stanza?
(a) For the bird to land near him to eat
(b) To be taught
(c) To come back into sight
(d) To continue its song for a very long time

## ANSWERS

| | | | | | | | | | | | | | | | | | | | |
|---|---|---|---|---|---|---|---|---|---|---|---|---|---|---|---|---|---|---|---|
| 1. | (b) | 2. | (b) | 3. | (d) | 4. | (a) | 5. | (d) | 6. | (d) | 7. | (c) | 8. | (c) | 9. | (d) | 10. | (b) |
| 11. | (c) | 12. | (a) | 13. | (b) | | | | | | | | | | | | | | |

Chapter 25

# The Broken Wings

*Sarojini Naidu*

## About the Poet

Sarojini Naidu was born on 13th, February, 1879 in Hyderabad. She was an Indian independence activist and poet. She was born in a Bengali Hindu family at Hyderabad and was educated in Chennai, London and Cambridge. She took part in the National Movement, became a follower of Mahatma Gandhi and fought for the attainment of Swaraj. She became the President of Indian National Congress and later she was appointed as the Governor of Uttar Pradesh Known as the 'Nightingale of India', she was also a noted poet. Her poetry includes children's poems, nature poems, patriotic poems and poems of love and death. She also wrote poetry in praise of Muslim figures like Imam Hussain.

Her first volume of poetry, The Golden Threshold (1905), was followed by the Bird of Time (1912) and in 1914 she was elected a fellow of the Royal Society of Literature. Her collected poems, all of which she wrote in English, have been published under the titles 'The Sceptred Flute' (1943) and The Feather of the Dawn (1961).

On 2nd March, 1949, Sarojini Naidu died at Lucknow, Uttar Pradesh, while listening to a song, sung by the nurse attending to her, which put her to eternal sleep.

## Summary

### Suppressed Spirit of the Indians due to Dominance of the British

The poem 'The Broken Wing' was published in 1917. It is dedicated to the 'dream of today' and the 'hope of tomorrows'. This poem portrays a picture of India under the British rule at a time when the freedom struggle had just begun. The centuries of dominance had not only broken the spirit of the Indians but also had taken its toll on those who could influence the common people the most. Such people include the poets, playwrights and other artists.

### Dawn of Awakening

These people are symbolised as songbird in the poem. Their voice had been suppressed for a long time. Any resistance on their part was dealt harshly with brute force and strict censorship. But now the people of India have awakened. The great dawn is the impending liberation while the mournful night is the period of dominance.

### Poet's Appeal to the Intellectuals

The prevalent atmosphere in the country is that of joy of expectation symbolised by the opening of buds. The returing winds symbolise the hope of independence. As the birds at dawn get themselves ready to fly towards the glorious light of a fresh morning, the people of India also get set to walk the splendid path of liberty. At this point of time, the poetess appeals to the intellectuals who have borne the brunt of oppression like a bird with a broken wing to gather courage and join the people committed for noble cause of freedom.

### Song bird's Positive Response to the Call of Liberty

The song bird being brave responds to the call of liberty and freedom leaving aside its sufferings and bruised heart. The centuries of repression may have weakened the body, it certainly has not exhausted the spirit. Its body may have been constrained yet its voice remains unconquered.

### Brave Attempt to Seek Freedom

It will not let a bleeding wing hamper its long awaited flight to freedom. The poetess concludes the poem by saying that the wounded bird flies higher and higher to meet its heart's desire i.e. freedom. The rhyme of the poem is 'aa bb'.

# Practice Questions

**1.** What does the poem 'The Broken Wing' portray?
(a) a picture of India under the British rule.
(b) a picture of women in the ancient India.
(c) a picture of education in pre. Independence era.
(d) a picture of farmers just after independence

**2.** Who are symbolised as song bird in the poem?
(a) The nightingale
(b) The intellectuals, the poets, the playwrights and other artist.
(c) The women of India
(d) The singers of India

**3.** What has suppressed the Voice of song bird in the poem?
(a) Wide-spread drought in the country
(b) Lack of quality food and water
(c) Brute force and strict censorship by the British
(d) A chronic disease.

**4.** What is the great dawn symbolic of in the poem?
(a) Early morning (b) Long day
(c) Wonderful time
(d) Impending Liberation

**5.** What does 'The mournful night' in the poem mean?
(a) Period of dominance and suppression
(b) Period of Femines
(c) Drought period
(d) Period of Sati (Women sacrifice) Culture

**6.** According to the poem, what is the current atmosphere in the nation?
(a) Gloomy
(b) Full of corruption
(c) Full of hope and expectation
(d) Full of jealousy and torture

**7.** Who are set to tread the path of liberty in the poem?
(a) The women (b) The children
(c) The intellectuals (d) The people of India

**8.** Who in the poem will not ignore the call of liberty?
(a) The women
(b) The Indians
(c) The British
(d) The bruised and suppressed intellectuals

**9.** What does the broken wing represent in the poem?
(a) Hurt, injured and suppressed artists and intellectuals
(b) Tortured women
(c) Mal-nourished children
(d) A bird without wings

**10.** What is the rhyme scheme of the poem?
(a) ab cd (b) aa bb
(c) ab ab (d) ab ca

**11.** How many sections is the poem 'The Broken Wing' divided into?
(a) Two (b) Three
(c) Four (d) Five

**12.** When was Sarojini Naidu born?
(a) 13, February, 1878
(b) 13th, February, 1879
(c) 26th, February, 1878
(d) 27th, February,1890

**13.** Where was Sarojini Naidu educated?
(a) Mumbai (b) Chennai
(c) Cambridge
(d) Chennai and Cambridge

**14.** 'The Broken Wing' was published in .......... .
(a) 1915 (b) 1916 (c) 1917 (d) 1918

**15.** What was 'The Broken Wing' dedicated to?
(a) Dream of Today
(b) Dream of Tomorrow
(c) Hope of Tomorrow
(d) Dream of Today and Hope of Tomorrow

**16.** Sarojini Naidu was appointed the Governor of .........
(a) West Bengal (b) Uttar Pradesh
(c) Odisha (d) Maharashtra

**17.** When did Sarojini Naidu die?
(a) 1948 (b) 1947 (c) 1949 (d) 1946

**18.** What was Sarojini Naidu's original name?
(a) Padmini Gangopadhyay
(b) Sarojini Chattopadhyay
(c) Aparna Mukhyopadhyay
(d) Sarojini Bandopadhyay

**19.** Where was Sarojini Naidu born?
(a) Serampore (b) Buxar
(c) Hyderabad (d) Plassey

**20.** Which of the following is true of Sarojini Naidu?
(a) First Indian President of Indian National Congress
(b) First Indian woman President of Indian National Congress
(c) First woman President of Indian National Congress
(d) Youngest President of Indian National Congress

**21.** Where did Sarojini Naidu die?
(a) Vijayawada (b) Golconda
(c) Secunderabad (d) Lucknow

## ANSWERS

| | | | | | | | | | | | | | | | | | | | |
|---|---|---|---|---|---|---|---|---|---|---|---|---|---|---|---|---|---|---|---|
| 1. | (a) | 2. | (b) | 3. | (c) | 4. | (d) | 5. | (a) | 6. | (c) | 7. | (d) | 8. | (d) | 9. | (a) | 10. | (b) |
| 11. | (c) | 12. | (b) | 13. | (d) | 14. | (c) | 15. | (d) | 16. | (b) | 17. | (c) | 18. | (b) | 19. | (c) | 20. | (b) |
| 21. | (d) | | | | | | | | | | | | | | | | | | |

Chapter 26

# Gitanjali (Song No. 1)

*Rabindranath Tagore (The Poet and the Pauper)*

## Summary

Thou has made me endless' is the first poem in the series of poems entitled Gitanjali which fetched Rabindranth Tagore the Nobel Prize for Literature in the year 1913, but written in 1910 sets the lyric continuing unto the last with its rhyme and rhythm, song note and word-flow, lyricism and musical tuning.

### Thanksgiving and Acknowledgement of God's Gift

A small poem it is in the form of submission and prayer, thanksgiving and acknowledgement of the same. God's gift of life has been acknowledged with thanks and oblation. Though utterly new for the West and the Occident, it is one drawn from Indian culture and philosophy, thought and tradition, spirituality and ethics, religion and metaphysics. Adi Shankararacharya's thoughts can be traced as the kernels of the idea.

### Poet's Devotion towards Vaishnava Tradition

The devotion with which Tagore recalls God is the one of the Vaishnava tradition and the Bhakti marga shown in the Gita. As interpreted in the Gita, discarding the older clothes and leaves as wear we and trees the newer ones so is the case with this body of ours before entering into new.

### God Controls everything in Life

The poet puts it that this life is his, the giver and taker of it all and nothing happens to it without the wish of whose for which we should be thankful to him. It is you who has made it all, who has given life. As the origin of the universe and life is beyond expiation and we can never know the truths so are the mysteries of life. God has made us endless and such is his pleasure. Again and again we shall take lives and meet lour ends. There is no way out. Everything is but into the hands of the Lord-God the maker of all. The vessel he fills and empties as well from time to time.

### God as Flute Player

The little flute of reed he carries over the hills and the dales to sing, to tune it beautifully, submerging it all with the mellifluous music of love and song and the melody of life played. At the touch of his hands, the joy of his knows no bounds. What can be more elated than to hold the hand of the divine? The gifts of God come to in their own from time to time, age to age. God keeps giving and man at the receiving end of the bounties.

When Tagore talks of intimate divine and his fluting, the picture of Krishna dances before the eyes though he prays to a secular God.

Though, he uses and applies in Indian imagery and thought-content to base on, the poem is a remarkable specimen of devotion. The high note of lyricism dots and punctuates the poem. As a lyric, he is sentimental and emotional to express the things. As usually untitled, form one in the series of lyrics embedded, 'Thou hast made me endless' is a superb lyric exquisitely beautiful for its thought and imagery. The poem is one flower embedded in the garland of flowers offered to the Deity.

### Influenced by various religious

The song like content of the lyric is admirable and is rich in imagery. It is devotion which adds beauty to the poem; it is thought and content which strengthen it.

The language which the poet uses in it but the Biblical language and he has after reading the Bible. Had it not been, Tagore would not have excelled. Household philosophies of the folks have also given the beauty of thought and idea to the poem. The influences of Kabir, Jayadeva, Shankaracharya and other others hang heavy upon him. He died on 7th august, 1941.

# Practice Questions

**1. When was Rabindranath Tagore born?**
(a) 7th May, 1861 (b) 12th June, 1858
(c) 22nd March, 1865 (d) 31st August ,1871

**2. Where was Rabindranath Tagore born?**
(a) Calcutta (b) Murshidabad
(c) Serampore (d) Chandranagore

**3. What is Rabindranath Tagore's father name?**
(a) Narendranath (b) Hridayanath
(c) Rajmohan (d) Debendranath

**4. What is Rabindranath Tagore's mother name?**
(a) Sarada Devi (b) Sharmila
(c) Sarojini Devi (d) Padmaja

**5. Rabindranath Tagore married Bhabtarini Devi in 1883. How was she known later on?**
(a) Mallika Devi (b) Mrinalini Devi
(c) Aparna (d) Suchitra

**6. Which university was founded by Rabindranath Tagore?**
(a) Benaras Hindu University (b) Calcutta University
(c) Visva bharati University (d) Bombay University

**7. In which year was Rabindranath Tagore awarded Nobel Prize for Literature?**
(a) 1901 (b) 1913
(c) 1928 (d) 1930

**8. In which year did Rabindranath Tagore surrender the knighthood as a protest against Jallianwalla-bagh massacre?**
(a) 1919 (b) 1924
(c) 1935 (d) 1939

**9. Which magazine was edited by Rabindranath Tagore?**
(a) Amritbazar Patrika (b) Bangadarshan
(c) Ganashakti (d) Imprint

**10. When did Rabindranath Tagore die?**
(a) 7th August, 1941
(b) 21st June, 1947
(c) 8th April, 1936
(c) 18th August, 1945

**11. Name the first poem in the series of Gitanjali.**
(a) Thou has made me endless
(b) Life of My Life
(c) Pluck This Little Flower
(d) The Time That My Journey Takes

**12. How does the poet acknowledge the gift of God in the poem?**
(a) With repentance
(b) With pride
(c) With attitude
(d) With thanks and obligation

**13. With what has body been compared in the poem?**
(a) Trees (b) Vessels
(c) Buildings (d) Books

**14. What is endless according to the poem?**
(a) Body (b) Mountains
(c) Soul (d) Spirits

**15. How does life get refreshed according to the poem?**
(a) God intermittently repairs and takes care of it
(b) Doctors take care of it
(c) Technology protects it
(d) The man himself refreshes it

**16. What does a flute represent in the poem?**
(a) Music (b) Learning
(c) God (d) Man/Woman

**17. Who is the flute player in the poem?**
(a) Man (b) Woman (c) God (d) Nature

**18. What fills the poet's heart with joy and pleasure in the poem?**
(a) His own intelligence
(b) God's invisible touch
(c) Women's company
(d) Beauty of nature

**19. What is God's greatest gift to the poet?**
(a) His life (b) His intelligence
(c) Beauty of nature (d) His nation

**20. What according to the poem is the poet's special room?**
(a) His life (b) His body
(c) His poetry (d) His heart

## ANSWERS

| | | | | | | | | | | | | | | | | | | | |
|---|---|---|---|---|---|---|---|---|---|---|---|---|---|---|---|---|---|---|---|
| 1. | (a) | 2. | (a) | 3. | (d) | 4. | (a) | 5. | (b) | 6. | (c) | 7. | (b) | 8. | (a) | 9. | (b) | 10. | (a) |
| 11. | (a) | 12. | (d) | 13. | (b) | 14. | (c) | 15. | (a) | 16. | (d) | 17. | (c) | 18. | (b) | 19. | (a) | 20. | (d) |

Chapter 27

# I Wandered Lonely as a Cloud (Daffodils)

*William Wordsworth*

## About the Poet

William Wordsworth was born on 7th April, 1770 in Cockermouth, Cumberland, in the Lake District, United Kingdom. His father, John Wordsworth, was the attorney of the Earl of Lansdale. The magnificent landscape deeply affected Wordsworth's imagination and gave him a love of nature. He lost his parents in his childhood. He was a major English Romantic poet and with Samuel Taylor Coleridge, he helped to launch the Romantic Age in English literature with their joint publication 'Lyrical Ballads' (1798).

Wordsworth's magnum opus is generally considered to be 'The Prelude', a semi-autobiographical poem of his early years that he revised and expanded a number of times. It was posthumously titled and published, before which it was generally known as 'The Poem to Coleridge'. His major works include 'Lyrical Ballads with Other Poems' (1800), Preface to the Lyrical Ballads, 'Poems, in Two Volumes' (1807), 'Resolution and Independence', 'French Revolution' (1810), 'Guide to the Lakes' (1810), 'To the Cuckoo', 'The Excursion' (1814) and 'Laodamia' (1815, 1845).

Wordsworth was Britain's poet laureate from 1843 until his death from pleurisy on 23rd April, 1850.

## Summary

In the poem 'I Wandered Lonely as a Cloud (Daffodils)', the speaker describes an incident when he was walking around the hills and valleys, but he felt all lonely. Suddenly, as he passed a lake, he noticed a big group of yellow daffodils waving in the breeze. This wasn't just some scattered patch of daffodils. We're talking about thousands of daffodils and thousands around this particular bay. And all these flowers were dancing.

Yes, the daffodils danced, and so did the waves of the lake. But the daffodils danced better. The speaker's loneliness was replaced by joy, but he didn't even realise what a gift he has received until later.

Now, the poet describes what he gained from the experience. Afterwards, when he was lonely or feeling pensive, he could remember the daffodils, seeing them with his 'inward eye,' and be content.

### Form

The four six-line stanzas of this poem follow a quatrain-couplet rhyme scheme. 'ABABCC' Each line is metred in iambic tetrametre.

## Practice Questions

**1.** William Wordsworth was ............

(a) Irish (b) English (c) Scottish (d) Welsh

**2.** William Wordsworth was a poet of ............

(a) nature (b) romance
(c) beauty (d) loves

**3.** William Wordsworth was born in ............

(a) 1850 (b) 1772 (c) 1852 (d) 1770

**4.** William Wordsworth died in ............

(a) 1770 (b) 1772 (c) 1850 (d) 1852

**5.** William Wordsworth was a poet of natural objects and ............ people.

(a) country (b) common
(c) aristocratic (d) gentry

**6.** 'I Wandered Lonely as a Cloud'. Here 'I' refer to ............

(a) the reader (b) the cloud
(c) the daffodils (d) the poet

**7.** 'Continuous as the stars that shine, and twinkle on the milky way,' in the above lines, the daffodils have been compared to ............

a) the clouds b) the other flowers
c) the stars d) milky way

**8.** 'They stretched in never ending line along the margin of a bay'. Here 'they' refers to ............

(a) the stars (b) the daffodils
(c) the clouds (d) the hills

**9.** The daffodils were growing ............

(a) along the margin of a bay
(b) by the side of a pool
(c) by the riverside
(d) in a garden

**10.** The poet saw ............ daffodils.

(a) a few (b) white
(c) blue (d) a large number of

**11.** 'A poet could not but be gay in such a jocund company!'. Here 'jocund company' refers to the ............

(a) friends of the poet (b) waves
(c) daffodils (d) stars

**12.** When the poet was looking at the daffodils, ............

(a) he felt sad to see them
(b) he was totally lost in their beauty
(c) he thought they were ugly
(d) he felt like dancing

**13.** 'What wealth the show to me had brought'. By 'wealth' the poet means ............

(a) happiness (b) gold
(c) pleasure (d) money

**14.** A host of golden daffodils, a 'host' means ............

(a) a small number (b) one who entertains
(c) a guest (d) a large number

**15.** 'Never-ending line' means ............

(a) a curved line (b) a short line
(c) a continuous line (d) line of stars

**16.** 'Ten thousand saw I at a glance, Tossing their heads in sprightly dance'. Here sprightly dance means ............

(a) a slow dance (b) lively dance
(c) dance of the spirits (d) religious dance

**17.** What is mean by 'solitude' in the poem?

(a) being alone (b) being together
(c) being in trouble (d) being sad

**18.** Explain the meaning of 'glee' as used in the poem.

(a) joy (b) sadness
(c) gloom (d) happiness

**19.** 'A poet could not but be gay' means ............

(a) the poet could not sleep
(b) the poet was very sad
(c) the poet was happy
(d) the poet could not be happy

**20.** What is mean by 'bliss' as used in the poem?

(a) great love (b) great joy
(c) great blessing (d) great loneliness

**21.** 'I wondered lonely as a cloud'. What is the image here?

(a) Metaphor (b) Simile
(c) Antithesis (d) Personification

**22.** 'Fluttering and dancing in the breeze'. Extract a figure of speech?

(a) Personification (b) Simile
(c) Metaphor (d) Rhyme scheme

**23.** 'Ten thousand I saw at a glance, Tossing their heads in sprightly dance', This line refers to

(a) inward eye (b) milky way
(c) pensive mood (d) daffodils

**24.** Why does the speaker compare himself to a cloud at the beginning of the poem?

(a) That's how he feels as he looks down on a lake from higher up
(b) He believes that poets have thoughts that rise as high as the clouds
(c) He is outdoors performing a scientific experiment
(d) He spills ink in the shape of a cloud on his journal page

**25.** How does the speaker feel before he sees the daffodils?

(a) Indifferent (b) Lonely
(c) Joyful (d) Angry

**26.** **How do the words 'fluttering and dancing', at the end of the first stanza, influence what the speaker wants you to feel about daffodils?**

(a) The words add a positive energy to the image of the daffodils
(b) The speaker thinks of dancing daffodils as a silly joke
(c) The words make the daffodils seem lonely and depressed
(d) The speaker believes that fluttering daffodils bring bad luck

**27.** **In the second stanza, the stars in the Milky Way are compared to ...........**

(a) the clouds overhead
(b) the speaker's sister, who silently walks beside him
(c) the towns that the speaker has already wandered past
(d) the many daffodils growing in a line

**28.** **Besides daffodils, what else dances in the poem?**

(a) Stars (b) Waves
(c) Clouds (d) The speaker

**29.** **The daffodils bring 'wealth' to the speaker because they ...........**

(a) give him something to write about
(b) increase the value of his lakeside property
(c) serve as a gift for his sister
(d) provide him with rich memories

**30.** **The last stanza of the poem is set ...........**

(a) on the banks of the lake the speaker has wandered to
(b) in the Milky Way, above the clouds
(c) at a later time, on a couch in the speaker's home
(d) at another lake where daffodils do not grow as well

**31.** **When memories of the daffodils appear to the speaker's 'inward eye,' he feels ...........**

(a) deprived (b) pleasure
(c) depressed (d) blissful

**32.** **Like the speaker of' 'I Wandered Lonely as a Cloud,' Dorothy Wordsworth also ...........**

(a) imagines that the daffodils are dancing
(b) believes that people feel lonely in nature
(c) thinks that the Milky Way extends farther than scientists know
(d) believes that wealth is the key to their success

**33.** **'For oft when on my couch I lie/In vacant or in pensive mood'. What is his tone in this section?**

(a) Happy (b) Bored
(c) Depressed (d) Excited

**34.** **What is the 'inward eye' upon which the daffodils flash?**

(a) His eye (b) His memory
(c) His mirror (d) A movie

**35.** **The poet belongs to the school of ...........**

(a) criticism (b) romanticism
(c) rationalism (d) tourism

## ANSWERS

| | | | | | | | | | | | | | | | | | | | |
|---|---|---|---|---|---|---|---|---|---|---|---|---|---|---|---|---|---|---|---|
| 1. | (b) | 2. | (a) | 3. | (d) | 4. | (c) | 5. | (a) | 6. | (d) | 7. | (c) | 8. | (b) | 9. | (a) | 10. | (d) |
| 11. | (c) | 12. | (b) | 13. | (a) | 14. | (d) | 15. | (c) | 16. | (b) | 17. | (a) | 18. | (d) | 19. | (c) | 20. | (b) |
| 21. | (b) | 22. | (a) | 23. | (d) | 24. | (a) | 25. | (b) | 26. | (a) | 27. | (d) | 28. | (b) | 29. | (d) | 30. | (c) |
| 31. | (b) | 32. | (a) | 33. | (c) | 34. | (b) | 35. | (b) | | | | | | | | | | |

Chapter 28

# The World is Too Much with Us

*William Wordsworth*


## Summary

The poem 'The World is Too Much with Us' is a famous sonnet. It was composed by Wordsworth sometime in 1802. It was first published in Poems in Two Volumes (1807). In this poem the poet says that love of worldly wealth can bring us no peace while love of nature can make us happy. The poem is a Petrarchan sonnet. It has been divided into two parts. The first part consists of the first eight lines. It is called the Octave. The second part consists of the last six lines. It is called the sestet. The idea of the sonnet is that we have become materialistic and have lost touch with nature. The money-making business is too much with us and almost all the time we are occupied with "getting and spending". It is a waste of our powers of the senses. Nature has a treasure of beautiful and vital influence.

Having turned our back on nature, we have devoted ourselves to worldly pursuits and temporal possessions. He exclaims that he would rather be a pagan than a materialist. The poem is an inspiring one and inspires us to feel consolation and ease in the lap of nature.


## Practice Questions

**1.** When was Wordsworth born?
(a) 7th April, 1770 (b) 7th May, 1770
(c) 7th June, 1770 (d) 7th July, 1770

**2.** Where was Wordsworth born?
(a) Walmer, Kent (b) Cockermouth, Cumberland
(c) Dublin (d) Lombard, London

**3.** What is the name of Wordsworth's father?
(a) Henry Wordsworth (b) John Wordsworth
(c) Edward Wordsworth (d) Tom Wordsworth

**4.** What is the name of Wordsworth's mother?
(a) Anne (b) Mary (c) Lara (d) Maud

**5.** In which year Wordsworth put to Cockermouth Grammar School?
(a) 1717 (b) 1770 (c) 1776 (d)1786

**6.** In which school was Wordsworth sent when he was eight years old?
(a) St. Charls (b) St. John
(c) Hawkshead (d) Dove

**7.** Till which year Wordsworth studied in St. John's College, Cambridge?
(a) 1742 (b) 1781
(c) 1799 (d) 1791

**8.** When did Wordsworth got married with Mary Hutchinson?
(a) 2nd October, 1802 (b) 4th October, 1802
(c) 5th November, 1803 (d) 1st December, 1804

**9.** Who is the friend of Wordsworth?
(a) Shakespeare (b) John Donne
(c) ST Coleridge (d) Robert Bridges

**10.** Who was Caroline?
(a) Wordsworth's sister (b) Wordsworth's mother
(c) Wordsworth's daughter (d) Wordsworth's wife

**11.** What was the name of Wordsworth's sister?
(a) Dorothy (b) Mary (c) Caroline (d) Elizabeth

**12.** In which year 'Lyrical Ballads' was published?
(a) 1784 (b) 1798 (c) 1748 (d) 1999

**13.** In which year Wordsworth married Mary Hutchinson?
(a) 1801 (b) 1814
(c) 1892 (d) 1802

**14.** French Revolution began in
(a) 1798 (b) 1780
(c) 1786 (d) 1789

**15.** Wordsworth went to Orleans where he came in contact with some officers of
(a) Newly Army (b) Republican Army
(c) French Army (d) Europe Army

**16.** Wordsworth's gloomy poem is
(a) The Borderes (b) The Prelude
(c) The Waggoner (d) The Excursion

**17.** What was the relation between Wordsworth and Mary Hutchinson before their marriage?
(a) Cousin (b) Friend
(c) Beloved (d) None of these

**18.** Who along with Wordsworth published 'Lyrical Ballads'?
(a) Caroline (b) Coleridge
(c) Robert Bridges (d) Sara Hutchinson

**19.** When did Wordsworth received his B.A. degree?
(a) 1790 (b) 1792 (c) 1789 (d) 1791

**20.** When was Wordsworth sent to the Gramm School at Hawkshead?
(a) In 1787 (b) In 1770 (c) In 1778 (d) In 1775

**21.** When was William Wordsworth die?
(a) 25th April, 1855 (b) 20th April, 1865
(c) 23rd April, 1850 (d) 24th April, 1850

**22.** Where was Wordsworth buried?
(a) Grasmere Churchyard (b) Stratford Churchyard
(c) Westminster Abbey (d) Twickenham

**23.** Who was called the 'High Priest of Nature'?
(a) William Shakespeare (b) William Wordsworth
(c) William Blake (d) William Augustus

**24.** In which year was Wordsworth appointed 'Poet Laureate'?
(a) 1841 (b) 1843
(c) 1842 (d) 1846

**25.** Which edition of his collected poems was published in 1815?
(a) First (b) Fourth
(c) Six (d) Eight

**26.** When did Wordsworth compose the poem 'Peter Bell'?
(a) 1794 (b) 1782
(c) 1798 (d) 1771

**27.** Name the poem which was published after Wordsworth's death?
(a) Peter Bell (b) The Waggoner
(c) The Excursion (d) The Prelude

**28.** Whom did Wordsworth meet when he first visited Scotland?
(a) Sir William Scott (b) Sir Philip Sidney
(c) Sir Heger (d) Sir Walter Scott

**29.** Who was called 'The Harbinger of Nature', 'Philosopher of Nature' and 'Mystical Pantheist'?
(a) Ben Jonson (b) William Wordsworth
(c) T S Eliot (d) John Donne

**30.** Who gave the definition–"Poetry is the spontaneous overflow of powerful feelings"?
(a) William Wordsworth (b) Ezra Pound
(c) Hazlitt (d) Philip Larkin

**31.** 'The World is Too Much with Us' is a popular
(a) Elegy (b) Lyric
(c) Ode (d) Sonnet

**32.** The poet is sad to see the people growing
(a) materialistic (b) free (c) full of joy (d) lazy

**33.** The people do not pay attention to the
(a) materialism (b) beautiful objects of nature
(c) blessings of the wealth (d) None of these

**34.** Poet prefers to be a
(a) priest (b) thiest (c) pagan (d) materialistic

**35.** What type of sonnet is 'The World is Too Much with Us'?
(a) Petrarchan sonnet (b) Shakespearean sonnet
(c) Miltonic sonnet (d) None of these

**36.** Proteus and Triton are
(a) Goddesses (b) Sea Gods (c) Devils (d) Dragon

**37.** What does Wordsworth condemns?
(a) Nature (b) Blessings
(c) Worldly pursuits (d) All of these

**38.** Too much indulgence in gross materialism creates
(a) baneful influence upon man's life
(b) a gross animosity among people
(c) base attitude towards money
(d) None of these

**39.** Money earnings, by fair and foul means, is the only
(a) natural thing (b) goal of man's life
(c) divine power (d) capitalism

**40.** The growing materialism makes man
(a) full of mental peace (b) the Guardian
(c) pagan (d) selfish

**41.** Due to our carelessness, the natural objects do not
(a) condemn us (b) harm us
(c) attract us (d) All of these

**42.** What is important in the world?
(a) Money (b) Nature
(c) God (d) Family

**43.** Who opens her heart to the moon?
(a) Flower (b) Sea
(c) Valleys (d) None of these

**44.** Who blows his wreathed horn?
(a) Proteus (b) Triton
(c) Both (a) and (b) (d) None of these

**45.** What is the style of the poem?
(a) Romantic
(b) Dignified
(c) Both (a) and (b)
(d) None of the above

**46.** The Poem 'The World is Too Much with Us' contains
(a) 16 lines (b) 13 lines
(c) 14 lines (d) 12 lines

**47.** How many stanzas are there in 'The World Is Too Much with Us'?
(a) 5 stanzas (b) 4 stanzas
(c) 8 stanzas (d) 3 stanzas

**48.** Why does the music of nature not attract us?
(a) People are busy in worldy pleasure
(b) Busy in enjoying
(c) Busy in praying to God
(d) People became materialistic

**49.** How do men spend their life?
(a) Watching movies
(b) Making and spending money
(c) Both (a) and (b)
(d) Fun

**50.** When was 'The World Is Too Much with Us' published in two volumes?
(a) 1803 (b) 1807 (c) 1800 (d) 1808

**51.** What have the men lost?
(a) Nature's Joy (b) Family
(c) Education (d) Self respect

**52.** What is the rhyme scheme of the sonnet?
(a) abbaabba; cdcdcd (b) ababbaba; ccddee
(c) abbababa; cddced (d) abbaabba; cdcdcd

**53.** What is the metre of the sonnet?
(a) Iambic pentameter (b) Hexameter
(c) Tetra meter (d) None of these

## ANSWERS

| | | | | | | | | | | | | | | | | | | | |
|---|---|---|---|---|---|---|---|---|---|---|---|---|---|---|---|---|---|---|---|
| 1. | (a) | 2. | (b) | 3. | (b) | 4. | (a) | 5. | (c) | 6. | (c) | 7. | (d) | 8. | (b) | 9. | (c) | 10. | (c) |
| 11. | (a) | 12. | (b) | 13. | (d) | 14. | (d) | 15. | (c) | 16. | (b) | 17. | (a) | 18. | (b) | 19. | (d) | 20. | (c) |
| 21. | (c) | 22. | (c) | 23. | (b) | 24. | (b) | 25. | (a) | 26. | (c) | 27. | (d) | 28. | (d) | 29. | (b) | 30. | (a) |
| 31. | (d) | 32. | (a) | 33. | (b) | 34. | (c) | 35. | (a) | 36. | (b) | 37. | (c) | 38. | (b) | 39. | (b) | 40. | (d) |
| 41. | (c) | 42. | (b) | 43. | (b) | 44. | (b) | 45. | (a) | 46. | (c) | 47. | (b) | 48. | (a) | 49. | (b) | 50. | (b) |
| 51. | (a) | 52. | (a) | 53. | (b) | | | | | | | | | | | | | | |

Chapter 29

# The Tables Turned

*William Wordsworth*

## Summary

### Adverse Effect of Just Reading Books

The poet begins by telling his friend to stop reading books; he'll become fat from being sedentary. Then, he asks why he chooses to be so serious, while there is a beautiful evening outside.

He warns him that he might grow obese if he coops himself up in a room while studying. Does this remind you of the stress and strain that students in India are put through in order to achieve good grades and do well in competitive exams? Do you think we should continue with the status quo in education?

### The Student is Missing the Beauty of Nature

Then the poet points out that the student is missing out on the wonderful scenery outside with sunshine bathing the mountains decked with lush green fields. Nowadays, even the natural environment is being pushed to the fringes.

### Students should Visit the Natural Environment as Part of Their Education

Children and students are being robbed of natural surroundings. In such a scenario, it is important to ensure that children and students visit natural environments and are also guided to be sensitive to natural environments. Activities like gardening and visiting neighbourhood parks should also form an important aspect of their educational years.

### Nature gives Wisdom While Studying Books is Laborious

The poet then points out that studying books brings in drudgery. William Wordsworth, who respects nature, asks his friend to listen to the sweet songs of birds which can bring in more wisdom than any number of books.

### Nature Teaches Students Humanity and Goodness

The poet strongly reiterates that nature brings about wisdom which keeps us healthy and cheerful. Do you feel that a student's health and even innate joy is compromised in the rat race kind of learning with competitive exams and the race for top grades? Nature can have a soothing effect on students and help them to think and act with sensitivity and depth.

William Wordsworth also says that spending time in the midst of nature can also teach students more about humanity, goodness as well as evil, than mere bookish learning.

### Students must Close their Books and Learn from Nature

It brings the sweetness of nature and its knowledge. According to the poet, knowledge has been distorted by the way human beings try to cruelly dissect it.

William Wordsworth ends the poem by asking his friend to close his books and stop studying science and art and instead learn from nature in a sensitive and open-hearted manner.

### Form

'The Tables Turned' consists of eight four-line stanzas in interlocking rhymes (abab). It is in ballad form, written in iambic with four beats in the first and third lines of each stanza, and three beats in the second and fourth lines.

## Practice Questions

**1.** **Describe 'The Table Turned' in a line by William Wordsworth.**
(a) Students should only read their books
(b) Students should learn from nature apart from books
(c) They should not be a part of outside the world of books
(d) They only should gain knowledge from bookish world

**2.** **What word does the speaker use to describe human intellect?**
(a) Meddling
(b) Useless
(c) Sweet
(d) Wise

**3.** **What activities does the poet want to describe to do in the poem?**
(a) Cooking food
(b) Playing indoor games
(c) Gardening and visting parks
(d) Sleeping and eating

**4.** **According to the speaker, nature is a valuable**
(a) resource
(b) teacher
(c) mother
(d) leader

**5.** **How are the stanzas divided?**
(a) Into octets
(b) Into couplets
(c) Into sestets
(d) Into quatrains

**6.** **What two birds appear in the poem?**
(a) A finch and a sparrow
(b) A mockingbird and a warbler
(c) A linnet and a throstle
(d) A raven and a crow

**7.** **How many stanzas are in the poem?**
(a) Seven
(b) Four
(c) Eight
(d) Five

**8.** **What does the speaker refer to as 'barren leaves' in the final stanza?**
(a) Science and art
(b) Sages
(c) Books
(d) Birds and trees

**9.** **What is the form of the given poem?**
(a) Sonnet
(b) ballad
(c) elegy
(d) Free verse

**10.** **What does the poet mean by the line 'Let Nature be your teacher' in the poem?**
(a) Understand the beauty and complexity of nature
(b) Play in the field
(c) Stop working and reading
(d) None of the above

## ANSWERS

| | | | | | | | | | | | | | | | | | | | |
|---|---|---|---|---|---|---|---|---|---|---|---|---|---|---|---|---|---|---|---|
| 1. | *(b)* | 2. | *(a)* | 3. | *(c)* | 4. | *(b)* | 5. | *(d)* | 6. | *(c)* | 7. | *(c)* | 8. | *(a)* | 9. | *(b)* | 10. | *(a)* |

Chapter 30

# The Solitary Reaper

*William Wordsworth*

## Summary

'The Solitary Reaper' opens with the speaker directing our attention to a solitary reaper (someone who cuts down crops—like corn or rye—by hand).

He says that anyone passing by should either stop here, or 'gently pass' so as not to disturb her, as she is singing in a field somewhere. She's a highland lass, and she's singing while she works and the valley overflows with the beautiful, sad sound. The speaker says that the sound is more welcome than any chant of the nightingale to weary travellers in the desert, and that the cuckoo-bird in spring never sang with a voice so thrilling.

Impatient, the poet asks, 'Will no one tell me what she sings?' He speculates that her song might be about 'old, unhappy, far-off things, / and battles long ago,' or that it might be humbler, a simple song about 'matter of today.' Whatever she sings about, he says, he listened 'motionless and still,' and as he travelled up the hill, he carried her song with him in his heart long after he could no longer hear it.

### Form

The four eight-line stanzas of this poem are written in a tight iambic tetrameter. Each follows a rhyme scheme of 'ABABCCDD', though in the first and last stanzas the 'A' rhyme is off (field/self and sang/work).

## Practice Questions

**1.** The 'Solitary Reaper' is written by
(a) William Wordsworth
(b) William Shakespeare
(c) Robert Frost
(d) Thomas Campbell

**2.** Where is the Solitary reaper allegedly from?
(a) The Irish Coast
(b) The English Countryside
(c) The Scottish Highlands
(d) The Swiss Alps

**3.** Which of the following is a word NOT used to describe the Solitary Reaper's song?
(a) Melancholy
(b) Thrilling
(c) Despairing
(d) Plaintive

**4.** How many lines are in each stanza?
(a) Six (b) Eight (c) Four (d) Two

**5.** How many stanzas are in the poem?
(a) Four (b) One
(c) Three (d) Two

**6.** To which two birds' songs does the speaker compare the Solitary Reaper's song?
(a) A swallow and a finch
(b) A mockingbird and a warbler
(c) A crow and an eagle
(d) A nightingale and a cuckoo-bird

**7.** What is the reaper described as bending over in the last stanza?
(a) Her sickle (b) A dead bird
(c) A pile of grain (d) The cliffside

**8.** The 'Solitary Reaper' was
(a) sowing seeds (b) watering the plants
(c) reaping the harvest (d) pulling out the weeds

**9.** The singing of the solitary reaper is compared to the
(a) Nightingale and Robin
(b) Cuckoo and Peacock
(c) Nightingale and Cuckoo
(d) Cuckoo and Owl

**10.** The instrument that the Solitary Reaper was using
(a) a spade (b) an axe
(c) a sickle (d) a knife

**Directions** *(Q. Nos. 11-34) Read the extracts from the poem that are given below and choose the appropriate option to answer the questions that follow the extract.*

**A.** Alone she cuts and binds the grain,
And sings a melancholy strain;
O listen! for the vale profound
Is overflowing with the sound.

**11.** Identify 'she' from the above stanza.
(a) A traveller (b) The poet
(c) Solitary Reaper (d) None of the above

**12.** How does the poet know that the song is melancholy when he cannot understand the words?
(a) From the girl's expression
(b) From the words of the song
(c) From the tune
(d) From her dress

**13.** What effect does the girl's song have over the surroundings?
(a) The valley echoes with the song
(b) Has no effect
(c) All people desert the valley
(d) The valley is indifferent

**B.** A voice so thrilling ne'er was heard
In spring-time from the cuckoo bird,
Breaking the silence of the seas
Among the farthest Hebrides.

**14.** What is cuckoo bird famous for?
(a) Cheerfulness (b) Thrill
(c) Driving away tiredness
(d) Welcoming the spring

**15.** How does the Solitary Reaper's song score over the song of the cuckoo?
(a) It is more far-reaching
(b) It echoes more
(c) It is more musical and fresh
(d) It does not have any effect

**16.** What does 'Hebrides' mean here?
(a) A group of trees
(b) A group of islands off near Scotland
(c) Far off valleys
(d) Sea

**C.** Will no one tell me what she sings?
Perhaps the plaintive numbers flow
For old, unhappy, far off things,
And battles long ago.

**17.** Explain the use of 'perhaps' in the second line.
(a) The poet is not sure
(b) He is double-minded
(c) He is indifferent
(d) None of the above

**18.** 'Flow' – what quality of the Solitary Reaper's song is expressed here?
(a) Its fluidity (b) Its evocativeness
(c) Its music (d) Its spontaneity

**19.** What is the poet's guess?
(a) The theme is of spring
(b) Of happiness and forgotten things
(c) Of battles and sad events in the past
(d) Of stories

**D.** Or is it some more humble lay,
Familiar matter of today?
Some natural sorrow, loss or pain,
That has been, may be again.

**20.** 'It' in the first line refers to
(a) the valley (b) the song
(c) the solitary reaper (d) her dress

**21.** Explain 'humble lay'.
(a) A song about ordinary events
(b) A song about extraordinary things
(c) A song about modest things
(d) A song about rich people

**22.** What does the poet wish to convey by saying 'that has been and may be again'?
(a) A natural loss, and pain
(b) A natural event
(c) Natural sorrow which can occur again
(d) Both (a) and (c)

**E.** Whatever the theme, the maiden sang
As if her song could have no ending;
I saw her singing at her work
And o'er the sickle bending

**23.** What other activities is the maiden doing besides singing?
(a) She is ploughing (b) Binding the corn
(c) Cutting grass (d) None of the above

**24.** What makes the maiden's song extraordinary?
(a) Its musicality (b) Its eternal nature
(c) Its theme (d) Her voice

**25.** What effect does the song have over the poet?
(a) Mesmerising
(b) Impressive
(c) Invigorating (d) No effect

**F.** **I listen'd, motionless and still**
**And, as I mounted up the hill,**
**The music in my heart I bore,**
**Long after it was heard no more.**

***26.*** **Where does the poet go?**
(a) Down the valleys
(b) Doesn't go anywhere
(c) Climbed up the mountain
(d) Nowhere

***27.*** **How did the song affect the poet?**
(a) Left a permanent mark on his heart
b) It impressed him
(c) Served as an inspiration
(d) Had no effect

***28.*** **What does the poet want to convey by 'long after it was heard no more'?**
(a) Music is entertaining
(b) Music is eternal and can give pleasure even when you do not hear it
(c) Sad music is always remembered
(d) The universal and permanent impression of music.

**G.** **Alone she cuts and binds the grain,**
**And sings a melancholy strain**
**O listen! for the vale profound**
**Is over flowing with the sound.**

***29.*** **'Melancholy strain' in the second line refers to**
(a) sad song
(b) happy song
(c) thrilling song
(d) sweet song

***30.*** **Identify the 'figure of speech' in the above lines.**
(a) Personification (b) Metaphor
(c) Imagery (d) Alliteration

***31.*** **The last two lines mean**
(a) her voice is resounding in the valley
(b) she is singing at a high pitch
(c) her voice is reaching outside the valley
(d) she is asking everyone to listen to her

**H.** **No nightingale did ever chant**
**More welcome notes to weary bands**
**Of travellers in some shady haunt**
**Among Arabian Sands**
**A voice so thrilling never was heard**
**In spring – time from the cuckoo – bird**
**Breaking the silence of the seas**
**Among the farthest Hebrides**

***32.*** **According to the poet, nightingales sing**
(a) to welcome the travellers
(b) to please themselves
(c) to welcome the tired travellers
(d) to get relief from their own pains

***33.*** **When and where do the nightingales sing?**
(a) in spring season in desert of Arabia
(b) in autumn season in deserts
(c) in spring season in deserts of Thar
(d) in spring season in deserts of Egypt

***34.*** **The effect of the voice of the cuckoo bird is**
(a) that it refreshes the tired travellers
(b) that it is spread everywhere
(c) that it seems to welcome travellers
(d) breaks the silence of the seas

## ANSWERS

| | | | | | | | | | | | | | | | | | | | |
|---|---|---|---|---|---|---|---|---|---|---|---|---|---|---|---|---|---|---|---|
| 1. | (a) | 2. | (c) | 3. | (c) | 4. | (b) | 5. | (a) | 6. | (d) | 7. | (a) | 8. | (c) | 9. | (c) | 10. | (c) |
| 11. | (c) | 12. | (c) | 13. | (a) | 14. | (d) | 15. | (a) | 16. | (b) | 17. | (a) | 18. | (d) | 19. | (c) | 20. | (b) |
| 21. | (a) | 22. | (c) | 23. | (b) | 24. | (b) | 25. | (a) | 26. | (c) | 27. | (a) | 28. | (d) | 29. | (a) | 30. | (c) |
| 31. | (a) | 32. | (c) | 33. | (a) | 34. | (d) | | | | | | | | | | | | |

Chapter 31

# After Apple Picking

*Robert Frost*

## About the Poet

Robert Frost was an American poet who was born on 26th March, 1874 in San Francisco, United States. His family moved to Lawrence, Massachusetts, in 1884 following his father William Prescott Frost Jr.'s death. He became interested in reading and writing poetry during his high school years in Lawrence, enrolled at Dartmouth College in Hanover, New Hampshire, in 1892, and later at Harvard University in Boston, though he never earned a formal college degree.

Frost drifted through a string of occupations after leaving school, working as a teacher, cobbler, and editor of the Lawrence Sentinel. His first published poem, "My Butterfly," appeared on November 8, 1894, in the New York newspaper The Independent.

Frost was honored frequently during his lifetime, receiving four Pulitzer Prizes for Poetry. He became one of America's rare "public literary figures, almost an artistic institution." He was awarded the Congressional Gold Medal in 1960 for his poetic works. On July 22, 1961, Frost was named poet laureate of Vermont. Frost was nominated for the Nobel Prize in Literature 31 times.

Some of his famous poems are: Acquainted with the Night, After Apple-Picking, Assertive, At Woodward's Gardens, Birches, Christmas Trees, The Code Heroics, The Death of the Hired Man, Dust of Snow, Fire and Ice, Fireflies in the Garden, The Flower-Boat etc. On 29 January 1963, Robert Frost died of complications from prostate surgery in Boston, Massachusetts.

## Summary

A guy has been picking apples all day up on a ladder. He hasn't picked every last apple, but night is coming and he is tired. He remembers the strange vision he had that morning when he looked at a bunch of grass through a sheet of ice he removed from a drinking trough. It looked like the world was melting, and then he dropped the piece of ice. He may or may not be falling asleep as he has these thoughts. He thinks of how he will dream about apples.

He's getting sick of harvesting apples – there are so many of them, and he has to be careful not to let them fall. If an apple falls, it has to be chucked into the heap to use for making cider. Those cider apples are considered almost worthless.

He imagines that these thoughts about worthless apples and dropping things will haunt his sleep. He wonders if it will be a long, deep sleep, like the hibernation of a woodchuck, or whether it will just be a normal 'human' sleep.

### Form

This is a rhyming poem that follows no preordained rhyme scheme. 'After Apple-Picking' is basically iambic, and mostly in pentameter, but line-length variants abound. Line 1, for example, is long by any standard.

Line 32 is very short: one foot. The poem's shorter lines of di-, tri-, and tetrameter serve to syncopate and sharpen the steady, potentially droning rhythm of pentameter. They keep the reader on his toes, awake, while the speaker drifts off into oblivion.

# Practice Questions

1. **In which year Robert Frost was born?**
(a) 1865 (b) 1874 (c) 1859 (d) 1492

2. **What was Robert Frost's middle name**
(a) Edward (b) Lee (c) Sam (d) Nemo

3. **What were Robert Frost's parents names?**
(a) Franklin and Susan (b) Bill and Susan
(c) William and Isabelle (d) Rocky and Adrian

4. **Where was Robert Frost born?**
(a) Danville, Virginia (b) Denver, Colorado
(c) San Francisco, California (d) Hender Sonville, Tennessee

5. **Where did Robert Frost attend college?**
(a) Dartmouth (b) Yale (c) Harvard (d) Vol State

6. **How many times was Frost awarded the Pultizer prize?**
(a) One (b) Two (c) Four (d) None at all

7. **Which was Frost's first published poem?**
(a) After Apple Picking (b) Road not Taken
(c) My Butterfly (d) Christmas trees

8. **When was the poem 'After Apple Picking' written?**
(a) 1897 (b) 1902 (c) 1914 (d) 1920

9. **What does 'apple picking' symbolise in the poem?**
(a) Daily routine (b) Poet's act of writing poetry
(c) Memory of writing poetry (d) Boring daily life

10. **What is the speaker's state of mind in the poem 'After Apple Picking?**
(a) Very excited (b) Tired and reflective
(c) Ready to goahead (d) Very confused

11. **What is the message which this poem After Apple Picking' gives us?**
(a) Work makes us tired
(b) The opportunities we do and don't take in life
(c) Waiting for the final journey
(d) The speakes is on the verge of sleep after working tirelessly.

12. **What is the form of poetry used in the poem After Apple picking?**
(a) Dramatic Morologue (b) Sonnet
(c) Lyric (d) Epic

13. **The literal meaning of the poem is**
(a) speaker is on the verge of sleep
(b) reflecting on his work of apple picking
(c) there are still unfinished jobs for him
(d) All of the above

14. **The poem has used the word 'sleep' several times in the poem. What does it symbolise?**
(a) Actual sleep (b) Unwillingness to work
(c) Death (d) Poet's fear

15. **How would you interpret the 'ladder' in the poem?**
(a) Using the ladder to pick up apples
(b) Climbing up his career
(c) Ascending into heaven (Approaching death)
(d) Used just for the sake of it

16. **A 'wood chuck' in the poem refers to**
(a) an animal (b) human (c) a bird (d) a fish

17. **What imagery has been used by the poet to describe apple picking?**
(a) Speaker filling up buckets with apples but some falling down
(b) Speaker standing on the ladder for long
(c) His feet hurting due to standing for long hours
(d) All of the above

18. **What figure of speech is there in the following lines:**
"The wood chunk could say, whether it's like his long sleep a I describe its coming on."
(a) Similie (b) Personification (c) Paradox (d) Metaphor

19. **Where is the narrator in the poem**
(a) In the apple orchard (b) In the bed
(c) Somewhere else (d) In his study room

20. **The form and meter used in the poem is**
(a) Tetra meter (b) Iambic Pentameter
(c) Lamb meter (d) Trochee meter

21. **What does the title of the poem suggest us about the time in which it is set?**
(a) During apple picking (b) At poet's bed room
(c) At a conference
(d) Poet's reflection after apple picking

22. **What happens to the apple if it fall down on the earth?**
(a) It is thrown out (b) Again put in the basket
(c) Chucked in the heap to use for making cider
(d) Given to some one

23. **What is the general mood of the poet as depicted in the poem 'After Apple Picking'?**
(a) Very happy (b) Sad (c) Dissatisfied (d) Highly excited

24. **Which images or words describe the ouset of winter in the poem?**
(a) Grass is hoary (b) Water's surface is frozen
(c) Wood chunk going in hibernation
(d) All of the above

25. **Frost was named Poet Laureate of Vermont on**
(a) 14th December, 1956 (b) 22nd July, 1961
(c) 22nd January, 1961 (d) Never

## ANSWERS

| | | | | | | | | | | | | | | | | | | | |
|---|---|---|---|---|---|---|---|---|---|---|---|---|---|---|---|---|---|---|---|
| 1. | (b) | 2. | (b) | 3. | (c) | 4. | (c) | 5. | (a) | 6. | (c) | 7. | (c) | 8. | (c) | 9. | (b) | 10. | (b) |
| 11. | (b) | 12. | (a) | 13. | (d) | 14. | (c) | 15. | (c) | 16. | (a) | 17. | (d) | 18. | (d) | 19. | (b) | 20. | (b) |
| 21. | (d) | 22. | (c) | 23. | (c) | 24. | (d) | 25. | (b) | | | | | | | | | | |

# Chapter 32

# The Road Not Taken

*Robert Frost*


## Summary

The poet has come into the deep autumnal wood where two roads have diverged into two ways like a fork. Immediately the poet understands that as a traveller, travelling both the roads is impossible. Here the two roads symbolise two ways to go in life. The poet first thought of travelling both the roads and then discarded the idea. Then he finds himself in dilemma (not able to decide) about the choice of roads. He found that the first road has bent in the undergrowth (bush). The undergrowth here represents the unknown world.

The poet selects the road that appears at first glance to be less travelled. This stanza suggests that he has an independent spirit and does not wish to follow the crowd. After a moment, he changes his mind, concluding that both roads are equally worn out. Leaves cover both roads equally. No one this morning has yet taken either path, for the leaves lie undisturbed. This symbolises that the choices in life open to the poet are both unknown to him. The poet remains committed to his decision to take the road he had previously selected, saying that he will save the other road for another day.

This symbolises that he will make the other choice in life only if he is not satisfied with the results of the first choice. He observes, that he will probably never pass this way again, as one path leads to another, and thus will never have an opportunity to take the other road. This symbolises that he will not be able to take the second choice in life at all.

In years to come, the poet says, he will be telling others about the choice he made, meaning that he will talk about what decision in life he took. While doing so, he will sigh, either with relief that he made the right choice, or with regret that he made the wrong choice. Whether right or wrong, the choice will have had a significant impact on his life.


## Practice Questions

**1.** Who is the poet of the poem?
(a) William Wordsworth (b) Thomas Campbell
(c) Alfred Lord Tennyson (d) Robert Frost

**2.** The entire poem is
(a) a simile (b) a metaphor
(c) a personification (d) a ballad

**3.** When was Robert Frost born?
(a) 26th March, 1874 (b) 29th January, 1963
(c) 26th June, 1874 (d) 29th May, 1963

**4.** The poet stood at the intersection of
(a) crossroads (b) two roads
(c) a roundabout (d) three roads

**5.** The poet felt sorry because
(a) he could not see the roads well
(b) he could not travel on both the roads
(c) he did not know the direction
(d) the roads were bumpy

**6.** The poet took the road
(a) to the right (b) to the left
(c) the one less travelled by
(d) the one most people travelled by

**7.** What does the poem depict?
(a) conflicts in life
(b) choices we make in life
(c) confusion in our life
(d) problems we face in life

**8.** What did the poet see in the yellow wood?
(a) Two paths diverging in different directions
(b) Trees in the forest
(c) Green grass
(d) Animals

**9.** How was one path different from the other?
(a) One was greener (b) One had more grass
(c) It seemed less used (d) All of the above

**10.** When the poet chose one of the paths, what did he hope to do?
(a) Come back and try the other path
(b) Not go back
(c) Go home
(d) Not to stop in the woods

**11.** In the line "Oh I kept the first for another day!", "the first" refers to ..........
(a) Narrator's choice (b) The road
(c) Fate (d) Green grass

**12.** Frost uses the image of two diverging roads to symbolise....
(a) Sorrow and regret
(b) Life's choice
(c) The love of nature
(d) The spirit of independence

**13.** According to the poet, the second road has "the better claim" because it.....
(a) was a familiar path
(b) has never been used
(c) had more grass
(d) had been traveled less on

**14.** This poem might have special relevance for a student if he is.....
(a) planning a move to the country
(b) deciding which college to attend
(c) concerned about the environment
(d) managing his time to study

**15.** What does the narrator decide to do?
(a) take the second road
(b) take the well travelled road
(c) save the decision for later
(d) not to travel anymore

**16.** Which of the following statements is the closest interpretation of the line "yet knowing how way leads on to way"?
(a) You can never go home alone
(b) It's easy to get lost in a path
(c) One path takes you to the next
(d) It's easy to decide the road to travel further

**17.** According to the narrator, the two roads looked....
(a) about the same (b) very different
(c) muddy and unpleasant (d) covered with grass

**18.** Looking back on his decision, the narrator feels.....
(a) relieved
(b) regretful
(c) meditative
(d) embarrassed

**19.** The narrator envisions that in later years he will....
(a) feel sad
(b) tell his story
(c) see his error
(d) write about his experience

**20.** Define the mood of the poet when he says, "If I should ever come back".
(a) confident
(b) indecisive
(c) optimistic
(d) pessimistic

## ANSWERS

| | | | | | | | | | | | | | | | | | | | |
|---|---|---|---|---|---|---|---|---|---|---|---|---|---|---|---|---|---|---|---|
| 1. | (d) | 2. | (b) | 3. | (a) | 4. | (b) | 5. | (b) | 6. | (c) | 7. | (b) | 8. | (a) | 9. | (d) | 10. | (a) |
| 11. | (b) | 12. | (b) | 13. | (d) | 14. | (b) | 15. | (a) | 16. | (c) | 17. | (a) | 18. | (c) | 19. | (b) | 20. | (b) |

Chapter 33

# Stopping by Woods on a Snowy Evening

*Robert Frost*

## Summary

The poet is riding on his horse when he passes through a forest. He is tempted to spend more time in the woods to witness the snowfall. He is aware that the owner of the place lives far away from there, so he won't come to know about his visit. The poet relaxes and enjoys the beauty of nature and the snowfall. He wants to spend more time and praise the beautiful surroundings.

The poet says that he wants to spend some time in the forest to witness snowfall. But, he thinks that his horse might find it strange to stop in the forest in the middle of the journey without any reason. Moreover, there was no farmhouse nearby. It is a dark winter evening. Perhaps, the darkest evening of the year. Everything was covered with snow and the lake was frozen. He wanted to enjoy the beauty of nature. The poet says that the horse shakes his bells to ask his master if he had made a mistake by stopping in the middle of the journey. Generally, the traveller stops near a farmhouse, so the horse was curious to know as why he had stopped near the woods. Moreover, the atmosphere was calm and composed. One could only hear the jingling of bells and the blowing of wind through trees and of the snowflakes falling on the trees.

The poet appreciates the surroundings by saying that the woods are lovely, dark and deep. He wants to spend more time in the peaceful forest. He loves the dark evening, snowfall and the forest. Though, he wants to stay there for sometime, but he has to fulfil many duties and responsibilities back home.

He can't escape from discharging his duties. He has made some promises which he has to keep against his own desires. He has to cover a long way before reaching his destination. There will be lots of temptations in life like this but he has to keep moving forward.

## Practice Questions

1. Robert Frost was a/an ............ poet.
   (a) Canadian (b) Australian
   (c) Swiss (d) American

2. What does 'woods' mean here?
   (a) snow (b) wood (c) forest (d) farm

3. The season described in the poem is ............
   (a) summer (b) winter (c) autumn (d) spring

4. The poet was riding on a ............
   (a) horse (b) donkey
   (c) mule (d) cycle

5. Why did the poet want to stop by the woods?
   (a) to take rest
   (b) to reach his destination
   (c) to avoid a stormy night
   (d) to enjoy the scene

6. The woods were filled up with ............
   (a) ice (b) hail (c) snow (d) flowers

7. It was the ........... evening of the year.
   (a) coldest (b) darkest
   (c) most beautiful (d) finest

**8.** **The horse shakes its harness bells to ask if there is some ............**

(a) mistake (b) problem (c) danger (d) error

**9.** **Why could the poet not stop to enjoy the beauty of the scene?**

(a) he had promised someone to return
(b) he had miles to go
(c) he had a long way to go
(d) he was in a hurry

**10.** **'My little horse must think it queer'. What does the word 'queer' mean here?**

(a) strange (b) pleasant
(c) nice (d) evening

**11.** **What is the rhyme scheme for stanza 3?**

(a) ABCA (b) AABB (c) ABAB (d) AABC

**12.** **What is the setting of this poem?**

(a) In the woods on a bright, snowy afternoon
(b) Near the woods on a dark, snowy evening
(c) In a village in a dark, snowy evening
(d) By a frozen lake on a bright, snowy afternoon

**13.** **What is the effect of the word "but" in the second line?**

(a) It makes it seem like the speaker does not actually like the woods much and wants to leave
(b) It makes it seem like the speaker can still keep promises while staying by the woods
(c) It makes it seem like the promises the speaker has to keep are lovely dark and deep
(d) It makes it seem like the speaker has to choose between keeping promises and the lovely woods

**14.** **What might be a main theme of this poem?**

(a) The pull of being alone in nature against the pull of responsibility
(b) The pull of sleeping in nature against the pull of sleeping at home
(c) The ability of nature to make a person feel tired and sleepy
(d) The fear of staying too long on someone else's land

**15.** **Why might the poet have repeated the line "and miles to go before I sleep"?**

(a) To make the woods seem even more attractive and lovely
(b) To make the speaker seem forgetful and less smart than earlier in the poem
(c) To make readers pay special attention to the meaning of the line
(d) To make the speaker seem like he or she is already asleep

## ANSWERS

| | | | | | | | | | | | | | | | | | | | |
|---|---|---|---|---|---|---|---|---|---|---|---|---|---|---|---|---|---|---|---|
| 1. | (d) | 2. | (c) | 3. | (b) | 4. | (a) | 5. | (d) | 6. | (c) | 7. | (b) | 8. | (a) | 9. | (d) | 10. | (a) |
| 11. | (d) | 12. | (c) | 13. | (d) | 14. | (a) | 15. | (c) | | | | | | | | | | |

Chapter 34

# The Last Ride Together

*Robert Browning*

## About the Author

Robert Browning was born on 7th May, 1812, in Camberwell, England. His mother was an accomplished pianist and a devout evangelical Christian. His father, who worked as a bank clerk, was also an artist, scholar, antiquarian, and collector of books and pictures. His rare book collection of more than 6,000 volumes included works in Greek, Hebrew, Latin, French, Italian, and Spanish. Much of Browning's education came from his well-read father.

He was an English poet and playwright whose mastery of the dramatic monologue made him one of the foremost Victorian poets. His poems are known for their irony, characterisation, dark humour, social commentary, historical settings, and challenging vocabulary and syntax.

Browning's early career began promisingly, but collapsed. The long poems *Pauline* and *Paracelsus* received some acclaim, but in 1840 the difficult *Sordello*, which was seen as willfully obscure, brought his poetry into disrepute.

In 1846 Browning married the older poet Elizabeth Barrett, and went to live in Italy. By the time of her death in 1861, he had published the crucial collection *Men and Women*. The collection *Dramatis Personae* and the book-length epic poem *The Ring and the Book* followed and made him a leading British poet.

Some of his major works are 'Pauline: A Fragment of a Confession' (1833), 'Paracelsus', (1835), 'Strafford' (Play) (1837), 'Sordello' (1840), 'My Last Duchess', 'The Pied Piper of Hamelin', 'The Lost Leader', 'Home Thoughts from Abroad' and 'Meeting at Night etc'.

Robert Browning died on the same day that his final volume of verse, 'Asolando: Fancies and Facts' was published, on 12th December, 1889.

## Summary

'The Last Ride Together' is a poem by English poet Robert Browning, first published in his 1855 collection 'Men and Women'. In the first stanza, the narrator blames the end of his romance on fate. He bemoans that everything he has tried has failed, and it seems the end of his love affair is set. Despite this, he expresses his love and appreciation for the woman he has spent years with, and blesses her name.

The lover's sweetheart has not reciprocated his love. He now knows his fate that she cannot love him and that his boundless love for her is of no avail. He does not blame his beloved. He does not want her promise for future love but requests her to grant him a last ride with her. Having heard this, the lover's sweetheart bent her deep dark eyes filled with pride and pity. She made him motionless for quite some time. But she consented to ride with him. He felt happy and thought that he would get heavenly bliss in her company. She began to ride with him. It gave intense joy to the lover. This joy excelled the joy and pleasure that can be had by looking at the objects of nature. But this joy was mixed with the fear of losing the beloved. The joy of ride dispelled the gloom of the soul. He thought there was no need to brood and gamble against the past. He had the consolation that his last request to ride together was granted.

The lover began to feel that he was not solitary in the sorry scheme of things. In fact all people try but achieve very little. Done is little and the undone is vast. The lover then brings to his mind the state of life of a statesman who makes big plans but achieves very little. A soldier dies for his country but gets a poor reward for his service. Similar is the fate of a poet who aims at the ideal but he achieves very little. The sculptor produces a statue of the Venus in which is embodied the highest ideal of beauty.

The musician, too, composes his songs but their fashions change. The comparison of the lover's joy with that of others transports him to thinks if his earthly bliss, but he would certainly aspire to win her in heaven. The lover feels heavenly joy is superior to the joy of meeting his beloved in heaven. He does not need heavenly bliss in his ridings with his beloved. If he ride together continuously his short-ride would change into everlasting ride and it would be a heaven for him upon this Earth.

## Form

The rhyme scheme is unusual-aabbcddeeec. All the end rhymes are full except for Sun's/once and wind/behind. Full rhyme brings a familiar closure to most lines but the sequence is a rare one, starting with two couplets and finishing with three rhymes in a row concluded by the last, which rhymes with the fifth.

# Practice Questions

**1.** Where was Robert Browning born?
(a) Spain (b) Italy
(c) England (d) France

**2.** Robert Browning's father worked as a clerk is a bank but he was fond of collecting
(a) old coins (b) old manuscripts
(c) books and pictures (d) sports material

**3.** When was Robert Browning's poem 'Pauline: A Fragment of a Confession' Published?
(a) 1842 (b) 1836
(c) 1828 (d) 1833

**4.** Which four languages, apart from English, did Browning learn by the time the was 14?
(a) Latin, Greek, Spanish and Italian
(b) Latin, Greek, French and Italian
(c) Latin, Greek, French and Gaelic
(d) Latin, Italian, French and German

**5.** Which University did Robert Browning to go in 1828?
(a) University of Cambridge
(b) University of Durham
(c) University of Oxford
(d) University of London

**6.** Which work by another poet created a great impression on him in 1845?
(a) William Thackeay's 'Barry Lyndon'.
(b) Edgan Allan poe's 'The Raven'
(c) Elizabeth Barrett's 'Poems'
(d) Friedrich's Engels' 'Condition of the Working Class in England'

**7.** Browning would be most appropriately described as what type of poet?
(a) Victorian Poet
(b) Labeside Poet
(c) Neo-Classicist poet
(d) Pre-Raphelite poet

**8.** Did Browing return to Italy in later life?
(a) Never
(b) Browning Zemain in Florence for the rest of his life
(c) Browning and his son paid frequent visits to Italy
(d) Browning remained in London only

**9.** In which Collection of poem did this poem 'The Last Ride Together' publish?
(a) Men and Women
(b) The Ring and the Book
(c) Sordello
(d) Pauline and Paracelsus

**10.** What does 'The last Ride Together' suggest?
(a) It was an ordinary horse ride with his lover
(b) A journey imagined by the poet in his heart and soul
(c) It was a dream
(d) None of the above

**11.** What does the first stanza of the poem suggest?
(a) Poets dejection
(b) Poet's attempt to accept his fate as a dejected lover
(c) Poet's lover has agreed to go with him for the last time
(d) Poet's deep love for his lover

**12.** What two wishes does the poet request his lady love?
(a) Allowed to cherish the memories of his love and happiness
(b) Requests to go on a last ride with her
(c) Requests her to marry him
(d) Both A and B

**13.** What does the expression 'Since this was written and needs must be' refer to in the poem?
(a) His meeting with his lover
(b) Rejection of lover by lady love was ordained by God
(c) Referring to lover's agreeing for the last ride
(d) God has destined them to meet in another life

**14.** How did the lady react over the lover's last wish?
(a) She readily agreed
(b) She out rightly refused
(c) She was in a dilemma
(d) The was utterly confused

**15.** What two emotion are reflected in lady love's eyes as described by the poet?
(a) Her pride (b) Lady's sad mood
(c) Lady taking pity on her lover (d) Both b and c

**16.** What is the form of this poem 'The last Ride Together'?
(a) Sonnet (b) Lyric
(c) Elegy (d) Dramatic Monologue

**17.** **The lines 'When pity would be softening through' contains which figure of speech?**

(a) Metaphor (b) oxymoron
(c) Personification (d) Alliteration

**18.** **The poet was excited as his lady love has consented for the last ride together. Still he had some fear. What was it?**

(a) Fear of annoying the lady love
(b) Tear of losing his lady love forever
(c) Fear of his lady love rejective the ride at the last moment
(d) far of dying with joy

**19.** **What is Browning's Philosophy of life as described in this poem 'Last Ride Together'?**

(a) Change should be welcomed
(b) Man should focus more on Present
(c) No body should fall in love
(d) Rejection is part of life

**20.** **What are the elements that make the lover's monologues in this poem a zalhir weak and ironical expression of a frustrated man?**

(a) the use of so many exclamations
(b) Notes of Interroglation and Uncalled comparisons
(c) The monologue itself, the lover hardly talks to the lady
(d) Long speech full of comparison

**21.** **Why does the lover in this poem compares his achievements with achievements of a poet. Why?**

(a) To justify his failure
(b) A poet does not get due recognition
(c) To prove that he is a winner though he has lost his lady love
(d) Re-compares just for comparison's sake, no reason behind it

**22.** **According to the poet how lover's achievement of a last ride in better than a Statesman's achievements?**

(a) A statesman gets only a few lines obituary
(b) Statesman's achievement always falls short of ambition and endeavour
(c) The lover has experienced heavenly bliss during the last ride with his lady love
(d) Due recognizition is not accorded to the

**23.** **What is the rhyming scheme of this poem?**

(a) AA BB CC DD EE
(b) AABBCDDEEEC
(c) AA BB AA BB
(d) ABC ABC ABC

**24.** **What metre is followed by the poet in this poem 'The Last Ride Together'?**

(a) Iambic Pentametre
(b) Iambic Tetrametre
(c) Iambic hexametre
(d) Iambic trimetre

**25.** **On what note does the poem end?**

(a) Pessimist (b) Philosophical
(c) Optimist (d) Romantic rote

## ANSWERS

| | | | | | | | | | | | | | | | | | | | |
|---|---|---|---|---|---|---|---|---|---|---|---|---|---|---|---|---|---|---|---|
| 1. | (c) | 2. | (c) | 3. | (d) | 4. | (b) | 5. | (d) | 6. | (c) | 7. | (a) | 8. | (c) | 9. | (a) | 10. | (b) |
| 11. | (b) | 12. | (d) | 13. | (b) | 14. | (c) | 15. | (d) | 16. | (d) | 17. | (c) | 18. | (b) | 19. | (b) | 20. | (c) |
| 21. | (a) | 22. | (b) | 23. | (b) | 24. | (b) | 25. | (c) | | | | | | | | | | |

Chapter 35

# Of Studies

*Francis Bacon*

## About the Author

Bacon is the Father of English Essay. Evaluating Bacon as an essayist Legouis writes in 'A History of English Literature': It was by his essays that Bacon proved himself a great writer of his own language. Bacon was born in 1561. It was not easy to present the life and character of "The wisest, brightest, meanest of mankind". So, Alexander Pope, the 18th century satirist, sums up the character of the great Lord Bacon, to a large extent but not the more important part is written in Latin; Bacon's style of writing is aphoristic and compact. His works are full of practical wisdom.

Bacon's philosophy of life can be constructed from his striping observations on various aspects of man's personal and social life. In his essays, he takes up the role of a practical moralist and presents a philosophy of his own. As a moralist, Bacon makes no pretence to system.

## Summary

Francis Bacon is a very important figure in the history of knowledge, and we can learn a lot from his essay, 'Of studies'. Bacon points that it is study that depicts our enjoyed moment, attraction and capabilities. Of Studies' was published in 1597.

### Three Chief Uses of Studies

Bacon, here, first tells us the three chief uses of studies, he then speaks of those who spend too much time in studies, those who use studies too much for ornament and those who form judgements wholly by the rules emerging from their studies.

### Value of Practical Experience

The writer then goes on to speak of the value of practical experience but even more abruptly, goes on to say that craft men condemn studies, simple men admire them and wise men use them.

### Category of Books

Bacon tells us why we should study and then abruptly classifies books into three or four categories-those that are to be tasted, those that are to be swallowed, those that are to be chewed and digested and finally those that may be read 'By Deputy'.

### Role of Studies in Development of a Man

In the paragraph that follows, he speaks of the contribution that reading, conference and writing make towards the development of a man.

### Studies Sharpen Our Mind

The central theme of the essay is that specific fields of study sharpen the mind in specific ways. Study, Bacon asserts, is for the mind what exercise is for the body. We would exercise one way to be able to run faster and another way to be able to dance. And, we would choose the type of exercise depending on what we wanted to achieve and also on an honest assessment of our weakness.

# Practice Questions

**1.** Bacon belonged to the
(a) 15th century (b) 16th century
(c) 17th century (d) 18th century

**2.** Bacon was essentially known as a
(a) poet (b) prose writer (c) novelist (d) critic

**3.** Who was the father of Francis Bacon?
(a) Sir Nicholas Bacon (b) Sir Charles Bacon
(c) Sir John Bacon (d) None of these

**4.** Who was the mother of Francis Bacon?
(a) Anne Bacon (b) Anne James
(c) Marry Bacon (d) Julie Bacon

**5.** In which year 'Of Studies' was published?
(a) 1610 (b) 1601 (c) 1620 (d) 1602

**6.** Where was Francis Bacon born?
(a) Liverpool (b) London (c) Cambridge (d) Paris

**7.** Where did Francis Bacon complete his Law study?
(a) Inner temple (b) Middle temple
(c) Lincoln's inn (d) Gray's inn

**8.** According to Bacon the chief use of study is
(a) ability (b) ornament
(c) delight (d) adornment

**9.** Where did Francis Bacon die?
(a) England (b) Marlborough
(c) Shrewsbury (d) Netherwood

**10.** Study of history improves wisdom and natural philosophy improves depth of
(a) intellect (b) mind (c) heart (d) None of these

**11.** In the age of twelve, Francis Bacon's college was
(a) Cambridge College (b) London University
(c) Oxford University (d) Trinity College

**12.** The Renaissance term means
(a) rebirth (b) evidence
(c) period (d) None of these

**13.** Bacon's first collection of essays was published in
(a) 1597 (b) 1605 (c) 1616 (d) 1625

**14.** To Bacon to spend too much time in studies is
(a) affection (b) affectation
(c) studious (d) sloth

**15.** "Studies serve for delight, for ornament and for ability". Who wrote these lines?
(a) Lamb (b) Bacon
(c) DH Lawrence (d) Swift

**16.** For abilities which are natural is like natural plants that need
(a) pruning by study (b) sunlight
(c) air (d) water

**17.** Bacon's essays are ........... in style.
(a) aphoristic (b) compact
(c) condensed (d) All of these

**18.** Bacon's essays are known as
(a) Dispersed Meditations (b) Handbook
(c) Essays of Elia (d) None of these

**19.** "Some books are to be tasted, others to be swallowed, and some few to be chewed and digested". The above line appears in the essay.
(a) On Spelling
(b) Recollections of Childhood
(c) Of Studies
(d) An Apology for Idlers

**20.** Which of the following is incorrect about Bacon's essays?
(a) They belonged to the reign of James I
(b) He was not clogged with long sentences like the writers of his age
(c) He was inclined to American authors who studied brevity
(d) He was imprisoned for bribery

**21.** Bacon's major contribution is
(a) His practical wisdom has universal appeal
(b) His wisdom is devoid of moral pretensions
(c) His wisdom is for the man of the world
(d) All of these

**22.** Bacon's style
(a) terse and pithy (b) packed with thought
(c) reflects the intellectual power in the great mind
(d) All of the above

**23.** A pioneer in the field of philosophical prose was
(a) Bacon (b) Lamb
(c) Steele (d) Addison

**24.** Bacon belonged to the ...................... faith.
(a) Indian (b) Anglican
(c) Puritan (d) Elizabethan

**25.** Bacon was the translator of .......... essays.
(a) Ciero (b) Plato (c) Montaigne (d) Pope

**26.** ................ maketh a full man.
(a) Speaking (b) Reading
(c) Writing (d) Listening

**27.** What does 'Of Studies' display?
(a) Wide learning (b) Deep scholarship
(c) Sound wisdom (d) All of these

**28.** Bacon explains the multifarius aspect of studies in
(a) Human affairs (b) Love affairs
(c) Nature is environment (d) None of these

**29.** What is the chief use of studies for delight?
(a) One's private life (b) One's public life
(c) For adventure (d) None of these

**30.** What is the dominant spirit of the essay?
(a) Didactism (b) Patriotism
(c) Secularism (d) Democracy

**31.** Which of the following is the professional work of Bacon?
(a) Maxims of the Law (b) The De Augment
(c) The New Atlantis
(d) The Novum organum

**32.** Which of the following is the literary work of Bacon?
(a) A Popthegms New and Old
(b) Reading on the Statute of Uses
(c) The Advancement of Learning
(d) The De Augments

**33.** Bacon's famous essay 'Of Studies' is full of
(a) aphorisms (b) criticisms
(c) admiration (d) excitement

**34.** Truth may perhaps come to the price of a
(a) diamond (b) gold
(c) pearl (d) None of these

**35.** History makes men wise; poet witty; mathematics subtle and natural philosphy
(a) shallow (b) deep
(c) intense (d) low

**36.** What purpose do studies serve?
(a) Creation (b) Ornaments
(c) Innovation (d) Invention

**37.** What kind of view simple men have about studies?
(a) Admiring (b) Criticism
(c) Support (d) Pull over

**38.** A man who studies a lot is temperamentally ............
(a) active (b) inactive (c) smart (d) lazy

**39.** What did Bacon advise in all the cases of excessiveness in studies?
(a) Avoided (b) Rejected
(c) Accepted (d) Admired

**40.** Studies develop the man's natural.........
(a) Ability (b) Inability
(c) Value (d) None of these

**41.** Different kinds of ............ have different effects upon the reader.
(a) books (b) compact discs
(c) equipments (d) None of the these

**42.** Bacon was an
(a) essayist (b) historian (c) thinker (d) All of these

**43.** "The English reader will find difficulties in Bacon's language of style." Who said this for Bacon?
(a) Mr. Wright (b) Mr. Machiavelli
(c) Mr. Humes (d) Hudson

**44.** Who calls the essays of Bacon "Good Advice for Satan's Kingdom"?
(a) Henry Hudson (b) William Blake
(c) Joseph Addison (d) Charles Lamb

**45.** Who influenced Bacon's political morality?
(a) Plato (b) Socrates
(c) Aristotle (d) Machiavelli

**46.** Bacon's essays was written in
(a) French and English (b) Latin and French
(c) Latin and English (d) Greek and Latin

**47.** "Proper Study of mankind is man", a dictum of the Augustan age means that
(a) they emphasised the importance of only men and not women
(b) they believed in the study of physical nature
(c) they believed in the study of human nature
(d) None of these

**48.** The Royal Society of science is the result of ......... emphasis on the collection of facts.
(a) Bacon (b) Byron
(c) Yeats (d) None of these

**49.** Name the writer who called an essays 'Dispersed Meditations'?
(a) Addison (b) Johnson
(c) Lamb (d) Bacon

**50.** The author of the novel 'The New Atlantis' is
(a) Sir Thomas Moore (b) Dean Church
(c) Goethe (d) Francis Bacon

**51.** Which constituency did Francis Bacon represent in the Parliament in 1586-1588?
(a) Middlesex (b) Ipswich (c) Tounton (d) Kent

**52.** Bacon believes that the human mind easily misuses its ......... in many ways.
(a) reason (b) intellect
(c) gray matter (d) purpose

**53.** Bacon says that ........... is more precious than anything on Earth.
(a) intellect
(b) philosophy
(c) true understanding
(d) a meeting of the minds

**54.** Bacon believes that the meeting between the two entities must return to its
(a) womb (b) previous incarnation
(c) original condition (d) self

**55.** Many things may be improved by using instruments of
(a) God (b) fellowship
(c) logic (d) intuition

**56.** Bacon states that people tend to lean towards false and hasty
(a) conclusion (b) allise (c) decision (d) beliefs

**57.** Bacon suggests that man should try to focus on their ............power.
(a) true (b) limited
(c) God given (d) inevitable

**58.** When was Francis Bacon born?
(a) 22nd January, 1561 (b) 4th May, 1549
(c) 16th July, 1548
(d) 11th November, 1564

**59.** Experience is essential to add to the value of ............
(a) land (b) gold
(c) building (d) studies

**60.** What makes people witty?
(a) Prose (b) Maths
(c) Poetry (d) Philosophy

**61.** How studies are used by the wise men?
(a) Intellectual way (b) Mathematical way
(c) Advantageous way (d) All of these

**62.** Bacon is remembered only for his
(a) drama (b) prose
(c) essay (d) fiction

**63.** What qualities the essay 'Of Studies' bear for human beings? It is
(a) significant (b) helpful
(c) entertaining (d) All of these

**64.** The mode of the study is
(a) reading (b) writing
(c) confidence (d) All of these

**65.** The study of logic and rhetoric develop a man's
(a) muscles (b) intellilgence
(c) debating power (d) None of these

**66.** One should not read books merely to contradict others but to
(a) judge the cost of the book
(b) judge the number of pages in the book
(c) judge the value of the material the book contains
(d) judge the time taken to make us sleepy

**67.** Bacon's style of writing is
(a) sorrowful (b) terse and pity
(c) the usage of intellectual power of mind
(d) All of these

**68.** The essay 'Of Truth' belongs to
(a) Charles Lamb (b) Francis Bacon
(c) William Hazlitt (d) None of these

**69.** Crafty people think that their cleverness can better serve their ends than
(a) student's knowledge (b) bookish knowledge
(c) teacher's knowledge (d) None of these

**70.** According to Bacon philosphy makes men
(a) wise (b) witty
(c) subtle (d) grave

**71.** In Bacon's essay, cunning persons don't like
(a) studies (b) games
(c) play (d) None of these

**72.** Studies become a source of pleasure when a man is
(a) in natural environment (b) all alone
(c) in social life (d) None of these

**73.** Bacon suggests that the general counsnels come best from those that are
(a) experienced (b) professionals
(c) learned (d) businessmen

**74.** "Crafty men condemn studies, simple men admire them and wise men use them." The above line appears in the essay.
(a) Of Adversity (b) Of Studies
(c) Of Marriage and Single Life (d) Of Friendship

**75.** "The disease of the body may have appropriate exercise". The above line belongs to
(a) Francis Bacon's essay (b) Charles Lamb
(c) Richard Steele (d) Joseph Addison

**76.** Bacon's books recommend studies as to be of
(a) three types (b) four types
(c) six types (d) None of these

**77.** To Bacon one must read to
(a) weigh and consider
(b) contradict and confute
(c) talk and discourse
(d) take for granted

**78.** Bacon's literary works are full of
(a) system
(b) practical wisdom
(c) adversity (d) None of these

**79.** What kind of view simple men have about studies, according to Bacon?
(a) Supportive (b) Entertaining
(c) Admiring (d) Helpful

**80.** Bacon's moral consideration gives to
(a) entertaining (b) morality
(c) aloofness (d) creativity

**81.** Francis Bacon died on
(a) 9th April, 1626
(b) 10th April, 1930
(c) 19th April, 1931
(d) 29th April, 1626

***82.*** "Bacon is the first of the English essayist and for sheer man and weight of genius, the greatest". Who said these lines?

(a) Hugh Walker (b) Joseph Addison
(c) Charles Lamb (d) None of these

***83.*** Bacon says if a man's mind is wavering, he should study

(a) English (b) Geography
(c) Mathematics (d) Science

***84.*** The term 'sloth' is

(a) to spend much time in sports
(b) to spend much time in sleeping
(c) to spend much time in studies
(d) to spend much time in discourse

***85.*** To prove the great importance of falsehood, Bacon cites example of alloy in precious metals like

(a) gold and silver (b) silver and bronze
(c) iron and copper (d) steel and iron

***86.*** What causes sloth?

(a) Speading too much time in discourse
(b) Speading too much time in studies
(c) Speading too much time in sleep (d) Speading too much time in rest

***87.*** Francis Bacon believes that it is .......... for him to write essays.

(a) frivolous (b) worthwhile
(c) crucial (d) pointless

## ANSWERS

| | | | | | | | | | | | | | | | | | | | |
|---|---|---|---|---|---|---|---|---|---|---|---|---|---|---|---|---|---|---|---|
| 1. | (b) | 2. | (b) | 3. | (a) | 4. | (a) | 5. | (b) | 6. | (b) | 7. | (d) | 8. | (c) | 9. | (a) | 10. | (b) |
| 11. | (d) | 12. | (a) | 13. | (a) | 14. | (d) | 15. | (b) | 16. | (a) | 17. | (d) | 18. | (a) | 19. | (c) | 20. | (c) |
| 21. | (a) | 22. | (c) | 23. | (a) | 24. | (b) | 25. | (c) | 26. | (b) | 27. | (d) | 28. | (a) | 29. | (a) | 30. | (a) |
| 31. | (a) | 32. | (a) | 33. | (a) | 34. | (c) | 35. | (b) | 36. | (b) | 37. | (a) | 38. | (d) | 39. | (a) | 40. | (a) |
| 41. | (a) | 42. | (a) | 43. | (a) | 44. | (b) | 45. | (d) | 46. | (c) | 47. | (c) | 48. | (a) | 49. | (d) | 50. | (d) |
| 51. | (c) | 52. | (a) | 53. | (c) | 54. | (c) | 55. | (c) | 56. | (a) | 57. | (a) | 58. | (a) | 59. | (d) | 60. | (c) |
| 61. | (c) | 62. | (c) | 63. | (d) | 64. | (d) | 65. | (c) | 66. | (c) | 67. | (c) | 68. | (b) | 69. | (c) | 70. | (d) |
| 71. | (a) | 72. | (b) | 73. | (c) | 74. | (b) | 75. | (a) | 76. | (b) | 77. | (a) | 78. | (b) | 79. | (c) | 80. | (c) |
| 81. | (a) | 82. | (a) | 83. | (c) | 84. | (a) | 85. | (c) | 86. | (b) | 87. | (c) | | | | | | |

Chapter 36

# Of Friendship

*Francis Bacon*

## Summary

### Man of Solitude Unfit for Society

Francis Bacon begins the essay by invoking the classical authority of Aristotle on basic human nature. First, he refers to Aristotle's view in Politics: Whosoever is delighted in solitude is either a wild beast or a God. According to Aristotle, a man by nature and behaviour may be degraded to such an extent that he may be called unfit for society. Again, he may be so self-sufficient that he may no need society. In the first case, he resembles a wild beast and in the second, he resembles Gods. Here it should be pointed out that Bacon is not ruling out the value of solitude; in fact, he is reserving solitude for higher kind of life, which is possible for a few great men like Epimenides, Numa, Empedocles, Apollonius and some Christian saints.

### Friendship : Essential for Good Health

Bacon's logic is that those who live in society should enjoy the bliss of friendship for more than one reason. First of all, friendship is necessary for maintaining good mental health by controlling and regulating the passions of the mind. In other words, Bacon here speaks of the therapeutic use of friendship though which one can lighten the heart by revealing the pent-up feelings and emotions: sorrows, joys, fears, hopes, suspicions, advice and the like. Then in order to justify the value of friendship, Bacon points out the practice of friendship on the highest social level. He informs us that the kings and princes, in order to make friends, would raise some persons who would be fit for friendship. Then Bacon tries to glorify friendship by translating the Roman term for friendship, Participes curarum, which means 'sharers of their cares'. He gives instances of raising of men as friends from the Roman history: Sylla and Pompey the Great, Julius Caesar and Antonius, Augustus and Agrippa, Tiberius Caesar and Sejanus, Septimius Severus and Plautianus. Bacon also refers to what Comineus wrote of Duke Charles the Hardy's deterioration of his mental faculty just because of his reserve and loneliness and extends his judgement to the case of Comineus' second master, Louis XI. The point which Bacon strongly wants to assert is that friendship functions for a man in a double yet paradoxically contrary manner: "...it redoubleth joys, and cutteth griefs in halfs".

### Friendship : Essential for Clarity of Understanding

According to Bacon, the second fruit of friendship is beneficial for the clarity of understanding. If a man has got a faithful friend, he can be consulted to clarify the confusions of the mind. He calls the counsel of a friend, citing Heraclitus, 'drier and purer' than that a man gives himself out of self – love which clouds his judgement. Bacon then counsel of this sort into two kinds: 'the one concerning manners and the other concerning business'. A friend's constructive criticism of the other friend's behaviour helps him more than a book of morality. In the matter of conducting practical business, Bacon thinks, a true friend's advice can also be helpful in undertaking a venture or averting a danger.

### A Friend is Another Self

Finally, Bacon speaks of the last fruit of friendship, which is manifold in the sense that there are so many things in life, which can be fulfilled only with the help of a friend.

In fact, at a rare moment Bacon gets emotional and quotes classical maxim that 'a friend is another self'.

### A Friend is Essence of Life

His point is that a man may have many a desire, which may not be realised in his life-time, but if he has got a true friend, his unfulfilled desire will be taken care of by his friend. Not only this, a friend, unlike the near and dear ones and enemies, can talk to him on equal terms whenever situation demands. Keeping all these things, Bacon concludes that if a man does not have a friend, he may well leave this world. That is to say, he is not fit for the human society to live in.

# Practice Questions

**1.** **When was Francis Bacon born?**
(a) 22nd January, 1561
(b) 4th May, 1549
(c) 16th July, 1548
(d) 11th November, 1564

**2.** **Where was Francis Bacon born?**
(a) Liverpool (b) London
(c) Cambridge (d) Paris

**3.** **Where did Francis Bacon study law?**
(a) Inner Temple (b) Middle Temple
(c) Lincoln's Inn (d) Gray's Inn

**4.** **Which constituency did Francis Bacon represent in Parliament in 1586-1588?**
(a) Middlesex (b) Ipswich
(c) Taunton (d) Kent

**5.** **To which government post was Francis Bacon appointed in 1618?**
(a) Advocate in Chief (b) Principal Auditor
(c) Lord Chancellor (d) Prime Minister

**6.** **When was Francis Bacon Lord Chancellor of England?**
(a) 1588-1594 (b) 1618-1621
(c) 1594-1598 (d) 1602-1614

**7.** **How much fine Francis Bacon had to pay when he was found guilty of corruption?**
(a) £20,000 (b) £40,000
(c) £10,000 (d) £28,000

**8.** **When did Francis Bacon die?**
(a) 25th March, 1628
(b) 9th April, 1626
(c) 11th September, 1634
(d) 17th December, 1636

**9.** **When did Francis Bacon publish Advancement of Learning?**
(a) 1605 (b) 1600 (c) 1598 (d) 1596

**10.** **Which book of Francis Bacon was published in 1609?**
(a) Novum Organum
(b) The Historie of the Raigne of King Henry the Seventh
(c) Sylva Sylvarum
(d) De Sapientia Veterum

**11.** **According to Bacon, without friends, the world is.......... .**
(a) Empty vessel (b) Forest
(c) Wasteland (d) None of these

**12.** **What, according to Bacon, is the principal fruit of friendship?**
(a) Close emotional bond (b) Clarity of thoughts
(c) Help in need (d) All of these

**13.** **How does Bacon compare the counsel from the friend with counsel within oneself?**
(a) It is not worthy
(b) Counsel within oneself is more important
(c) It should be not taken seriously
(d) It is drier and purer

**14.** **Who was Heraclitus?**
(a) A Greek philosopher (b) Bacon's friend
(c) A king (d) None of these

**15.** **What happens when a person communicates and discourses with a friend?**
(a) Person becomes wiser than himself
(b) Person cannot take right decision
(c) Friend makes him fool
(d) Friend takes his advantage for his own benefit

**16.** **Bacon compares the third fruit of friendship to.........**
(a) an apple (b) an orange
(c) a pomegranate (d) a mango

**17.** **Explain the expression, 'Magna civitas, magna solitude' as used in the essay 'Of Friendship'.**
(a) A friend in need is a friend indeed
(b) A civilian who lives in solitude
(c) A person without friends
(d) A great city is a great solitude

**18.** **A friendship must have .......... as its main strand(s).**
(a) feelings and passions (b) gifts and money
(c) false praise (d) time and faith

**19.** **A friendless, cut-off person is ........ to live in the society.**
(a) fit (b) unfit
(c) beneficial (d) harmful

**20.** **On whose request was the essay 'Of Friendship' initiated by Bacon?**
(a) William Words worth
(b) Aristotle
(c) His friend, Toby Matthew
(d) His friend, Michael Andrews

**21.** **Whom does Bacon first refer to in his essay 'Of Friendship'?**
(a) His friend, Toby Matthew
(b) His friend, Michael Andrews
(c) William Wordsworth
(d) Aristotle

**22.** **What is Bacon's logic behind friendship?**
(a) To maintain good mental health by controlling and regulating the passions of the mind
(b) To enjoy physical pleasures
(c) To protect oneself financially
(d) To seek heaven after death

**23.** **What does the Roman term for friendship 'Participes curarum' mean in Bacon's 'Of Friendship'?**
(a) Participating in cultural activities
(b) Sharers of their cares
(c) Stay away from active participation
(d) Haters of friendship

**24.** **According to Bacon, the second fruit of friendship is**
(a) Strengthening of power
(b) Lack of isolation
(c) Benefit of the clarity of understanding
(d) Comfort of support

**25.** **What is more helpful than a book of morality according to Bacon?**
(a) A friend's love
(b) A friend's mental support
(c) A friend's encouragement
(d) A friend's constructive criticism of the other friend's behaviour

**26.** **According to Bacon, what prolongs the life of a person even after his/her death?**
(a) Dignity of a person
(b) True friendship of a person
(c) Money and power of a person
(d) Intelligence of a person

**27.** **What is the 'art' that Bacon seeks to apply in his work?**
(a) The advancement of learning
(b) The parsing of opposites
(c) The construction of similes
(d) The interpretation of nature

**28.** **Which device of logic does Bacon reject?**
(a) The conjecture
(b) The syllogism
(c) The premise
(d) The conclusion

**29.** **What has been the enemy of natural philosophy in every age?**
(a) The teachings of Aristotle and Plato
(b) Poor experimental technique
(c) Problems of method and logic
(d) Superstition and the blind, immoderate zeal of religion

## ANSWERS

| | | | | | | | | | | | | | | | | | | | |
|---|---|---|---|---|---|---|---|---|---|---|---|---|---|---|---|---|---|---|---|
| 1. | *(a)* | 2. | *(b)* | 3. | *(d)* | 4. | *(c)* | 5. | *(c)* | 6. | *(b)* | 7. | *(b)* | 8. | *(b)* | 9. | *(a)* | 10. | *(d)* |
| 11. | *(c)* | 12. | *(a)* | 13. | *(d)* | 14. | *(a)* | 15. | *(a)* | 16. | *(c)* | 17. | *(d)* | 18. | *(b)* | 19. | *(b)* | 20. | *(c)* |
| 21. | *(d)* | 22. | *(a)* | 23. | *(b)* | 24. | *(c)* | 25. | *(d)* | 26. | *(b)* | 27. | *(d)* | 28. | *(b)* | 29. | *(d)* | | |

Chapter 37

# Father's Letter

*William Hazlitt*

## About the Author

William Hazlitt is considered as one of the greatest literary cities and essayists. He was born on 10th April, 1778 in Maidstone, Kent, England to William Hazlitt Sr., a Unitarian minister in England and Grace Loftus. His father was a sympathiser of the American struggle for independence. hazlitt inherited liberal views from his father. Hazlitt was a political liberal and wrote expressive defenses of the ideas of the French Revolution.

He is recognised as the best art critic of the Romantic period. He was educated mainly at home and at a local school. At the age of 13, he debuted in writing with a letter, which was published in the 'Shrewsbury Chronicle'. In 1793, he was sent to the new college at Hackney, a Unitarian Seminary. While studying at the college, Hazlitt had a loss of faith and returned home to Wem. On 14th January 1798, Hazlitt met Samuel Taylor Coleridge at the Unitarian Chapel in Shrewsbury. While visiting him at his residence in Nether Stowey, Hazlitt also came in contact with William Wordsworth. Artistic inclinations ran in the family and from 1798, Hazlitt took keen interest in painting. By 1802, he had made decent progress in painting and a portrait of his father that he had recently painted was accepted for an exhibition at the Royal Academy.

He moved to London in 1804 in order to shape up his writing career. On 19th July 1805, he published 'An Essay on the Principles of Human Action' with the help of William Godwin. In 1807, Hazlitt's preface to 'The Light of Nature Pursued' along with a compilation of parliamentary speeches: 'The Eloquence of the British Senate' were published. In 1808, Hazlitt married Sarah Stoddart, a friend of Mary Lamb and sister of John Stoddart, a journalist and the editor of 'The Times' newspaper.

In 1825, 'The Spirit of the Age: or, Contemporary Portraits' was published which was a collection of sketches of twenty–five prominent personalities of England. Throughout the last years of his life, he continued to write articles for 'The Atlas', 'The London Weekly Review', 'The Court Journal' and 'The Edinburgh Review'. He gave his last years were given to an unsuccessful biography of Napoleon Bonaparte in four volumes (1828–1830). Hazlitt was suffering from stomach cancer and died in 18th September 1830. In the present essay, William Hazlitt has written a letter to his son on the moral conduct of life. He is advising his son to be good and to do good in life always. He is sharing his own mistakes and advises his son not to repeat them to be successful in life. He wants his son to achieve everything in life by fair means.

## Summary

### His son Should Give his School a Chance before Deciding not to Go to It

He is telling his son that entrance to school is his first entrance to the world. He teaches him to always hope for the best and think positive. The son should give his school a chance before deciding not going to school. He tells the son to give people in school a chance to know him and he should also get to know them and make friends with them. William says we should not think bad for others nor should we do bad for them. We should try to overlook their faults and keep our complaints to minimum.

### Do not Value People on Their Appearances

He tells his son not to despise anyone, especially when they are suffering from poverty. Values are more important than appearances. One should value oneself and others too rather than their appearances.

### Learn to Accept the World

William tells his son that none in the world would treat him like his father at home, people would taught at him and do not care about him. The son should not feel bad about it instead learn from this because he is sent to school purposefully so that he can learn to accept the world. He would meet people with same qualities as him or even better then him, so he should learn to adjust with them and he cannot be the leader of the group all the time. There are other people in the world besides ourselves. There are competitors at every turn. The son is not a king's son who can dictate others but have to share fate with others and school helps in learning this behaviour.

## Do not Look Down on Others : Treat Everyone Equally

William says it is easy to think that we are ahead of people and look down upon others but this is a narrow minded thinking; everyone is equal and deserves equal opportunities. There are countless number of people on this Earth who have lived and died and not heard of any of the things you are master at, so it is in vain to have pride an yourself for such things.

It is a bad habit to speak disrespectfully for others for it will lead us to think ill for them. It is better to courteous and kind. We are good at secing fault of others and lose temper over them but it harms us only. The temmates, school fellows and other boys should be treated with same dignity as ours. One should be one's our master rather than controlling others.

## Do not Quarrel Over Small Matters

The son is advised not to quarrel with world over small things; and try to escape from it easily. This lead to think that others are fools and will not solve the problem. It is not right to keep a feeling of hatred for others. Impatience should be avoided and love should be promoted. The humans can have many fake faces but it is not right to hate them. The father says one day his son would thank him for this piece of advice.

## Improve your Manners and Appearance

The father wishes his son to learn French, Latin and dance. He asks to do regular exercises to be fit. He tells the importance of first impression. Dancing is a talent which can speak for a person. Unattention to own self leads to disrespect for others as well because we rely on world for opinions about ourselves and other people. Confusion in manners and gestures creates a bad impression while openness, freedom and self possession set others at ease and makes a good impression. Another advice given is that the son should not over indulge with books as it can lead to ill consequences in life. This can lead to sink a man in public and private estimation. Worldly luxuries should not be used much that they make the working limbs of no use.

## Do not Read Excessively

The father knows that his son is fond of reading so he advises his son not to excess it. To prevent this, he suggest him some ways like the son should make it a habit not to read when involved in conversation with others even during the trivial ones. Reading should be avoided at meal times and play hours as well. Life gives more knowledge than books. So mind should be open to this knowledge also.

## Learn French and Latin

The father wants his son to learn French and master it and he also wants him to learn Latin also because the father himself has learnt it. He wants him to study classics also for they help in the worldly affairs. They are an excercise of inlellect. It gives men liberal views, it accustoms mind to learn things foreign to itself, to prefer fame to life. He gives the example of Rome and Athens, the two great cities which have occupied their place in history forever. Now the father says just because the son has learnt Latin and Greek more than one language than he should not show off his talent to others because there are people who do not care about this talent. The son should not think himself above those whom he usually converse with learning different languages help to broaden the mind and spirit. He gives examples that if history and literature mention only few names of famous writers it does not mean their centemporaries were below them. So learning different languages that are knows some things in many ways and has become a learned. If others are more talented than are should not complain and be stick to one's our canduct and knowledge as no one is beneath or above.

## Do not Show Superiority

The father advises to not feel bad if others talk well on different subjects better than the son. Every one has his own talents. One should not put his worst qualities foremost. We should express ourselves in such a way that it does not offend or hurt others. Some opinions should be kept to oneself. Learn to listen to other and gain something from them.Not every time one can talk about one's our favourite topic. It is not possible to make friends with people by showing superiority to them. It is better to seek good will of others rather than their applause.

## Lead a Healthy Life

The father suggests that obstacles can be overcome if one decides to do so. Then, he says to keep health above all things in life. He advises to do regular exercises and abstain from drinking, drink more water and less of alcohol. He tells him not to gamble. He advises not to do foolish things if done once. We should not aim what is beyond our reach and should be indulge in calm persuits.

## Choose Friends Wisely

Then, he suggests the son to choose his friends wisely and adhere to them as long as he can. He should not take wrong advantage of them or try them. He suggests to read books and learn from them.

## Marry only the Girl You Love

Then he advises him about marriage. He says to marry only when he is ready and to the one he loves. He should not marry based on his friends recommendations. He suggests to marry a girl who is neither superior nor inferior to the son. He suggests the son not to fancy for the heroine of a romance or becoming a hero of if. The father advises about the qualities of a woman; how to impress them and how to handle them. The father shares his experiences with love and how he felt in his times.

## Select your own Profession and Work hard

Finally, he speaks about the profession for the son. He tells him that the son is independent to select his profession. He tells that being professional requires labour and competition. He advises never to compare with others and their achievements.

# Practice Questions

**1. What is the letter all about?**
(a) Moral conduct of life
(b) School life
(c) Advice for profession
(d) Advice to study

**2. Speaking bad for others leads one to think of us as being ......... to them.**
(a) good (b) superior
(c) ill (d) inferior

**3. Why does the son refuse to go to school?**
(a) he does not like the school
(b) The school is far away
(c) He is bored of it
(d) He does not want to leave the home

**4. The father suggested the son to marry the girl whom he ............. .**
(a) hates (b) his friends recommend
(c) loves (d) like

**5. When should reading be avoided?**
(a) At meal times (b) At play hour
(c) During conversations (d) All of the above

**6. What does the father suggest to abstain from?**
(a) Water (b) Drinking alcohol
(c) Regular exercise (d) Reading

**7. What things does the father want his son to learn?**
(a) French, Latin and dancing (b) School studies
(c) Sports (d) None of the above

**8. What advice is given to the son regarding his profession?**
(a) The son has to choose according to father
(b) The son is independent to choose his profession
(c) The son has to be a singer
(d) None of the above

**9. What advice is given regarding speaking about others?**
(a) We should speak disrespectfully about others
(b) We should believe all the negative things about others
(c) We should speak respectfully about others
(d) All of the above

**10. Why should one not think oneself as being superior to others?**
(a) Because others think the same about us
(b) Because we do not know others
(c) Because we should not show off our talents
(d) Because others can be the same or more talented than us

**11. Learning different languages helps to become**
(a) superior to others (b) inferior to others
(c) a learned (d) improves language

**12. Why did the father gave the example of Rome and Athens?**
(a) They are two great cities
(b) They have occupied their places in history forever
(c) Everyone has seen them shining
(d) All of the above

**13. Why did the father share his mistakes with his son?**
(a) He does not want his to repeat the same mistakes
(b) He is ashamed of his mistakes
(c) He is boasting of them to his son
(d) He want his son to repeat them

**14. What kind of people will one met at every turn of life?**
(a) Childish (b) Adults
(c) Competitors (d) Helpers

**15. How did the son behave at home?**
(a) He was not a spoilt child
(b) He was a well mannered boy
(c) He did make his deal by unfair means
(d) None of the above

**16. How is school different from home?**
(a) There is no difference between school and home
(b) There is no concerned father at school
(c) There are friends at school
(d) School is better than home

**17. Why is it important to study the classics?**
(a) It is an exercise of the intellect
(b) It helps to refine the taste
(c) It teaches great things present in this world
(d) All of the above

**18. Why does the father want his son to learn Latin?**
(a) Because the father learnt it himself
(b) Because the father want his son to be a Latin writer
(c) Because Latin is a good language
(d) None of the above

**19. What is suggested to be kept above all things?**
(a) Studies (b) Health (c) Love (d) Friends

**20. How is overindulgence in books harmful?**
(a) It decreases public and private estimation
(b) It does not give much knowledge
(c) It is of no use
(d) It can lead to failures

**21. Which one ingredient is considered to be great in the conduct of life?**
(a) Being superior to others
(b) Being inferior to others
(c) Being down to Earth
(d) Boasting in front of others

**22.** How one should treat one's teammates?
(a) With low esteem (b) With same dignity
(c) Dictate them (d) Curse them

**23.** Why is it important to listen to others?
(a) It helps to gain knowledge
(b) We learn new things
(c) It broadens the mind and spirit
(d) All of the above

**24.** What advice is given regarding selection of friends?
(a) One should adhere to them as long as one can
(b) One should choose them biasfully
(c) One should choose friends based on their financial status
(d) One should not make friends at all

**25.** Why is the son unable to make friends at school?
(a) Boys do not talk to him
(b) The son and other boys are strangers to each other
(c) The son is not able to speak
(d) Boys are not worthy to become friends

**26.** Why is it not good to affect the society of inferior ranks?
(a) They consider it as bad
(b) They can hit back
(c) They consider it as restrain open them
(d) They are not good people

**27.** Which characteristics should be hated as suggested by the father?
(a) Honesty (b) Loyalty (c) Jealousy (d) Injustice

**28.** How should the mistress be chosen?
(a) Below your rank
(b) Above your rank
(c) Based on friends recommendations
(d) Among your equals

**29.** Which fancy of woman should be avoided?
(a) Heroine of romance
(b) To become a hero of romance
(c) mistress will have sympathy with you
(d) All of the above

**30.** How can one become successful in a profession?
(a) By being laborious and honest
(b) By giving in to the fate
(c) By unfair means (d) None of these

**31.** How can one gain the reputation of wisdom?
(a) By offending others
(b) By Keeping their follies to themselves
(c) By showing their superiority
(d) By pointing out others follies

**32.** Why is the son sent to school?
(a) To make friends
(b) To read classics
(c) To keep him away from home
(d) To understand and learn about the worldly affairs

**33.** What are the other sources of knowledge apart from books?
(a) Talking to others
(b) Playing with others
(c) Experiences and observations
(d) Negligence and ignorance

**34.** What are the consequences of quarreling with others?
(a) It makes us wise
(b) It makes us think ill about others
(c) It makes us fool
(d) None of the above

**35.** How was the father's experience with love?
(a) Love turned its face from him
(b) He had a heavenly experience
(c) He had good hopes from love
(d) He did not love anybody

**36.** What is the son fond of?
(a) Playing
(b) Eating
(c) Reading (d) All of these

**37.** What does the son complain about?
(a) Hostel rooms are unclean
(b) School is not a good place
(c) His uniform is untidy
(d) Boys laugh at and do not care about him

**38.** What are good qualities of the son?
(a) Well–mannered boy
(b) Good nature and good sense
(c) Obedient son
(d) Friendly boy

**39.** When does one become a thing to laugh at?
(a) When one gives childish self importance to oneself
(b) When one respects others
(c) When one mockeries others
(d) When one does not care for others

**40.** Why does the son have to share the fate with others?
(a) Because he is inferior to them
(b) Because he is not a son of a king
(c) Because he does not have knowledge
(d) Because he is in the same class as theirs

**41.** What is the meaning of 'salt of the Earth' as mentioned in the essay?
(a) A bad person
(b) An offender
(c) Fundamental goodness of person
(d) A person who has evil thoughts for others

**42.** Why are recommendations of no use?
(a) They lead to insults
(b) Talent speaks louder than it
(c) It does not give money
(d) None of the above

**43.** Which language should be mastered by the son according to his father?
(a) English (b) Greek
(c) Latin (d) French

**44.** Why should one not overuse worldly luxuries?
(a) To keep the limbs working
(b) They lead to downfall
(c) They are unfair means
(d) All of the above

**45.** First impression depends upon two things. What are they?
(a) Coldness and Contempt
(b) Dress and Address
(c) Looks and Behaviour
(d) Language and Dialect

**46.** According to the father, what is a woman's triumph?
(a) Sympathy by man (b) Ignorance by man
(c) A man's pain (d) Love given by man

**47.** Who is not cared about by the women?
(a) Poets (b) Singers
(c) Men (d) All of these

**48.** What advice did the father give to his son regarding his love?
(a) Do not let thoughts came between self and love
(b) Do not abstract self in regions of truth
(c) Do not let the canker sink into your heart
(d) All of the above

**49.** Which creature is described as the meanest in the world?
(a) Lizard (b) Spider
(c) Parrots (d) Dogs

**50.** How can one pass as a fine man as suggested by the father?
(a) By keeping the colour in your cheek
(b) By keeping the fire in your eye
(c) By maintaining your health
(d) All of the above

# ANSWERS

| | | | | | | | | | | | | | | | | | | | |
|---|---|---|---|---|---|---|---|---|---|---|---|---|---|---|---|---|---|---|---|
| 1. | *(a)* | 2. | *(b)* | 3. | *(d)* | 4. | *(c)* | 5. | *(d)* | 6. | *(b)* | 7. | *(a)* | 8. | *(b)* | 9. | *(c)* | 10. | *(d)* |
| 11. | *(c)* | 12. | *(d)* | 13. | *(a)* | 14. | *(c)* | 15. | *(d)* | 16. | *(b)* | 17. | *(d)* | 18. | *(a)* | 19. | *(b)* | 20. | *(a)* |
| 21. | *(c)* | 22. | *(b)* | 23. | *(d)* | 24. | *(a)* | 25. | *(b)* | 26. | *(c)* | 27. | *(d)* | 28. | *(d)* | 29. | *(d)* | 30. | *(a)* |
| 31. | *(b)* | 32. | *(d)* | 33. | *(c)* | 34. | *(b)* | 35. | *(a)* | 36. | *(c)* | 37. | *(d)* | 38. | *(b)* | 39. | *(a)* | 40. | *(b)* |
| 41. | *(c)* | 42. | *(b)* | 43. | *(d)* | 44. | *(a)* | 45. | *(b)* | 46. | *(c)* | 47. | *(a)* | 48. | *(d)* | 49. | *(b)* | 50. | *(d)* |

Chapter 38

# Dream Children

*Charles Lamb*

## About the Author

Charles Lamb was born on 10th February 1775 in London. He died on 27th December 1834. He was an English essayist, poet and antiquarian. He was best known for his Essays of Elia and for the children's book Tales from Shakespeare, co-authored with his sister, Mary Lamb.

Friends with such literary luminaries as Samuel Taylor Coleridge, William Wordsworth, and William Hazlitt, Lamb was at the centre of a major literary circle in England. He has been referred to by E. V. Lucas, his principal biographer, as 'the most lovable figure in English literature'.

Lamb was born in London, the son of Elizabeth Field and John Lamb. Lamb was the youngest child, with a sister 11 years older named Mary and an even older brother named John; there were four others who did not survive infancy. His father John Lamb was a lawyer's clerk and spent most of his professional life as the assistant to a barrister named Samuel Salt, who lived in the Inner Temple in the legal district of London.

It was there in Crown Office Row that Charles Lamb was born and spent his youth. Lamb created a portrait of his father in his 'Elia on the Old Benchers' under the name Lovel. Lamb's older brother was too much his senior to be a youthful companion to the boy but his sister Mary, being born eleven years before him, was probably his closest playmate. Lamb was also cared for by his paternal aunt Hetty, who seems to have had a particular fondness for him. A number of writings by both Charles and Mary suggest that the conflict between Aunt Hetty and her sister-in-law created a certain degree of tension in the Lamb household. However, Charles speaks fondly of her and her presence in the house seems to have brought a great deal of comfort to him Written about a dream world, the essay Dream Children by Charles Lamb belongs to his famous work Essays of Elia (1823) published in London magazines. Referring to himself by the pseudonym Elia, Lamb has penned down the essays as personal accounts of his life devoid of any didactic or moral lessons. Enriched with humour, pathos and regret for the time long gone, Lamb's essays leave an everlasting impression on the minds and hearts of the readers. Notwithstanding, there has always been a small but enduring following for Lamb's works, as the long-running and still-active Charles Lamb Bulletin demonstrates. Because of his notoriously quirky, even bizarre, style, he has been more of a 'cult favourite' than an author with mass popular or scholarly appeal. Lamb was honoured by The Latymer School, a grammar school in Edmonton, a suburb of London where he lived for a time; it has six houses, one of which, 'Lamb', is named after Charles.

His selected works include Blank Verse, poetry, 1798, A Tale of Rosamund Gray, and old blind Margaret, 1798, John Woodvil, poetic drama, 1802, Tales from Shakespeare, 1807, The Adventures of Ulysses, 1808, Specimens of English Dramatic poets who lived about the time of Shakespeare, 1808, On the Tragedies of Shakespeare, 1811, Witches and Other Night Fears, 1821, The Pawnbroker's Daughter, 1825, Eliana, 1867, Essays of Elia, 1823, The Last Essays of Elia, 1833.

## Summary

Having told his children about their grandmother, Alice Winterton, Charles Lamb stares at the face of Alice. The dream children grew fainter from his view. Though, they spoke nothing yet they appeared to be saying that they were not the children of Alice nor the author. They went to the extent of saying that they were not children at all. Then, they, presented the harsh reality of Lamb's life before him that it was not he, but Bartram, whom the children of Alice would call father. The children further said that they were nothing and less than nothing.

### Story about Grandmother

The writer explained to the children that their grandmother was a very good lady and she was having a lot of respect and love from all for her goodness. She was very humble, honest and virtuous lady of tall stature. Lamb then told the children that grandmother, Field died and her funeral was attended by all poor and a few gentries of the neighbourhood. She was a good lady at head to heart. She was very faithful to others. She was respected and admired by all.

### Time Spent with Brother John

The writer explains about his grandmother to the children. Lamb along with John, his elder brother spent his holidays at his grand mother Field's great house, a hundred times bigger then their present one, in Norfolk.

### Grandmother Loved and Respected by All

She had been a tall, upright and graceful person and in her youth, she was considered the best dancer in the country, but she fell victim to a cruel disease, cancer, which bowed her down with pain though it could never bend her spirits because she was a good and religious woman. She was respected and loved by all for goodness. She was very much humble, honest and virtuous.

### How the Author won the Heart of the Mother of Dream Children

The writer told his children how he tried in vain to win the heart of their mother for seven years long. Lamb was stupefied with amazement, while he was still looking at them, the figures of his children started fainting and receding till nothing at last but two mournful features were seen in the uttermost distance.

They appeared to declare that they were children neither of Lamb nor of Alice. They were nothing but dreams.

### Loses Brother John Forever

Lamb awoke from the dream and found himself quietly seated in him bachelor arm chair, with his sister Mary by his side and his brother, John Lamb has gone forever.

## Practice Questions

**1. Why is the essay entitled 'Dream Children'?**

(a) Because the children, Lamb speaks of in the essay were actually the creations of his imagination or fancy
(b) Because the author was not married
(c) Because the author's wife had died
(d) Because the children do not accept the author as his father

**2. Who was 'Field' in the essay?**

(a) He was lamb's uncle
(b) Field, pseudonym for the actual person, was Lamb's grandmother
(c) He was Charles lamb's brother
(d) She was Charles Lamb's wife

**3. How does Lamb present Field before his dream children?**

(a) As a loving wife
(b) As a sweet child
(c) As extremely pious, fearless and compassionate grandmother
(d) As a cheat and fraudulent lady

**4. Why is the essay subtitled 'A Reverie'?**

(a) Because the author of the essay had children without marriage
(b) Because he had adopted children without marrying
(c) Because he missed his grandmother a lot in the essay
(d) Because he created an imaginary picture of a happy conjugal life in the essay

**5. How does Lamb present his brother John Lamb?**

(a) As a handsome, high-spirited, strong, fearless and a caring person in youth
(b) As an irritated youth
(c) As a careless elder brother
(d) As a drunkard

**6. When did John Lamb become lame-footed?**

(a) In his childhood
(b) In his old age
(c) In his youth
(d) He didn't become lame footed at all

**7. Whom does Lamb refer to as 'faithful bridget' by side?**

(a) His grandmother, Field
(b) His brother, John
(c) His sister, Mary Lamb
(d) His love, Ann Simmons

**8. What is the most striking feature of the essay?**

(a) The author's use of satire
(b) The author's use of irony
(c) The author's use of hyperbole
(d) The author's mingling of pathos and humour

**9. What type of essay is 'Dream Children'?**

(a) A personal essay
(b) A moral essay
(c) A social essay
(d) A sci-fi essay

**10. How does Lamb show his knowledge of child psychology?**

(a) With Wife's advice and suggestions
(b) With acute sense and understanding of how children react to the happenings in the world of the adults
(c) With pure imagination
(d) With experience of his own children

**11. "...till the old marble heads would seem to be live again...to be turned into marble with them"—Where does the expression occur?**

(a) Around the great country house in Norfolk
(b) In dreams
(c) At the twelve marble busts of Caesars
(d) At his children's dwelling place

**12.** Where does the expression 'busy-idle diversion' occur?
(a) While dreaming
(b) While conversing with his brother
(c) While talking to his grandmother
(d) While telling 'dream children' about his boyhood

**13.** What does the author mean by 'busy-idle diversion'?
(a) Staying busy without work
(b) Day dreaming
(c) Working very hard
(d) Being in deep slumber

**14.** "When he died though he had not been...died great while ago". Who is referred to as 'he'?
(a) Lamb's male dream child
(b) Lamb's brother, John Lamb
(c) Lamb's Father
(d) Lamb's childhood friend

**15.** "When he died though he had not been...died great while ago". Why does the author say so?
(a) Because he liked him
(b) Because It didn't make any difference to him
(c) Because he experienced an immeasurable vacuum in his life after his death
(c) Because he had never met him

**16.** "...such a distance there is between life and death"—Explain the significance of the line in light of the context.
(a) Lamb really understood how to enjoy life
(b) Lamb started taking care of his children
(c) Lamb gave value to his wife
(d) Lamb learnt the true difference between life and death after his brother's death

**17.** "...the soul of first Alice looked out at her eyes with such reality of re-presentment that I came in doubt". What does the word 're-presentment' mean here?
(a) His dream daughter resembling his dream girl
(b) To lead in a course
(c) To resolve the impending issue
(d) To disguise for fun

**18.** 'But James Elia was gone forever'—Who was James Elia?
(a) Author's dream girl
(b) Another name of his brother, John-Lamb
(c) His mother (d) His father

**19.** "Here Alice put out one of her dear mother's looks, too tender to be called upbraiding"—What does the word 'braiding' mean here?
(a) Permission (b) Disagreement
(c) Castigation or Censure (d) Revelation

**20.** How does Lamb record Alice's reactions to his story-telling?
(a) As funny (b) As ridiculous
(c) As comic
(d) As that of astonishment and piousness

**21.** How does Lamb record John's reactions to his story-telling?
(a) As foolish work (b) As an intelligent art
(c) As humorous (d) As satire

**22.** Who was 'Alice' in the essay?
(a) The wife of the author
(b) The dream daughter of the author
(c) The grandmother of the author
(d) The sister of the author

**23.** What did working at East India House provide Charles Lamb?
(a) A lifetime of stability
(b) An opportunity to travel
(c) A chance to meet friends
(d) A chance to meet fellow writers

**24.** In Charles Lamb's poem 'Dream Children,' what was the thrust of the poem?
(a) He reflected on an account of his life
(b) He wrote about his sister, Mary
(c) He lamented losing the woman he loved
(d) He wrote about life in the asylum

**25.** This famous essayist was known as 'Elia'.
(a) John Stuart Mill (b) Charles Lamb
(c) Voltaire (d) Guy De Maupassant

## ANSWERS

| | | | | | | | | | | | | | | | | | | | |
|---|---|---|---|---|---|---|---|---|---|---|---|---|---|---|---|---|---|---|---|
| 1. | (c) | 2. | (b) | 3. | (c) | 4. | (d) | 5. | (a) | 6. | (b) | 7. | (c) | 8. | (d) | 9. | (a) | 10. | (b) |
| 11. | (c) | 12. | (d) | 13. | (a) | 14. | (b) | 15. | (c) | 16. | (d) | 17. | (a) | 18. | (b) | 19. | (c) | 20. | (d) |
| 21. | (c) | 22. | (b) | 23. | (d) | 24. | (a) | 25. | (b) | | | | | | | | | | |

Chapter 39

# Discovery of India

*Pandit Jawaharlal Nehru*

## About the Author

### Teenage of Pandit Nehru

A charismatic nationalist leader, Jawaharlal Nehru (1889-1964) Indian nationalist leader and statesman fought for Indian independence from British rule for nearly three decades beginning in the late 1910s. He was deeply involved in the political opposition and was imprisoned numerous times for Civil Disobedience. The nationalist movement achieved its goal when India gained its freedom at midnight on 14th August, 1947. Upon Britain's withdrawal, Jawaharlal Nehru became independent India's first Prime Minister (1947-1964) and a leader of the Non Aligned Movement during the Cold War.

### Major Literacy works of Pt. Nehru

Jawaharlal Nehru wrote his major books, 'Toward Freedom' (1936), an autobiography; 'The Discovery of India' (1946); and 'Glimpses of World History' (1934), a series of letters to his daughter, Indira. He was a talented and expressive writer in English, and he and India's freedom struggle became more widely known through the extensive circulation of his writings in the West.

## Summary

### Nehru was Jailed for Quit India Movement

'The Discovery of India' was written by India's first Prime Minister Pt. Jawaharlal Nehru during his imprisonment in 1942-1946 at Ahmednagar Fort. Nehru was jailed for his participation in the Quit India Movement along with other Indian leaders, and he used this time to write down his thoughts and learning about India's history. 'Discovery of India' is widely regarded as a classic in India, and provides a concise precise of Indian history, philosophy and culture as viewed from the eyes of a liberal Indian fighting for independence of his country. Then, It was published in 1946 and has since acquired the status of a classic.

### Account of Great Indian Since Time Unknown

The story of 'Discovery of India' begins from prehistory to the last years of British colonial rule; some of the greatest heroes of India are mentioned. Analysing texts from the Vedas to the Upanishads, and epics such as the Mahabharata and the Ramayana, and personalities like the Buddha and Mahatma Gandhi, Jawaharlal Nehru brings to life an ancient culture and land that has been the base and headquarters of some of the world's great traditions of philosophy, science and art, and almost all its major religions.

### Nehru as a Human Being

Badenweiler, Lausanne of the Discovery of India is about the relationship with his wife, her death, and his thoughts of death. These are the two clues from the book that give us a very good idea about Jawaharlal Nehru, not as the Prime Minister of India, but as a human being.

### Quest for Unknown Truth

The quest: From here the very essence of the 'Discovery of India' begins. The panorama of his past, the search for India, the Bharat Mata, the variety and unity of India and all these reflect the beauty and glory of the Indian civilisation. The glory of the Indian civilisation can never be equaled in any way by the modern society of our country.

Actually this was the 'Discovery of India' from the minds of the author. Here, we will not come across a bunch of facts, about Indian history, to recollect all the years and names. But Discovery of India combines with the visions of the author, so here we are enlightened by the knowledge on the culture and tradition in India and at the same time, we are not going to be starved of our enthusiasm.

And the whole written and unwritten history of India is given in 'Discovery of India'. The Indus Valley Civilisation, the coming of the Aryans, Hinduism, caste system, the continuity of the great Indian culture, is in the book 'Discovery of India'. The epics, 'The Mahabharata', 'The Bhagvad Gita', 'Buddha', 'Ashoka' and through all the people, the Discovery of India has the contemporary records of the time, we can get a complete picture of India through the ages.

## Medieval Period and the Golden Era of the Guptas

The dawn of the medieval period, and the golden era of the Guptas, 'Discovery of India' gives a good insight of India's foreign relationships with the people of Iran, Greece. Then, there is the answer to the most perplexing question of Buddhism in India. Through the Arabs, the Mongols we come to the golden time of the Mughal Empire. And the lives of Babar, Akbar, the Marathas, all flash before our eyes, as we are led to the colonial times of the British rule, with all the minute details. The path takes through the times when the British came as tracers to India and later went to build a colonial empire.

## Friendship between Gandhi and Nehru

'Discovery of India' gives us a beautiful insight into the friendship between Gandhiji and Nehru, the role of Gandhiji, MA Jinnah, the coming of the War II and the final phase of the freedom movement after the war.

## Pin-Point Narration of India

Jawaharlal Nehru's narration of history and knowledge about India is excellent. Writing with pride about his motherland, he does not mince his words. Whilst singing the praises of his people's successes and great heritage, he also acknowledges their failures and weaknesses. His intense dislike for British rule comes through and it is his hope for India that prevails.

At times, 'Discovery of India' is also autobiographical and for anyone at all interested in the Nehru-Gandhi dynasty of today, 'Discovery of India' serves to provide the reader with the story of one of its founding members. This only adds to the uniqueness of the book 'Discovery of India' and makes it even more of an enjoyable read for the author has put a little of himself in Discovery of India – one of the most important ingredients of writing anything at all. At times, one feels that Jawaharlal Nehru has just stopped by for a chat in your living room. The style of writing is such that you never feel that he is 'lecturing' you or even 'teaching' you. He is discussing with you your heritage and really his abilities here show an in depth understanding of how to tell a story without sounding deadly dull.

## Prison as the Best of Universities

Nehru described prison as 'the best of universities', because during his several prison stints for civil disobedience he was able to focus on his studies and writings on political philosophy.

## Covers Issue beyond India

To read 'The Discovery of India' is to more than discover just India. Not limited to information about the subcontinent as it is today, the discovery foes from the world from Plato, Emerson, the history of lands like Afghanistan, China's ancient trade links with India and so much more. It is to venture into a discovery of the world itself. Discovery of India makes a person have inner knowledge and pride that he originates from so wonderful a land.

When one reads a book, there must be a purpose to this exercise - be it for entertainment, pleasure, knowledge or curiosity. In reading 'The Discovery of India' one is given the chance of experiencing all of these at once.

# Practice Questions

**1.** Jawaharlal Nehru penned two important books, the first one is 'Discovery of India'. Can you name the second?
(a) An autobiography
(b) Glimpses of world History
(c) A tryst with Destiny
(d) My experiments with truth

**2.** At the age of 26, Nehru married a girl of 16. What was her name?
(a) Sarojini Dubey (b) Kamla Kaul
(c) Lady Mount batten (d) Sister Nivedita

**3.** When Nehru became the Prime Minister of tree India, he delivered a speech. His speech has been given a special name. It is
(a) A Tryst with India (b) A Tryst with fate
(c) A Tryst with Destiny (d) A Tryst with Nation

**4.** Nehruji penned an autobiography which was published in the USA in 1936. What was its title?
(a) My Experiments with Truth (b) Towards Freedom
(c) Life of Freedom Fighter (d) Letters to Indira

**5.** Which of the following was not a contemporary of Jawaharlad Nehru?
(a) Sardar Vallavbhai Patel
(b) Michael Madhusudan Dutt
(c) Netaji Subhas Chandra Bose
(d) Muhammed Ali Jinnah

**6.** What is the name of Nehruji's Kashmiri friend whom he referred as blood brother?
(a) Sardar Patel
(b) Sheikh Abdulla
(c) Farroq Abdulla
(d) Maharaja Hari Singh

**7.** For how many times was nehru nominated for Nobel Peace Prize ?
(a) 4 times (b) 3 times (c) 11 times (d) 2 times

**8.** On which date Children's Day is celebrated internationally?
(a) 14th November (b) 30th December
(c) 20th November (d) 5th January

**9. On the book 'The Discovery of India' a popular TV Serial was produced by Shyam Benegal. Name it.**
(a) Bharat, Ek Khoj (b) Train to Pakistan
(c) Buniyaad (d) Hum Log

**10. Where was this book written by Pt. Nehru?**
(a) In a prison cell in Ahmednagar
(b) While studying in England
(c) While fail in USA
(d) After India became free in 1945

**11. In the book Nehruji indulges in a journey to the past. Why?**
(a) To consolidate ancient heritage and wisdom
(b) Frankly admit one's mistakes
(c) To prepare oneself for the change
(d) All of the above

**12. The book presents a good insight of India's foreign relationship with the people of**
(a) Burma
(b) Iran
(c) Greece
(d) Both (b) and (c)

**13. What was the aim of Nehruji while writing the book 'Discovery of India'?**
(a) To present India's past
(b) Constructive suggestion on the basis of historical knowledge
(c) To admit his mistakes
(d) To dwell on the tortures incurred by the Britishers

**14. Why does Nehru describe prison 'as best of universities'?**
(a) As he got enough time for studies
(b) Enjoyed solitary time
(c) He was able to focus on writing on political philosophy
(d) As he got many books to read

**15. What is the theme of the book 'The Discovery of India"?**
(a) Writing about historical facts about India
(b) Tributes to the rich cultural heritage of India
(c) History of world in nutshell
(d) Our trade ties with china

**16. Why was Nehruji jailed when he wrote this book in prison?**
(a) To participate in Quit India Movement
(b) For writing against the Britishers
(c) To support freedom fighters
(d) None of the above

**17. Through this book we come to know about Nehruji's wide knowledge in the areas of**
(a) Indus Valley Civilisation
(b) Influence of Muslim invaders
(c) India's slavery under Britishers and Indian's Mistakes
(d) All of the above

**18. What is the style of writing adopted by Nehru in 'The Discovery of India'?**
(a) Didactic (b) Philosophical
(c) Narrative and lively (d) Spiritual

**19. How does an Indian feel after reading this book?**
(a) It makes a person have inner knowledge and pride in ancient cultural heritage
(b) Feels sorry about present condition
(c) Hates the Britishers
(d) None of the above

**20. While singing the praises of ancient Indian's and present Indian's success and great heritage, Nehru also acknowledges**
(a) supremacy of the Britishers
(b) friendly relations with neighbours
(c) Indian people's failures and weaknesses
(d) self glorification

**21. What was the purpose behind writing this book?**
(a) To appreciate India's wisdom
(b) To condemn people's follies
(c) Use past as a spring board of action for a better future
(d) At describe world history

**22. Why Nehru's ji observation about the Afgani invaders is not appreciated?**
(a) Afghani never allowed freedom and expression
(b) They dragged away India's wealth into then countries
(c) They were not tolerant towards Indian religious and hated Indians
(d) All of the above

**23. What picture of the author emerges after reading this book?**
(a) Nehruji was deeply pained by the oppression of millions of Indians
(b) Nehruji had a large and comprehensive knowledge
(c) He is one of the greatest writer of English prose
(d) All of the above

**24. Why can we not call this book purely auto biographical?**
(a) Only in first few chapter Nehru talks about him personal life
(b) More or less, he talks about the glorious past of India
(c) He is more concerned about the poverty struck Indians waiting to get a better future
(d) He had nothing to say about his own life

## ANSWERS

| | | | | | | | | | | | | | | | | | | | |
|---|---|---|---|---|---|---|---|---|---|---|---|---|---|---|---|---|---|---|---|
| 1. | (b) | 2. | (b) | 3. | (c) | 4. | (b) | 5. | (b) | 6. | (b) | 7. | (c) | 8. | (a) | 9. | (a) | 10. | (a) |
| 11. | (d) | 12. | (d) | 13. | (b) | 14. | (c) | 15. | (b) | 16. | (a) | 17. | (d) | 18. | (c) | 19. | (a) | 20. | (c) |
| 21. | (c) | 22. | (d) | 23. | (d) | 24. | (c) | | | | | | | | | | | | |

Chapter 40

# My Mother

*Nirad C. Chaudhuri*

## About the Author

Nirad C. Chaudhuri was born on 23rd November, 1897 in Kishoreganj (now in Bangladesh). He was born into the family of a country lawyer. His mother didn't even know how to read, as was common with most women of those times. After receiving his primary education from Kishore ganj and Calcutta, he went to Ripon College, Calcutta.

His first article was published by Bengali poet, Bharat Chandra. He had always been a journalist, but it wasn't until he was 53 and he brought out his first book in English, 'The Autobiography of an Unknown Indian', in 1951. The book created much controversy at the time of its release as it infuriated a lot of Indians, especially the bureaucratic class. But here was a man who didn't care a damn about what others thought of him. That was what set him apart from many a writer of his time. Born in British India, his writings reflect the history of India in the context of British colonialism. He was one of the best known Indian fiction authors of 20th century.

His book, 'The Continent of Circe' won the prestigious 'Duff Cooper Memorial Award in 1966, making Chaudhuri the first Indian to have won the prize. He was presented with the Sahitya Akademi Award for his biography on Max Muller, 'Scholar Extraordinary' in 1975.

In 1970, he left India to settle in Oxford, England and spent his expatriate years, thinking and writing about India. He lived a very long and productive life. He was actively writing well up to the end of his life, publishing his last work at the age of 99. He died in 1999 of natural causes, just two months short of his 102nd birthday.

## Summary

### My Mother's Distinctive Features and Connections

'My Mother' is a part of the autobiography of Nirad C. Chaudhuri. It emphasises the distinctive features and convictions of his mother. He makes out the difference between her and an average Indian mother.

In 'My Mother', Nirad explains how his father and mother were bound to each other. They complemented each other in all ways. They were the same in different ways. If his mother was fragile then his father was robust. He says that his mother could not hide any feeling so the family members get to known her emotions and regulated their emotions accordingly. She was not much of an intellectual but she was logical.

### Her Physical Features

He explains the physical features of his mother. Her eyes were large and her lips were well cut but tending towards fullness in the lower one. There was an unsleeping alertness and inexhaustible animation on her face. There was openness, goodness and generosity on her face with positive energy.

### Her Likes and Dislikes

She was intolerant of demonstrativenses and showing feeling openly. She handled the situations differently from an average Indian mother. To explain this, Nirad gave an example of one year old baby falling from the height of 2 feet, an average Indian mother would react by screaming and banging her head an the floor thinking her child is dead. But, Nirad's mother never gave such reactions on any matter.

He tells us that his mother did not like falsehood, dishonesty, morad cowardice and meanness. She also despised silently taking advantage of a wrong opportunity. He gives example for this as well. It his mother divided sweets among them, then the one who took the bigger piece would get an angry look from her. So, they used to ask the mother to give them pieces herself.

### Learning from His Mother

Nirad tells us that he has learned a lot from his mother. He learned that god manners were a part of basic etiquettes and not external polish. His mother used to think bad manners as sin and not merely against a code of social behaviour. Nirad says that he used to make barbed observations since his childhood. He used to defend himself from her saying that he never speaks harshly of the underdog/weak.

# Practice Questions

**1.** **Which was the first book written by Nirad C. Chaudhuri?**
(a) A Passage to England
(b) The Autobiography of an Unknown Indian
(c) Three Horsemen of the New Apocalypse
(d) The Continent of Circe

**2.** **Bad manners, as considered by Nirad's mother were..........**
(a) against code of social conduct
(b) not a big thing
(c) sing
(d) good thing

**3.** **How did Nirad explain the bond between his father and mother?**
(a) Complement each other
(b) Similar in different ways
(c) Bound by common principles
(d) All of the above

**4.** **How is the nature of author's mother described in the essay?**
(a) Soft and fragile (b) Robust
(c) Angry (d) Impassive

**5.** **When was Nirad C. Chaudhuri born?**
(a) 20th November, 1857 (b) 23rd November, 1897
(c) 9th August, 1897 (d) 10th September, 1890

**6.** **Which novel did win Nirad the 'Duff Cooper Memorial Award'?**
(a) Three Horsemen of the New Apocalypse
(b) The Hand, Great Anarch!
(c) The Autobiography of an Unknoun Indian
(d) The Continent of Circe

**7.** **Which character faults were disliked by the author's mother?**
(a) Good maners (b) Loyalty
(c) Moral cowardice (d) All of these

**8.** **How would an average Indian mother react if her one year old baby falls from a height of 2 feet?**
(a) Scream and knock her head on floor Thinking baby as dead
(b) Scold her child for doing so
(c) Do not react at all
(d) None of the above

**9.** **At what age Nirad died?**
(a) 102 Years (b) 100 years (c) 103 years (d) 101 years

**10.** **Nirad's first article was published by**
(a) Bharat Chandra (b) Jawaharlal Nehru
(c) Sarat Chandra Bose (d) Subhas Chandra Bose

**11.** **Where was Nirad C. Chaudhuri born?**
(a) Calcutta (now Kolkata), West Bengal
(b) Kishoreganj (now is Bangladesh)
(c) Madras (now Chennai), Tamil Nadu
(d) None of the above

**12.** **Which book of Nirad C. Chaudhuri infuriated the Indian high class people?**
(a) Thy Hand, Great Anarch!
(b) The Continent of Circe
(c) Scholar Extraordinary
(d) The Autobiography of an Unknown Indian

**13.** **Which quality of mother could be seen when she was argumentative?**
(a) Logical
(b) Deceptive
(c) Illiterateness
(d) Rude behaviour

**14.** **How has the author described the eyes of his mother?**
(a) well- shaped
(b) large and liquid
(c) Small
(d) Bright and big

**15.** **What was the weakness of mothers face as described by the author in 'My Mother'?**
(a) Forehead
(b) Nose
(c) Lips
(d) Chin

**16.** **What could be interpreted form facial features of author's mother in 'My Mother'?**
(a) Unsleeping alertness and inexhaustible animation
(b) Negative energy
(c) Angry look
(d) Moral cowardice

**17.** **What did the author's mother intorelant of?**
(a) Panicking
(b) Complaining
(c) Demonstrativeness
(d) Crying

**18.** **When did the author's could give additional cuffing?**
(a) When they screamed louder than required for an injury
(b) When the children do not behave properly
(c) When they do not go to sleep
(d) When they laugh loudly

**19.** **Which characteristic of author's mother was typical of an Indian mother?**
(a) Being easy going
(b) Being Highstrung
(c) Being short-tempered
(d) None of the above

**20.** **What did the mother despise the most?**
(a) Taking sympathy
(b) Crying
(c) Taking silent advantage of a wrong opportunity
(d) Falsehood

**21.** **Why was there a rush for dinner at the author's hostel?**
(a) Dining hall was not large enough
(b) Students were more than the food available
(c) Food was served only once
(d) All of the above

**22.** **How did the boarders on the second floor in the hostel come down?**
(a) Making loud noises
(b)They did not come down
(c) They rushed to the dining room
(d) They came silently with their shoes in their hands.

**23.** **What did the author assume?**
(a) He should manipulate his turn at the dinners
(b) If he waits for his turn, he will get the food
(c) If he waits for his turn, he will not get the food
(d) He should go silently to the dining room.

**24.** **What was the author's mother remonstrate against?**
(a) Author's sharp and biting tongue
(b) Behavior of author's father
(c) Author's demonstrativeness
(d) None of the above

## ANSWERS

| | | | | | | | | | | | | | | | | | | | |
|---|---|---|---|---|---|---|---|---|---|---|---|---|---|---|---|---|---|---|---|
| 1. | (b) | 2. | (c) | 3. | (d) | 4. | (a) | 5. | (b) | 6. | (d) | 7. | (c) | 8. | (a) | 9. | (d) | 10. | (a) |
| 11. | (b) | 12. | (d) | 13. | (a) | 14. | (b) | 15. | (d) | 16. | (a) | 17. | (c) | 18. | (a) | 19. | (b) | 20. | (c) |
| 21. | (a) | 22. | (d) | 23. | (b) | 24. | (a) | | | | | | | | | | | | |

Chapter 41

# Figures of Speech

## Definition

A figure of speech is a phrase or word having different meaning than its literal meanings. It conveys meaning by identifying or comparing one thing to another, which has connotation or meaning familiar to the audience. That is why it is helpful in creating vivid rhetorical effect.

## Types of Figures of Speech

There are many types of figures of speech. Here are a few of them.

### Simile

In a simile, comparison is made between two distinctly different things, especially using, like, or and as.

*Examples*

1. It droppeth as the gentle rain from heaven.
2. Or from star-like eyes doth seek.

### Metaphor

It is a figure of speech that makes a comparison between two seemingly unlike things without using the connective words like, as, than or resembles.

*Examples*

1. Life is a dream.
2. I see a lily on thy brow.

### Personification

Personification gives life to inanimate objects or makes animals human.

*Examples*

1. "How far that little candle throws its beams!
   So shines a good deed in a naughty world".
2. Truth sits upon the lips of a dying man.

### Apostrophe

In Apostrophe, the speaker directly addresses an absent or dead person, an abstract quality or something non-human as if it were present and capable of responding.

*Examples*

1. Frailty, thy name is woman!
2. Little lamb, who made thee?

### Paradox

A paradox is a figure of speech in which a statement appears to contradict itself. Adjective: paradoxical.

In everyday communication, notes HF Platt, paradox "is mostly used for expressing astonishment or disbelief at something unusual or unexpected" (Encyclopedia of Rhetoric, 2001)

*Examples*

1. "Some of the biggest failures I ever had were successes." (attributed to American actress and singer Pearl Bailey)
2. "The swiftest traveler is he that goes afoot."
   (Henry David Thoreau, Walden, 1854)

### Irony

Irony is a figure of speech in which words are used in such a way that their intended meaning is different from the actual meaning of the words. It may also be a situation that ends up in quite a different way than what is generally anticipated. In simple words, it is a difference between appearance and reality.

*Examples*

1. The butter is as soft as a slab of marble.
2. Oh great! Now you have broken my new camera.

# Practice Questions

I. *Point out the figures of speech in the following.*

**1.** My love is like a red, red rose.
(a) Personification (b) Metaphor
(c) Simile (d) Paradox

**2.** She hangs like a star in the dew of our song.
(a) Metaphor (b) Simile
(c) Irony (d) Personification

**3.** Look like the innocent flower.
(a) Personification (b) Metaphor
(c) Simile (d) Paradox

**4.** Life is a tale told by an idiot.
(a) Personification (b) Metaphor
(c) Simile (d) Paradox

**5.** Life is but a walking shadow.
(a) Metaphor (b) Simile
(c) Irony (d) Personification

**6.** Hope is the poor man's bread.
(a) Simile (b) Metaphor
(c) Irony (d) Personification

**7.** Opportunity knocks at the door but once.
(a) Irony (b) Simile
(c) Metaphor (d) Personification

**8.** This sea that bares her bosom to the moon.
(a) Personification (b) Simile
(c) Irony (d) Metaphor

**9.** Truth sits upon the lips of dying men.
(a) Metaphor (b) Simile
(c) Irony (d) Personification

**10.** Live like a hermit.
(a) Paradox (b) Metaphor
(c) Simile (d) Personification

**11.** She skims like a bird on the foam of a stream.
(a) Personification
(b) Metaphor
(c) Simile
(d) Paradox

**12.** The city's voice itself is soft like solitude's.
(a) Personification (b) Simile
(c) Metaphor (d) Paradox

**13.** Life is as tedious as a twice-told tale.
(a) Metaphor (b) Simile
(c) Personification (d) Paradox

**14.** She is the pillar of the state.
(a) Personification (b) Metaphor
(c) Paradox (d) Simile

**15.** If you wish to preserve your secret, wrap it up in frankness."
(a) Paradox (b) Metaphor
(c) Simile (d) Personification

**16.** "I have found the paradox, that if you love until it hurts, there can be no more hurt, only more love."
(a) Personification (b) Metaphor
(c) Simile (d) Paradox

**17.** "War is peace."
"Freedom is slavery."
"Ignorance is strength."
(a) Personification (b) Metaphor
(c) Paradox (d) Simile

**18.** I posted a video on YouTube about how boring and useless YouTube is.
(a) Personification (b) Metaphor
(c) Irony (d) Paradox

**19.** The name of Britain's biggest dog was 'Tiny'.
(a) Personification (b) Irony
(c) Simile (d) Paradox

**20.** You laugh at a person who slipped stepping on a banana peel, and the next thing you know, you've slipped too.
(a) Personification (b) Metaphor
(c) Simile (d) Irony

## ANSWERS

| | | | | | | | | | | | | | | | | | | | |
|---|---|---|---|---|---|---|---|---|---|---|---|---|---|---|---|---|---|---|---|
| 1. | (c) | 2. | (b) | 3. | (c) | 4. | (b) | 5. | (a) | 6. | (b) | 7. | (d) | 8. | (a) | 9. | (d) | 10. | (c) |
| 11. | (c) | 12. | (b) | 13. | (b) | 14. | (b) | 15. | (a) | 16. | (d) | 17. | (c) | 18. | (c) | 19. | (d) | 20. | (d) |

Chapter 42

# Forms of Poetry and Stanza

## The Sonnet

- Sonnet is a short poem of fourteen lines expressing one single thought, feeling, sound or strain. It is of lyrical nature to be sung with a musical instrument.
- Sonnet is originally associated with the name of great Italian poet. Petrarch, the father of Sonnet-Italian or Petrarchan sonnet. Petrarchan Sonnet is composed of two parts–Octave (8 lines) and Sestet (6 lines).
- In England, sonnet writing began during the reign of Queen Elizabeth. Wyatt Surrey and Spenser were the earlier ones. Then came Shakespeare, he gave new structure, beauty and flexibility to the Sonnet.
- Shakespeare wrote 154 sonnets. This new form of Sonnet introduced by him is known as the Shakespearean or English Sonnet. It concludes with a couplet. (Second kind of Sonnet).
- After Shakespeare, there came up a third kind of Sonnet. It is a combination of two kinds of Sonnet - Petrarchan and English Sonnet. It is called Irregular Sonnet.
- Poets generally wrote 'sonnet sequences' all of which had the theme of 'Love'. Some poets, especially Milton, changed this practice of writing in sequences. Wordsworth took further liberties with the Italian Sonnet and broke up the rhyme scheme of the octave to be 'abba acca' in place of 'abba abba'.
- The sonnet was introduced to England by Wyatt and developed by Surrey and was there after, widely used, notably in the sonnet sequences of Shakespeare, Sidney, Spenser and other poets of the Golden period.

## The Elegy

1. The Elegy is a poem of mourning or sorrow. It is often written on the death of a person.
2. It is full of pathetic feelings. Sometimes the poet discusses some philosophical thought in place of giving expression to his personal grief.
3. The Elegy is a mourning song in which the poet mourns the death of some friend or relative. It is as spontaneous as a lyric and like the ode.
4. The Elegy is often serious and philosophical in tone. It is a poem of serious, pensive or reflective mood in memory of something loved and lost.
5. In the current literary language, an elegy is a short lyric of the poet's lament or expression of sorrow over the death of someone dear. Its theme must be reflective and melancholic.
6. 'Elegy on the Death of a Mad Dog' and 'In Memoriam' are the best examples of elegy.
7. The Elegy can be divided into two parts :
   (i) Personal Elegy (ii) Impersonal Elegy

## The Ode

1. The ode may be defined as "a rhymed lyric often in the form of an address, generally dignified or exalted in subject and style."

2. Its theme may be an important public event like a National Jubilee, the death of a distinguished personage, the commemoration of the founding of a great university etc.
3. Like its parent form, the lyric, an ode is of Greek origin. It is dignified and exalted in tone.
4. There are four kinds of ode – Pindaric Ode, Horatian ode, Regular or Irregular ode.
5. An ode is longer than lyric, but it is the result of hard labour, not spontaneous. It is always serious and elevated in tone.

## The Lyric

1. Lyric was most popular form of poetry during the 16th century.
2. A lyric is a short poem. The word 'Lyric' is derived from the Greek work 'lyre' a musical instrument.
3. It is personal in mood and emotions.
4. THe first great poet who introudced lyric in English literature in England was Sir Thomas Wyatt.
5. In the beginning lyrics were composed by ancient Greeks. The greatest writers of lyrics were Pindar, Aeschylus and Sopocles.
6. Ben Jonson has written a number of lyrics that are ideal and superb.
7. The subject matter of a lyric is emotion and feeling, it appeals more to the heart than to the intellect.
8. It is a subjective poem. It has a simple and single emotion. In English lyric there is powerful personal emotion.

## The Satire

1. The word satire is derived from the Greek word 'Satyrs', a type of Greek comedy.
2. Satire is a technique or literacy device which is used by the writer to criticise or expose something.
3. Satire has been also called the oldest form of Social Commentary.
4. The writer uses fictional characters in a satire but they stand for real characters or people to expose and condemn the ills prevailing in the society.
5. Satirist uses irony and humour to emphasise the flaws prevalent in a sociely.
6. People may pick up a satirical book or watch a satirical movie hoping to be entertained but end up thinking about issues and perspectives they never thought of before.
7. The writer's intention of using satire is improving society by criticising their follies and foibles. The writer sees a problem and wants it corrected.
8. Alexander Pope's 'Rape of Lock' and George orwell's 'Animal Farm' are perfect example of satires in literature.

# Practice Questions

## The Sonnet

**1.** What is Sonnet?
(a) A prose of special nature
(b) A sacred poem of a reputed poet
(c) A poem of fourteen lines
(d) A criticism of a poet

**2.** How many lines does a sonnet have?
(a) 10 (b) 14 (c) 12 (d) 15

**3.** The sonnet is known to have originated in
(a) Spain (b) Greece
(c) England (d) Italy

**4.** The word 'sonnet' comes from ....... origin.
(a) Greek (b) Spanish (c) Latin (d) Italian

**5.** There are ............... types of sonnets.
(a) three (b) two
(c) four (d) five

**6.** Who was the first one to use sonnet in England?
(a) Shakespeare (b) Petrarch
(c) Milton (d) Sir Thomas Wyatt

**7.** ............... was the first to use this form of lyric to express his love for his beloved Lauka.
(a) Petrarch (b) Shakespeare
(c) Milton (d) Earl of Surrey

**8.** Petrarchan sonnet has two parts
(a) Octave and sestet
(b) Quatrains and couplet
(c) Octave and couplet
(d) Quatrains and sestet

**9.** There are............... lines in octave of Petrarchan sonnet.
(a) ten (b) eight
(c) six (d) four

**10.** The octave of Petrarchan sonnet presents a ................
(a) question/problem
(b) describes something
(c) confesses mistake
(d) addresses someone

**11.** The rhyming scheme of sestet is .........
(a) cde cde (b) cd cd ef
(c) cd ef ef (d) cd cd cd

**12.** Petrarchan sonnet is also called ................
(a) the Shakespearean Sonnet (b) the Miltonic Sonnet
(c) the Jacobian Sonnet (d) None of these

**13.** In which year were Shakespeare's sonnets first published?
(a) 1600 (b) 1609
(c) 1619 (d) 1630

**14.** How many sonnets does Shakespeare's collection contain?
(a) 154 (b) 160
(c) 164 (d) 170

**15.** What are the last two lines of a Shakespearean sonnet called?
(a) Quatrain (b) Triple
(c) Couplet (d) Sestet

**16.** How is the rhyme's scheme of the couplet represented?
(a) gg (b) ab
(c) cc (d) ee

**17.** Shakespeare's sonnets are addressed to
(a) Queen Elizabeth (b) A Dark lady
(c) Mr W.H. (d) Both (b) and (c)

**18.** This type of sonnet is made up of three quatrains and one couplet.
(a) Petrarchan sonnet (b) Free verse
(c) Shakespearean sonnet (d) Poetry

**19.** The main characteristic of sonnet are
(a) highly personal
(b) in form of love song
(c) musical and addressed to someone
(d) All of the above

**20.** Spenserian sonnet is an important varient of
(a) Petrarchan Sonnet
(b) Shakespearean Sonnet
(c) Classical Sonnet
(d) None of these

**21.** Faerie Queene is written in the form of
(a) Petrarchan Sonnet
(b) Spenserian Sonnet
(c) Shakespearean Sonnet
(d) Miltonic Sonnet

**22.** Spenser's motto in writing his Faerie Queene was
(a) to please and humour Queen Elizabeth
(b) to justify holiness as the greatest virtue
(c) to save the honour of womanhood
(d) to fashion a gentleman in virtuous and gentle discipline

**23.** The last six lines of a Miltonic Sonnet are divided into two groups of three lines each what is the group of three lines called
(a) Tercet (b) Tricet (c) Triplet (d) Trilet

**24.** The rhyming scheme 'abab bcbc, cd cd, ee' belongs to
(a) Miltonic Sonnet
(b) Petrarchan Sonnet
(c) Spenserian Sonnet
(d) Shakespearean Sonnet

## The Elegy

**25.** An Elegy is a type of lyric and focusses on expressing emotions and thoughts using
(a) heroic couplet
(b) an octave and a sestet
(c) formal language and structure
(d) alliteration

**26.** An Elegy is a
(a) historical poem (b) figurative story
(c) song of lamentation (d) short story

**27.** Which is a special kind of lyrics?
(a) Sonnet (b) Ode (c) Elegy (d) Epic

**28.** The best elegies are characterised by
(a) personal sorrow to general sorrow of mankind
(b) a gentle melancholy
(c) dignified and solemn in tone
(d) All of the above

**29.** The first elegy was written by
(a) Thomas Gray (b) Spenser
(c) Milton (d) John Donne

**30.** The elegy 'Astrophel' is about
(a) the death of Sir Philip Sidney
(b) the death of villagers
(c) the death of Sir Richard (d) None of these

**31.** Tennyson's 'In Memoriam' is a good example of
(a) Impersonal elegy (b) Personal elegy
(c) Pastoral elegy (d) None of these

**32.** 'Elegy written in a Country Churchyard' was written by
(a) Tennyson (b) Thomas Gray
(c) Milton (d) PB Shelley

**33.** A pastoral elegy is a lament of a
(a) poet (b) villager
(c) king (d) shepherd

**34.** An elegy written with a particular convention and rural background, is called
(a) Pastoral elegy (b) Personal elegy
(c) Impersonal elegy (d) None of these

**35.** In England, pastoral elegies have been written down from
(a) the restoration age (b) the renaissance age
(c) the victorian age (d) the romantic age

**36.** Milton's Lycidas is
(a) a lyric (b) a sonnet
(c) a pastoral elegy (d) a personal elegy

**37.** Elegy is said to be originated from
(a) Greek (b) England
(c) Italy (d) France

**38.** An elegy is a brief lyric of
(a) ceremony (b) religious event
(c) mourning (d) None of these

**39.** What is Sidney's Arcadia?
(a) A pastoral verse tale (b) A pastoral romance
(c) A pastoral elegy (d) A pastoral lyric

**40.** Shelley wrote a Pastoral Elegy on the death of Keats, what is its title?
(a) Lycidas (b) Endymion
(c) Adonais (d) Thyrsis

## The Ode

**41.** An ode is generally defined as a serious long poem in which the poet pours out his
(a) aspirations (b) anger
(c) horror (d) terror

**42.** Ode is a type of
(a) lyrical verse (b) short poem
(c) narrative poem (d) non-narrative poem

**43.** Classical ode or Pindaric ode is structured in three major parts
(a) Strophe, Antistrophe, Epode
(b) Strophe, Epode, Antistrophe
(c) Epode, Strophe, Antistrophe
(d) Antistrophe, Epode, Strophe

**44.** Strophe forms the ............... part of ode.
(a) first (b) second
(c) third (d) fourth

**45.** Pindaric ode's another name is
(a) The Dorian Ode (b) Horatian Ode
(c) Irregular Ode (d) Regular Ode

**46.** Pindaric Odes were written for
(a) the honour of victory
(b) the mourning
(c) singing in simple and sober style
(d) None of the above

**47.** ............... is the example of pindaric Ode.
(a) The progress of Poesy (b) The Bard
(c) Both (a) and (b) (d) None of these

**48.** The most common rhyme scheme of English ode is
(a) ababcdecde
(b) aa bb cc dd
(c) abbai, abba
(d) Both (a) and (b)

**49.** Ode is a poem that written for an
(a) occasion (b) religion
(c) Both (a) and (b) (d) None of these

**50.** The forms of odes are
(a) Pindaric, Horatian and irregular
(b) Irregular, Horatian
(c) Pindaric and Horatian
(d) Both (a) and (c)

**51.** The earliest odes in the English literature were
(a) Epithalamion, Prothalamion by Spenser
(b) Ode to evening by Collins
(c) Ode to Nightingale by Keats
(d) None of the above

**52.** Horatian ode is also known as
(a) The Dorian ode (b) The Irregular ode
(c) Lesbian ode (d) The English ode

**53.** Dryden's 'ode on solitude' is an example of
(a) Pindaric ode (b) Horatian ode
(c) Irregular ode (d) None of these

**54.** Romantic ode expresses
(a) personal emotions
(b) emotional and romantic responses
(c) patriotism and national adoration
(d) None of the above

**55.** The greatest writer of victorian ode is
(a) Wordsworth (b) Watson
(c) Collins (d) Tennyson

**56.** 'Ode to West Wind' is written by
(a) Shelley (b) Keats
(c) Wordsworth (d) Tennyson

**57.** 'Couch' is an ode singing of
(a) the old glories of the past
(b) death of the duke of Wellington
(c) celebrations
(d) victory

**58.** Which one is known as the irregular ode?
(a) Strophe (b) Anti-strophe
(c) Epode (d) Cowleyan ode

**59.** Cowleyan ode was established by
(a) Horace (b) Abraham Cowley
(c) Pindar (d) Collins

**60.** John Keats 'Ode to Autumn' is a ............... ode.
(a) Pindaric (b) Horatian
(c) Cowleyan (d) None of these

**61.** Which one is known as the Regular ode?
(a) Strophe (b) Anti strophe
(c) Epode (d) None of these

**62.** Which odes were generally written for public occasions?
(a) Pindaric odes (b) Horatian odes
(c) Cowleyan odes (d) None of these

**63.** What is the most distinctive feature of an ode?
(a) It is longer than a lyric
(b) It is in the form of an address
(c) It is written on a sublime subject
(d) It is written on a historical theme

**64.** Who is the most important poet who has written Pindaric Odes in English?
(a) Thomas Gray (b) John Keats (c) PB Shelley (d) Walter Scott

**65.** Who is the poet of an 'ode to himself'?
(a) Abraham Cowley (b) John Donne
(c) Ben Jonson (d) Robert Herrick

**66.** This is a form of a classical ode
(a) Gray's odes (b) Pindaric ode
(c) Shelley's Adonais (d) None of these

**67.** Odes had originated in religious celebrations and were performed at
(a) festivals and other important occasions
(b) stage
(c) classrooms
(d) parties hall

**68.** Odes normally included the following
(a) Prayers or praise to the Gods
(b) Stories or myth from the heroic past
(c) Moral maxims and personal references
(d) All of the above

## The Lyric

**69.** Lyric is derived from the Greek word
(a) Lyre (b) Lyrika (c) Lyrikos (d) Lirio

**70.** Lyric is a Greek
(a) music (b) rhythm (c) song (d) ode

**71.** Lyric was sung with a musical instrument called
(a) lyre (b) sitar (c) drum (d) gitar

**72.** Lyric is an expression of a
(a) single emotion (b) single music
(c) double thought (d) None of these

**73.** The test of a good lyric is
(a) sincerity (b) variety
(c) morality (d) puerility

**74.** A short singing poem, which expresses a single emotion usually personal, is known as
(a) interlude (b) free verse
(c) lyric (d) epilogue

**75.** Who has written the famous lyrical poem 'L'Allegro'?
(a) Dryden (b) Milton
(c) Donne (d) Cowley

**76.** Which of the following lyrics is written by Robert Herrick?
(a) A Christmas Carol (b) The Gifts of God
(c) Song to Celia (d) Go and Catch a Falling Star

**77.** Lyric was introduced by the great poet
(a) Shakespeare (b) Milton
(c) Sir Thomas Wyatt (d) None of these

**78.** The subject matter of a lyric appeals to
(a) intellect (b) heart
(c) senses (d) brain

**79.** Who define 'lyric' as 'The Perf ect Singing God'
(a) AC Swinburne (b) Coleridge
(c) Tennyson (d) Wordsworth

**80.** ............... is an important element of lyric.
(a) Objectivity (b) Spirituality
(c) Emotions (d) Subjectivity

**81.** The theme of impersonal lyric is
(a) festivals (b) public events
(c) marriage (d) All of these

**82.** Elizabethan lyric is sweet and musical but it characterised by
(a) emotions (b) artificiality
(c) didactic (d) separation

**83.** The Elizabethan lyric is different from the romantic lyric, in terms of its
(a) structure (b) rhyming scheme
(c) spontaneity (d) fixed pattern

**84.** Alliterations and other verbal devices are frequently used to make the lyric
(a) musical (b) more sweet
(c) understandable (d) All of these

**85.** The cavalier poet are great lovers of
(a) history (b) religion
(c) nature (d) modernity

**86.** Among the Romantic lyric, the work of ............... remain unexcelled.
(a) Wordsworth (b) Blake
(c) Keat (d) Shelley

**87.** ............... is a great writer of dramatic lyric.
(a) Tennyson (b) Browning
(c) Milton (d) None of these

**88.** Lyric 'Prospice' is written by
(a) Milton (b) Tennyson
(c) Browning (d) Blake

**89.** 'The Rime of the Ancient Mariner' is written by
(a) ST Coleridge (b) Wordsworth
(c) PB Shelley (d) John Keats

**90.** Modern Lyric covers a wide range of subject and qualities. It is
(a) artificial (b) realistic
(c) grand (d) subjective

## The Satire

**91.** The word satire is derived from
(a) French word (b) Greek word
(c) English word (d) Sanskrit word

**92.** A satire uses what type of characters in satire?
(a) Real character (b) Religious characters
(c) Fictional characters (d) None of these

**93.** The purpose of satire is.......
(a) to make people laugh
(b) to provide philosophical thoughts
(c) just a causal reading
(d) to expose the problem prevailing in society

**94.** The writer users satire in his writing with the intertion of
(a) criticism only
(b) entertaining people
(c) bringing improvement
(d) make people think

**95.** Which are two main components of satire?
(a) Ornamental language and poetry
(b) Irony and humour
(c) Preaching and logical explanation
(d) Use of Lyrics and dramatization

**96.** Which best describes the relationship between Impersonation and satire?
(a) Impersonation and satire are synonyms
(b) Impersonation is a tool of satire
(c) Impersonation is opposite of satire
(d) Satire is a tool of impersonation.

**97.** Which is not a type of satire?
(a) Hovation (b) Juvenalism
(c) Calm (d) Menippean

**98.** Alexander Pope's 'Rape of the Lock' is an example of ......
(a) parody (b) Romantic literature
(c) satire (d) ironic

**99.** Who wrote 'Animal Farm' – (a satire)?
(a) Tennyson (b) Jonathan Swift
(c) George Or Well (d) Bernard Shaw

## ANSWERS

| | | | | | | | | | | | | | | | | | | | |
|---|---|---|---|---|---|---|---|---|---|---|---|---|---|---|---|---|---|---|---|
| 1. | (c) | 2. | (b) | 3. | (d) | 4. | (d) | 5. | (b) | 6. | (d) | 7. | (a) | 8. | (a) | 9. | (b) | 10. | (a) |
| 11. | (a) | 12. | (b) | 13. | (a) | 14. | (a) | 15. | (c) | 16. | (a) | 17. | (d) | 18. | (c) | 19. | (d) | 20. | (b) |
| 21. | (b) | 22. | (a) | 23. | (c) | 24. | (c) | 25. | (c) | 26. | (c) | 27. | (c) | 28. | (d) | 29. | (b) | 30. | (a) |
| 31. | (b) | 32. | (b) | 33. | (d) | 34. | (a) | 35. | (b) | 36. | (c) | 37. | (a) | 38. | (c) | 39. | (c) | 40. | (a) |
| 41. | (a) | 42. | (a) | 43. | (a) | 44. | (a) | 45. | (a) | 46. | (a) | 47. | (a) | 48. | (c) | 49. | (a) | 50. | (a) |
| 51. | (a) | 52. | (c) | 53. | (b) | 54. | (b) | 55. | (d) | 56. | (a) | 57. | (a) | 58. | (d) | 59. | (b) | 60. | (b) |
| 61. | (c) | 62. | (a) | 63. | (b) | 64. | (b) | 65. | (c) | 66. | (b) | 67. | (a) | 68. | (d) | 69. | (c) | 70. | (c) |
| 71. | (a) | 72. | (a) | 73. | (a) | 74. | (c) | 75. | (b) | 76. | (b) | 77. | (c) | 78. | (b) | 79. | (a) | 80. | (d) |
| 81. | (d) | 82. | (b) | 83. | (c) | 84. | (a) | 85. | (c) | 86. | (d) | 87. | (b) | 88. | (c) | 89. | (a) | 90. | (b) |
| 91. | (b) | 92. | (c) | 93. | (d) | 94. | (c) | 95. | (b) | 96. | (b) | 97. | (c) | 98. | (c) | 99. | (c) | | |

Chapter 43

# Indian Writing in English

## Inspired by Western Modals

Indian writing in English has a vibrant history with gigantic expansion globally. In the beginning, the Indian writers were inspired by Western models towards prose, translation, biographies and political essays. The first book in English by an Indian was written in 1793 by Sake Dean Mahomed titled 'The Travels of Dean Mahomed'. The emergence of the Indian English novel underwent assorted phases from imitation, assimilation and finally to genuine self expression. However, most early Indian writing in English was non-fictional work, such as biographies and political essays.

## Bankim Chandra Chatterjee as Father of Indian Novel

The first Indian English novel, titled 'Rajmohan's Wife' was published in the year 1864 by Bankim Chandra Chatterjee, and it marked a significant epoch in the history of Indian writing in English. He is considered to be the father of the novel in Indian literature. The 'Poison Tree' (1873) and 'Krishnakanta's Will' (1878) were other two popular novels of Chatterjee that prompted Krishna Kripalani to compare him with international novelists. Other contributions in this period were Rajlakshmi Devi's 'The Hindu Wife' (1876), 'H. Dutt's Bijoychand' (1888), 'Roshinara' by Kali Krishna Lahiri's (1881) and 'Kshetrapal Chakravarti's Sarata and Hingana (1895).

## Rabindranath Tagore entered into Indian English Writing

This began to change in the late 1800s, when famous Indian authors who wrote mostly in their mother tongue, began to try their hand at writing in English. In the early 1900s, Rabindranath Tagore began translating his works from Bengali to English with the release of his first substantial poems by 1877 and was acclaimed for his best-known works novels, stories, songs, dance-dramas and essays.

## Beginning of Children Stories

Starting in 1917, Dhan Gopal Mukerji wrote many children's stories that were set in India. He was awarded the Newbery medal in 1928 for 'Gay Neck, the Story of a Pigeon'.

## Era of R.K. Narayanan and Mulk Raj Anand

Soon after, a new generation of Indian authors, who wrote almost exclusively in English, hit the bookshelves, beginning in 1935, 'Swami and Friends' by RK Narayan and 'Untouchable by' Mulk Raj Anand's. Raja Rao's 'Kanthapura' followed in 1938. What made Narayan's, Anand's and Rao's writing different from the Indian authors before them was that their stories were about the contemporary man on the street. There was also Indianness to their work, in terms of the words they used and their style of writing. This resonated with the new, but growing ranks of Indians reading English literature. Their works were the forerunners to the magnificent diversity of Indian writing in English that we see today.

## Crusaders of Contemporary and Modern Era

The crusaders of the contemporary and modern era include Salman Rushdie, Amitav Ghosh, Vikram Seth and many more. They elucidate and substantiate strength of the emerging modern voice of India, which has the vibrancy and energy of a gushing artesian along with an unmatched resolve to experiment and explore new avenues of writing novels. A host of contemporary post – colonial writers like Rushdie, Arundhati Roy, Meena Alexander, Anita Nair and Jhumpa Lahiri have initiated the process of decolonising the 'Colonial English' and using it as a medium to express Indian thoughts and sensibilities with a distinctive Indian style.

## National Freedom Movement Inspired Literature in India

The freedom movement spearheaded by Gandhi inspired a flurry of activity in the literary world. There was a flourish of novels in both regional and as well as in the national stream. This burst of energy in regional literature, laid the ground work of fine – tuning and enhancing the vibrancy and the scope of the Indian English Fiction. The dual combination of independent movement and nationalist consciousness gave much impetus and spur to the outflow of novels in which affection for motherland was the crux and this served to invoke the patriotic sentiments of the masses. Post -

independent India also produced number of novels involving the causes and aftermaths of the freedom movement. The novels that belong to this category include A Time to be Happy Nayantara Sahgal (1952), by Khwaja Ahmed Abbas 'Inquilab (1955), 'Waiting for the Mahatma' by Rk Narayan (1955) etc.

## Role of Women Novelists

Women novelists have played a crucial and momentous role in enhancing the quality and quantity of the Indian English Fiction. They have further added the woman's perspective and feministic dimensions to the novels. These rich contributions have widened the spectrum of issues deliberated in the novel.

In the 19th century, more and more women actively participated in India's reformist movement against the British rule. It again led to the women's literature.

At that time, their write - ups mainly concentrated on the country's freedom struggle. Over the years, the world of feminist ideologies began to influence the English literature of India. Among the women writers Sarojini Naidu, the great poetess charmed the readers with her writings. Feminism themes have also been used by authors like Nayantara Sahgal and Rama Mehta. Regional fiction theme has been aptly used by Kamala Das, Anita Nair and Susan Viswanathan. Novelists like Kamala Markandaya and Anita Desai captured the spirit of Indian cultures and its traditional values. During 1990's India became a popular literary nation as a number of women authors made their debut in this era. Chitra Banerjee Divakaruni, Suniti Namjoshi and Anuradha Marwah Roy used realism as main theme of their novels. The novels of authors like Namita Gokhale or Shobha De are really out - spoken.

Most of these female novelists are known for their bold views that are reflected in their novels. Basically, these are the novels of protest and an outburst of reservations and contaminations.

## Indian Literature on the Verge of being the Best Seller

These authors make use of Indian phrases alongside English words and have tried to reproduce a blend of the Indian and the Western cultures.

While Indian poets, novelists, essayists, dramatists have been making momentous and considerable contributions to world literature since the pre-independence era, the past few years have witnessed a thriving of Indian English writing in the global market. The works of Indian authors writing in English are often to be found on the best-seller list. They are also incurring and earning an immense amount of critical fame.

# Practice Questions

**1.** The Jataka stories are related to the previous lives of whom?
(a) Krishna (b) Mahabir
(c) Budha (d) Guru Nanak

**2.** In which year Salman Rushdie cancelled his visit of Jaipur Literature Festival for threats to his life?
(a) 2008 (b) 2010
(c) 2011 (d) 2012

**3.** Wings of Fire is an autobiography of
(a) Indira Gandhi
(b) A. P. J. Abdul Kalam
(c) Subhash Chandra Bose
(d) Pranab Mukherjee

**4.** The fictional South Indian city 'Malgudi' is a creation of
(a) Ruskin Bond (b) Mulk Raj Anand
(c) Rabindranath Tagore (d) RK Narayan

**5.** Who has received the Sahitya Akademi Award for his short story collection, 'Our Trees Still Grow in Dehra?
(a) RK Narayan (b) Chetan Bhagat
(c) Ruskin Bond (d) Anita Desai

**6.** For which book Salman Rushdie won the Booker Prize?
(a) The Satanic Verses
(b) Midnight's Children
(c) Fury
(d) Shalimar the Clown

**7.** In which year Salman Rushdie won the Booker Prize?
(a) 1981 (b) 1984
(c) 1987 (d) 1990

**8.** Which Indian writer is also a member of the US President's Committee on the Arts and Humanities, appointed by US President Barack Obama?
(a) Arundhati Roy (b) VS Naipaul
(c) Jhumpa Lahiri (d) Salman Rushdie

**9.** Where the Head Office of the Sahitya Akademi is located?
(a) Kolkata (b) New Delhi
(c) Lucknow (d) Pune

**10.** In which year National Book Trust was founded?
(a) 1947 (b) 1949
(c) 1952 (d) 1957

**11.** In 2011, who won the Pulitzer Prize for the book 'The Emperor of All Maladies: A Biography of Cancer'?
(a) Siddhartha Mukherjee (b) Geeta Anand
(c) Jhumpa Lahiri (d) Gobind Behari Lal

**12.** Jhumpa Lahiri won the Pulitzer Prize in the section of
(a) Public Service (b) Fiction (c) Poetry (d) Drama

**13.** Who is the author of the book 'Hajar Churashir Maa'?
(a) Aparna Sen (b) Taslima Nasrin
(c) Ashapoorna Devi (d) Mahasweta Devi

**14.** Who was the first elected fellow of Sahitya Akademi Fellowship?
(a) C Rajagopalachari (b) DR Bendre
(c) Dr S Radhakrishnan (d) Gopinath Kaviraj

**15.** Which foundation instituted Saraswati Samman annual award?
(a) KK Birla Foundation
(b) TATA Foundation
(c) Smile Foundation
(d) M Gandhi Foundation

**16.** Who translated the book 'The Story of My Experiments with Truth' written by MK Gandhi from Gujrati to English?
(a) Mahadev Desai (b) JB Kripalani
(c) Mohanlal Pandya (d) Vinoba Bhave

**17.** 'The Autobiography of an Unknown Indian' is an autobiography of
(a) Inder Kumar Gujral
(b) Nirad C. Chaudhuri
(c) Mahatma Gandhi
(d) Jawaharlal Nehru

**18.** Who wrote the famous novel 'Anandamath'?
(a) Sarat Chandra Chattopadhyay
(b) Bankim Chandra Chattopadhyay
(c) Rabindranath Tagore
(d) Michael Madhusudan Dutt

**19.** The first English translation of the Bhagavad Gita was done by
(a) Charles Wilkins
(b) William Jones
(c) Warren Hastings
(d) Henry Thomas Colebrooke

**20.** Who is the first woman to receive Sahitya Akademi Award?
(a) Mahasweta Devi (b) Bani Basu
(c) Ashapoorna Devi (d) Amrita Pritam

**21.** Who is the first winner of Sahitya Akademi Award for Hindi?
(a) Acharya Narendra Dev (b) Nagendra
(c) Makhanlal Chaturvedi (d) Amritlal Nagar

**22.** Indian origin writer VS Naipaul won the Nobel Prize in Literature in the year?
(a) 1998 (b) 2001
(c) 2003 (d) 2008

**23.** Who wrote the the National Anthem of Bangladesh's 'Amar Shonar Bangla'?
(a) Kazi Nazrul Islam
(b) Michael Madhusudan Dutt
(c) Faraaz Kazi
(d) Rabindranath Tagore

**24.** Which Bengali poet is also known as 'Bidrohi Kobi (Rebel Poet)' during independence movement?
(a) Jibanananda Das
(b) Rabindranath Tagore
(c) Kazi Nazrul Islam
(d) Daulat Qazi

**25.** When the famous novel 'Godaan' of Munshi Premchand was first published?
(a) 1930 (b) 1936
(c) 1940 (d) 1942

**26.** What is the other pen name of Munshi Premchand?
(a) Nawab Rai (b) Dhanpat Das
(c) Gopal Sharma (d) Prem Das

**27.** In which novel, the fictitious town 'Malgudi' was first mentioned?
(a) The Bachelor of Arts
(b) The English Teacher
(c) Under the Banyan Tree
(d) Swami and Friends

**28.** From which year Sahitya Akademi Award was started?
(a) 1949 (b) 1951 (c) 1954 (d) 1962

**29.** Satyajit Ray's famous film 'shatranj ke Khilari' is based on a novel written by
(a) Prem Chand (b) RK Narayan
(c) Girish Karnad (d) Anita Desai

**30.** The fictional character 'Mowgli' is the creation of
(a) Ruskin Bond (b) RK Narayan
(c) Mulk Raj Anand (d) Rudyard Kipling

**31.** Which one is the first novel of Chetan Bhagat?
(a) One Night at the Call Center
(b) 2 States
(c) Five Point Someone
(d) The 3 Mistakes of My Life

**32.** The story in the book 'God of Small Things' is based on which state
(a) Goa (b) Kerala
(c) Andhra Pradesh (d) Tamil Nadu

**33.** Who is the writer of of the book 'Train to Pakistan'?
(a) Amrita Pritam (b) Khushwant Singh
(c) Anita Desai
(d) Subodh Javadekar

**34.** Which one is the longest Indian novel ever published in a single volume in the English language?
(a) Revolution 2020
(b) The God of Small Things
(c) A Suitable Boy
(d) Train to Pakistan

**35.** Who is the first women to received Jnanpith Award?
(a) Amrita Pritam (b) Ashapoorna Devi
(c) Mahadevi Verma (d) Mahasweta Devi

**36.** Who is the first winner of Jnanpith Award?
(a) G Sankara Kurup (b) Ashapoorna Devi
(c) Umashankar Joshi (d) Amrita Pritam

**37.** For which book Kiran Desai won the Man Booker Prize?
(a) Life of Pi (b) The White Tiger
(c) Last Orders
(d) The Inheritance of Loss

**38.** Beside Arundhati Roy and Kiran Desai, who is the other one to win Man Booker Prize from India?
(a) Aravind Adiga (b) Amitav Ghosh
(c) Rohinton Mistry (d) Anita Desai

**39.** Who is the writer of the book 'Devdas'?
(a) Satyajit Ray (b) Bankim Chandra Chattopadhyay
(c) Mahasweta Devi
4. Sarat Chandra Chattopadhyay

**40.** Who is the writer of the book 'A Suitable Boy'?
(a) Vikram Seth
(b) Arundhati Roy
(c) Salman Rushdie
(d) Kiran Desai

**41.** Famous Indian writer Dhanpat Rai Srivastav is also known as
(a) Lakshminath Bezbaroa
(b) Rabindranath Tagore
(c) Premchand
(d) Sumitranandan Pant

## ANSWERS

| | | | | | | | | | | | | | | | | | | | |
|---|---|---|---|---|---|---|---|---|---|---|---|---|---|---|---|---|---|---|---|
| 1. | (a) | 2. | (d) | 3. | (b) | 4. | (d) | 5. | (c) | 6. | (b) | 7. | (a) | 8. | (c) | 9. | (b) | 10. | (d) |
| 11. | (a) | 12. | (b) | 13. | (d) | 14. | (c) | 15. | (a) | 16. | (a) | 17. | (b) | 18. | (b) | 19. | (a) | 20. | (d) |
| 21. | (c) | 22. | (b) | 23. | (d) | 24. | (c) | 25. | (b) | 26. | (a) | 27. | (d) | 28. | (c) | 29. | (a) | 30. | (d) |
| 31. | (c) | 32. | (b) | 33. | (b) | 34. | (c) | 35. | (b) | 36. | (a) | 37. | (d) | 38. | (a) | 39. | (d) | 40. | (a) |
| 41. | (c) | | | | | | | | | | | | | | | | | | |

Chapter 44

# Swami and Friends

*R.K Narayan*

## About the Author

RK Narayan is considered as one of leading figures of early Indian literature in English. He was born in Chennai, India in 1906 in a working class South Indian family. His father was a school headmaster and because his father had to be frequently transferred for his job, RK Narayan spent most of his childhood in the loving care of his grandmother, Parvati. It was his grandmother who taught him arithmetic, mythology and Sanskrit. He also attended many different schools in Chennai like Mission Lutheran School, Christian College High School, etc.

He was interested in English literature since he was very young. He was consistently encouraged to involve himself into literature. That is why, after finishing his graduation, he decided to stay at home and write. His work involves novels like: 'The Guide', 'The Financial Man', 'Mr. Sampath', 'The Dark Room', 'The English Teacher', 'A Tiger for Malgudi', etc. RK Narayan won numerous accolades for his literary work: Sahitya Akademi Award, Padma Bhushan, AC Benson Medal by the Royal Society of Literature, honorary membership of the American Academy of Arts and Literature, Padma Vibhushan, etc.

## Summary

'Swami and his Friends' was the first novel of RK Narayan, which he started writing in the autumn of 1930, on a sudden burst of inspiration. It was as if a window had opened, and through it Narayan saw a little town and its railway station, the Mempi Forest and the Nallapa's Grove, the Albert Mission School, Market Road, the River Sarayu. Its inhabitants appeared and Malgudi was born.

'Swami and his Friends' (1935) was published with the help of Graham Greene. The novel describes all the small confusions and dislocations of the child reaching the end of a pleasant childhood and facing the grave tasks of adulthood. The setting that one day swam into Narayan's view was Malgudi, the colonial district town with its post office and bank; middle-class suburb, small roadside shops and low-caste slums, and missionary school and government bungalows. It is the new world of urbanising India that Swami is expected to find his place in. But Swami is essentially a chaotic and amoral Krishna of Hindu epics. It is his great restlessness within this restricted world and the premonitions of the dullness that awaits him which make for that unique mix of 'sadness and beauty'.

Swami feels oppressed by authority of the Christians at school, his strict father but he is also attracted by its promise of stability and identity. His great infatuation is with Rajam, the police officer's son, with his bungalow and toy rail engine: the symbols of the world of colonial progress and modernity that Swami, too, is being asked to enter. That exalted world, once the exclusive preserve of Brahmins, is changing fast: it is no accident that Swami's greatest source of fear in Malgudi is the low-caste, slum-dwelling ball boy at his father's tennis club.

The game of cricket, with its simultaneously rule-bound and anarchic nature, offers Swami, as it does millions of Indians, emotional release from the strains and pressures of adjusting to his ever-altering circumstances. But the captain of the cricket team is Rajam himself, before whom Swami tries hard to pose as a modern rational adult, an act in which even his old affectionate grandmother becomes a shameful embarrassment, someone to hide from, when Rajam visits his house.

When Swami, giving in to his natural rebelliousness, runs away from home just before an important cricket match, he knows not only fear and uncertainty but also guilt. His feeling that he has been irresponsible and cowardly, that he has failed to act like a man, colours the heartbreaking last two pages.

The randomness of events and emotions describes Rajam's departure for the bigger world outside Malgudi. A nervous Swami has gone to the railway station with another grown-up friend, Mani, to see Rajam off. He has a present, 'Andersen's Fairy Tales' for Rajam. But Rajam, whose own attitude towards Swami has alternated between harsh indifference and brisk curiosity, is already remote. The train starts to move; Rajam takes the book but says nothing: childhood has ended for him and he won't prolong it any further for Swami.

Swaminathan and Mani stood as if glued where they were, and watched the train. The small red lamp of the last van could be seen for a long time; it diminished in size every minute, and disappeared around a bend. All the loud, rattling and hissing of the moving train softened in the distance into something that was half a sob and half a sigh. Swaminathan said, "Mani, I am glad he has taken the book. Mani, he waved to me. He was about to say something when the train started. Mani, he did wave to me and to me alone. Don't deny it."

'Yes, yes,' Mani agreed.

Swaminathan broke down and sobbed.

'Swami and his Friends' was at once hailed by critics as a great work of art. The novel describes the rainbow world of childhood and early boyhood of boys of the likes of Swami growing up in the interior of South India. It seems that Narayan's personal experience at school has gone into the making of the novel. We get a vivid portrayal of the thoughts, emotions and activities of school boys. It is as though everyday reality has taken over Narayan's pen and written this universal epic of all our boyhood days.

The novel is remarkable for the author's understanding of child psychology and for his depiction of the carefree, buoyant world of school boys in a most realistic and convincing manner. It renders people and their actions as they appear to boys at school stage. Swami is one of Narayan's immortal creations.

Chandran, Raju, Jagan and others came much after in his fiction. Some writers have the tendency to convert their childhood into shrines and further on they try to mystify their own boyhood. Narayan has consciously avoided that because he never wrote any more tales of boyhood after 'Swami and his Friends'.

In addition to depicting Narayan's skill in characterisation, the novel also highlights the brilliance of his never-cloying humour. Despite minor defects like its looseness in construction, the novel is a remarkable first achievement, and it displays Narayan's peculiar genius to the hilt. Graham Greene, for example, considered it 'A book in ten thousand' and Compton Mackenzie observed that 'he had never read any other book about India in the least like it'.

## Practice Questions

**1.** What is the name of RK Narayan's first novel?
(a) The Bachelor of Arts
(b) The Far Pavilions
(c) Swami and Friends
(d) The Dark Room

**2.** The fictional town of Malgudi is the setting for most of Narayan's novels. However, Malgudi is intended to be a fictionalisation of Narayan's lifelong home, which was
(a) Jodhpur, in Northwestern India
(b) Mumbai (formerly Bombay), on India's West coast
(c) Chennai (formerly Madras), on India's South-East coast
(d) Srinagar, in far Northern India, in the Himalayan mountains

**3.** RK Narayan was one of the first Indian writers to
(a) write novels
(b) write fiction in English
(c) win a nobel prize
(d) write a screen play

**4.** RK Narayan spent most of his childhood in the care of his
(a) parents (b) uncle
(c) grandmother (d) sister

**5.** Which author helped RK Narayan get his novels published?
(a) Graham Greene
(b) Arundhati Roy
(c) James Joyce
(d) Salman Rushdie

**6.** Name Narayan's first novel that was published in 1935.
(a) The Guide (b) Swami and his Friends
(c) The English Teacher
(d) Malgudi Days

**7.** What is the name of fictional town where a lot of Narayan's stories are set ?
(a) Mussoorie (b) Malgudi
(c) Pukhar (d) Eradu

**8.** What is the theme of the novel 'Swami and his Friends'?
(a) Memories of happy childhood
(b) Enforcing discipline
(c) Confusions of a child about to enter adulthood
(d) None of these

**9.** Out of four class friends who makes Swami laugh more than any one else?
(a) Rajam (b) Mani (c) Sankar (d) Samuel (The Pea)

**10.** What are some of the qualities of a boy Rajam which makes him rival of Mani?
(a) Fearlessness (b) Intelligence
(c) Wealth (d) All of these

**11.** On his visit of Rajam's house Swami gets impressed by
(a) Rajam's mother
(b) his big house, and expensive toys
(c) Rajam's father
(d) Rajam's grandmother

**12.** **Why did Swami's friends call him Rajam's tail ?**
(a) Rajam is police officer's son
(b) Rajam helps Swami in home work
(c) Swami is in awe of Rajan and follows him everywhere
(d) Rajam visits Swami's house many times

**13.** **Why does Swami hate Mondays?**
(a) It is discontinuation of fun
(b) Monday means activity, discipline, Class work and Home work
(c) he feels bored and tired after Sunday's fun
(d) he is not interested in studies.

**14.** **What is the name of Swami's class teacher?**
(a) Mr Pillai (b) Mr Ebenezar
(c) Nayagam (d) Mr Mani

**15.** **Why did Swami get a complaint letter written by his father for the head master?**
(a) Complaining against the education system
(b) Complaining against some rowdy boys
(c) Complain against Swami's class teacher
(d) Complain against Fanatic Christian teacher Mr. Ebenezar

**16.** **Which behaviour of Swami's friend's made him very sad?**
(a) They slopped talking to him
(b) They grew hostile towards
(c) Did not share any food with him
(d) both (a) and (b)

**17.** **Swami's grandmother has been described as an old lady who**
(a) talks too much
(b) boasts too much about her past
(c) both (a) and (b)
(d) very affectionate towards Rajam, Swami's friends

**18.** **How did Mani and Swami enjoy at the last day of the school before Summer Vacations?**
(a) By shouting loudly
(b) Dancing
(c) Throwing ink of other boy
(d) Playing Cricket

**19.** **Why did Swami make hectic efforts to procore six paises?**
(a) He wanted to buy a hoop
(b) Coachmen has asked him to get six paise
(c) His friend needed this money
(d) None of the above

**20.** **Which place in the club did Swami find the safest place**
(a) The card room
(b) The library
(c) Tennis court
(d) The restaurant in the club

**21.** **Why did Swami's schooling at Albert Mission School come to a sudden end?**
(a) Swami was beaten mercilessly by the headmaster
(b) Swami's class teacher punished him the whole day
(c) Swami's friends refused to talk to him
(d) He was thrown out of school

**22.** **What was the name suggested by Swami for cricket team which was formed by him and his other two friends ?**
(a) Victory Union Eleven
(b) Malgudi Cricket Club
(c) Chennai Cricket Club
(d) Albert Eleven

# ANSWERS

| | | | | | | | | | | | | | | | | | | | |
|---|---|---|---|---|---|---|---|---|---|---|---|---|---|---|---|---|---|---|---|
| 1. | (c) | 2. | (c) | 3. | (b) | 4. | (c) | 5. | (a) | 6. | (b) | 7. | (b) | 8. | (c) | 9. | (d) | 10. | (d) |
| 11. | (b) | 12. | (c) | 13. | (b) | 14. | (c) | 15. | (d) | 16. | (d) | 17. | (c) | 18. | (c) | 19. | (b) | 20. | (a) |
| 21. | (b) | 22. | (c) | | | | | | | | | | | | | | | | |

Novel

Chapter 45

# The Guide

*R.K Narayan*

## Summary

'The Guide' is a powerful story about spiritual transformation and self-realisation. The narrative itself is both fantastical and comical, as the path the main character, Raju, takes to understanding is not intentional. In essence, Narayan's story shows how a man intent on deception, including self-deception, comes to find clarity based in large part on his life of deception. Raju lives in an old-fashioned village called Malgudi. In Malgudi, Raju aspires to be whatever other people want him to be. As such, he is a chameleon of a character, always becoming someone based on someone's current need. One such example of Raju's malleability is when he begins managing a shop at the Malgudi train station, and is known by the village people as 'Railway Raju.' In this role, Raju bills himself as an expert guide, and professes to be able to obtain any and all items a person is searching for.

One day a couple named Marco and Rosie arrived at Malgudi Railway Station. He took Rosie to watch a Cobra dance as she demanded; Rosie amazed everyone there with her dance by giving a snake girl performance. Raju always praises her dance and spoke out his love for her. He aids her in making the decision to become a professional dancer. His advice pays off, and Rosie soon becomes famous on account of her dancing skills. With this new opportunity, Raju becomes 'Raj,' an influential man with an elevated social standing, thanks to Rosie. Things seem to be looking up for Raju, and yet complications soon arise. Raju eventually ends up in prison because of his machinations. While there, Raju again changes his persona and causes others to not only respect him, but to like him and come to his aid if need to be.

Raju is finally released from prison, but is unsure where to go or what to even do with his life. At this point, Raju takes shelter in an abandoned temple. In this holy place on the banks of the Sarayu River, Raju is able to think a bit more and give himself time to come up with his next plan.

While hiding out in the temple, Raju meets a strange man named Velan. The two begin talking and discussing life, and after a time, Velan actually thinks of Raju as a holy man. With his talent for becoming whatever is beneficial to his circumstances, Raju picks up on Velan's mistake and plays along with the trick. When Raju is later forced to admit that he is not a holy man after all and subsequently must reveal where he is from and who he really is, he is somewhat shocked to find that his admission and guilt, which he initially thought would free him from the burdensome role of a holy man, actually has the opposite effect he was looking for.

His revelation of the truth actually propels him further into the role of a holy man, thus making Raju's malleability a path that has brought him to this point, the true incarnation of a 'Swamiji,' a holy man. The reader sees in the narrative that, at this point in Raju's transformation, he is finally able to overcome his previous need to be whatever people wanted him to be. He no longer needs to be everything to everybody, and has come to a place where he genuinely serves others from a place of selflessness. At this moment, his past endeavours, including his ties to Malgudi, prison, Rosie, and fame, all peel away. Raju sees himself for what he truly is, just another individual. With this clarity, he is now able to help others without an ulterior motive. His path has become clear, and he follows it selflessly.

Raju's transition from con man to holy man is both comical and didactic. Narayan's narrative shows how people can be destined for great things without even realiszing it. At the same time, it shows how people's pasts are not entirely what defines them. People can change and do good in life.

They can go from self-centered individuals to people of character, like Raju. Ultimately, perhaps, the narrative shows that there are often greater forces at work than what mankind perceives in a moment of choice, whether a good choice or not. There is hope for mankind, despite outward appearances. Raju's journey is testament to this hope.

## Practice Questions

**1. Where did Rosie and Marco stay?**
(a) In Room 28 (b) In Room 67
(c) In Room 74 (d) In Room 32

**2. Who arrives at the temple during Raju's hunger strike?**
(a) Nalini (b) His mother (c) The press (d) Marco

**3. What sentence did Raju receive at his trial?**
(a) Two years in prison
(b) Two months in prison
(c) Two years in prison with six months of community service
(d) Two months in prison and one year probation

**4. What was Marco's view of Rosie's passion?**
(a) He thought it was nice but unnecessary
(b) He encouraged it
(c) He forbid it (d) He was bored by it

**5. Who do the children convince to accompany them to the temple?**
(a) The village officials
(b) Children from a neighbouring village
(c) The village elders
(d) Their parents

**6. What did Raju begin selling in the railway shop?**
(a) Umbrella (b) Used school books
(c) Guide books (d) Train tickets

**7. What did Raju receive in the mail that he tried to keep from Nalini?**
(a) Divorce papers from Marco
(b) A copy of Marco's book
(c) A poor review of Nalini's performance
(d) A set of blackmail pictures

**8. What is Raju's favorite season?**
(a) The harvesting season (b) The planting season
(c) The rainy season (d) The dry season

**9. What does Raju notice around the temple?**
(a) The river rises to a record high
(b) The villagers are ill
(c) It fails to rain
(d) It becomes increasingly muggy

**10. What did Raju promise his mother when he took on his new job?**
(a) He would always provide for her
(b) She would never have to worry again
(c) She could visit him at his new job
(d) He would still look after the railway shop

**11. What does Raju's role become at the temple?**
(a) Praying in silence for long periods of time
(b) Teaching the parents about life and spiritual matters
(c) Teaching the children when the school master is away
(d) Keeping order in the temple

**12. What nickname did Raju have at the railway?**
(a) Railway Raj (b) Rail-Raj
(c) Raju of the Rails (d) Railway Raju

**13. What kills the crocodile?**
(a) A hunter (b) Dehydration (c) Raju (d) Disease

**14. How much money does the cattle herder earn?**
(a) A total of 4 annas a month
(b) 4 annas a week per home
(c) A total of 4 annas a week
(d) 4 annas a month per home

**15. How does Velan respond to hearing the truth about Raju?**
(a) He is unswayed in his devotion
(b) He riots against the Swami
(c) He is shocked into disbelief
(d) He feels deeply betrayed

**16. What is found in the crocodile?**
(a) A medal (b) Ten thousand rupees
(c) An heirloom (d) Jewelry

**17. What role did Raju's uncle play in the family?**
(a) He cleaned up after the family
(b) He handled all of the family's affairs
(c) He was the black sheep of the family
(d) He bought homes for all of the children

**18. Who gave Raju his nickname?**
(a) The station master (b) The travellers
(c) His father (d) Himself

**19. Who offers Raju an update on the village violence?**
(a) Velan's uncle (b) Velan's sister
(c) Velan's brother (d) Velan's nephew

**20. What does Raju tell the villagers to do about the new conditions in the village?**
(a) There is nothing they can do
(b) Chant at the temple
(c) Bring more offerings
(d) Pray harder

**21. Who was Raju's assistant?**
(a) Mani (b) Jabar
(c) Indyana (d) Alexander

**22. What was Raju's fate after he became preoccupied with Rosie?**
(a) He lost all other relationships
(b) He finally found peace
(c) He lost his business
(d) He was assaulted by Marco

**23. Who did Raju ask for a loan to pay the creditor?**
(a) Rosie (b) Gaffur
(c) His mother (d) His uncle

**24. How did Raju propose raising money to pay the creditor?**
(a) He suggested getting a job at the barber shop
(b) He suggested robbing the station master
(c) He suggested selling his home
(d) He suggested making money from Rosie's dancing

**25.** What business decision did Raju make after his father passed?
(a) He expanded the current shop
(b) He opened another shop
(c) He closed the hut shop
(d) He hired more help

**26.** Before joining Raju on the steps of the temple, what does Velan do?
(a) Ask Raju's permission to join him
(b) Introduce himself
(c) Pick berries for them to share
(d) Wash in the river

**27.** What town had Velan been visiting before meeting Raju?
(a) Mangal (b) Madras (c) Malgudi (d) Mysore

**28.** Why was Velan out of town?
(a) He was conducting business
(b) He was seeking medicine
(c) He was visiting the carnival
(d) He was visiting family

**29.** What does the barber deduce about Raju?
(a) He recently left jail (b) He robbed a man
(c) He was in an accident (d) He left his wife

**30.** What did Raju dislike about his last residence?
(a) He couldn't handle the extreme temperatures
(b) He loathed waking early in the morning
(c) He disliked the hard work it required
(d) He despised the other residents

**31.** What is the name of Raju's love interest?
(a) Meena (b) Lalitha
(c) Rosie (d) Devi

**32.** What is said to be hiding in the river?
(a) A murderer (b) Raju
(c) A crocodile (d) A water monster

**33.** What does Raju offer the boy by the river?
(a) An apple (b) A plantain
(c) A kiwi (d) A mango

**34.** Where did Raju and Marco meet?
(a) At the railway station (b) At the barber shop
(c) At the market (d) In jail

**35.** Where did Raju's father work?
(a) At the doctor's office
(b) In his own shop
(c) In the market square
(d) At the railway station

**36.** What did Raju's father purchase to go with the jutka?
(a) A horse (b) A basket
(c) A farm pen (d) A money bag

**37.** What does Velan give Raju in appreciation of helping his sister?
(a) A book of prayers (b) A fruit tray
(c) A bag of gold (d) A statue of a God

**38.** Where did Raju learn the story that he tells Velan in the temple?
(a) From his mother
(b) From his father
(c) From his cousin
(d) From his grandmother

**39.** How did Raju's mother describe their animals?
(a) A strict commodity (b) As joyous company
(c) A sufficient bother (d) A necessary evil

**40.** What was Raju's punishment from his father?
(a) He had to attend school
(b) He had to leave India for a month
(c) He had to go without dinner
(d) He was slapped by his father

**41.** How does Raju propose solving the problem of educating the children?
(a) He offers to teach the children
(b) He offers to hire a school teacher
(c) He is willing to help on their farms
(d) He suggests the children could be educated in the evenings

**42.** How did Raju feel about his affair with Rosie?
(a) Blessed (b) Insecure
(c) Lucky (d) Entitled

**43.** Who did become friends of Raju in the beginning of Chapter 5?
(a) Gideon (b) Geoffery
(c) Garison (d) Gaffur

**44.** To whom does Velan's sister agree to marry?
(a) Her uncle
(b) Her cousin
(c) Her brother
(d) Her neighbour

**45.** When Raju and Velan meet, what does Velan say that causing him problems?
(a) His business associate (b) His mother
(c) His wife (d) His step-sister

**46.** What is a jutka?
(a) A piece of money (b) A fruit
(c) A taxi (d) An animal

**47.** What lesson did Raju learn around the railway?
(a) Conning money out of passengers
(b) Anticipating the passengers'needs
(c) Where to hide at the station
(d) How to sneak onto a train without passage

**48.** What does Velan's sister claim Raju has to do to change someone?
(a) Look at them
(b) Speak to them
(c) Lay hands on them
(d) Bless them

**49.** Why did Raju's father punish him by the railway?
(a) He used foul language
(b) He stole from the railway
(c) He tried to run away
(d) He punched another child

**50.** What industrial progress was finally made in Chapter 3?

(a) The railway was finished
(b) The cotton gin was used
(c) An assembly line began in the factory
(d) Cars made an appearance in the streets

**51.** What new nickname does Raju earn from the villagers?

(a) Sensei (b) Swami (c) Holy One (d) Buddha

**52.** How much did Raju owe the creditor?

(a) 250 rupees (b) 6000 rupees
(c) 100 rupees (d) 8000 rupees

**53.** Where did Nalini live at the end of Chapter 10?

(a) Malgudi (b) Mysore (c) Malasia (d) Madras

**54.** Where did Marco spend his time?

(a) In Mempi (b) In Mangala
(c) In Malgudi (d) In Mysore

**55.** What job at the railway did R=aju inherit in Chapter 3?

(a) Directing passengers
(b) Running the station shop
(c) Sweeping the station floor
(d) Driving a train

**56.** What did Raju's father get permission to do at the railway?

(a) Ride for free
(b) Polish the trains
(c) Open a shop at the station
(d) Pass out newspapers

**57.** What job did Raju take on in Chapter 5?

(a) Snake charmer
(b) Professional tour guide
(c) Station master
(d) School master

## ANSWERS

| | | | | | | | | | | | | | | | | | | | |
|---|---|---|---|---|---|---|---|---|---|---|---|---|---|---|---|---|---|---|---|
| 1. | (a) | 2. | (c) | 3. | (a) | 4. | (c) | 5. | (d) | 6. | (b) | 7. | (b) | 8. | (c) | 9. | (c) | 10. | (d) |
| 11. | (b) | 12. | (d) | 13. | (b) | 14. | (d) | 15. | (a) | 16. | (d) | 17. | (b) | 18. | (b) | 19. | (c) | 20. | (a) |
| 21. | (a) | 22. | (b) | 23. | (c) | 24. | (b) | 25. | (d) | 26. | (d) | 27. | (a) | 28. | (d) | 29. | (a) | 30. | (b) |
| 31. | (c) | 32. | (c) | 33. | (b) | 34. | (a) | 35. | (b) | 36. | (a) | 37. | (b) | 38. | (a) | 39. | (c) | 40. | (a) |
| 41. | (d) | 42. | (b) | 43. | (d) | 44. | (b) | 45. | (d) | 46. | (c) | 47. | (b) | 48. | (a) | 49. | (a) | 50. | (a) |
| 51. | (b) | 52. | (d) | 53. | (d) | 54. | (a) | 55. | (b) | 56. | (c) | 57. | (b) | | | | | | |

Chapter 46

# The Lost Child

*Mulk Raj Anand*

## About the Author

Mulk Raj Anand was the born in Peshawar to Lal Chand—a coppersmith and soldier—and Ishwar Kaur. From an early age, Mulk Raj Anand was pained by the problems of Indian society that stemmed from the issues of religion and caste.

He began to write from a young age; some of his early works were inspired by the love he had for a Muslim girl who was unfortunately already married. He was also angered by the suicide of a relative who had been ostracized for sharing food with a Muslim. These events inspired him to vent his frustration through words.

He went to Khalsa College, Amritsar, and then to the University of Punjab from where he graduated in 1924. While at the college, he became involved in the non co–operation Movement in 1921 and was imprisoned for a short while.

Thereafter, he went to University College, London on a scholarship before enrolling at the Cambridge University. He earned his PhD in 1929. In England, he actively became involved in left wing politics.

### Career

He became a writer in English language as English language publishers were more open to publish the kind of themes he wrote on. His writing career began in England where he used to publish short reviews in TS Eliot's magazine, 'Criterion'.

During the 1930s and 1940s, he was very active in politics and spoke regularly at the meetings of India League which was founded by Krishna Menon.

Over this period he became acquainted with the likes of intellectuals, such as, Bertrand Russell and Michael Foot, and authors like Henry Miller and George Orwell. He was deeply influenced by MK Gandhi.

His first novel, 'Untouchable' was published by the British firm, Wishart in 1935. The story was about a day in the life of Bakha, a boy who has to become a toilet cleaner just because he belongs to the untouchable caste. The novel was seen as a poignant reminder of the atrocities of the caste system in India.

In 1935, he played an important role in the founding of the Progressive Writers' Association in London along with the writers Sajjad Zaheer and Ahmed Ali.

His heart wrenching novel 'Two Leaves and a Bud' (1937) again dealt with the way the lower caste people are exploited in India. It was the story of a poor peasant who is brutally killed by a British officer who tries to rape his daughter.

He joined the International Brigade in the Spanish Civil War in 1937. As a socialist, he wrote numerous articles and essays on Marxism, Fascism, Indian independence and other political issues.

In 1939, he began lecturing in literature and philosophy at the London County Council Adult Educational Schools and the Workers' Educational Association where he taught till 1942.

In 1939, he wrote 'The Village', which was the first part of the trilogy that would include the novels 'Across the Black Waters' (1940) and 'The Sword and the Sickle' (1942). The trilogy was about was about a rebellious adolescent and his experiences in the World War I.

Throughout the 1930s and 1940s, he divided his time between London and India. At both places he was involved in politics—he was associated with the British Labour Party as well as the Indian National Congress.

Anand worked as a broadcaster and scriptwriter in the film division of the BBC in London during the World War II. He returned to India after the war. He founded the fine-arts magazine, 'Marg' in 1946.

He spent the next several years from 1948 to 1966 teaching at various universities. During the 1960s he served as Tagore Professor of Literature and Fine Art at the University of Punjab. He served as the fine art chairman at Lalit Kala Akademi from 1965 to 1970. He also became the president of Lokayata Trust in 1970.

## Summary

### Fair Held in the Festival of Spring

A child along with his parents went to a fair in the village during the spring festival. Large number of people were going towards the fair by different modes of transport. The little boy ran between his parent's legs full of laughter and enjoyment. He was very excited.

### Child's Desire for Toys

As the child passed in front of a toy shop, his attention was drawn to the varied toys displayed there and he stopped for a while. He was asked by his parents to come with them which he obeyed but his eyes were struck on the beautiful toys. He knew his father would not buy any toy for him, yet he expressed his wish to buy a particular toy. He was asked to come ahead and was shown colourful mustards field which spread far and wide.

The fields also had dragonflies and butterflies. The child was mesmerised by the natural beauty spread around and forgot his demand for toys.

### The Actual Fair

Inside the fair, there were many attractions like sweets (*barfi*) balloons, garlands etc. The child also desired to have all these things but was refused by the parents.

A juggler was playing a flute to a snake which was coiled in a basket. The child wanted to have a closer look at the snake but was asked by his parents to come with them. There was a huge crowd at a swing where people of all age groups were enjoying going round and round. The shrieks and laughter of people sitting on the swing tempted the child and he asked his parents to allow him to ride on it.

### The Child Gets Lost

When the child did not get any answer, he turned, but, there was no sign of his parents. He looked for them all around him, in front, both sides, behind, but they were not to be seen anywhere. The child started crying very loudly shouting father-mother. He ran from one place to another crying and shouting, he looked for them near the grass, near a shrine which was very crowded. The child got so frightened that he kept running between the legs of people looking for his parents.

### Helped by a Stranger

A man, who was a stranger to the child, took notice of the crying child, picked him up in his arms and asked him many questions to find out how he was lost.

### Behaviour of the Lost Child

The man tried to calm down the child. He offered to take him on the roundabout. However, the child declined. The man also offered and took him to the juggler, to the horse, to the sweet shop, to the balloon shop to the flower seller's shop but all in vain.

Incidentally, these were the things which the child had demanded from his parents. But, now when he had lost his parents, he showed no interest in any of these things. He just wanted his parents. Nothing was more important to him at that time.

## Practice Questions

**1. What festival were the people going to celebrate?**
(a) The festival of Holi
(b) The festival of Spring
(c) The festival of Dussehra
(d) The festival of Diwali

**2. How were the people dressed for the festival?**
(a) Shabbily (b) Gaily
(c) Carelessly (d) Scantily

**3. How were the people going to the festival?**
(a) Going on foot
(b) Riding on horses
(c) Carried in bamboo and bullock carts
(d) All of the above

**4. To whom was the little boy going?**
(a) With his father
(b) With his mother
(c) With his father and mother
(d) None of the above

**5. How was the little boy feeling while going to the fair?**
(a) Nervous
(b) Frightened
(c) Sad and unhappy
(d) Full of life and laughter

**6. What did the parents say when the child lagged behind?**
(a) Come, child, come
(b) Come, or you'll be lost
(c) Come, have these toys
(d) Come, we're getting late

**7. What did the child do when his parents said, 'Come, child, come'?**
(a) He refused to move
(b) He hurried towards them
(c) He looked at them angrily
(d) He began to cry

**8. What did the father do when the child said, 'I want that toy'?**
(a) He at once bought the toy for the child
(b) He said, 'Look, child, what is before you!
(c) He looked at the child red-eyed
(d) He began to beat the child

**9. What did the mother do when the child said, 'I want that toy'?**
(a) She asked the father to buy that toy for the child
(b) She looked at the child red-eyed
(c) She said they had no money for the toy
(d) She said, 'Look, child, what is there before you!'

**10. How did the flowering mustard-field look?**
(a) White like silver
(b) Red like a rose
(c) Pale like melting gold
(d) Lovely like a rainbow

**11. What did the child do as they passed by the mustard-field?**
(a) He collected some flowers
(b) He ran after butterflies and caught some of them
(c) He would try to catch dragon-flies as one of them settled down to rest there
(d) He lay down to rest there

**12. Who said to the child, "Come, child, come, come on to the footpath"?**
(a) The father
(b) The mother
(c) Both the father and the mother
(d) Neither the father nor the mother

**13. What was it that attracted the child on the footpath?**
(a) The butterflies (b) The dragon-flies
(c) The doves
(d) The little insects and worms

**14. What did the parents do when they reached a shady grove?**
(a) They collected some flowers for the child
(b) They lay down to rest for some time
(c) They sat down on the edge of a well
(d) They listened to the cooing of doves

**15. What happened as the child entered the grove?**
(a) A shower of young flowers fell on him
(b) A dove flew above his head
(c) His father started shouting at him
(d) His mother collected some flowers for him

**16. What did the child start doing when a shower of young flowers fell on him?**
(a) He started collecting the flowers from the ground
(b) He started gathering the raining petals in his hands
(c) He started dancing with joy
(d) He started climbing up the flowering tree

**17. What did the child do when he heard the cooing of doves in the grove?**
(a) He started cooing like the doves
(b) He tried to catch the doves
(c) He ran towards his parents shouting, 'The dove! The dove!'
(d) He told his parents that he wanted to have the dove

**18. What shop was there at the entrance of the fair?**
(a) A toy shop (b) A balloon shop
(c) A sweetmeat-shop (d) A flower shop

**19. What was the child's favourite sweet?**
(a) Gulab Jamun (b) Rasagulla
(c) Burfi (d) Jalebi

**20. What did the child say as they passed by sweetmeat-shop?**
(a) He said, 'I want that burfi'
(b) He said, 'I want that jalebi'
(c) He said, 'I want that rasagulla'
(d) He said, 'I want that gulab jamun

**21.** **The child asked for toy but then he moved on without waiting for an answer. Why?**
(a) He knew his plea would not be heeded
(b) He knew his parents were poor
(c) He knew his parents had no money
(d) He knew it was bad to be greedy

**22.** **What did the child want to have at the flower-shop?**
(a) A garland of roses (b) A garland of violets
(c) A garland of gulmohar (d) A garland of lilies

**23.** **The child asked for a garland of flowers but then he moved on without waiting for an answer. Why?**
(a) He knew his parents would refuse to buy him those flowers
(b) He knew his parents would say they were cheap flowers
(c) Both (a) and (b) above
(d) Neither (a) nor (b)

**24.** **The child wanted to have balloons yet he walked on. Why?**
(a) He knew his parents would never buy him the balloons
(b) He knew his parents would say he was too old to play with such toys
(c) Both (a) and (b) above
(d) Neither (a) nor (b)

**25.** **The child was attracted by the music of the snake-charmer, yet he moved on. Why?**
(a) His parents had forbidden him to hear such coarse music
(b) His parents were saying, "Come, child, come"
(c) The child was afraid of the cobra
(d) The child did not want to be left behind

**26.** **At what point in the fair did the child lose his parents?**
(a) At the sweetmeat-shop (b) At the flower-shop
(c) At the balloon-seller's (d) At the roundabout

**27.** **What did the child do when he didn't find his parents with him?**
(a) He cried, 'Father, Mother'
(b) He ran here and there in all directions
(c) Both (a) and (b)
(d) Neither (a) nor (b)

**28.** **What did the lost child say when a man asked him, 'Whose baby are you?'**
(a) The child said, 'I want my father, I want my mother'
(b) The child said, 'I want to go home'
(c) The child said, 'I live in a village'
(d) The child said, 'I am feeling hungry'

## ANSWERS

| | | | | | | | | | | | | | | | | | | | |
|---|---|---|---|---|---|---|---|---|---|---|---|---|---|---|---|---|---|---|---|
| 1. | (b) | 2. | (b) | 3. | (d) | 4. | (c) | 5. | (d) | 6. | (a) | 7. | (b) | 8. | (c) | 9. | (d) | 10. | (c) |
| 11. | (c) | 12. | (b) | 13. | (d) | 14. | (c) | 15. | (a) | 16. | (b) | 17. | (c) | 18. | (c) | 19. | (c) | 20. | (a) |
| 21. | (a) | 22. | (c) | 23. | (b) | 24. | (c) | 25. | (a) | 26. | (d) | 27. | (c) | 28. | (a) | | | | |

# PRACTICE PAPERS

# MADHYA PRADESH

## Higher Secondary Teacher Eligibility Test

# Practice Paper 1

**1.** The ....... still has not taken our order.
(a) porter (b) manager
(c) waiter (d) shopkeeper

**2.** The Nile is the longest of all the .......
(a) lakes (b) oceans (c) seas (d) rivers

**3.** The eggs are sold by .......... dozen.
(a) a (b) an
(c) the (d) None of these

**4.** Last month we went to see .......... National book fair with our teacher.
(a) Some (b) the (c) a (d) an

**5.** ............ you like to have tea or coffee?
(a) Could (b) Would (c) Can (d) Will

**6.** We ............ respect our parents.
(a) must (b) should (c) ought to (d) will

**7.** The professional .............. doesn't follow ethics cannot be considered a professional.
(a) which he (b) who
(c) who he (d) whose

**8.** Do you know where I can take the bus .............. goes to Chandigarh?
(a) which (b) when
(c) who (d) that

**9.** He said, "I do not wish to see any of you, go away."
(a) He said that he had not wished to see any of them and ordered them to go away.
(b) He said that he did not wish to see any of them and ordered them to go away.
(c) He told that he did not wish to see any of them and ordered them to go away.
(d) He said that he does not wish to see any of us and ordered us to go away.

**10.** He said to her, "What a cold day!"
(a) He told her that it was a cold day.
(b) He exclaimed that it was a cold day.
(c) He exclaimed sorrowfully that it was a cold day.
(d) He exclaimed that it was a very cold day.

**11.** My neighbour said to me, "I am going out for a few days."
In reported speech the above sentence will be
My neighbour told me that
(a) he was going out for a few days
(b) he is going out for a few days
(c) he will go out for a few days
(d) we are going out for a few days

**12.** Choose the correct indirect speech of the italicised sentence from the options given below.
"What are you doing old man?" said the king.
(a) The king told the old man that what he was doing.
(b) The king asked the old man what he was doing.
(c) The king asked what the old man is doing.
(d) The king told the old man what he was doing.

**13.** One's promises must be kept.
(a) One's promises must keep.
(b) One's promises were kept.
(c) One's promises are kept.
(d) One must keep one's promises.

**14.** Fill in the blank to complete sentence in passive voice.
A number of plays were written .......... Shakespeare.
(a) from (b) of (c) in (d) by

**15.** Choose the synonym of the word 'malady' from the alternative given below.
(a) Disease (b) Melody
(c) Joy (d) Comedy

**16.** Choose the synonym for the word 'derogatory.'
(a) Resolution (b) Solace
(c) Humiliating (d) Forlorn

**17.** Choose the antonym of the word 'Blemish'.
(a) Stigma (b) Strength
(c) Adornment (d) Bolt

**18.** Choose the antonym of the word Dismal.
(a) Dreadful (b) Gloomy (c) Jovial (d) Cheerful

**19.** Our guest speaker this week is ............ writer Mr. Chetan Bhagat.
(a) eminent (b) imminent
(c) iminent (d) None of these

**20.** Our ............ concern is that the project may not be completed before the June dead line.
(a) principle (b) principal
(c) principel (d) None of these

**21.** An office with no work, but high pay.
(a) Honorary (b) Sinecure
(c) Ex-officio (d) Reticent

**22.** One who deserts his religion.
(a) Deserter (b) Apostate
(c) Opportunist (d) Turn coat

**23.** The boy's allergy to dust caused his skin to ......... .
(a) itch (b) rub
(c) blemish (d) flush

**24.** I would like to ........ touch with my friends but I have so little time.
(a) be in (b) be out (c) lose (d) keep in

**25.** Which word below contains a prefix?
(a) Uncle (b) Unhappy
(c) Under (d) Understand

**26.** What is the suffix in the word Reformation?
(a) on (b) mation
(c) ation (d) ion

**Directions** (Q. Nos. 27-33) *Read the following passage carefully and answer the questions that follow.*

In spite of all the honours that we heaped upon him, Pasteur, as has been said, remained simple at heart. Perhaps the imagery of his boyhood days, when he drew the familiar scenes of his birthplace and the longing to be a great artist, never wholly left him. In truth he did become a great artist, though after his sixteenth year he abandoned the brush forever.

Like every artist of worth, he put his whole soul and energy into his work and it was this very energy that in the end wore him out. For to him, each sufferer was more than just a case that was to be cured. He looked upon the fight against hydrophobia as a battle and he was absorbed in his determination to win. The sight of injured children, particularly, moved him to an indescribable extent. He suffered with his patients and yet he would not deny himself a share in that suffering. His greatest grief was when sheer physical exhaustion made him give up his active work. He retired to the estate of Villeneuve Etang, where he had his Kennels for the study of rabies and there he passed his last summer, as his great biographer, Vallery Robot, has said, "practicing the gospel virtues."

The attitude of this man to the science, he had done so much to perfect, can be best summed up in a sentence that he is reputed once to have uttered, concerning the materialism of many of his contemporaries in similar branches of learning to his own: "the more I contemplate the mysteries of nature, the more my faith becomes like that of a peasant." But even then, in retirement he loved to see his former pupils, and it was then he would reiterate his life's principles: 'Work,' he would say, "never cease to work." He passed as simply as a child, the greatest man France had ever produced, derived from a plebiscite among the French people. Napoleon, the idol of France was placed fifth. No greater tribute could have been given to Louis Pasteur, the tanner's son, the scientist, the man of peace and the patient worker for humanity.

**27.** What advice Pasteur always gave to his pupils?
(a) Never to stop working
(b) To work according to one's health
(c) Work and rest at the same time
(d) Work to earn money

**28.** How did Pasteur engage himself in the estate?
(a) He took enough rest as he was very exhausted
(b) Conducted study on rabies
(c) Practiced the Gospel Virtues
(d) Both (b) and (c)

**29.** How did Pasteur view those who suffered from diseases?
(a) He gave them best treatment
(b) As subjects of pity
(c) The sufferer was more than just a case for him
(d) He dealt carefully not to give pain in wounded areas

**30.** Give one word for the phrase- Vote by the people of the country to decide a matter of national importance.
(a) Election (b) Plebiscite
(c) Hydrophobia (d) Contemporaries

**31.** Who was ranked fifth after the achievements of Louis Pasteur?
(a) Napoleon (b) Hitler
(c) Nelson Mandela (d) Thomas Addison

**32.** Even accolades and honours did not change the simple man that Pasteur was
(a) because he did not like false praises
(b) he was very simple and child like at heart
(c) he wanted more than what he had achieved
(d) he was very egoistic

**33.** Opposite word for 'humanity' is
(a) callousness (b) early man
(c) homogeneous (d) people

**34.** Why do we need to use abbreviations during note making along with key?
(a) Saves times
(b) While reading able to understand abbreviation.
(c) It is part of question on note-making
(d) Both (b) and (c)

**35.** What points should be kept in mind while making summary?
(a) Write in your own language in required word limit
(b) Combine all main headings
(c) Use headings of notes to make summaries
(d) Write one part of the passage

**36.** When was Jane Austen born?
(a) 16th, December 1775 (b) 16th, October 1775
(c) 16th, December 1776 (d) None of these

**37.** When did Austen meet Tom?
(a) When she was 17 (b) When she was 20
(c) When she was 30
(d) None of the above

**38.** A Tale of Two Cities was published in weekly installments from April to November of what year?
(a) 1845 (b) 1859
(c) 1879 (d) 1890

**39.** What sound does Lucie often hear echoing off the street when she is in her home?
(a) Footsteps
(b) Brawling
(c) The yells of the crowd at public executions
(d) A choir singing

**40.** What was the first lesson that Dev's first day in London taught him?
(a) One should not sleep with windows open
(b) Who wants tea must get up and make it
(c) One should not go to bed early in London
(d) One should have sufficient warm clothings

**41.** Who is Dev in the novel?
(a) He is the brother of Adit
(b) He is the husband of Sarah
(c) He is a friend of Adit who has come to London for high is studies
(d) He is the one who provides shelter to Adit in London

**42.** Khushwant went abroad for further studies for ............ years.
(a) two (b) five (c) three (d) four

**43.** What was peculiar about 'the last evening'?
(a) Grandmother did not pray (b) Grandmother did not speak
(c) Grandmother had fever (d) Grandmother kept sleeping

**44.** Nicola is
(a) an old man (b) a youngman
(c) a middle-aged man (d) None of these

**45.** Who was the father of the theatre of ideas in England?
(a) Shaw (b) Galsworthy
(c) WB Yeats (d) None of these

**46.** How long have Prospero and Miranda been on their island?
(a) Ten years (b) Fifteen years
(c) Twelve years (d) One day

**47.** What was the name of Caliban's mother?
(a) Ariel (b) Claribel (c) Sycorax (d) Setebos

**48.** Which character speaks the first line of the play?
(a) Bernardo (b) Francisco (c) Hamlet (d) Horatio

**49.** In which of the following years was Hamlet most likely written?
(a) 1570 (b) 1601 (c) 1581 (d) 1610

**50.** Rabindranath Tagore married Bhabtarini Devi in 1883. How was she known later on?
(a) Mallika Devi (b) Mrinalini Devi
(c) Aparna (d) Suchitra

**51.** In which year was Rabindranath Tagore awarded Nobel Prize for Literature?
(a) 1901 (b) 1913 (c) 1928 (d) 1930

**52.** How should we treat the down–trodden people?
(a) We should punish them
(b) They should be forced to worship God
(c) They should be neglected
(d) We should give them support, love and care

**53.** What should we learn before bowing our heads in prayer?
(a) to bow in humility
(b) to offer flowers upon the feet of God
(c) to bow against the priest
(d) to ligts the candles

**54.** 'Pourest thy full heart' In profuse strains of unpremediated art.'
To which bird are these lines addressed by Shelley?
(a) Raven (b) Nightingale
(c) Skylark (d) Cuckoo

**55.** How does the speaker compare the Skylark to a 'high born maiden'?
(a) The Maiden has beauty like the bird's song
(b) They both are up high where they are out of sight
(c) The Maiden gives her heart as a Skylark sings with their heart
(d) The poet does not make this comparison

**56.** What does 'The mournful night' in the poem mean?
(a) Period of dominance and suppression
(b) Period of Femines
(c) Drought period
(d) Period of Sati (Women sacrifice) Culture

**57.** Who in the poem will not ignore the call of liberty?
(a) The women
(b) The Indians
(c) The British
(d) The bruised and suppressed intellectuals

**58.** The poet saw ........... daffodils.
(a) a few (b) white
(c) blue (d) a large number of

**59.** When the poet was looking at the daffodils, ............
(a) he felt sad to see them
(b) he was totally lost in their beauty
(c) he thought they were ugly
(d) he felt like dancing

**60.** French Revolution began in
(a) 1798 (b) 1780 (c) 1786 (d) 1789

**61.** When did Wordsworth received his B.A. degree?
(a) 1790 (b) 1792 (c) 1789 (d) 1791

**62.** According to the speaker, nature is a valuable to
(a) resource (b) teacher (c) mother (d) leader

**63.** Bacan's essays was written in
(a) French and English (b) Latin and French
(c) Latin and English (d) Greek and Latin

**64.** The instrument that the Solitary Reaper was using
(a) a spade (b) an axe (c) a sickle (d) a knife

**65.** How does the poet know that the song is melancholy when he cannot understand the words?
(a) From the girl's expression
(b) From the words of the song
(c) From the tune
(d) From her dress

**66.** How many times was frost awarded Pultizer prize?
(a) One (b) Two
(c) Four (d) None at all

**67.** When was the poem 'After Apple Picking' written?
(a) 1897 (b) 1902
(c) 1914 (d) 1920

**68.** This poem might have special relevance for a student if he is.....
(a) planning a move to the country
(b) deciding which college to attend
(c) concerned about the environment
(d) managing his time to study

**69.** What does the narrator decide to do?
(a) take the second road (b) take the well travelled road
(c) save the decision for later (d) not to travel anymore

**70.** Why could the poet not stop to enjoy the beauty of the scene?
(a) he had promised someone to return
(b) he had miles to go
(c) he had a long way to go
(d) he was in a hurry

**71.** 'My little horse must think it queer'. What does the word 'queer' mean here?
(a) strange (b) pleasant (c) nice (d) evening

**72.** In which Collection of poem did this poem 'The Last Ride Together' publish?
(a) Men and Women (b) The Ring and the Book
(c) Sordello (d) Pauline and Paracelsus

**73.** GB Shaw was born in
(a) 1856 (b) 1858 (c) 1860 (d) None of these

**74.** Which of the following is incorrect about Bacon's essays?
(a) They belonged to the reign of James I
(b) He was not clogged with long sentences like the writers of his age
(c) He was inclined to American authors who studied brevity
(d) He was imprisoned for bribery

**75.** Bacon's major contribution is
(a) His practical wisdom has universal appeal
(b) His wisdom is devoid of moral pretensions
(c) His wisdom is for the man of the world
(d) All of the above

**76.** "Proper Study of mankind is man," a dictum of the Augustan age means that
(a) they emphasised the importance of only men and not women
(b) they believed in the study of physical nature
(c) they believed in the study of human nature
(d) None of the above

**77.** Which constituency did Francis Bacon represent in the Parliament in 1586-1588?
(a) Middlesex (b) Ipswich
(c) Tounton (d) Kent

**78.** Which book of Francis Bacon was published in 1609?
(a) Novum Organum
(b) The Historie of the Raigne of King Henry the Seventh
(c) Sylva Sylvarum
(d) De Sapientia Veterum

**79.** According to Bacon, without friends, the world is........... .
(a) Empty vessel (b) Forest
(c) Wasteland (d) None of these

**80.** What, according to Bacon, is the principal fruit of friendship?
(a) Close emotional bond (b) Clarity of thoughts
(c) Help in need (d) All of these

**81.** How did the son behave at home?
(a) He was not a spoilt child
(b) He was a well mannered boy
(c) He did make his deal by unfair means
(d) None of the above

**82.** Why does the father want his son to learn Latin?
(a) Because the father learnt it himself
(b) Because the father want his son to be a Latin writer
(c) Because Latin is a good language
(d) None of the above

**83.** What advice is given regarding selection of friends?
(a) One should adhere to them as long as one can
(b) One should choose them biasfully
(c) One should choose friends based on their financial status
(d) One should not make friends at all

**84.** Where does the expression 'busy-idle diversion' occur?
(a) While dreaming
(b) While conversing with his brother
(c) While talking to his grandmother
(d) While telling 'dream children' about his boyhood

**85.** "Here Alice put out one of her dear mother's looks, too tender to be called upbraiding"—What does the word 'braiding' mean here?
(a) Permission (b) Disagreement
(c) Castigation or Censure (d) Revelation

**86.** On the book 'The Discovery of India' a popular TV Serial was produced by Shyam Benegal. Name it.
(a) Bharat, Ek Khoj (b) Train to Pakistan
(c) Buniyaad (d) Hum Log

**87.** What is the theme of the book 'The Discovery of India'?
(a) Writing about historical facts about India
(b) Tributes to the rich cultural heritage of India
(c) History of world in nutshell
(d) Our trade ties with china

**88.** Why we cannot call this book purely auto biographical?
(a) Only in first few chapter Nehru talks about him personal life
(b) More or less, he talks about the glorious past of India
(c) He is more concerned about the poverty struck Indians waiting to get a better future
(d) He had nothing to say about his own life

**89.** When was Nirad C. Chaudhuri born?
(a) 20th November, 1857 (b) 23rd November, 1897
(c) 9th August, 1897 (d) 10th September, 1890

**90.** Which book of Nirad C. Chaudhuri infuriated the Indian high class people?
(a) Thy Hand, Great Anarch!
(b) The Continent of Circe
(c) Scholar Extraordinary
(d) The Autobiography of an Unknown Indian

**91.** Life is but a walking shadow.
(a) Metaphor (b) Simile
(c) Irony (d) Personification

**92.** "I have found the paradox, that if you love until it hurts, there can be no more hurt, only more love."
(a) Personification (b) Metaphor (c) Simile (d) Paradox

**93.** An Elegy is a type of lyric and focusses on expressing emotions and thoughts using
(a) heroic couplet (b) an octave and a sestet
(c) formal language and structure (d) alliteration

**94.** Lyric is a Greek
(a) music (b) rhythm (c) song (d) ode

**95.** Which one is the longest Indian novel ever published in a single volume in the English language?
(a) Revolution 2020 (b) The God of Small Things
(c) A Suitable Boy (d) Train to Pakistan

**96.** Who is the first women to received Jnanpith Award?
(a) Amrita Pritam (b) Ashapoorna Devi
(c) Mahadevi Verma (d) Mahasweta Devi

**97.** Which place in the club did Swami find the safest place
(a) The card room (b) The library
(c) Tennis court (d) The restaurant in the club

**98.** What was the name suggested by Swami for cricket team which was formed by him and his other two friends ?
(a) Victory Union Eleven (b) Malgudi Cricket Club
(c) Chennai Cricket Club (d) Albert Eleven

**99.** What did Raju receive in the mail that he tried to keep from Nalini?
(a) Divorce papers from Marco
(b) A copy of Marco's book
(c) A poor review of Nalini's performance
(d) A set of blackmail pictures

**100.** How did the flowering mustard-field look?
(a) White like silver (b) Red like a rose
(c) Pale like melting gold (d) Lovely like a rainbow

**101.** The children were happy to look after the ...... of puppies they found in the park.
(a) litter (b) have (c) flock (d) catch

**102.** When I met Anu, I invited ...... to my house.
(a) them (b) her (c) they (d) us

**103.** ...... fotball is not only his hobby but also his profession.
(a) Played (b) Play (c) Playing (d) Player

**104.** The passengers ...... wear their seat belts at all times.
(a) could (b) must (c) will (d) may

**105.** Ten books of this library ...... .
(a) is missing (b) are missing
(c) has been missing (d) has missed

**106.** Remember, this is not a safe road ...... .
(a) to travel (b) to travel by
(c) travelling (d) travel

**107.** I have ...... influence in the political field now.
(a) little (b) a little (c) some (d) the little

**108.** ...... unit means a measurement.
(a) A (b) An (c) No article (d) The

**109.** Choose the correct sentence based on the adverb given in the bracket.
We don't see her. (often)
(a) We don't often see her. (b) We often don't see her.
(c) We don't see her often. (d) Often we don't see her.

**110.** Fill the blank with suitable prefix.
I was shocked at her rude ...... .
(a) ness (b) ment
(c) ence (d) None of these

**111.** Identify the best replacement for the given underlined part in the sentence.
If he <u>had</u> time he will call you.
(a) would have (b) would have had
(c) has (d) No improvement

**112.** Select the correct form of the given sentence.
I agreed to you.
(a) I agreed with you (b) I agreed for you
(c) I agreed on you (d) None of these

**113.** Choose the correct direct form of the given sentence. She said that her brother was getting married.
(a) She said, "Her brother is getting married".
(b) She told, "Her brother is getting married".
(c) She said, "My brother is getting married".
(d) She said, "My brother was getting married".

**114.** Which of the following sentence is in passive voice?
(a) He was assisted by a group of students.
(b) Please mind your business.
(c) I kept quiet throughout the meeting.
(d) They came late and lost the match.

**115.** Choose the correct synonym.
Acquaint
(a) Withhold (b) Conceal
(c) Familiarise (d) Risky

**116.** Whom does Caroline want Mr. Bingley to marry
(a) Jane (b) Miss De Bourgh
(c) Georgiana Darcy (d) Miss Hurst

**117.** Khushwant Singh has compared her grandmother to
(a) summer landscape in the mountains
(b) the Moon
(c) the Sun
(d) winter landscape in the mountains

**118.** Which of the following is not by Shaw ?
(a) The Apple Cart (b) Mrs. Warren's Profession
(c) As you like it (d) None of these

**119.** What is Caliban ?
(a) The son of a witch-hag (b) A complex figure
(c) A fool (d) All of these

**120.** What is the name of fictional town where a lot of Narayan's stories are set?
(a) Mussoorie (b) Malgudi
(c) Pukhar (d) Eradu

## ANSWERS

| | | | | | | | | | | | | | | | | | | | |
|---|---|---|---|---|---|---|---|---|---|---|---|---|---|---|---|---|---|---|---|
| 1. | (c) | 2. | (d) | 3. | (c) | 4. | (b) | 5. | (b) | 6. | (c) | 7. | (b) | 8. | (d) | 9. | (b) | 10. | (d) |
| 11. | (a) | 12. | (b) | 13. | (d) | 14. | (d) | 15. | (a) | 16. | (d) | 17. | (b) | 18. | (d) | 19. | (a) | 20. | (b) |
| 21. | (b) | 22. | (b) | 23. | (a) | 24. | (d) | 25. | (b) | 26. | (c) | 27. | (a) | 28. | (d) | 29. | (c) | 30. | (b) |
| 31. | (a) | 32. | (b) | 33. | (a) | 34. | (d) | 35. | (a) | 36. | (a) | 37. | (b) | 38. | (b) | 39. | (a) | 40. | (b) |
| 41. | (c) | 42. | (b) | 43. | (a) | 44. | (c) | 45. | (a) | 46. | (c) | 47. | (c) | 48. | (a) | 49. | (b) | 50. | (b) |
| 51. | (b) | 52. | (d) | 53. | (a) | 54. | (c) | 55. | (c) | 56. | (a) | 57. | (d) | 58. | (d) | 59. | (b) | 60. | (d) |
| 61. | (d) | 62. | (b) | 63. | (b) | 64. | (c) | 65. | (c) | 66. | (c) | 67. | (c) | 68. | (b) | 69. | (a) | 70. | (d) |
| 71. | (a) | 72. | (a) | 73. | (a) | 74. | (c) | 75. | (a) | 76. | (c) | 77. | (c) | 78. | (d) | 79. | (c) | 80. | (a) |
| 81. | (d) | 82. | (a) | 83. | (a) | 84. | (d) | 85. | (c) | 86. | (a) | 87. | (b) | 88. | (c) | 89. | (b) | 90. | (d) |
| 91. | (a) | 92. | (d) | 93. | (c) | 94. | (c) | 95. | (c) | 96. | (b) | 97. | (a) | 98. | (c) | 99. | (b) | 100. | (c) |
| 101. | (a) | 102. | (b) | 103. | (c) | 104. | (b) | 105. | (b) | 106. | (b) | 107. | (a) | 108. | (c) | 109. | (c) | 110. | (a) |
| 111. | (c) | 112. | (a) | 113. | (c) | 114. | (a) | 115. | (c) | 116. | (c) | 117. | (d) | 118. | (c) | 119. | (d) | 120. | (b) |

# MADHYA PRADESH
## Higher Secondary Teacher Eligibility Test

# Practice Paper 2

**1.** I do not travel with much .......
(a) furniture (b) food (c) work (d) luggage

**2.** ....... is on the banks of river Hooghly.
(a) Kelkata (b) Kolkata (c) Calcutta (d) None of these

**3.** The next .......... passengers are without ticket.
(a) three (b) fewer (c) many (d) all

**4.** There is .......... scope of his recovery.
(a) the little (b) fewer (c) little (d) None of these

**5.** What is revealed about Madame Defarge?
(a) That she is Darnay's sister
(b) That she and Lucy are sisters
(c) That she is the sister of the woman raped by Darnay's uncle
(d) That she is an aristocrat by birth

**6.** The doctor must be greedy, that's why he demanded so much money.
Here the word must shows
(a) certainty (b) possibility (c) belief (d) suspicion

**7.** Can you speak more than two languages?
Here the word can shows
(a) capacity (b) ability (c) skill (d) compliance

**8.** The man .............. received that recommendation letter works for the government.
(a) that she (b) who she
(c) from whom she (d) to whom she

**Directions** (Q. Nos. 9 and 10) *Which type of noun the underlined word is?*

**9.** Solomon was the wisest of all kings.
(a) Common noun (b) Proper noun
(c) Abstract noun (d) Collective noun

**10.** The soldiers were rewarded for their bravery.
(a) Common noun (b) Proper noun
(c) Abstract noun (d) Material noun

**11.** Choose the correct indirect form of the sentence.
The man said. "Let me have the first chance."
(a) The man proposed that he should have the first chance.
(b) The man proposed to have the first chance.
(c) The man desired that he had the first chance.
(d) The man claimed that he had the first chance.

**12.** Change the following into indirect speech by choosing correct alternative. Our teacher said to us, "Sugar dissolves in water."
(a) Our teacher told us that sugar dissolved in water.
(b) Our teacher told us that sugar has dissolved in water.
(c) Our teacher said to us that sugar dissolves in water.
(d) Our teacher told us that sugar dissolves in water.

**13.** The recitation ........... the audience.
(a) was pleased (b) pleased
(c) have been pleased (d) will be pleased

**14.** Change the following into passive voice.
Do not insult your elder.
(a) Let not your elders be insulted.
(b) Your elders let not be insulted.
(c) Let your elders not be insulted by you.
(d) Let us not insult your elders.

**Directions** (Q. Nos. 15 and 16) *Choose the correct synonym for the underline word.*

**15.** We were taken aback at the fulsome praise heaped upon our former enemy.
(a) elaborated (b) extravagant (c) excessive (d) exorbitant

**16.** The five experiments gave disparate results.
(a) similar (b) encouraging (c) strange (d) different

**Directions** (Q. Nos. 17 and 18) *Choose the correct antonym for the underline word.*

**17.** He plunged into the turbid waters of the stream.
(a) deep (b) muddy (c) clear (d) fresh

**18.** We are excited about playing in the school team.
(a) serious (b) depressed (c) bored (d) silent

**19.** A section of the Hindus believe in ............ worship.
(a) idle (b) ideal (c) Idol (d) None of these

**20.** Due to drinking very cold water, I developed a ............ throat.
(a) soar (b) sore (c) sour (d) None of these

**21.** The government is under no obligation to offer contracts to companies which choose to flout guidelines.
(a) condemn (b) ignore (c) defy (d) neglect

**22.** The study of ancient societies is called.
(a) Anthropology (b) Archaeology
(c) History (d) Ethnology

**23.** Be quiet. It is rude to ......... people when they are speaking.
(a) Interfere (b) interrupt
(c) prevent (d) introduce

**24.** ......... of money prevented us from taking a holiday this year.
(a) Limit (b) Freeze
(c) Emptiness (d) Lack

**25.** The word missionary has a suffix. Find it out.
(a) nary (b) ary (c) ry (d) onary

**26.** The adjective 'beautiful' contain which suffix?
(a) iful (b) ul (c) tiful (d) ful

**Directions** (Q. Nos. 27-32) *Read the following passage carefully and answer the questions that follow.*

True, it is the function of the army to maintain law and order in abnormal times. But in normal times there is another force that compels citizens to obey the laws and to act with due regard to the rights of others. The force also protects the lives and the properties of law abiding men. Laws are made to secure the personal safety of its subjects and to prevent murder and crimes of violence.

They are made to secure the property of the citizens against theft and damage to protect the rights of communities and castes to carry out their customs and ceremonies, so long as they do not conflict with the rights of others. Now the good citizen, of his own free will obey these laws and he takes care that everything he does is done with due regard to the rights and well-being of others.

But the bad citizen is only restrained from breaking these laws by fear of the consequence of his actions. And the necessary steps to compel the bad citizen to act as a good citizen are taken by this force. The supreme control of law and order in a State is in the hands of a Minister who is responsible to the State Assembly and acts through the Inspector General of Police.

**27.** The expression 'customs and ceremonies' means
(a) fairs and festivals
(b) habits and traditions
(c) usual practices and religious rites
(d) superstitions and formalities

**28.** A suitable title for the passage would be
(a) The Function of the Army
(b) Laws and the People's Rights
(c) The Fear of the Law and Citizen's Security
(d) The Functions of The Police

**29.** Which of the following is not implied in the passage?
(a) Law protects those who respect it
(b) Law ensures people's religious and social rights absolutely and unconditionally
(c) A criminal is deterred from committing crimes only for fear of the law
(d) The forces of law help to transform irresponsible citizens into responsible ones

**30.** According to the writer, which one of the following is not the responsibility of the police?
(a) To protect the privileges of all citizens
(b) To check violent activities of citizens
(c) To ensure peace among citizens by safeguarding individual rights
(d) To maintain peace during extra-ordinary circumstances

**31.** Which of the following reflects the main thrust of the passage?
(a) It deals with the importance of the army in maintaining law and order
(b) It highlights role of the police as superior to that of the army
(c) It discusses the roles of the army and the police in different circumstances
(d) It points to the responsibility of the Minister and the Inspector General of Police

**32.** "They are made to secure the property of citizens against theft and damage", means that the law
(a) helps in recovering the stolen property of the citizens
(b) assist the citizens whose property has been stolen or destroyed
(c) initiate process against offenders of law
(d) safeguard people's possessions against being stolen or lost

**Directions** (Q. Nos.33 and 34) *Answer the following questions by filling the blanks with the most appropriate article from the given options.*

**33.** What did you get for your birthday?
I got ........ lot of good presents.
(a) a (b) the (c) an (d) No article

**34.** Where are you going for your vacations?
I am going to ........ hill station in Himachal Pradesh.
(a) an (b) a (c) the (d) No article

**35.** What feature initially attracts Darcy to Elizabeth?
(a) Her smile (b) Her cheerfulness
(c) Her intelligence (d) Her eyes

**36.** Why doesn't Bingley visit Jane while she is in London?
(a) He doesn't know that she's there
(b) Lady Catherine forbids him from going
(c) He thinks that Jane does not like him
(d) Darcy advises him against it

**37.** Who does Miss Pross believe is the ideal suitor for Lucie Manette?
(a) Sydney Carton (b) Charles Darnay
(c) Her brother, Solomon
(d) She believes that no man is good enough for Lucie.

**38.** What does Mr Lorry try to persuade Mr Stryver not to do?
(a) Propose to Lucie Manette
(b) Invest his money in Tellson's Bank
(c) Drop Sydney Carton as a business colleague
(d) Visit Paris at a time of political turmoil

**39.** Who was Adit's landlady in his early days in England?
(a) Mrs Sympson (b) Sarah
(c) Mrs Miller (d) None of these

**40.** When was Anita Desai born?
(a) 24th June, 1935 (b) 24th June, 1936
(c) 24th June, 1937 (d) 24th July, 1938

**41.** Khushwant Singh could not believe that her grandmother once had been
(a) young (b) pretty
(c) married (d) All of these

**42.** Whose portrait hung in the drawing room of Khushwant Singh ?
(a) His father's (b) His grandmother's
(c) His grandfather's (d) His mother's

**43.** Raina belongs to
(a) Italy (b) Bulgaria (c) Serbia (d) None of these

**44.** Louka is
(a) Raina's cousin (b) Raina's maid servant
(c) Raina's neighbour (d) None of these

**45.** What task are both Caliban and Ferdinand forced to perform?
(a) Marrying Miranda (b) Singing drunkenly
(c) Collecting berries (d) Carrying wood

**46.** Who persuades Sebastian to try to kill Alonso?
(a) Antonio (b) Gonzalo (c) Ariel (d) Alonso

**47.** What does Polonius say about Ophelia's relationship with Hamlet?
(a) He simply wants her to be happy
(b) He believes that Hamlet is a good match for her
(c) He does not believe that Hamlet has feelings for her
(d) He forbids her from seeing him anymore.

**48.** What does Hamlet overhear while waiting for the ghost to appear?
(a) The revelry of the King (b) The sounds of battle
(c) Ophelia crying (d) His own conscience

**49.** What is God's greatest gift to the poet?
(a) His life (b) His intelligence
(c) Beauty of nature (d) His nation

**50.** What according to the poem is the poet's special room?
(a) His life (b) His body (c) His poetry (d) His heart

**51.** What is true worship according tothe poet?
(a) To follow what God wants
(b) To offer flowers to God
(c) To recite prayers for God
(d) To devote one self in the service of God

**52.** What, according to the poet, God wants us to do?
(a) To sing God's praise
(b) To serve the mankind with love and equality
(c) To bow down to God
(d) To renounce the world for God

**53.** Shelley wrote with what artistic drive?
(a) Impulse (b) Deep thought
(c) Life experience (d) Love for literature

**54.** What is the speaker's request to the Skylark in the last stanza?
(a) For the bird to land near him to eat
(b) To be taught
(c) To come back into sight
(d) To continue its song for a very long time

**55.** When did Sarojini Naidu die?
(a) 1948 (b) 1947 (c) 1949 (d) 1946

**56.** What was Sarojini Naidu's original name?
(a) Padmini Gangopadhyay (b) Sarojini Chattopadhyay
(c) Aparna Mukhyopadhyay
(d) Saro ini Bandopadhyay

**57.** 'Fluttering and dancing in the breeze'. Extract a figure of speech?
(a) Personification (b) Simile
(c) Metaphor (d) Rhyme scheme

**58.** 'Ten thousand I saw at a glance, Tossing their heads in sprightly dance', This line refers to
(a) inward eye (b) milky way
(c) pensive mood (d) daffodils

**59.** When was 'The World Is Too Much with Us' published in two volumes?
(a) 1803 (b) 1807 (c) 1800 (d) 1808

**60.** What have the men lost?
(a) Nature's Joy (b) Family
(c) Education (d) Self respect

**61.** A Tale of Two Cities opens in 1775. Which of the following does not characterise this period?
(a) The British colonies in America have just presented a list of grievances to the King of England.
(b) Crime and capital punishment plague the streets of London.
(c) The guillotine stands as a much-feared fixture on the streets of Paris.
(d) The French aristocracy causes great suffering among the lower classes.

**62.** What does the speaker refer to as 'barren leaves' in the final stanza?
(a) Science and art (b) Sages
(c) Books (d) Birds and trees

**63.** What is cuckoo bird famous for?
(a) Cheerfulness (b) Thrill
(c) Driving away tiredness (d) Welcoming the spring

**64.** How does the Solitary Reaper's song score over the song of the cuckoo?
(a) It is more far-reaching (b) It echoes more
(c) It is more musical and fresh (d) It does not have any effect

**65.** The form and meter used in the poem is
(a) Tetra meter (b) Iambic Penta meter
(c) Lamb meter (d) Trochee meter

**66.** What does the title of the poem suggest us about the time in which it is set?
(a) During apple picking (b) At poet's bed room
(c) At a conference
(d) Poet's reflection after apple picking

**67.** Which of the following statements is the closest interpretation of the line "yet knowing how way leads on to way?"
(a) You can never go home alone
(b) It's easy to get lost in a path
(c) One path takes you to the next
(d) It's easy to decide the road to travel further

**68.** According to the narrator, the two roads looked....
(a) about the same (b) very different
(c) muddy and unpleasant (d) covered with grass

**69.** Why are the drivers of the Dover mail coach hesitant to stop for Jerry Cruncher's message?
(a) They fear that he is a highwayman attempting to rob the passengers.
(b) They fear that stopping will put them behind schedule for delivering the mail in a timely fashion.
(c) They have been charged with the safety of Jarvis Lorry, one of the coach's passengers.
(d) Jerry Cruncher's troublesome reputation precedes him.

**70.** What is the effect of the word "but" in the second line?
(a) It makes it seem like the speaker does not actually like the woods much and wants to leave
(b) It makes it seem like the speaker can still keep promises while staying by the woods
(c) It makes it seem like the promises the speaker has to keep are lovely dark and deep
(d) It makes it seem like the speaker has to choose between keeping promises and the lovely woods

**71.** How did the lady react over the lover's last wish?
(a) She readily agreed (b) She out rightly refused
(c) She was in a dilemma (d) The was utterly confused

**72.** What two emotion are reflected in lady love's eyes as described by the poet?
(a) Her pride (b) Lady's sad mood
(c) Lady taking pity on her lover (d) Both (b) and (c)

**73.** In Bacon's essay, cunning persons don't like
(a) studies (b) games
(c) play (d) None of these

**74.** Studies become a source of pleasure when a man is
(a) in natural environment (b) all alone
(c) in social life (d) None of these

**75.** Bacon suggests that the general counsnels come best from those that are
(a) experienced (b) professionals
(c) learned (d) businessmen

**76.** "Crafty men condemn studies, simple men admire them and wise men use them." The above line appears in the essay.
(a) Of Adversity (b) Of Studies
(c) Of Marriage and Single Life (d) Of Friendship

**77.** The name of Britain's biggest dog was 'Tiny'.
(a) Personifiction (b) Irony
(c) Simile (d) Paradox

**78.** You laugh at a person who slipped stepping on a banana peel, and the next thing you know, you've slipped too.
(a) Personification (b) Metaphor
(c) Simile (d) Irony

**79.** The writer users satire in his writing with the intertion of
(a) criticism only (b) entertaining people
(c) bringing improvement (d) make people think

**80.** Which are two main components of satire?
(a) Ornamental language and poetry
(b) Irony and humour
(c) Preaching and logical explanation
(d) Use of Lyrics and dramatization

**81.** Who wrote the famous novel 'Anandamath'?
(a) Sarat Chandra Chattopadhyay
(b) Bankim Chandra Chattopadhyay
(c) Rabindranath Tagore
(d) Michael Madhusudan Dutt

**82.** The first English translation of the Bhagavad Gita was done by
(a) Charles Wilkins (b) William Jones
(c) Warren Hastings (d) Henry Thomas Colebrooke

**83.** What is the name of RK Narayan's first novel?
(a) The Bachelor of Arts (b) The Far Pavilions
(c) Swami and Friends (d) The Dark Room

**84.** The fictional town of Malgudi is the setting for most of Narayan's novels. However, Malgudi is intended to be a fictionalisation of Narayan's lifelong home, which was
(a) Jodhpur, in Northwestern India
(b) Mumbai (formerly Bombay), on India's West coast
(c) Chennai (formerly Madras), on India's South-East coast
(d) Srinagar, in far Northern India, in the Himalayan mountains

**85.** How did Raju's mother describe their animals?
(a) A strict commodity (b) As joyous company
(c) A sufficient bother (d) A necessary evil

**86.** What was Raju's punishment from his father?
(a) He had to attend school
(b) He had to leave India for a month
(c) He had to go without dinner
(d) He was slapped by his father

**87.** How does Raju propose solving the problem of educating the children?
(a) He offers to teach the children
(b) He offers to hire a school teacher
(c) He is willing to help on their farms
(d) He suggests the children could be educated in the evenings

**88.** How did Raju feel about his affair with Rosie?
(a) Blessed (b) Insecure (c) Lucky (d) Entitled

**89.** What did the child say as they passed by sweetmeat-shop?
(a) He said, 'I want that burfi'
(b) He said, 'I want that jalebi'
(c) He said, 'I want that rasagulla'
(d) He said, 'I want that gulab jamun'

**90.** The child asked for toy but then he moved on without waiting for an answer. Why?
(a) He knew his plea would not be heeded
(b) He knew his parents were poor
(c) He knew his parents had no money
(d) He knew it was bad to be greedy

**91.** What did the child want to have at the flower-shop?
(a) A garland of roses (b) A garland of violets
(c) A garland of gulmohar (d) A garland of lilies

**92.** Which device of logic does Bacon reject?
(a) The conjecture (b) The syllogism
(c) The premise (d) The conclusion

**93.** What has been the enemy of natural philosophy in every age?
(a) The teachings of Aristotle and Plato
(b) Poor experimental technique
(c) Problems of method and logic
(d) Superstition and the blind, immoderate zeal of religion

**94.** How was the father's experience with love?
(a) Love turned its face from him
(b) He had a heavenly experience
(c) He had good hopes from love
(d) He did not love anybody

**95.** What is the son fond of?
(a) Playing (b) Eating
(c) Reading (d) All of these

**96.** "...such a distance there is between life and death"—Explain the significance of the line in light of the context.
(a) Lamb really understood how to enjoy life
(b) Lamb started taking care of his children
(c) Lamb gave value to his wife
(d) Lamb learnt the true difference between life and death after his brother's death

**97.** "...the soul of first Alice looked out at her eyes with such reality of re-presentment that I came in doubt". What does the word 're-presentment' mean here?
(a) His dream daughter resembling his dream girl
(b) To lead in a course
(c) To resolve the impending issue
(d) To disguise for fun

**98.** The book presents a good insight of India's foreign relationship with the people of
(a) Burma (b) Iran
(c) Greece (d) Both (b) and (c)

**99.** What was the aim of Nehruji while writing the book 'Discovery of India'?
(a) To present India's past
(b) Constructive suggestion on the basis of historical knowledge
(c) To admit his mistakes
(d) To dwell on the tortures incurred by the Britishers

**100.** What was the author's mother remonstrate against?
(a) Author's sharp and biting tongue (b) Behavior of author's father
(c) Author's demonstrativeness (d) None of these

**101.** Why did Swami make hectic efforts to procore six paises?
(a) He wanted to buy a hoop.
(b) Coachmen has asked him to get six paise.
(c) His friend needed this money.
(d) None of the above

**102.** The Jataka stories are related to the previous lives of whom?
(a) Krishna (b) Mahabir (c) Buddha (d) Guru Nanak

**103.** The Cavalier poet are great lovers of
(a) history (b) religion (c) nature (d) modernity

**104.** Point out the figure of speech in the following line.
Opportunity knocks at the door but once.
(a) Irony (b) Simile
(c) Metaphor (d) Personification

**105.** Which was the first book written by Nirad C. Chaudhuri?
(a) A Passage to England
(b) The Autobiography of An Unknown India
(c) Three Horsemen of the New Apocalypse
(d) The Continent of Circle

**106.** To which government post ws Francis Bacon appoint in 1618?
(a) Advocate in Chief (b) Principal Auditor
(c) Lord Chancellor (d) Prime Minister

**107.** Robert Frost was a/an ...... poet.
(a) Canadian (b) Australian (c) Swiss (d) American

**108.** Pick out the word which is the same in meaning to the word given in bold.
He had a **penchant** for fine phrases.
(a) bias (b) liking (c) training (d) desire

**109.** Select the correct antonym of the underlined word.
Tanya <u>gathered</u> some wood for the campfire.
(a) burnad (b) soaked
(c) collected (d) scattered

**110.** ...... Ram, all his friends were present there.
(a) Accept (b) Except
(c) Adapt (d) Adopt

**Directions (Q. Nos. 111 and 112)** ***Select the alternative which is the best substitute of the given sentence.***

**111.** Anything written in a letter after it is signed
(a) Posterity (b) Postdiction (c) Postscript (d) Corrigendum

**112.** One who deserts his religion
(a) Deserter (b) Turn-coat (c) Fanatic (d) Apostate

**113.** Select the one which best expresses the same sentence in passive voice.
Should you ever tell a lie?
(a) Should a lie be ever told by you?
(b) Should a lie be ever told by everyone?
(c) Should a lie be ever told ?
(d) Should a lie ever be told?

**114.** Choose the indirect speech of the given sentence.
Ram said, "You need not talk to me".
(a) Ram said that I need not talk to him.
(b) Ram told that I need not to talk to him.
(c) Ram told that I need not talk to him.
(d) Ram asked me not talk to him.

**115.** The week the rupee dropped ...... its lowest level.
(a) on (b) to (c) at (d) for

**116.** Fill the blank with correct past tense forms.
I ...... (write) to her last week.
(a) wrote (b) have been writing
(c) had been writing (d) written

**117.** Which part of the word 'impossible' is the prefix?
(a) im (b) poss (c) ib (d) le

**118.** I ...... want to know what happened.
(a) exactly (b) purely (c) simply (d) highly

**119.** ...... man that we saw turned out to be a thief.
(a) A (b) The (c) That (d) This

**120.** It gives me immense pleasure ...... you of her engagement.
(a) to inform (b) inform (c) informing (d) to informing

## ANSWERS

| | | | | | | | | | | | | | | | | | | | |
|---|---|---|---|---|---|---|---|---|---|---|---|---|---|---|---|---|---|---|---|
| 1. | (d) | 2. | (b) | 3. | (a) | 4. | (c) | 5. | (c) | 6. | (b) | 7. | (b) | 8. | (c) | 9. | (b) | 10. | (c) |
| 11. | (a) | 12. | (d) | 13. | (b) | 14. | (c) | 15. | (c) | 16. | (d) | 17. | (c) | 18. | (b) | 19. | (c) | 20. | (b) |
| 21. | (b) | 22. | (a) | 23. | (b) | 24. | (d) | 25. | (b) | 26. | (d) | 27. | (c) | 28. | (d) | 29. | (b) | 30. | (d) |
| 31. | (c) | 32. | (d) | 33. | (a) | 34. | (b) | 35. | (c) | 36. | (a) | 37. | (c) | 38. | (a) | 39. | (d) | 40. | (c) |
| 41. | (d) | 42. | (c) | 43. | (b) | 44. | (b) | 45. | (d) | 46. | (c) | 47. | (d) | 48. | (a) | 49. | (a) | 50. | (d) |
| 51. | (a) | 52. | (b) | 53. | (a) | 54. | (b) | 55. | (c) | 56. | (b) | 57. | (a) | 58. | (d) | 59. | (b) | 60. | (a) |
| 61. | (c) | 62. | (a) | 63. | (d) | 64. | (a) | 65. | (b) | 66. | (d) | 67. | (c) | 68. | (a) | 69. | (a) | 70. | (d) |
| 71. | (c) | 72. | (d) | 73. | (a) | 74. | (b) | 75. | (c) | 76. | (b) | 77. | (d) | 78. | (d) | 79. | (c) | 80. | (b) |
| 81. | (b) | 82. | (a) | 83. | (c) | 84. | (c) | 85. | (c) | 86. | (a) | 87. | (d) | 88. | (c) | 89. | (b) | 90. | (a) |
| 91. | (c) | 92. | (b) | 93. | (d) | 94. | (a) | 95. | (c) | 96. | (d) | 97. | (a) | 98. | (d) | 99. | (b) | 100. | (a) |
| 101. | (b) | 102. | (a) | 103. | (c) | 104. | (d) | 105. | (b) | 106. | (c) | 107. | (d) | 108. | (b) | 109. | (d) | 110. | (b) |
| 111. | (c) | 112. | (d) | 113. | (a) | 114. | (a) | 115. | (b) | 116. | (a) | 117. | (a) | 118. | (c) | 119. | (b) | 120. | (a) |

# MADHYA PRADESH
## Higher Secondary Teacher Eligibility Test

# Practice Paper 3

1. The French army was defeated at Waterloo.
(a) Common noun (b) Collective noun
(c) Proper noun (d) Abstract noun

2. I want to while away my time .......... new places in world.
(a) visit (b) visiting (c) visits (d) visited

3. The bottle contained .......... amount of water.
(a) the few (b) the little (c) many (d) a little

4. .......... number of students leave this school every year.
(a) A (b) An
(c) The (d) Zero article

5. The conservatives should win the next election.
(a) Obligation (b) Probability
(c) Desirability (d) Conjecture

6. Choose the correct word to complete the given sentence. ...... I speak to the principal for one day leave?
(a) Can (b) May
(c) Must (d) Should

7. Many people hope that Canada can resolve its economic problems.
(a) Noun clause (b) Adjective clause
(c) Adverb clause (d) Either (a) or (c)

8. Wherever there is a large American city, there will be poverty.
(a) Noun clause (b) Adjective clause
(c) Adverb clause (d) Either (a) or (b)

**Directions** (Q. Nos. 9 and 10) *Fill in the blanks by choosing the correct option.*

9. Leena and Payal are very excited because ........... are going to Disneyland.
(a) that (b) those (c) there (d) they

10. Mahima and Kajal are doctors and ........ profession is very noble.
(a) her (b) hers
(c) them (d) their

11. The tailor said to him, "Will you have the suit ready by tomorrow evening?"
(a) The tailor asked him that he will have the suit ready by the next evening.
(b) The tailor asked him that he would had the suit ready by the next evening.
(c) The tailor asked him if he would have the suit ready by the next evening.
(d) The tailor asked him if he will like to have the suit ready by the next evening.

12. The students said, "We want to learn a foreign language." In reported speech the above sentence will be The students said that
(a) they want to learn a foreign language
(b) they wanted to learn a foreign language
(c) we want to learn a foreign language
(d) we wanted to learn a foreign language

13. Point out the active voice in the following sentence. This notice has been altered.
(a) Alteration has been made is this notice.
(b) Some one has altered the notice.
(c) Already the notice has been altered.
(d) The notice has been altered previously.

14. "I know him" the passive voice form of the sentence will be
(a) He is known by me (b) He knows me.
(c) He is known to me (d) None of these

15. Choose the correct synonym of the word 'Despise'.
(a) Affection (b) Hate (c) Jealous (d) Love

16. Choose the correct synonym of the word 'Chaos'.
(a) Disorder (b) Blank (c) Gap (d) Difference

17. Choose the correct Antonym for the word given 'Arrogant'.
(a) Humble (b) Cowardly
(c) Egoistic (d) Gentlemanly

18. Choose the correct Antonym for the word given 'Debtor'
(a) Reluctant (b) Rigid (c) Static (d) Creditor

19. I like the ............ of roses is my room.
(a) cent (b) sent
(c) scent (d) None of these

20. He presented me a book ............ in a beautiful cover.
(a) rap (b) wrapped
(c) rape (d) None of these

21. One of the time-tested ways of remembering a series of items is known as a/an
(a) recollection (b) schematizing
(c) mnemonic (d) ingenuity

22. Nations that do not trust each other look upon each other
(a) calmly (b) hopefully
(c) askance (d) retrospectively

23. If you were a more ......... person, you would have not left me alone.
(a) polite (b) considerate (c) kind (d) humorous

24. I am feeling really ......... today. The weather is terrible and I got some bad news this morning too.
(a) lazy (b) punctual (c) miserable (d) starving

**25.** What prefix you will use to make the opposite of word 'credible?
(a) Un (b) em (c) In (d) Ir

**26.** What suffix you will use in the noun 'miser' to make it an adjective?
(a) able (b) y (c) ary (d) ent

**Directions** (Q. Nos. 27-32) *Read the following passage carefully and answer the questions that follow.*

The small village of Somnathpur contains an extraordinary temple, built around AD 1268 by the Hoyasalas of Karnataka-one of the most prolific temple builders. Belur and Helebid are among their better known works. While these suffered during the invasion of the 14th century, the Somnathpur temple stands more or less intact in near-original condition.

This small temple captivates with the beauty and vitality of its detailed sculpture, covering almost every inch of the walls, pillars and even ceilings. It has three shikharas and stands on a star shaped platform with 24 edges. The outer walls have a profusion of detailed carvings: the entire surface runs over by a carved plaque of stone.

There were vertical panels covered by exquisite figures of Gods and Goddesses. Vishnu seemed the most popular, with many of his incarnations being depicted. Shiv, Brahma and Indra weren't left out and there were plenty of female deities too like Durga and Saraswati. There were shapely nymphs too, some carrying an ear of maize.

The elaborate ornamentation, very characteristic of Hoyasalas sculptures, was a remarkable feature.

On closer look and it is worth it- the series of friezes on the outer walls revealed intricately carved caparisoned elephants, charging horsemen, stylised flowers, warriors, musicians crocodiles and swans.

The temple was actually commissioned by Soma Dandanayaka or ( Somnath), he named the temple after him, the minister of the Hoyasalas king, Narsimha the Third. The temple was built to house three versions of Krishna. The inner center of the temple was Kalyana Mandapa.

Leading from here were three corridors, each ending in a shrine, one for each kind of Krishna-Venugopala, Janardana and Prasanna Keshava, though only two remain in their original form. In the darkness of the sanctum, I tried to discern the different images. The temple's sculptural perfection is amazing and it includes the doors of the temple and the three elegantly carved towers.

**27.** After whom was the temple named?
(a) Kalyana Mandapa (b) Lord Shiva
(c) Minister of the Hoyasalas King (d) Lord Krishna

**28.** What would the word 'maize' mean here?
(a) Grain (b) Deer
(c) Symbol of prosperity (d) Symbol of weakness

**29.** The most remarkable feature of Hoyasalas sculptures was
(a) elaborate ornamentation (b) beautiful clothing
(c) sharply cut sculptures (d) real expression

**30.** What stands on the 24 edges star shaped raised platform?
(a) Shrines (b) Temple
(c) Shikharas (d) Pillars

**31.** What will be the most suitable antonym of 'reveal'?
(a) Impart (b) Disclose (c) Conceal (d) Refuse

**32.** The word 'intricately' can also mean
(a) easy (b) complicated
(c) tangled (d) simple

**33.** When did Wordsworth received his B.A. degree?
(a) 1790 (b) 1792 (c) 1789 (d) 1791

**34.** When was Wordsworth sent to the Gramm School at Hawkshead?
(a) In 1787 (b) In 1770 (c) In 1778 (d) In 1775

**35.** Rain was coming, so why does Jane not take a carriage to Netherfield?
(a) The carriage had a leak was currently being repaired
(b) Mr Bennet refused to allow Jane to go to the party, so she secretly snuck out of the house
(c) Mrs Bennet wanted Jane to get caught in the rain and be unable to return home immediately; she hoped Mr Bingley would return to Netherfield before Jane left
(d) Lizzy had taken the carriage to Meryton

**36.** Why does Lizzy decide to go to Netherfield?
(a) Caroline Bingley invited her to join the party
(b) She wanted to see Darcy
(c) Jane was sick
(d) She had left her coat there on her last visit

**37.** How does Carton describe himself to Darnay?
(a) Ambitious, vengeful, unforgiving
(b) Generous, devoted, friendly
(c) Disappointed, misanthropic, unloved
(d) Excitable, paranoid, fearful

**38.** How do Stryver and Carton know each other?
(a) Stryver defended Carton once.
(b) Carton saved Stryver's life.
(c) They went to school together.
(d) They are cousins.

**39.** How does Sarah escape her dilemma?
(a) By separating from Adit
(b) By opting for the new man in life
(c) By deciding to go with Dev
(d) By creating a world of illusions of her own about India and embrace it

**40.** Sarah's love for India and its customs is revealed when
(a) she is with Miss Moffit, admiring everything Indian
(b) she criticises English culture
(c) she agrees to come to India
(d) None of the above

**41.** What was the turning point in Khushwant's friendship with his grandmother?
(a) When Khushwant Singh started practising law
(b) When Khushwant Singh went abroad
(c) When Khushwant Singh got married
(d) When they went to the city to live with their parents

**42.** The grandmother's body was covered in a ............shroud.
(a) white (b) blue
(c) red (d) yellow

**43.** What are Ferdinand and Miranda doing when Prospero reveals them to the lords?
(a) Spying on the lords (b) Playing chess
(c) Chopping wood (d) Stealing clothing

**44.** Where was William Shakespeare born?
(a) Kingston-upon-Thames (b) Berwick-upon-Tweed
(c) Shipston-on-Stour (d) Stratford-upon-Avon

**45.** Which of the following characters survive the play?
(a) Fortinbras, Horatio, and Osric
(b) Prince Hamlet, Polonius, and Gertrude
(c) Claudius, Rosencrantz, and Guildenstern
(d) Ophelia, Laertes, and King Hamlet

**46.** What does Hamlet claim to be able to tell the difference between when the wind is from the South?
(a) A flea and a fire log (b) A nymph and a nihilist
(c) A hawk and a handsaw (d) A shark and St. Timothy

**47.** Who is the flute player in the poem?
(a) Man (b) Woman (c) God (d) Nature

**48.** What fills the poet's heart with joy and pleasure in the poem?
(a) His own intelligence (b) God's invisible touch
(c) Women's company (d) Beauty of nature

**49.** Who are the 'downtrodden' as mentioned in the poem?
(a) people who are hungry and poor
(b) people who are treated so badly by rich and powerful people
(c) people who do not worship God
(d) People who never treat anyone with love and affection

**50.** How should we treat the down–trodden people?
(a) We should punish them
(b) They should be forced to worship God
(c) They should be neglected
(d) We should give them support, love and care

**51.** In his poem 'To a Skylark', Shelley viewed the skylark as …………
(a) an annoyance (b) a small, brown bird
(c) a good singer (d) a spirit

**52.** In his poem 'To a Skylark', Shelley compared the skylark to …………
(a) a glow worm (b) a princess in a tower
(c) a rose flower (d) All of these

**53.** According to the poem, what is the current atmosphere in the nation?
(a) Gloomy (b) Full of corruption
(c) Full of hope and expectation (d) Full of jealousy and torture

**54.** Who are set to tread the path of liberty in the poem?
(a) The women (b) The children
(c) The intellectuals (d) The people of India

**55.** What is mean by 'solitude' in the poem?
(a) being alone (b) being together
(c) being in trouble (d) being sad

**56.** Explain the meaning of 'glee' as used in the poem.
(a) joy (b) sadness (c) gloom (d) happiness

**57.** What is the metre of the sonnet?
(a) Iambic pentameter (b) Hexameter
(c) Tetra meter (d) None of these

**58.** Which sonnet was composed by Wordsworth in 1802?
(a) Tintern Abbey
(b) The World is Too Much with Us
(c) Ode to Duty
(d) The Solitary Reaper

**59.** Describe 'The Table Turned' in a line by William Wordsworth.
(a) Students should only read their books
(b) Students should learn from nature apart from books
(c) They should not be a part of outside the world of books
(d) They only should gain knowledge from bookish world.

**60.** What word does the speaker use to describe human intellect?
(a) Meddling (b) Useless
(c) Sweet (d) Wise

**61.** What other activities is the maiden doing besides singing?
(a) She is ploughing (b) Binding the corn
(c) Cutting grass (d) None of the above

**62.** What makes the maiden's song extraordinary?
(a) Its musicality (b) Its eternal nature
(c) Its theme (d) Her voice

**63.** What figure of speech is there in the following lines: "The wood chunk could say, whether it's like his long sleep a I describe its coming on."
(a) Similie (b) Personification (c) Paradox (d) Metaphor

**64.** What is important in the world?
(a) Money (b) Nature
(c) God (d) Family

**65.** Frost uses the image of two diverging roads to symbolise….
(a) Sorrow and regret (b) Life's choice
(c) The love of nature
(d) The spirit of independence

**66.** According to the poet, the second road has "the better claim" because it.....
(a) was a familiar path (b) has never been used
(c) had more grass (d) had been traveled less on

**67.** What might be a main theme of this poem?
(a) The pull of being alone in nature against the pull of responsibility
(b) The pull of sleeping in nature against the pull of sleeping at home
(c) The ability of nature to make a person feel tired and sleepy
(d) The fear of staying too long on someone else's land

**68.** Why might the poet have repeated the line "and miles to go before I sleep"?
(a) To make the woods seem even more attractive and lovely
(b) To make the speaker seem forgetful and less smart than earlier in the poem
(c) To make readers pay special attention to the meaning of the line
(d) To make the speaker seem like he or she is already asleep

**69.** In which Collection of poem did this poem 'The Last Ride Together' publish?
(a) Men and Women (b) The Ring and the Book
(c) Sordello (d) Pauline and Paracelsus

**70.** What does 'The last Ride Together' suggest?
(a) It was an ordinary horse ride with his lover
(b) A journey imagined by the poet in his heart and soul
(c) It was a dream
(d) None of the above

**71.** Bacon belonged to the …………………… faith.
(a) Indian (b) Anglican
(c) Puritan (d) Elizabethan

**72.** Bacon was the translator of ……….. essays.
(a) Ciero (b) Plato (c) Montaigne (d) Pope

**73.** ................ maketh a full man.
(a) Speaking (b) Reading
(c) Writing (d) Listening

**74.** What does 'Of Studies' display?
(a) Wide learning (b) Deep scholarship
(c) Sound wisdom (d) All of these

**75.** Bacon compares the third fruit of friendship to.........
(a) an apple (b) an orange
(c) a pomegranate (d) a mango

**76.** Whom does Bacon first refer to in his essay 'Of Friendship'?
(a) His friend, Toby Matthew (b) His friend, Michael Andrews
(c) William Wordsworth (d) Aristotle

**77.** According to Bacon, what prolongs the life of a person even after his/her death?
(a) Dignity of a person
(b) True friendship of a person
(c) Money and power of a person
(d) Intelligence of a person

**78.** Why is it important to study the classics?
(a) It is an exercise of the intellect
(b) It helps to refine the taste
(c) It teaches great things present in this world
(d) All of the above

**79.** How one should treat one's teammates?
(a) With low esteem (b) With same dignity
(c) Dictate them (d) Curse them

**80.** 'But James Elia was gone forever'—Who was James Elia?
(a) Author's dream girl
(b) Another name of his brother, John-Lamb
(c) His mother (d) His father

**81.** What did working at East India House provide Charles Lamb?
(a) A lifetime of stability
(b) An opportunity to travel
(c) A chance to meet friends
(d) A chance to meet fellow writers

**82.** How does an Indian feel after reading this book?
(a) It makes a person have inner knowledge and pride in ancient cultural heritage
(b) Feels sorry about present condition
(c) Hates the Britishers
(d) None of the above

**83.** What picture of the author emerges after reading this book?
(a) Nehruji was deeply pained by the oppression of millions of Indians
(b) Nehruji had a large and comprehensive knowledge
(c) He is one of the greatest writer of English prose
(d) All of the above

**84.** What did the mother despise the most?
(a) Taking sympathy
(b) Crying
(c) Taking silent advantage of a wrong opportunity
(d) Falsehood

**85.** What was the author's mother remonstrate against?
(a) Author's sharp and biting tongue
(b) Behavior of author's father
(c) Author's demonstrativeness
(d) None of the above

**86.** Identify the Figure of Speech
"War is peace."
"Freedom is slavery."
"Ignorance is strength."
(a) Personification (b) Metaphor
(c) Paradox (d) Simile

**87.** I posted a video on YouTube about how boring and useless YouTube is.
(a) Personification (b) Metaphor
(c) Irony (d) Paradox

**88.** Among the Romantic lyric, the work of ............... remain unexcelled.
(a) Wordsworth (b) Blake
(c) Keat (d) Shelley

**89.** ............... is a great writer of dramatic lyric.
(a) Tennyson (b) Browning
(c) Milton (d) None of these

**90.** Who is the writer of the book 'A Suitable Boy'?
(a) Vikram Seth (b) Arundhati Roy
(c) Salman Rushdie (d) Kiran Desai

**91.** Famous Indian writer Dhanpat Rai Srivastav is also known as
(a) Lakshminath Bezbaroa (b) Rabindranath Tagore
(c) Premchand (d) Sumitranandan Pant

**92.** What is the name of Swami's class teacher?
(a) Mr Pillai (b) Mr Ebenezar
(c) Nayagam (d) Mr Mani

**93.** Why did Swami get a complaint letter written by his father for the head master?
(a) Complaining against the education system
(b) Complaining against some rowdy boys
(c) Complain against Swami's class teacher
(d) Complain against Fanatic Christian teacher Mr. Ebenezar

**94.** Which behaviour of Swami's friend's made him very sad?
(a) They slopped talking to him
(b) They grew hostile towards
(c) Did not share any food with him
(d) Both (a) and (b)

**95.** Who gave Raju his nickname?
(a) The station master (b) The travellers
(c) His father (d) Himself

**96.** What does Raju tell the villagers to do about the new conditions in the village?
(a) There is nothing they can do (b) Chant at the temple
(c) Bring more offerings (d) Pray harder

**97.** What was Raju's fate after he became preoccupied with Rosie?
(a) He lost all other relationships
(b) He finally found peace
(c) He lost his business
(d) He was assaulted by Marco

**98.** What did the child start doing when a shower of young flowers fell on him?
(a) He started collecting the flowers from the ground
(b) He started gathering the raining petals in his hands
(c) He started dancing with joy
(d) He started climbing up the flowering tree

**99.** What did the child do when he heard the cooing of doves in the grove?
(a) He started cooing like the doves
(b) He tried to catch the doves
(c) He ran towards his parents shouting, 'The dove! The dove!'
(d) He told his parents that he wanted to have the dove

**100.** What shop was there at the entrance of the fair?
(a) A toy shop (b) A balloon shop
(c) A sweetmeat-shop (d) A flower shop
101. Identify the type of noun, underlined in the given sentence

**101.** Identify the type of noun, underlined in the given sentence.
Cleanliness is next to godliness.
(a) Proper (b) Common
(c) Collective (d) Abstract

**102.** They looked at ......
(a) their (b) it (c) we (d) my

**103.** Identify the type of underlined word.
He would tell me if he thought we were in danger.
(a) Transitive verb
(b) Intransitive verb
(c) Linking verb
(d) Auxiliary verb

**104.** Several criminals ...... have managed to escape into the woods.
(a) should (b) might
(c) had to (d) ought to

**105.** That red-haired lady in the fur hat ...... across the street
(a) live (b) lives
(c) living (d) were lived

**106.** Choose the correct form of the given sentence.
The white and the black dog is dead.
(a) The white and black dog are dead
(b) The white and the black dog are dead
(c) The white and blacks dog are dead
(d) None of the above

**107.** He never minds ...... the deserving persons.
(a) to help (b) helping
(c) in helping (d) for helping

**108.** ...... first item in today's programme is a song.
(a) The (b) A (c) Any (d) Some

**109.** He ...... goes to office in the weekends as his office remains shut.
(a) always (b) never (c) often (d) sometime

**110.** Which of the following is not a suffix?
(a) Ful (b) Ing
(c) Re (d) Ness

**111.** When he died, Ramanujan ...... behind three notebooks.
(a) was leaving (b) had left
(c) left (d) leaves

**112.** Choose the sentence with correct use of preposition.
A big crowd assembled to the outside.
(a) A big crowd assembled on the outside
(b) A big crowd assembled at the outside
(c) A big crowd assembled outside
(d) None of the above

**113.** I waitad for him ...... the clock struck seven.
(a) until (b) unless (c) upto (d) as

**114.** Choose the correct indirect speech of the given sentence.
The boys are sure to say, "We are going by ourselves".
(a) The boys will say that we are going by ourselves
(b) The boy will say that they are going by themselves
(c) The boys would say that they were going by the themselves
(d) The boys will say that would be going by themselves

**115.** Choose the correct synonym of the world - DESTITUTION
(a) Humility (b) Moderation (c) Poverty (d) Beggary

**116.** Choose the word which is the exact opposite of the given word.
Repel
(a) Attend (b) Concentrate
(c) Continue (d) Attract

**117.** You ...... of onions ! What did you eat?
(a) wreak (b) reek (c) wreck (d) reeked

**118.** Select the alternative which is the best substitute of the given sentence.
Person who believes that god is everything and everything is god
(a) Agnostic (b) Theist
(c) Pantheist (d) Pantechnicon

**119.** Explain 'humble lay'.
(a) A song about ordinary events
(b) A song about extraordinary things
(c) A song about modest things
(d) A song about rich people

**120.** According to Bacon, the chief use of study is
(a) ability (b) ornament
(c) delight (d) adornment

## ANSWERS

| | | | | | | | | | | | | | | | | | | | |
|---|---|---|---|---|---|---|---|---|---|---|---|---|---|---|---|---|---|---|---|
| 1. | (b) | 2. | (b) | 3. | (d) | 4. | (a) | 5. | (c) | 6. | (d) | 7. | (a) | 8. | (c) | 9. | (b) | 10. | (d) |
| 11. | (c) | 12. | (b) | 13. | (b) | 14. | (c) | 15. | (b) | 16. | (a) | 17. | (a) | 18. | (d) | 19. | (c) | 20. | (b) |
| 21. | (c) | 22. | (c) | 23. | (b) | 24. | (c) | 25. | (c) | 26. | (a) | 27. | (c) | 28. | (c) | 29. | (a) | 30. | (b) |
| 31. | (c) | 32. | (b) | 33. | (d) | 34. | (c) | 35. | (c) | 36. | (c) | 37. | (c) | 38. | (c) | 39. | (d) | 40. | (a) |
| 41. | (d) | 42. | (c) | 43. | (b) | 44. | (d) | 45. | (a) | 46. | (c) | 47. | (c) | 48. | (b) | 49. | (b) | 50. | (d) |
| 51. | (d) | 52. | (d) | 53. | (c) | 54. | (d) | 55. | (a) | 56. | (d) | 57. | (b) | 58. | (b) | 59. | (b) | 60. | (a) |
| 61. | (b) | 62. | (b) | 63. | (d) | 64. | (b) | 65. | (b) | 66. | (d) | 67. | (a) | 68. | (c) | 69. | (a) | 70. | (b) |
| 71. | (b) | 72. | (c) | 73. | (b) | 74. | (d) | 75. | (c) | 76. | (d) | 77. | (b) | 78. | (d) | 79. | (b) | 80. | (b) |
| 81. | (d) | 82. | (a) | 83. | (d) | 84. | (c) | 85. | (a) | 86. | (c) | 87. | (c) | 88. | (d) | 89. | (b) | 90. | (a) |
| 91. | (c) | 92. | (c) | 93. | (d) | 94. | (d) | 95. | (b) | 96. | (a) | 97. | (b) | 98. | (b) | 99. | (c) | 100. | (c) |
| 101. | (d) | 102. | (b) | 103. | (d) | 104. | (b) | 105. | (b) | 106. | (b) | 107. | (b) | 108. | (a) | 109. | (b) | 110. | (c) |
| 111. | (a) | 112. | (c) | 113. | (a) | 114. | (b) | 115. | (c) | 116. | (d) | 117. | (b) | 118. | (c) | 119. | (a) | 120. | (c) |

# MADHYA PRADESH

## Higher Secondary Teacher Eligibility Test

# Practice Paper 4

**1.** Identify the type of underlined noun in the following sentence.
Solomon was the wisest of all things.
(a) Proper (b) Common
(c) Collective (d) Abstract

**2.** The thieves hid the loot in a ...... of hay.
(a) bunch (b) stack
(c) bowl (d) group

**3.** Which among the following is a reflexive pronoun?
(a) Themselves (b) Yours
(c) Hers (d) Both (b) and (c)

**4.** Stella and Maria haven't met ...... for a long time.
(a) each other (b) each
(c) other (d) others

**5.** 'Queen' is for ......, 'king' is for gentleman.
(a) woman (b) girl
(c) princess (d) lady

**6.** Choose the third form of the verb of word 'Arise'.
(a) Arose (b) Arosed
(c) Arisen (d) Arised

**7.** The lion is ...... the deer.
(a) choosing (b) cheering
(c) changing (d) chasing

**8.** Choose the correct word to replace the given underlined word.
One is bounded in duty to help the ageing parents.
(a) bound (b) binding
(c) bind (d) No improvement

**9.** ...... I have more cheese on my sandwich.
(a) Must (b) Could
(c) Would (d) Have to

**10.** She expects that her son ...... .
(a) can return (b) may return
(c) should return (d) could return

**11.** Select the option which is the correct form of the sentence.
Deepak alongwith his aunts were present in the party.
(a) Deepak alongwith his aunts were present in the parties.
(b) Deepak alongwith his aunts was present in the party.
(c) Deepak alongwith his aunt were present in the party.
(d) No error

**12.** The members of the committee ...... to the proposal.
(a) have consented
(b) was consented
(c) had been consented
(d) has consented

**13.** His mother always forbids him ...... with Nisha.
(a) from speaking (b) to speak
(c) not to speak (d) speaking

**14.** The boys in the hostel are averse ...... port in the strike.
(a) to take (b) to taking (c) for taking (d) taking

**15.** She has got ...... headache.
(a) A (b) An (c) The (d) No article

**16.** ...... people can speak English correctly.
(a) A few (b) Few (c) Elder (d) The few

**Directions** (Q. Nos. 17-21) *Read the following passage and choose the most suitable answer from the options given below them.*

Organisations are institutions in which members compete for status and power. They compete for resource of the organisation, e.g. finance to expand their own departments, for career advancement and for power to control the activities of others. In pursuit of these aims, grouped are formed and sectional interests emerge. As a result, policy decisions may serve the ends of political and career systems rather than those of the concern. In this way, the goals of the organisation may be displaced in favour of sectional interests and individual ambition.

These preoccupations sometimes prevent the emergence of organic systems. Many of the electronic firms in the study had recently created research and development departments employing highly qualified and well paid scientists and technicians. Their high pay and expert knowledge were sometimes seen as a threat to the established order of rank, power and privilege.

Many senior managers had little knowledge of technicality and possibilities of new developments and electronics. Some felt that close cooperation with the experts in an organic system would reveal their ignorance and show their experience was now redundant.

**17.** The theme of the passage is
(a) groupism in organisations
(b) individual ambitions in organisations
(c) frustration of senior managers
(d) emergence of sectional interests in organisations

**18.** Organic system as related to the organisation implies its
(a) growth with the help of expert knowledge
(b) growth with input from science and technology
(c) steady all around development
(d) natural and unimpeded growth

**19.** Policy decision in organisation would involve
(a) cooperation at all levels in the organisation
(b) modernisation of the organisation
(c) attracting highly qualified personnel
(d) keeping in view the larger objectives of the organisations

**20.** The author makes out a case for
(a) organic system
(b) research and development in organisations
(c) an understanding between senior and middle level executives
(d) a refresher course for senior managers

**21.** The author tends to the senior managers as
(a) ignorant and incompetent
(b) a little out of step with their work environment
(c) jealous of their younger colleagues
(d) robbed of their rank, power and privilege

**Directions** (Q. Nos. 22-56) *Choose the most suitable option from the given ones.*

**22.** Which poem ends 'I shall but love thee better after death'?
(a) How Do I Love Thee
(b) Ode to a Grecian Urn
(c) In Faith I Do not Love Thee with Mine Eyes
(d) Let Me not to the Marriage of True Minds

**23.** Which poet is considered a national hero in Greece?
(a) John Keats (b) Lord Byron
(c) Solan (d) Sappho

**24.** Which kind of poem is Edward Lear associated with?
(a) Nature (b) Epics
(c) Sonnets (d) Nonsense

**25.** In Coleridge's poem 'The Rime of the Ancient Mariner' where were the three gallants going?
(a) A funeral (b) A wedding
(c) Market (d) To the races

**26.** Harold Nicholson described which poet as 'Very yellow and glum. Perfect manners'?
(a) Cummings
(b) T S Elliot
(c) John Greenleaf Whittier
(d) Walt Whitman

**27.** What was strange about Emily Dickinson?
(a) She rarely left home
(b) She wrote in code
(c) She never attempted to publish her poetry
(d) She wrote her poems in invisible ink

**28.** Rupert Brooke wrote his poetry during which conflict?
(a) Boer War (b) Second World War
(c) Korean War (d) First World War

**29.** Which poet Laureate wrote about a church mouse?
(a) Betjeman (b) Hughes
(c) Marvel (d) Larkin

**30.** Which American writer published 'A Brave and Startling Truth' in 1996?
(a) Robert Hass (b) Jessica Hagdorn
(c) Maya Angelou (d) Micheal Palmer

**31.** Who wrote about the idyllic 'Isle of Innisfree'?
(a) Dylan Thomas (b) Ezra Pound
(c) WB Yeats (d) Cummings

**32.** Sylvia Plath married which English poet?
(a) Masefield (b) Causley
(c) Hughes (d) Larkin

**33.** Carl Sandburg's 'Planked Whitefish' contains what kind of imagery?
(a) Sea scenes (b) Rural Idyll
(c) War (d) Innocent childhood

**34.** Which influential American poet was born in Long Island in 1819?
(a) Emily Dickinson (b) Paul Dunbar
(c) John Greenleaf Whittier (d) Walt Whitman

**35.** In 1960 'The Colossus' was the first book of poems published by which poetess?
(a) Elizabeth Bishop (b) Sylvia Plath
(c) Marianne Moore (d) Laura Jackson

**36.** In his poem, Kipling said 'If you can meet with triumph and ..............'?
(a) Glory (b) Ruin
(c) Disaster (d) Victory

**37.** What is the earliest surviving European poem?
(a) The Homeric epic (b) The Gilgamesh epic
(c) The Deluge epic (d) The Hesiodic ode

**38.** Which of the following is not a poetic tradition?
(a) The Epic (b) The Comic
(c) The Occult (d) The Tragic

**39.** What is the study of poetry's meter and form called?
(a) Prosody (b) Potology
(c) Rheumatology (d) Scansion

**40.** Shakespeare composed much of his plays in what sort of verse?
(a) Alliterative verse (b) Sonnet form
(c) Iambic pentameter (d) Dactylic hexameter

**41.** Which poet invented the concept of the variable foot in poetry?
(a) William Carlos Williams (b) Emily Dickinson
(c) Gerard Manly Hopkins (d) Robert Frost

**42.** Who wrote this famous line: 'Shall I compare thee to a summer's day/ Thou art more lovely and more temperate...'
(a) TS Eliot (b) Lord Tennyson
(c) Charlotte Bronte (d) Shakespeare

**43.** From what century does the poetic form the folk ballad date?
(a) The 12th (b) The 14th
(c) The 17th (d) The 19th

**44.** From which of Shakespeare's plays is this famous line: 'Did my heart love till now?/ For swear it, sight/ For I never saw a true beauty until this night'
(a) A Midsummer Night's Dream (b) Hamlet
(c) Othello (d) Romeo and Juliet

**45.** What is a poem called whose first letters of each line spell out a word?
(a) Alliterative (b) Epic
(c) Acrostic (d) Haiku

**46.** Auld Lang Syne is a famous poem by whom?
(a) Sir Walter Scott (b) William Butler Yeats
(c) Henry Longfellow (d) Robert Burns

**47.** How has Stephen Dunn been described in the Oxford Companion to 20th Century Poetry?
(a) A poet of middleness
(b) Capturing a sense of spiritual marooness
(c) One of the leading prairie poets
(d) Has some distinction as a critic

**48.** 'The Cambridge school' refers to a group who emerged when?
(a) The 1900's (b) The 1960's
(c) The 1920's (d) The 1930's

**49.** Margaret Atwood was born in which Canadian city?
(a) Vancouver (b) Toronto (c) Ottowa (d) Montreal

**50.** Which of the following words describe the prevailing attitude of High-Modern Literature?
(a) Skeptical (b) Authoritative
(c) Impressionistic (d) Both (a) and (c)

**51.** Which Welsh poet wrote 'Under Milk Wood' ?
(a) Anthony Hopkins (b) Richard Burton
(c) Tom Jones (d) Dylan Thomas

**52.** Who wrote 'Canterbury Tales'?
(a) Geoffrey Chaucer (b) Dick Whittington
(c) Thomas Lancaster (d) King Richard II

**53.** Who wrote 'The Hound of the Baskervilles'?
(a) Agatha Christie (b) H Ryder-Haggard
(c) PD James (d) Arthur Conan Doyle

**54.** William Shakespeare is not the author of
(a) Titus Andronicus (b) Taming of the Shrew
(c) White Devil (d) Hamlet

**55.** ......... is a late 20th century play written by a woman.
(a) Queen Cristina (b) Top Girls
(c) Camille (d) The Homecoimg

**56.** Which of the following writers wrote historical novels?
(a) Jane Austen and Charlotte Bronte
(b) Sir Walter Scott and Maria Edgeworth
(c) William Wordsworth and Samuel Taylor Coleridge
(d) Mary Shelley and Percy Bysshe Shelley

**Directions** (Q. Nos. 57-61) *Read the following passage and choose the most suitable answer of the questions from the options given below them.*

The rainy season has returned, and the man is back at his work, he is Pannalal Patel, the man who has completed 96 years, and is still going strong. Pannalal was once a 'terrorist' then he turned into a Gandhian. At present, his mission is 'Meen Mangal' or 'the well-being of fish', as he calls it. Come the rains and Pannalal would release millions of young salmons into rivers following through the neighbourhood. He says that water without fish is just as absurd as fish without water. On Independence Day Eve, he had, as if, an appointment with the Ajoy, the river he loves and adores. Choked up with silt and sand from bank to bank, the river remains almost dry throughout the year except in the rainy season. Once called 'the crazy river' for often changing its course. Ajoy is now better known for the great destruction it causes, at intervals of some years, by flooding the villages on its banks. It then washes away people and cattle and houses and brings great misery. The appointed day arrived. It was a cloudy afternoon at Palitpur, the venue of the programme where a new bridge has been built across the river. Short speeches were made. Songs were sung. Mr Patel took a handful of the young salmon and threw them into the water–once, twice, thrice. Others followed him. The hero of the day looked happy, and a smile lit up his wrinkled face. But some fisherman in the crowd were rather sceptical about the usefulness of the programme. Will the fish, when grown up, return to the same water and be caught in their nets ? Perhaps not. They talked among themselves. Mr Patel, however, does not bother himself about who catches how much fish in which waters. He himself is a complete vegetarian. His only concern is the well-being of fish.

**57.** Pannalal Patel, who is very old, is still
(a) strong (b) fond of fishing
(c) very alert (d) can walk fast

**58.** Pannalal had an appointment with the river Ajoy
(a) on 15th August (b) on 14th August
(c) on 15th August morning (d) on 14th August evening

**59.** The Ajoy floods its banks
(a) every rainy season (b) very rarely
(c) every few years (d) quite often

**60.** According to Pannalal, water without fish is
(a) unthinkable (b) tasteless
(c) impure (d) unprofitable

**61.** The object of Pannalal's programme at Palitpur was the welfare of
(a) the fishermen (b) the Ajoy
(c) society (d) fish

**Directions** (Q. Nos. 62-70) *Choose the right option that can fill the blank in the most appropriate way.*

**62.** The workers are .......... what is due to them.
(a) hell bent on getting (b) hell bent for getting
(c) hell bent upon getting (d) hell bent at getting

**63.** When it was feared that the serfs might go too far and gain their freedom from serfdom, the protestant leaders joined the princes ...........them.
(a) into crushing (b) in crushing
(c) without crushing (d) at crushing

**64.** ............, I would have been able to read for a while before bed time.
(a) If the room was brighter (b) If the room are brighter
(c) Had the room been brighter (d) If the room had been brighter

**65.** The record for the biggest tiger hunt has not been.........since 1911 when Lord Hardinge. Then Viceroy of India, shot a tiger than measured 11 feet and 6 inches.
(a) improved (b) broken
(c) bettered (d) met

**66.** .........brought about his downfall.
(a) His intense desire (b) His desire for power
(c) His fatal desire (d) His powerful desire

**67.** Will you kindly............. the knot?
(a) untie (b) break
(c) loose (d) open

**68.** He ................ to me that he would be coming late.
(a) sent word (b) had sent a word
(c) sent words (d) sent a word

**69.** John.................. me that he hasn't done it yet.
(a) told (b) tells
(c) was telling (d) had told

**70.** If he ............ time he will call you.
(a) would have (b) would have had
(c) has (d) had

**71.** Mrs. bennet's reaction to Lydia's marriage is best described as
(a) indifferent (b) condemnatory
(c) cautiously pleased (d) unreservedly jubilant

**72.** Jane is younger than Elizabeth.
(a) False (b) True
(c) Not mentioned in the Novel (d) Both are twins

**73.** What form of execution has just been invented?
(a) The guillotine (b) The electric chair
(c) The firing squad (d) Drawing and quartering

**74.** Who has been termed as 'spineless immigrant lover' in the novel?
(a) Sarah (b) Dev
(c) Adit (d) None of these

**75.** In 'Portrait of a Lady', Khushwant Singh describes about his
(a) mother (b) grandmother (c) aunt (d) niece

**Directions** (Q. Nos. 76-84) *Read each sentence to find out whether there is any grammatical error in it. The error, if any will be in one part of the sentence. The letter of that part is the answer. If there is no error, the answer is '4'. (Ignore the errors of punctuation, if any).*

**76.** (a) We discussed about the problem so thoroughly
(b) on the eve of the examination
(c) that I found it very easy to work it out.
(d) No error

**77.** (a) An Indian ship
(b) laden with merchandise
(c) got drowned in the Pacific Ocean.
(d) No error

**78.** (a) I could not put up in a hotel
(b) because the boarding and lodging charges
(c) were exorbitant.
(d) No error

**79.** (a) The Indian radio
(b) which was previously controlled by the British rulers
(c) is free now from the narrow vested interests.
(d) No error

**80.** (a) If I had known (b) this yesterday
(c) I will have helped him. (d) No error

**81.** Choose the correct form of the given sentence.
The death is a great leveller.
(a) A death is a great leveller. (b) An death is a great leveller.
(c) Death is a great leveller. (d) None of the above

**82.** He and his friends work ...... .
(a) hardly (b) hard (c) only (d) diligent

**83.** If you take away the prefix and the suffix, what is left of the word 'Unemployed'?
(a) Unemploy (b) Employed (c) Employ (d) Employe

**84.** If you want to say that someone is not helpful, which word would you use?
(a) Inhelpful (b) Unhelpful
(c) Helpfulness (d) None of the above

**Directions** (Q. Nos. 85-89) *Read the following passage carefully and answers the questions.*

**On the day of the Christmas concert the entire orchestra entered the gymnasium where a large throng of pupils and parents were gathered. The school choir had gathered on the balcony with candles and the orchestra began 'Silent Night'. Slowly the lights dimmed, leaving us in darkness except for the hundred glimmering candles held by the choir as they softly sang the carol. Slowly, and just as dramatically, the orchestra began to falter - in direct proportion to the dimming of the lights, when the lights faded out completely, so did the orchestra, because no one could read his music except for me, for my music was in my head. From a corner of the stage, the sound of my violin filled the gymnasium. The choir and I went through verse after verse. When it was all over, the ovation was positively thunderous.**

**85.** The narrator is
(a) a priest (b) the leader of pupils
(c) an instrumentalist (d) a singer

**86.** Why did the orchestra begin to falter?
(a) The orchestra was not led properly
(b) The dimming of lights caused it
(c) The violin dominated the other instruments
(d) There was no coordination in the chorus

**87.** How could the choir sing when the lights dimmed?
(a) They had memorised the songs
(b) They could sing in candle lights
(c) There was some natural light at the choir side
(d) The narrator helped them sing

**88.** The statements that 'the ovation was positively thunderous' means that
(a) there was a joyful expression of appreciation by people
(b) the audience joined the singers and sang aloud
(c) the audience made circles and danced in ecstasy
(d) the audience made a noise resembling thunder

**89.** How was it possible for the narrator to continue with his music?
(a) He was at the corner of the stage where he could get light
(b) His instrument did not need electric power
(c) He played in candle light
(d) He did not need to read his music

**Directions** (Q. Nos. 90-94) *In the questions below the sentences have been given in Active/Passive voice. From the given alternatives, choose the one which best expresses the given sentence in Passive/Active voice.*

**90.** After driving Professor Kumar to the museum she dropped him at his hotel.
(a) After being driven to the museum, Professor Kumar was dropped at his hotel.
(b) Professor Kumar was being driven dropped at his hotel.
(c) After she had driven Professor Kumar to the museum she had dropped him at his hotel.
(d) After she was driven Professor Kumar to the museum she had dropped him at his hotel.

**91.** I remember my sister taking me to the museum.
(a) I remember I was taken to the museum by my sister.
(b) I remember being taken to the museum by my sister.
(c) I remember myself being taken to the museum by my sister.
(d) I remember taken to the museum by my sister.

**92.** Who is creating this mess?
(a) Who has been created this mess?
(b) By whom has this mess been created?
(c) By whom this mess is being created?
(d) By whom is this mess being created?

**93.** They greet me cheerfully every morning.
(a) Every morning I was greeted cheerfully.
(b) I am greeted cheerfully by them every morning.
(c) I am being greeted cheerfully by them every morning.
(d) Cheerful greeting is done by them every morning to me.

**94.** Darjeeling grows tea.
(a) Tea is being grown in Darjeeling.
(b) Let the tea be grown in Darjeeling.
(c) Tea is grown in Darjeeling.
(d) Tea grows in Darjeeling.

**95.** Fill the blank with correct past tense form.
He ...... (be) weak in English in the beginning.
(a) being (b) been (c) was (d) had been

**96.** The thief explained how he ...... from the jail.
(a) escapes (b) had escaped
(c) escaped (d) has escaped

**97.** In the tragic incident, none of the passengers ...... .
(a) could survived (b) survive
(c) survived (d) is surviving

**98.** I was angry ...... him ...... lying to me.
(a) with, for (b) to, for
(c) with, on (d) to, with

**99.** A jeep hit him while he was going ...... the main road.
(a) on (b) across
(c) behind (d) through

**100.** Select the option which is the correct form of the sentence.
He has no faith for God.
(a) He has no faith with God. (b) He has no faith in God.
(c) He has no faith to God. (d) None of the above

**101.** She writes slowly ...... neatly.
(a) but (b) and (c) else (d) since

**102.** Although she works hard ...... she fails.
(a) but (b) and (c) yet (d) than

**103.** Choose the correct indirect speech of the given sentence.
She said to him, 'Why don't you go today?'
(a) She asked him why he did not go that day.
(b) She said to him why he don't go that day.
(c) She asked him not to go that day.
(d) She asked him why he did not go today.

**104.** Choose the correct direct speech of the given sentence.
Rekha told Aman that he was lying.
(a) Rekha told Aman, " He was lying".
(b) Rekha said to Aman, "You are lying".
(c) Rekha said to Aman, "You were lying".
(d) Rekha said to Aman "He is lying".

**105.** Choose the best alternative to complete the sentence given below.
I didn't know ...... .
(a) what he mean (b) what did he mean
(c) what did he meant (d) what he meant

**106.** Choose the synonym of the given word. Error
(a) Misadventure (b) Misgiving
(c) Ambiguity (d) Blunder

**107.** Pick out the same meaning word to the italicised word in the given sentence.
Reading of poetry is not *congenial* to his taste.
(a) preferable (b) helpful
(c) beneficial (d) suited

**Directions** (Q. Nos. 108-110) *Choose the word which is exact opposite in meaning to the given word.*

**108.** Hypocritical
(a) Gentle (b) Sincere
(c) Amiable (d) Dependable

**109.** Evasive
(a) Free (b) Honest
(c) Liberal (d) Frank

**110.** Industrious
(a) Indifferent (b) Indolent
(c) Casual (d) Passive

**111.** The ...... to this hill is very difficult.
(a) avenge (b) revenge
(c) assent (d) ascent

**112.** Which is an example of homophones?
(a) Bear and bare
(b) Cat and Dog
(c) Read and unread
(d) Pretty and beautiful

**113.** Which word is a homophone of 'four'?
(a) fir (b) hair
(c) for (d) foreign

**114.** The ...... of the cats are sharp.
(a) paws
(b) pauses
(c) pause
(d) None of the above

**Directions** (Q. Nos. 115-117) *Select the alternative which is the best substitute of the words / sentence.*

**115.** A man of odd habits
(a) Eccentric (b) Cynical
(c) Introvert (d) Moody

**116.** Willing to be guided or controlled
(a) Adorable (b) Adamant
(c) Amenable (d) Abominable

**117.** Regard something as being due to a cause
(a) Adventitious (b) Superfluous
(c) Incidental (d) Ascribe

**118.** The first scene of the play, 'Arms and the Man' opens late in November in the year
(a) 1885 (b) 1886
(c) 1887 (d) None of the above

**119.** Dragoman is an imaginary
(a) river
(b) hill
(c) pass
(d) None of the above

**120.** What is Caliban?
(a) The son of a witch-hag
(b) A complex figure
(c) A fool
(d) All of the above

# ANSWERS

| | | | | | | | | | | | | | | | | | | | |
|---|---|---|---|---|---|---|---|---|---|---|---|---|---|---|---|---|---|---|---|
| 1. | (a) | 2. | (b) | 3. | (a) | 4. | (a) | 5. | (d) | 6. | (c) | 7. | (d) | 8. | (a) | 9. | (b) | 10. | (b) |
| 11. | (b) | 12. | (a) | 13. | (b) | 14. | (b) | 15. | (a) | 16. | (a) | 17. | (d) | 18. | (b) | 19. | (c) | 20. | (c) |
| 21. | (a) | 22. | (a) | 23. | (b) | 24. | (d) | 25. | (b) | 26. | (b) | 27. | (a) | 28. | (d) | 29. | (a) | 30. | (c) |
| 31. | (c) | 32. | (c) | 33. | (c) | 34. | (d) | 35. | (b) | 36. | (c) | 37. | (a) | 38. | (c) | 39. | (a) | 40. | (c) |
| 41. | (a) | 42. | (d) | 43. | (a) | 44. | (d) | 45. | (c) | 46. | (d) | 47. | (a) | 48. | (b) | 49. | (c) | 50. | (d) |
| 51. | (d) | 52. | (a) | 53. | (d) | 54. | (c) | 55. | (c) | 56. | (b) | 57. | (a) | 58. | (d) | 59. | (c) | 60. | (a) |
| 61. | (d) | 62. | (c) | 63. | (b) | 64. | (c) | 65. | (b) | 66. | (b) | 67. | (a) | 68. | (a) | 69. | (b) | 70. | (c) |
| 71. | (d) | 72. | (a) | 73. | (a) | 74. | (c) | 75. | (b) | 76. | (a) | 77. | (c) | 78. | (a) | 79. | (c) | 80. | (c) |
| 81. | (c) | 82. | (b) | 83. | (c) | 84. | (b) | 85. | (c) | 86. | (c) | 87. | (d) | 88. | (a) | 89. | (d) | 90. | (a) |
| 91. | (b) | 92. | (d) | 93. | (b) | 94. | (c) | 95. | (b) | 96. | (a) | 97. | (d) | 98. | (a) | 99. | (b) | 100. | (b) |
| 101. | (a) | 102. | (c) | 103. | (a) | 104. | (b) | 105. | (d) | 106. | (d) | 107. | (d) | 108. | (b) | 109. | (b) | 110. | (b) |
| 111. | (d) | 112. | (a) | 113. | (c) | 114. | (d) | 115. | (a) | 116. | (c) | 117. | (d) | 118. | (a) | 119. | (c) | 120. | (d) |

# MADHYA PRADESH
## Higher Secondary Teacher Eligibility Test

# Practice Paper 5

**1.** Which of the following sentences is in active voice?
(a) I requested him to come in time.
(b) He was asked to keep quiet.
(c) A house was bought for fifty lakhs.
(d) He was hit bad by a ball.

**2.** Which of the following sentence is in passive voice?
(a) They live in this city.
(b) He will be taken care of.
(c) He teaches Chemistry.
(d) Ram is flying a kite.

**Directions** (Q. Nos. 3 and 4) *Choose the best alternative to complete the sentence.*

**3.** He said
(a) that the weather colder than usual
(b) the weather be colder than usual
(c) the weather was colder than usual
(d) the weather it is colder than usual

**4.** I believe
(a) him he is right
(b) he is right
(c) he be right
(d) that he right

**Directions** (Q. Nos. 5-7) *Select the one which best expresses the same sentence in Indirect/Direct speech.*

**5.** The spectators said, "Bravo! Well played, Ravi."
(a) The spectators called Ravi Bravo because he had played well.
(b) The spectators said that Ravi played well and applauded him.
(c) The spectators encouraged Ravi saying that he played well.
(d) The spectators applauded Ravi, saying that he had played well.

**6.** "Have you ever seen Taj Mahal?" he said.
(a) He asked him whether he has ever seen Taj Mahal.
(b) He asked him whether he ever seen Taj Mahal.
(c) He said that had he ever seen Taj Mahal.
(d) He asked him whether he had ever seen Taj Mahal.

**7.** The father warned his son that he should be beware of him.
(a) "Beware of him, son", warned his father.
(b) The father warned his son, "Be careful about him".
(c) "Beware of him, son", warned the father.
(d) The father said to his son, "Be aware of him".

**8.** Although my father is sick ...... he goes to the office.
(a) if (b) unless
(c) yet (d) for

**9.** The Sun rose ...... the fog disappeared.
(a) still (b) and
(c) as soon as (d) as

**10.** Select the option which is the correct form of the sentence.
This horse runs as fast like the tiger.
(a) This horse runs as fast as the tiger.
(b) This horse runs as fast as like the tiger.
(c) This horse runs as fast like as the tiger.
(d) None of the above

**11.** Indian Airlines had no positive response ...... the incident occurred ...... the failure ...... an aeroplane engine.
(a) to, in, of (b) of, in, to
(c) in, to, of (d) to, into, from

**12.** He drained what was left ...... his drink.
(a) from (b) in
(c) of (d) off

**13.** We have lot of things in common ...... music.
(a) beside (b) below
(c) among (d) besides

**14.** Which is the correct form of the given sentence?
Rupesh applied for a Principal.
(a) Rupesh applied to the post of a Principal.
(b) Rupesh applied for the post of a Principal.
(c) Rupesh applied on the post of a Principal
(d) None of the above

**15.** Fill the blank with correct present tense form.
The Sun ...... (shine) by day.
(a) shining (b) has been shining
(c) shines (d) is shining

**16.** Identify the best replacement from the options given below.
I have still to meet a person who is perfectly satisfied with his job.
(a) am still to meet (b) am yet to meet
(c) might still meet (d) No improvement

**Directions** (Q. Nos. 17-21) *Read the following passage and choose the most suitable answer from the options given below them.*

**Corduroy is fast establishing itself at this year's fabric, while the ribbed cotton itself provides utilitarian tenaciary, texture and warmth. It is the fabric's long held associations may provide a hint to its current revival as a fabric for all seasons. It is Corduroy's link with the good breeding and country living that made it an essential ingredient in the gentleman's wardrobe along with Wellington boots and decent wooly. It combines the comfortable nonsense appeal of cotton with the perfectly correct luxury finish of velvet. Corduroy has the ability to appear either supremely sophisticated or rough and ready.**

**17.** Which one of the following best describes the passage?
(a) It tell us about the usefulness of corduroy
(b) It talks us about the virtues of corduroy
(c) It persuades us to buy corduroy
(d) It makes as understand the everlasting appeal of corduroy to the young

**18.** According to the author, the special quality of corduroy is that
(a) it needs no ironing
(b) it combines the virtues of both cotton and velvet
(c) it contains the correct mixture of cotton and velvet
(d) both the rich and that not-so rich can afford to buy it

**19.** Corduroy is a fabric for all seasons because
(a) it can be worn not only in winter but also in summer
(b) of its peculiar texture and warmth
(c) it is made popular by catchy advertisements
(d) gentleman can wear it in both formal and informal occasions

**20.** According to the passage, corduroy is essential in a gentleman wardrobe because
(a) it goes with Wellington boots
(b) its current revival gives a taste of the latest fashion
(c) it has its associations with good upbringing and a conservative lifestyle
(d) it can be an idea alternative to the woollen clothes

**21.** When the writer refers to corduroy's 'utilitarian tenacity' he means that
(a) though expensive, it is economic in the long run
(b) it is useful because it is durable
(c) it has remained fashionable over several years
(d) it does not need frequent washing

**Directions** (Q. Nos. 22-56) *Choose the most suitable option from the given ones.*

**22.** Who wrote 'Ten Little Niggers'?
(a) Sir Arthur Conan Doyle
(b) Irvine Welsh
(c) Agatha Christie
(d) None of the above

**23.** Which of the following is Thomas Hardy's book?
(a) The Poor Man and the Lady
(b) The Return of Native
(c) Chollttee
(d) None of the above

**24.** Which of the following is not a work of John Keats?
(a) Endymion (b) To Some Ladies
(c) To Hope (d) None of these

**25.** Who wrote the poems, 'On Death' and 'Women, Wine, and Snuff'?
(a) John Milton (b) John Keats
(c) PB Shelley (d) William Wordsworth

**26.** "Of Man's first disobedience, and the fruit Of that forbidden tree whose mortal taste Brought death into the world, and all our woe, With loss of Eden."
This is an extract from
(a) Paradise Lost (b) Paradise Regained
(c) Samson Agonistes (d) Divorce Tracts

**27.** William Shakespeare was born in the year
(a) 1564 (b) 1544 (c) 1578 (d) 1582

**28.** Which of the following is not a Shakespeare's tragedy?
(a) Dracula (b) Othello
(c) Macbeth (d) Hamlet

**29.** Who wrote 'The Winter's Tale'?
(a) George Bernard Shaw (b) John Dryden
(c) Christopher Marlowe (d) William Shakespeare

**30.** What is the difference between a simile and a metaphor?
(a) No difference. Simply two different ways of referring to the same thing
(b) A simile is more descriptive
(c) A simile uses as or like to make a comparison and a metaphor doesn't
(d) A simile must use animals in the comparison

**31.** What is the word for a 'play on words'?
(a) pun (b) simile
(c) haiku (d) metaphor

**32.** Which represents an example of alliteration?
(a) Language Arts
(b) Peter Piper Picked Peppers
(c) I Like Music
(d) A Beautiful Scenery with Music

**33.** What is the imitation of natural sounds in word form?
(a) Personification (b) Hyperboles
(c) Alliteration (d) Onomatopoeia

**34.** The theme is ...
(a) a plot
(b) a character
(c) an address
(d) the point a writer is trying to make about a subject

**35.** Concentrate on these elements when writing a good poem.
(a) Characters, main idea and theme
(b) Purpose and audience
(c) Theme, purpose, form and mood
(d) Rhyme and reason

**36.** Which is not a poetry form?
(a) Epic (b) Tale
(c) Ballad (d) Sonnet

**37.** Which is an example of a proverb?
(a) Get a 'stake' in our business.
(b) You can't have your cake and eat it, too
(c) The snow was white as cotton.
(d) You're driving me crazy.

**38.** Which is an exaggeration?
(a) Alliteration (b) Haiku
(c) Hyperbole (d) Prose

**39.** Which of the following is not a poet?
(a) William Shakespeare (b) Terry Saylor
(c) Elizabeth B Browning (d) Emily Dickinson

**40.** Who has defined 'poetry' as a fundamental creative act using languages?
(a) H W Longfellow (b) Ralph Waldo Emerson
(c) Dylan Thomas (d) William Wordsworth

**41.** What is a sonnet?
(a) A poem of six lines
(b) A poem of eight lines
(c) A poem of twelve lines
(d) A poem of fourteen lines

**42.** What is study of meter, rhythm and intonation of a poem called as?
(a) Prosody (b) Allegory
(c) Scansion (d) Assonance

**43.** Which figure of speech is it when a statement is exaggerated in a poem?
(a) Onomatopoeia (b) Metonymy
(c) Alliteration (d) Hyperbole

**44.** There was aware of her true love, at length come riding by this is a couplet from the Bailiff's Daughter of Islington. What figure of speech is used by the poet?
(a) Metaphor (b) Synecdoche
(c) Euphemism (d) Irony

**45.** Which culture is known for their long, rhymic poetic verses known as Qasidas?
(a) Hindu (b) Celtic
(c) Arabic (d) Arameic

**46.** Complete this Shakespearean line "Let me not to the marriage of true minds bring........."
(a) Impediments (b) Inconveniences
(c) Worries (d) Troubles

**47.** Which of the following is a Japanese poetic form?
(a) Jintishi (b) Villanelle
(c) Ode (d) Tanka

**48.** What is the title of the poem that begins thus 'what is this life, if full of care, we have no time to stand and stare'?
(a) Comfort (b) Leisure
(c) Relaxation (d) Tranquility

**49.** Which of the following is not an English poet (i.e. from England)?
(a) Victor Hugo (b) Alexander Pope
(c) John Milton (d) Samuel Taylor Coleridge

**50.** Who was often called as the Romantic Poet as most of his poems revolved around nature?
(a) William Blake
(b) William Shakespeare
(c) William Morris
(d) William Wordsworth

**51.** What is a funny poem of five lines called?
(a) Quartet (b) Limerick
(c) Sestet (d) Palindrome

**52.** How did WH Auden describe poetry?
(a) An awful way to earn a living
(b) A game of knowledge
(c) The soul exposed
(d) An explosion of language

**53.** Sassoon and Brooke wrote what kind of poetry?
(a) Light verse (b) Romantic
(c) Political satire (d) War poems

**54.** Where did TS Eliot spend most of his childhood?
(a) Denver (b) St Louis
(c) Cuba (d) Toronto

**55.** Ted Hughes was married to which American poetess?
(a) Carolyn Kizer (b) Mary Oliver
(c) Sylvia Plath (d) Marianne Moore

**56.** How old was Rupert Brooke at the time of his death?
(a) 24 (b) 31 (c) 21 (d) 28

**57.** We shall go for a picnic if the weather ...... good.
(a) is (b) was
(c) has been (d) had been

**58.** When the doctor ...... the patient was already .......... .
(a) arrived ; died
(b) arrived ; dead
(c) arrive ; dead
(d) arriving ; dying

**59.** Choose the correct prefix/suffix to fill the blank. You shouldn't eat chicken that is ...... cooked.
(a) anti (b) mis (c) under (d) less

**60.** Which prefix can be used with the following words? Take, Chief, Behave
(a) Non (b) Dis
(c) In (d) Mis

**61.** Find out the word that has got a wrong prefix.
(a) Invincible (b) Indelible
(c) Malnourished (d) Unaccessible

**Directions** (Q. Nos. 62-70) *Choose the right option that can fill the blank in the most appropriate way.*

**62.** Will you ......... in this hour of need?
(a) lend me any rupees
(b) borrow me a few rupees
(c) lend me a few rupees
(d) lend me few rupees

**63.** During his long discourse, he did not ......... that point.
(a) touch upon (b) touch on
(c) touch of (d) touch

**64.** He found a ............ in the room.
(a) wooden and broken chair
(b) broken wooden chair
(c) broken and wooden chair
(d) wooden broken chair

**65.** He could not..............in the dark room.
(a) look at (b) see
(c) see through (d) look anything

**66.** The greatest thing in style is to have a ........... metaphor.
(a) knowledge (b) command
(c) need (d) use of

**67.** While crossing the highway, a five years old child was knocked ..................... by a passing car.
(a) away (b) up
(c) down (d) out

**68.** Hoping not to be disturbed, I sat down in my easy chair to read the book,...............................
(a) I had won as a prize
(b) I have won as prize
(c) I had to win as a prize
(d) I won as a prize

**69.** More than one person ............................ in accident.
(a) were killed (b) are killed
(c) have been killed (d) was killed

**70.** No one could explain how a calm and balanced person like him could ........................ such a mindless act on his friends.
(a) perpetuate (b) perpetrate
(c) precipitate (d) penetrate

**Directions** (Q. Nos. 71-75) *Read the following passage and choose the most suitable answer from the options given below them.*

The assault on the purity of the environment is the price that we pay for many of the benefits of modern technology. For the advantage of automotive transportation we pay a price in smog-induced diseases; for the powerful effects of new insecticides, we pay a price in dwindling wildlife and disturbances in the relation of living things and their surroundings; for nuclear power, we risk the biological hazards of radiation. By increasing agricultural production with fertilisers, we worsen water population.

The highly developed nations of the world are not only the immediate beneficiaries of the good that technology can do that are also the first victims of environmental diseases that technology breeds. In the past, the environmental effects which accompanied technological progress were restricted to a small and relatively short time. The new hazards are neither local nor brief. Modern air pollutions cover vast areas of continents: Radioactive fall out from the nuclear explosion is worldwide. Radioactive pollutants now on the Earth surface will be found there for generations, and in case of Carbon-14, for thousands of years.

**71.** The widespread use of insecticides has
(a) reduced the number of wild animals
(b) caused imbalance in the relationship between living beings and their environment
(c) eliminated diseases by killing mosquitoes and flies
(d) caused biological hazards

**72.** The passage emphasis that modern technology
(a) is an unmixed blessing
(b) has caused serious hazards to life
(c) has produced powerful chemicals
(d) has benefited highly developed nations

**73.** According to the passage, the increasing use of fertilisers is responsible for
(a) abundance of food
(b) disturbance in the ecological system
(c) water pollution
(d) increase in diseases

**74.** The harmful effects of modern technology are
(a) widespread but short-lived (b) widespread and long-lasting
(c) limited and long-lasting (d) severe but short-lived

**75.** Radioactive pollutants
(a) are limited in their effect
(b) will infect the atmosphere for thousands of years
(c) will be on the surface of Earth for a very long time
(d) will dissipate in short span of time

**Directions** (Q. Nos. 76-79) *Read each sentence to find out whether there is any grammatical error in it. The error, if any will be in one part of the sentence. The letter of that part is the answer. If there is no error, the answer is '4'. (Ignore the errors of punctuation, if any).*

**76.** (a) If you lend him a book
(b) he will lend it to someone else
(c) and never you will get it back.
(d) No error

**77.** (a) According to the Bible,
(b) it is meek and humble
(c) who shall inherit the Earth.
(d) No error

**78.** (a) Do the roses in your garden smell
(b) more sweetly
(c) than those in ours?
(d) No error

**79.** (a) Block of Residential flats
(b) are coming up
(c) near our house
(d) No error

**80.** Choose the correct sentence based on the adverb given in the brackets.
I take too long in the shower. (always)
(a) I take always too long in the shower.
(b) I always take too long in the shower.
(c) I take too long always in the shower.
(d) I take too long in the shower always.

**81.** Sanjay is ...... better today.
(a) fairly (b) rather (c) very (d) too

**82.** We were ...... considering selling the house.
(a) heavily (b) seriously (c) brightly (d) fully

**83.** Please get me ...... vegetables from the market.
(a) few (b) any (c) some (d) the

**84.** You can buy these maps at ...... station. They all have them.
(a) a lot of (b) several
(c) some (d) any

**85.** ...... boy standing behind the tree, is my cousin.
(a) The (b) A
(c) An (d) No article

**86.** Ramesh earns ₹ 10000 ...... month.
(a) a (b) the
(c) an (d) No article

**87.** There was ...... accident near ...... market this morning.
(a) the, a (b) an, the
(c) a, the (d) the, the

**88.** She showed ...... concern for her step-daughter.
(a) a little (b) little
(c) few (d) some

**89.** Her brother had ...... work.
(a) a lot of (b) a number of
(c) the few (d) few

**Directions** (Q. Nos. 90-100) *In the questions below the sentences have been given in Active/Passive voice. From the given alternatives, choose the one which best expresses the given sentence in Passive/Active voice.*

**90.** A child could not have done this mischief.
(a) This mischief could not be done by a child.
(b) This mischief could not been done by a child.
(c) This mischief could not have been done by a child.
(d) This mischief a child could not have been done.

**91.** James Watt discovered the energy of steam.
(a) The energy of steam discovered James Watt.
(b) The energy of steam was discovered by James Watt.
(c) James Watt was discovered by the energy of steam.
(d) James Watt had discovered energy by the steam.

**92.** She makes cakes every Sunday.
(a) Every Sunday cakes made by her.
(b) Cakes are made by her every Sunday.
(c) Cakes make her every Sunday.
(d) Cakes were made by her every Sunday.

**93.** She spoke to the official on duty.
(a) The official on duty was spoken to by her.
(b) The official was spoken to by her on duty.
(c) She was spoken to by the official on duty.
(d) She was the official to be spoken to on duty.

**94.** The doctor advised the patient not to eat rice.
(a) The patient was advised by the doctor not to eat rice.
(b) The patient was advised by the doctor that he should not eat rice.
(c) The patient was being advised by the doctor that he should not rice by the doctor.
(d) The patient has been advised not to eat rice by the doctor.

**Directions** (Q. Nos. 95 and 96) *Choose the correct synonym of the given words.*

**95.** Canny
(a) Obstinate (b) Handsome
(c) Clever (d) Stout

**96.** Foray
(a) Excursion (b) Contest
(c) Ranger (d) Intuition

**Directions** (Q. Nos. 97 and 98) *Select the word which is same in meaning to the given underlined word.*

**97.** The function was attended by some <u>eminent</u> persons.
(a) important (b) rich
(c) cultured (d) related

**98.** Special areas in the town have been allocated for <u>commercial</u> activities.
(a) social (b) official
(c) business (d) clerical

**Directions** (Q. Nos. 99 and100) *Choose the word exact opposite of the given word.*

**99.** Rarely
(a) Hardly (b) Definitely
(c) Frequently (d) Periodically

**100.** Commissioned
(a) Started (b) Closed
(c) Finished (d) Terminated

**Directions** (Q. Nos. 101 and 102) *Select the correct antonym of the given underlined word.*

**101.** Jia felt a lot of <u>pride</u>.
(a) Happiness (b) Shame
(c) Joy (d) Enjoyment

**102.** Tanya <u>gathered</u> some wood for the campfire.
(a) Burned (b) Soaked
(c) Collected (d) Scattered

**103.** You ...... of onions ! what did you eat?
(a) wreak (b) reek (c) wreck (d) reeked

**104.** He is bent upon taking........ .
(a) avenge (b) ark
(c) arc (d) revenge

**105.** Which of the following is a homonym pair?
(a) Counsil - Counsel
(b) Course - Curse
(c) Buyer - Bare
(d) Corpse - Crops

**106.** Which of the following is not a homonym pair?
(a) Patrol - Petrol (b) Pare - Pair
(c) Pain - Pane (d) Fear - Fare

**Directions** (Q. Nos. 107 and 108) *Select the one which is the best substitute of the given sentences.*

**107.** To send an unwanted person out of the country
(a) Exclude (b) Ostracise
(c) Deport (d) Expatriate

**108.** A short stay at a place
(a) Halt (b) Interlude
(c) Intermission (d) Sojourn

**109.** I ...... for my pen. Have you seen it?
(a) will look (b) looking
(c) look (d) am looking

**110.** She asked her mother, how ...... the oven.
(a) use (b) to use
(c) using (d) used to

**111.** ...... his lesson, he went out to play cricket.
(a) Learnt (b) Learning
(c) Having learnt (d) Learned

**112.** Choose the correct alternative to improve the given underlined word.
The teacher made the students <u>to solve</u> their problems.
(a) solve (b) solving
(c) in solving (d) No improvement

**113.** ...... you read when you were five?
(a) Can (b) Could
(c) May (d) Might

**114.** Make haste lest you ....... late.
(a) should get (b) should not get
(c) may not got (d) shall got

**115.** I had a hard time staying ...... during the boring speech.
(a) awoke (b) awake
(c) awaken (d) awakened

**116.** Identify the type of verb, underlined in the sentence.
Frustrated with the official's call, Ethan <u>kicked</u> the bench.
(a) Transitive verb
(b) Intransitive verb
(c) Linking verb
(d) Auxiliary verb

**117.** Don't blame yourself for the mistake. ...... is perfect.
(a) Nobody (b) Anybody
(c) Everybody (d) Somebody

**118.** He is not a good friend but he is an acquaintance of ........... .
(a) mine (b) myself (c) me (d) I

**119.** Life of a/an ...... is luxurious.
(a) farmer (b) shopkeeper
(c) engineer (d) king

**120.** The leaping ...... of dolphins was fun to watch.
(a) army (b) school
(c) colony (d) nest

# ANSWERS

| | | | | | | | | | | | | | | | | | | | |
|---|---|---|---|---|---|---|---|---|---|---|---|---|---|---|---|---|---|---|---|
| 1. | (a) | 2. | (b) | 3. | (c) | 4. | (b) | 5. | (d) | 6. | (d) | 7. | (c) | 8. | (c) | 9. | (b) | 10. | (a) |
| 11. | (a) | 12. | (c) | 13. | (d) | 14. | (b) | 15. | (c) | 16. | (a) | 17. | (b) | 18. | (b) | 19. | (b) | 20. | (b) |
| 21. | (b) | 22. | (c) | 23. | (b) | 24. | (d) | 25. | (b) | 26. | (a) | 27. | (a) | 28. | (a) | 29. | (d) | 30. | (c) |
| 31. | (a) | 32. | (b) | 33. | (d) | 34. | (d) | 35. | (c) | 36. | (b) | 37. | (b) | 38. | (c) | 39. | (b) | 40. | (c) |
| 41. | (d) | 42. | (a) | 43. | (d) | 44. | (b) | 45. | (c) | 46. | (a) | 47. | (a) | 48. | (b) | 49. | (c) | 50. | (d) |
| 51. | (b) | 52. | (b) | 53. | (d) | 54. | (b) | 55. | (c) | 56. | (d) | 57. | (c) | 58. | (d) | 59. | (c) | 60. | (d) |
| 61. | (d) | 62. | (c) | 63. | (b) | 64. | (b) | 65. | (b) | 66. | (a) | 67. | (c) | 68. | (a) | 69. | (a) | 70. | (b) |
| 71. | (b) | 72. | (b) | 73. | (c) | 74. | (b) | 75. | (c) | 76. | (c) | 77. | (b) | 78. | (b) | 79. | (b) | 80. | (b) |
| 81. | (b) | 82. | (b) | 83. | (c) | 84. | (d) | 85. | (a) | 86. | (a) | 87. | (b) | 88. | (b) | 89. | (a) | 90. | (c) |
| 91. | (b) | 92. | (b) | 93. | (a) | 94. | (a) | 95. | (c) | 96. | (a) | 97. | (a) | 98. | (c) | 99. | (d) | 100. | (d) |
| 101. | (b) | 102. | (d) | 103. | (b) | 104. | (d) | 105. | (a) | 106. | (d) | 107. | (c) | 108. | (d) | 109. | (d) | 110. | (b) |
| 111. | (c) | 112. | (a) | 113. | (b) | 114. | (a) | 115. | (b) | 116. | (a) | 117. | (a) | 118. | (a) | 119. | (d) | 120. | (b) |